D1555643

Value-Form and the State

This major new work of Marxist theory covers philosophy, economics, politics, and sociology. It provides a challenging interdisciplinary alternative to current thinking in social science which, the authors argue, is based on spurious positivist methodology and an unnecessary separation of disciplines.

Geert Reuten and Michael Williams develop a neglected approach in the Hegelian-Marxist tradition, which focuses on social form, and take as their own starting point the value-form. They present an outline of the capitalist economy, showing how its development is grounded in the tendencies of accumulation, and look in detail at civil society and the bourgeois state. They go on to explore the interconnection of the state and economic policy, discussing which forms of economic policy are necessary and which are contingent.

Integrating insights from many different schools of thought, Reuten and Williams resolve outstanding problems on the fields of value theory, the tendencies of accumulation, and of state theory. They unite theories of the economic, social, and political determinants of economic policy, helping us to understand both economic processes and the state's attempts to deal with them. Distinguishing policies and institutions contingent to the capitalist system from those necessary, the authors clarify which options are still open to both governments and social groups for policy changes within the system (and which would lead beyond it).

The Authors

Geert Reuten teaches Philosophy of Economics and History of Economic Thought at the Faculty of Economics of the University of Amsterdam. Michael Williams teaches Political Economy at the Victoria University of Wellington, New Zealand.

Value-Form and the State

The tendencies of accumulation and the determination of economic policy in capitalist society

Geert Reuten and Michael Williams

R

Routledge
London and New York

First published 1989
by Routledge
11 New Fetter Lane, London EC4P 4EE
29 West 35th Street, New York, NY 10001

Typeset by Witwell Ltd, Southport
Printed and bound in Great Britain by
Billing & Sons Ltd, Worcester

British Library Cataloguing in Publication Data

Reuten, Geert, 1946–
    Value-form and the state: the tendencies of
    accumulation and the determination of economic
    policy in capitalist society.
    1. Marxist economics
    I. Title II. Williams, Michael, 1941–
    335.4

    IBSN 0–415–00088–2
    IBSN 0–415–03893–6   pbk

Library of Congress Cataloging in Publication Data

Reuten, G. A.
        Value-form and the state: the tendencies of accumulation and
        the determination of economic policy in capitalist society/Geert
        Reuten and Michael Williams.
            p.   cm.
        Bibliography: p.
        Includes index
        ISBN 0–415–00088–2
        ISBN 0–415–03893–6 pbk
        1. Value   2. Social structure.   3. State, The.   4. Marxian
    economics.   I. Williams, Michael, 1941–   .II. Title.
    HB201.R44   1989
    338.9–dc19

                                                            88–32178
                                                            CIP

General Contents

Detailed Contents

List of Figures

Preface

This book has two closely related aims. The first is to theorise the interconnection in capitalist society of the economy, the state and economic policy. In this respect it could be placed in the tradition of classical political economy of Smith, Ricardo and Mill, which, soon after Marx, was overshadowed by the far narrower 'economics' of the subjectivist and then the neoclassical tradition. Today, political processes insofar as they can be cast in an economics framework are allotted to a tiny sub-branch of economics – public choice theory. Otherwise one is referred to the allegedly different discipline of political science. Major disputes amongst economists on economic policy, even within the same school of thought, manifest the inadequacy of this separation. More fundamentally it precludes the understanding of society: one cannot keep separate in thought processes that are interconnected – at least if the aim is to theorise reality.

It is of course hard to overcome this separation, given that it has gone on for so long. We could not just go back to the classicals and Marx and pass over a century of – albeit one-sided – theoretical work. Moreover, to do so would mean neglecting the question as to why the separation emerged and has been sustained for so long. This takes us to the prior aim of the book, which is to develop a method from which the interconnection of economy, state and economic policy can be theorised. We distance ourselves from both the purely abstract formalism, and the empiricism, of economics, as well as from the empiricist philosophy of science on which it claims to be based. Abstract formalism and empiricism have, in our view, at least contributed to the emergence of the separation of economics and political science; and their persistence has been sustained by the widespread indifference to methodology and philosophy of science amongst mainstream economists.

The notion of interconnection, which is central to our work, derives from Hegel, who is, for us, the most profound critic yet of empiricist philosophy. Interconnection between empirical phenomena cannot be established by applying isolated abstract formal categories – as empiricism does. It rather has to be established in the development of the categories themselves from empirical phenomena, which are then both reconstituted and concretised so that as a result they can be grasped concretely. This dialectical process should reveal eventually how and to what extent economy, state and policy are necessarily, as opposed to merely contingently, connected within capitalist society. This systematic interconnection then reveals to what extent there is, within that society, freedom for systemic change of policy. Although we strongly reject Hegel's historicism, in developing our method we draw heavily on his logic, so that our work might be characterised as 'dialectical political economy'.

The coincidence of political economy and dialectics explains why throughout this book frequent reference is made to Marx and the Marxist tradition. Indeed both (as well as historicism) appear in Marx's *Capital*. However, Marx's mature work did not reach the conceptualisation of the state and economic policy, and the Marxist tradition has for the most part been no more successful in theorising their interconnection. Whilst this is partly due to the often dogmatic textual exegesis of many Marxists, it is also the case that Marxism had been influenced by the purely abstract formalism and the empiricism of economics. To the extent that Marxists distance themselves from empiricist philosophy, it is often historicism rather than dialectical logic that is counterposed to it. Relatedly Marxist political economy has been widely reduced to a one-sided Marxist economics. Nevertheless, taking the project of dialectical political economy seriously, we cannot simply neglect Marxist economics nor for that matter that of neoclassicals, Keynesians or Austrians, each of which has therefore been critically located within our presentation.

Part One provides a systematic account of the method of dialectical political economy. Such a project is never complete, but we feel that the subsequent Parts show that a systematic account of bourgeois society is feasible, and that it provides an understanding of the interconnection of social processes, and indeed capitalist society as a whole. We hope to have shown that our method can indeed be generally deployed within political economy.

This project could only have worked as a joint effort. We are both convinced that what we have produced together is much more than the sum of the parts. Whilst we have both contributed to all the Parts, and take full responsibility for their coherence, the final draft of the first three Parts has been written by Reuten, and of the last three by Williams. We should like to thank all those who have contributed to the production of this book at some stage. We are grateful to Neil de Marchi and Eg. Berns for their comments on (parts of) the manuscript and especially to Jörg Glombowski who has taken much time to comment on it in detail. We also thank Veith Bader, Meindert Fennema, Gerd Junne and Bob Rowthorn for their support at different stages of the project.

May 1988

Geert Reuten
University of Amsterdam
Faculty of Economics
Jodenbreestraat 23
1011 NH Amsterdam

Michael Williams
Victoria University of Wellington
Economics Group
PO Box 600, Wellington
New Zealand

For a note on the arrangement of the text see pp. 5–6

Part One:

Method and Introduction

Method and Introduction

PRELIMINARY REMARKS

The overt objective of this book is to provide an account of how economic policy is determined in contemporary capitalist society. But in one important respect it is an essay in methodology. The methodology of mainstream economics is based on the empiricist philosophy of (in particular) logical positivism and critical rationalism. This applies not only to neoclassical and Keynesian economics, but also to much of current Marxist economics. In our view, this methodology has come to a dead end, and some arguments for this view are briefly discussed in Section 1. However, our object is not to provide a methodological critique of economics, nor to set out a methodology drawn solely from within philosophy. The current state of economic science necessitates the development of methodology from within economics, but without neglecting its philosophical foundations. From this perspective, we will outline a methodology (Part One) and then deploy it in theoretical practice so as to test and evaluate its usefulness (Parts Two to Five).

Any critical approach towards the empiricist tradition soon comes into contact with the Hegelian critique of that tradition; this is indeed the starting point of our philosophy and our methodology. Hegel has provided a profound critique of empiricism, on the basis of which he founded his own philosophical system, not by rejecting empiricism but by critically appropriating it. Though Marx rejected the Hegelian dialectic per se, he nevertheless worked largely within the kind of systematic framework advocated by Hegel. He very often also worked with an Hegelian inspired dialectic. Because Marx is in fact the only great economist that ever worked within this tradition, he will be often referred to. He developed his own (incomplete) system by a critique of classical political economy, again not by rejecting it but by critically appropriating it into his own theoretical discourse.

3

Hegel and Marx represent the culmination of a systematic critique, on the basis of which they built a positive system of logical and political economic theory; both authors have been rejected without critical appropriation (or, more often, simply neglected) by the mainstream philosophical and political economic traditions. It is debatable as to what extent Hegel's and Marx's explicit philosophies of science are compatible with each other, and we have confronted this debate in our work. Starting from Hegel's critique of philosophy, a critical stand is taken against both dialectical and historical materialism as the basis for a theory of the development of the bourgeois epoch. Equally, we criticise Hegelian dialectics at the point at which it goes beyond absolute transcendental idealism towards an empirical idealism (as in Hegel's philosophy of history).

A dominant philosophical reference point for contemporary economics is the work of Karl Popper (in a popularised form). It is our contention that to a large extent it is because Popper rejected Hegel's philosophy that those economists who are interested in philosophy of science at all have found an excuse not to read Hegel. Be that as it may, Hegel's critique of empiricism has almost disappeared from the Anglo-Saxon dominated philosophy of economics. Because of this absence of any dialectical thought in the mainstream economics tradition, we have presented our own dialectically inspired methodology by stages. Section 2 introduces dialectical thought, and dialectical transcendental idealism in particular. Section 3 then sets out more systematically those elements that are specific to our own methodology. Only halfway through Section 3 do we explicitly take a critical stand towards Hegel's philosophy.

The key paragraph of Section 3 is that in which the mode of argument of the presentation is discussed (§9). Central to the method is that it aims to dispense with reliance on axioms: anything that requires to be assumed (anything that is posited immediately) has eventually to be grounded in the presentation. The starting point of the presentation (§8) is a single abstract concept which is posited immediately, and the grounds for doing so cannot be given in advance. Such an abstract grounding would always lead to regression towards infinity or to the positing of indisputable axioms. The grounding of that which is posited immediately is to be provided as the condition of its existence at a more concrete level in the subsequent argument.[1] To the extent that this grounding requires some new concept to be

---

1 This usage of the term 'grounding' is at odds with common usage, in which assertions are said to be grounded in (implicitly more abstract) argument and theory. Hegel (for example, 1817) goes to great lengths to distance himself from this everyday consciousness. As will become clear in the course of Part One, the two meanings coalesce when the presentation is 'complete'.

introduced, it in turn has to be grounded in its conditions of existence at an even more concrete level. In this way, the presentation moves forward until it has (in principle) derived all the necessary conditions of existence of the more abstract concepts at the most concrete level. This mode of systematic argument may be called 'systematic theory'. Because it is also dialectical, it is called 'dialectical systematic theory'. One further characteristic of the method is that, from the outset, that which is necessary *to the object of study is differentiated from that which is merely contingent. This 'necessary–contingent' distinction is inseparable from the mode of argument.*

The closer the account comes to the particular concrete phenomena of the object of investigation – economic policy in capitalist societies – the more contingent elements will be at work. For example, whilst welfare policy in some determinate form may be necessary, the particular phenomenal content of such policy is contingent. Such policy may thus have a different particular content in different countries, and within any one country at different times. This issue is discussed in the last paragraph of Section 3. To arrive at the very concrete level at which economic policy can be discussed at all requires an outline presentation of the necessary economic, social and political moments of capitalist society; as our method consists neither of analysis nor of model-building in the usual economist's sense, we cannot start immediately at that very concrete level. A large part of the presentation is thus taken up with the derivation of the basis of economic policy in capitalist society. This process is introduced in Section 4.

Some remarks should finally be made here as to the **organisation** *of the text. The* **systematic argument** *is set out in the* **numbered paragraphs** *(§5, etc.) of each chapter, and the argument may be followed by reading only these numbered paragraphs. They are usually followed by one or more* **addenda** *(identified by lower case letters a, b, c). These addenda contain supplementary material of three kinds: they may locate the main argument in relation to other work; they may refer back and forwards to earlier and later stages of the systematic presentation; or they may reformulate the main argument in perhaps more familiar but less rigorous language. At the beginning of each chapter will be found Preliminary Remarks and at the end a Summary. These again are not part of the systematic presentation. (It should be noted that Part One also follows this format, although it does not belong to the systematic presentation proper.) This format has been adopted for two related reasons. The first is the systematic rigour inherent in the method. The second is pragmatic, in that the reader may economise on reading without losing the thread of the systematic argument.*

Cross references within the text are given as follows: 2§3 refers to Chapter 2, paragraph 3; 2S4 refers to Chapter 2, section 4; references to Part One (which is not divided into chapters) are given as 0§3 or 0S4. Bibliographical references are always to the year of the first printing of the first edition of a work (Marshall 1890), perhaps followed by a page (1890: 26), paragraph (1890: II§5) or chapter (1890: ch.1) reference. (For further details see the note at the beginning of the Bibliography.)

SECTION 1   THE PHILOSOPHY AND METHODOLOGY OF MAINSTREAM ECONOMICS

§1. The application of the methodology of mainstream economics

The methodology of current mainstream economics is based on the empiricist philosophy of logical empiricism and/or critical rationalism.[2] Methodologists of economics seem, however, to agree that this methodology is more professed than practised. The idea that there are problems with the application of empiricism in economics is also familiar to those economists who are (even only dimly) aware of the elementary foundations of economic research. Economic practice is indeed far removed from empiricist aspirations: most research is not empirically oriented; of that research which is, a large part is directed at fitting instead of testing; and of that research which is directed at testing a negligible part is directed at falsifying (see, for example, Blaug 1980: 259; Katouzian 1980: 90; Leontief 1982: viii, xi; Caldwell 1982: 127–8; Canterbery & Burkhardt 1983: 22, 31).

Although this methodology has always lived a distorted life (not only in economics, but also in the natural sciences – cf. Kuhn 1962), empiricism as a philosophy of science cannot be dismissed merely by pointing to such distortion. A systematic critique of this philosophy is beyond the scope of this book, but a brief indication is appropriate. §2 therefore provides a brief outline of Bhaskar's (1975 and 1979) critique of logical empirism and critical rationalism which is coherent and penetrating, whilst its kernel is rather simple.[3]

§2. Bhaskar's critique of empiricism

The roots of the current mainstream philosophy of economics are in British empiricism. Its programmatic problems are displayed in the

---

2 For the purposes of the brief outline in this section, these may be lumped together under the heading of empiricism.
3 This appraisal of Bhaskar's critique should not be read to imply agreement with his own transcendental realist philosophy of science.

work of Hume (1739/40, 1748). These are, first, the antithesis of a knowing subject (mind) and a known real object (the real world of objects and events); and, second, the antithesis of the particular and the universal. The second problem is commonly referred to as the problem of induction: how the move can be made from particular matters of fact to knowledge of causal relations and universal theories. This is related to the problem of how it is possible to arrive at any knowledge at all where we do not have experience (see K. Williams 1975: 312).

Logical empiricism (Wiener Kreis) and critical rationalism (Popper-Hempel) aim to provide 'workable solutions' to these Humean problems, concerning first the concept of 'law', and secondly the demarcation of science from non-science. The critique in this paragraph is an immanent critique of these attempts. At a more fundamental level, one would need to come to terms with the antitheses themselves (see S2 below).

The crucial issue within the empiricist philosophy is the Humean concept of laws as constant conjunctions of events (plus some disputed contribution of mind). Such a constant conjunction of events, though not always considered as a sufficient condition, is generally considered as at least a necessary condition for a law. Related to this concept is the notion that laws find phenomenal expression as events or states of affairs, and that only the phenomenal is real (Bhaskar 1975: 64, 1979: 158). From this derive the two principles of the empiricist account of science: (1) laws are or depend upon empirical regularities (the empirical invariance principle); (2) laws are confirmed (or falsified) by their instances (Bhaskar 1975: 127, 1979: 159). From the first principle derive theories of causality, explanation, prediction, the symmetry of prediction with explanation, the development of science, etc. From the second derive various theories of demarcation and scientific rationality.

The kernel (and the novelty) of Bhaskar's critique lies in his application of the distinction between closed and open systems. In the natural sciences (apart from astronomy) experimental situations have the character of closed systems, and it is only in such situations that a *constant* conjunction of events can occur. Outside this, in the open system of the 'real world', disturbing or counteracting forces operate. (Thus, for example, the law of gravity will be related to a constant conjunction only in cases where there are no disturbing factors.) Laws then must either be restricted to closed systems (and so they do not seem to be universal laws), or the empirical status of laws in open systems must be questioned.

The empiricist is now caught in a terrible dilemma: for to the extent that the antecedents of law-like statements are instantiated in open systems, he must sacrifice either the universal character or the empirical status of laws. If, on the other hand, he attempts to avoid this dilemma by restricting the application of laws to closed systems (e.g. by making the satisfaction of a ceteris paribus clause a condition of their applicability), he is faced with the embarrassing question of what governs phenomena in open systems. (Bhaskar 1975: 65)

The argument is thus that from the perspective of empiricism there can be no universal laws. What is so remarkable about this very fundamental critique is that it sounds so familiar. The distinction between open and closed systems is not new (e.g. Klant 1972: 116ff., 179ff. touched upon it, in a similar connection); that even in the natural sciences theories cannot be applied universally is not new (e.g. Katouzian 1980: 158–9); and the problem of verification/falsification of law is not new (e.g. Kuhn 1962). What is, however, new is to argue all three together.

According to Bhaskar, for science to be an intelligible activity at all (as distinct from any other activities), the invariance principle must be dispensed with. Laws in both the natural and the social sciences are 'normic': they are tendencies. The crucial point is that laws are not open system empirical regularities and open system empirical regularities are not laws. On the one hand, disturbance both by different laws and by accidental/contingent events may prevent the phenomenal expression of normic laws (say the generation of actual empirical regularities). On the other, empirical regularities may be the outcome of the operation of different laws, or indeed be accidental or contingent: that is, there may be empirical regularities for which there is no natural or systemic necessity.

But the similar status of laws in the natural and the social sciences (naturalism), does not imply that social objects can be studied in the same way as natural objects (scientism). The point (mentioned in almost every elementary economics textbook) is that the social sciences do not have the opportunity (ontologically or because of moral objections) to experiment. The absence of closed systems in the social sciences implies that there are no decisive test situations for social scientific theories. But the conclusion to draw from this is not that there are no social laws. This would follow only if indeed 'the principle of empirical-invariance' were true. There are laws in both the natural and the social sciences but they are normic. The difference between natural and social science is that the conditions for the identification of laws are different (Bhaskar 1979: 163). The epistemological problem is then that society as an object of inquiry cannot be empirically identified independently of its effects; society as an object of inquiry is necessarily theoretical, in the sense that it is per se imperceivable. A further problem is that social laws manifest themselves only, if at all, in open systems (Bhaskar 1979: 57).

But even if pure empiricism is inapplicable, could not a pragmatic *attempt* be made to apply it as some methodologists have in fact claimed (for example, Klant 1972; cf. also Quine 1953). On the failure of such pragmatism Bhaskar is quite clear. The first problem is that empiricist criteria cannot do justice to the subject matter of social science. Because of this the object of study tends to be reduced to, or identified with, its empirical manifestations (cf. Bhaskar 1979: 167). In economics this is exemplified in empirical model building. The second problem – for example, with theoretical model building in economics – is that:

> ... the very absence of decisive test situations, coupled with continuing formal allegiance to a *predictive* criterion, serves at once to mystify methodology, protect entrenched (or otherwise privileged) theory, stunt alternatives and/or encourage (a belief in) the unresolvability of theoretical conflicts – which, in practice, of course means their resolution in favour of the status quo. (Bhaskar 1979: 167)[4]

To summarise: if one identifies laws with constant conjunctions of events then there are no non-superficial universal laws, in natural science or in social science. There can be non-universal laws only within the controlled domain of experimental situations, which have the character of closed systems. Therefore for science to be an intelligible activity one has to cut loose from the empiricist invariance principle. This implies not that there can be no laws (this would be the case only if the invariance principle were taken as axiomatic) but only that laws (which are always normic) are not immediately manifest in open systems. Science then is first of all a theoretical project. So there is at least one difference between the natural and the social sciences: because the latter lacks a closed system experimental situation, its conditions for the identification of laws are different.

---

4 Many philosophers of economic science have also pointed at the privileging of the status quo. For example, Caldwell (1982: 251): 'It should first be noted that dogmatism exists today. It does not derive from methodological pluralism, but from its opposite: alternative programs which do not meet the standards of scientific practice alleged to be followed by the mainstream are often summarily (hence dogmatically) rejected'.

Addendum: a. 'Normic laws' and the classical economist's concept of 'tendency'

a. Bhaskar's concept of laws as normic laws or tendencies appears to be akin to that of J. S. Mill, Marx and J. N. Keynes. (Bhaskar 1979: 161 seems to deny this; of course, the philosophical foundation of such a concept may be different for these authors.) Because we shall draw on it later, we may recall here Mill's 1836 concept of 'tendency' (note that this is not the Mill of the *System of Logic*, to which Bhaskar refers):[5]

> That which is true in the abstract, is always true in the concrete with proper *allowances*. When a certain cause really exists, and if left to itself would infallibly produce a certain effect, that same effect, *modified* by all the other concurrent causes, will correctly correspond to the result really produced (Mill 1836: 145). [These allowances and modifications should however not be read to be exceptions.] What is thought to be an exception to a principle is always some other and distinct principle cutting into the former: some other force which impinges against the first force, and deflects it from its direction. There are not a *law* and an *exception* to that law ... There are two laws ... bringing about a common effect by their conjunct operation (Mill 1836: 162). [The error is to have] predicated an actual result, when [one] should only have predicated a *tendency* to the result – a power acting with certain intensity in that direction. (Mill 1836: 161)

In a similar vein, J. N. Keynes argues:

> As a matter of fact, in the instances that actually occur of the operation of a given cause, counteracting causes sometimes will and sometimes will not be present; and, therefore, laws of causation are to be regarded as statements of tendencies only. (Keynes 1891: 86) ... the pure theory assumes the operation of forces under artificially simplified conditions ... (Keynes 1891: 89) ... laws are statements of *tendencies* only, and are therefore usually subject to the qualifying condition that *other things are equal*; and that, in the second place, many of its conclusions depend upon the realisation of certain *positive* conditions, which are not as a matter of fact always realised. (Keynes 1891: 90)

But it is most interesting that Keynes also provides a critique of the Mill of the *Logic*:

> The serious difficulties which sometimes attend the process of verification must not be overlooked. Mill goes so far as to say that "the ground of confidence in any concrete deductive science is not the *à priori* reasoning itself, but the accordance between its results and those of observation *à posteriori*," [Keynes refers to the *Logic*.] This statement needs to be slightly qualified. For we may have independent grounds for believing that

---

5 For a discussion of the (alleged) differences in this respect between Mill's *Essays* and his *Logic*, see De Marchi 1986.

our premisses correspond with the facts, and that the process of deduction is correct; and we may accordingly have confidence in our conclusions, in spite of the fact that there is difficulty in obtaining explicit verification. (Keynes 1891: 92)

Mill and Keynes thus long ago provided intimations of a critique of empiricism as a philosophical foundation for social science. It appears likely that these philosophers as economists would have agreed with Bhaskar's critique of empiricism.

SECTION 2   INTRODUCTION TO THE METHOD OF DIALECTICAL SYSTEMATIC THEORY

§3. Preliminary notions

The links from the brief critique of empiricism in Section 1 to the outline of our own method in this and the following Section are the empiricist dichotomous antitheses of subject and object, and particular and universal. In this paragraph a number of notions are stated without derivation or grounding. In this sense, from the point of view of the presentation, they are preliminary notions.

The first of these is what Norman (1976a: 12) has called the *dilemma of epistemology* (cf. also Callinicos 1983: 156): the well known problem that any principle which specifies some criterion as to what should be counted as truth, or as to what knowledge should be accepted as science, is always circular or regressive. As such a principle is itself a claim to knowledge, it must either appeal to itself (circularity), or to some other criterion (regression). Our own response to this dilemma is to set ourselves the task of providing a grounding of the argument within the presentation itself. It must be the intrinsic merits of the argument – not some external criterion – that has to convince the reader of its adequacy (see further S3). In this way, the dilemma is coped with, though not overcome. It should be noted that the decision not to rely on external criteria does not imply that 'anything goes' (Feyerabend 1975: 28); nor does the notion of the intrinsic merit of the argument imply relativism (which does seem to be implied by McCloskey 1983).

The second preliminary notion is related to what may be termed the *axiom of realism*, which derives from the long standing problems of the thought–reality dualism and reductionism. The axiom asserts that 'reality', or 'what is', is what it is notwithstanding our inter-subjective knowledge of it. Unfortunately, this formulation is dualistic and (apparently irreducibly) ambivalent. It is our contention that once this axiom has been posited, it should be

11

suspended,[6] since we cannot know more about reality than we do in fact consciously know. In this sense, reality cannot be different from the social inter-subjective conception of it. (In *this* sense, reality is constituted by social inter-subjective consciousness – cf. Hegel's Phenomenology.) This transcendental notion of reality leaves open its ontological status. Our preconception is that the essential core of reality is neither an autonomous thing-in-itself (Kant) nor the working out of the self-developing Idea in history (Hegel's Philosophy of History) nor social/natural tendencies/laws working themselves out autonomously in history (Marxist and other historicism). Reality is rather the active unity of being and consciousness. Whilst reality cannot *conceivably* exist without human consciousness, humankind is both natural and social, both conscious and active. Humankind is not merely the unity of being and consciousness (being conscious, 'Bewusst-sein'), it is an active unity (becoming conscious, 'Bewusst-werdung'). In actively changing its circumstances, humankind changes itself, and so its consciousness of itself, and so also of its being. (This, we contend, is Hegel's Phenomenology as transcended by Marx's Theses on Feuerbach. But there is no transcendence if – as many Marxists would have it – human activity is hypostatised as subjectless, which easily gives rise to historical 'laws of motion', however subtle.)[7] The thesis that active change changes consciousness resolves, but does *not* dissolve the thesis that changing consciousness changes reality.

The axiom of realism obviates absurdities such as the notion that reality is in some way created by consciousness alone. But it must then be suspended in order to avoid the equally absurd notion that reality is fixed independently of consciousness.

The third preliminary notion is that of the *universal–particular dichotomy*. This is related to the Humean problem of laws and in particular to the Hegelian notion of the concept ('Begriff').[8] It is based, in the first place on the negative assertion that there can be no direct and immediate sensory acquaintance with particular, objects or with sense data (Russell). Such acquaintance is always mediated by universal concepts, and would thus seem to presuppose them. Positively – as Hegel shows – sensory acquaintance with particulars

6 In the Husserlian phrase, 'bracketed'.
7 The thesis of the active unity of being and consciousness incorporates thought as an *activity* (cf. Hegel, for example, 1817: §20).
8 cf. Hegel 1817: §163. We have drawn mainly on Hegel's *Logic* of the *Encyclopaedia* (1817), the *Philosophy of Right* (1821) and his various introductions, in particular that to his *Phenomenology* (1807) and the *History of Philosophy* (1833). Besides these our brief account in the remainder of this paragraph draws on Norman 1976b, and in particular Norman 1976a: 27–31.

is possible only in so far as the particular *is* also a universal, characterised by a universal concept. The particular, then, is connected with other particulars of the same kind, and contrasted with particulars of other kinds. Thus 'we have acquaintance with particulars only in so far as this is *at the same time* a knowledge of universals' (Norman 1980: 28). So universals cannot be reduced to particulars, nor can they be separated from them. Rather, universal and particular are mutually interdependent: 'the applicability of the one concept is a necessary precondition for the applicability of the other, and vice versa.' (the 'identity of opposites' – Norman 1976a: 29; cf. Norman 1976b: 41). This constitution of something as both a particular and a universal is the basic form of internal opposition or contradiction. Contradiction, however, cannot persist without further mediation. The contradiction of 'sense-certainty' is transcended into what Hegel calls 'perception', which is the experience of things considered as *bearers of universal properties*.[9,10]

The universal–particular relation plays an important role in dialectical systematic theory. But, more generally, thinking fundamentally runs in terms of opposites: something can be 'above' only in relation to something else which is 'below'; the concept of 'truth' can be made intelligible only in relation to the concept of 'error'. 'In this sense, the opposed concepts constitute a unity, and because they are both united and opposed in this way, Hegel describes each such pair as a "contradiction"' (Norman 1980: 52).

Addendum: a. The axiom of realism suspended

a. Our reason for positing and then suspending the axiom of realism is to make it clear that we do not hold an empirical idealist position. We do not claim that there are no material substances, but only ideas; rather we abstain from any claim as to what sorts of entity may exist (cf. Norman 1976a: 109). The notion of an existing reality may therefore be taken as a provisional axiom. But this being said, it cannot meaningfully be held that reality exists

---

9 Note that these are mental acts; as Hegel 1817: §21A puts it: '... the laws of the celestial motions are not written on the sky. The universal is neither seen nor heard, its existence is only for the mind.'

10 In being transcended ('Aufhebung'), a contradiction is resolved rather than dissolved. Here the concept of perception thus derives from that of sense-certainty as a unity of opposites (see also S3). This concept of contradiction should not be confused with formal logical contradiction (see §10). In English, the Hegelian notion of 'Aufhebung' is variously translated by: superceding, overcoming, abolishing, abrogating, annulling, transcending, transforming (Findlay 1974: 156), or by suspending and resolving. We prefer to use one term to denote this particular concept – transcending – unless this is very odd in English or unless we want to stress a particular aspect.

independently of the concept of it. Whilst we may say that reality exists independently of *my* concept of it, it cannot be independent of *the* – inter-subjective – concept of it. To perceive an entity as 'a house' or as 'copper' is dependent on our conceptualisation of these entities. (But the 'I' (subjective), the 'us' (inter-subjective) and the entity (objective) imply that the perceptions of entities are not unconstrained – cf. Geurts 1974: 13, 58–69). To posit a reality independently of any concept of it – even if such reality could (hypothetically) truly exist – makes no sense, indeed has *no meaning*, no conceptual meaning.

The concept of reality has to be determined by science. Science has to determine what reality is – to determine its *object*. This does not mean that the determination of reality does not take place in everyday consciousness; by 'science', we mean the *systematic* production of knowledge by way of rational and inter-subjective discourse, which may indeed involve the systematisation of everyday consciousness. Reality is all there is; and all there is must mean all we know that there is, our consciousness: that is, all that has been determined in some way. In a transcendental sense, reality is thus all that has been produced by thought, all that is known. (Note that we do not say 'reality is all that is known of *it*': we do not posit a thing in itself, a 'Ding an sich', which has no inter-subjective conceptual meaning beyond 'no-meaning'.)

This position may usefully be called transcendental idealism. However it is not a *subjective* transcendental idealism (Kant). Reality is *all we* know. The 'all' proposes to do away with dualistic remnants, and the 'we' proposes inter-subjective or social knowledge. This is then an absolute transcendental idealism (Hegel); however, it is no more than a provisional epistemological label. We shall criticise in particular the historicism that is often associated with it (as well as with its materialist counterpart – 'Umkehrung'). As already indicated, we shall argue for the conception of reality as *systematic*, which itself is based on the possibility of reality.

---

§4. Subject-matter (preliminary introduction)

The subject-matter of our theory is 'the determination of economic policy in capitalist society'. The *analytical* way of dealing with such a theme would be to define first each of the terms 'society', 'capitalist', 'policy' and so on. However, this procedure involves a regression, and what usually happens is that it is eventually assumed at some point that the reader knows what the authors means. In one sense, our method is the other way around. To say what 'capitalism' is would be to presuppose what is to be derived; the object is rather to be determined systematically. The conception of economic policy then becomes a result rather than a presupposition. Nevertheless, the object of the theory is a 'real world phenomenon' (as qualified by the notions of the dilemma of epistemology and the axiom of realism –

§3). Our preliminary indication of this phenomenon is 'the bourgeois epoch'.

In the Preliminary Remarks it was stated that in a sense this work is an essay on method. The discussion above indicates that the method cannot usefully be separated from the content.[11]

In general terms, there are three related sources of working material for the theory. First, the *method* derives from a critical appraisal of the philosophical and political-economic critiques of Hegel and Marx, as well as from a critical appraisal of the more recent critique of Hegelianism and Marxism by the 'form analysis' of authors such as Backhaus, and Eldred, Hanlon, Kleiber and Roth.[12] Second, we make use of inter-subjective *perceptions* – the experience of things considered as bearers of universal properties (§3). Thirdly we make use of the working up of these perceptions by *everyday consciousness* and other fragments of more or less *reflected consciousness*. (The source of these is in conversation, newspapers, statistical records, journals, books and other media of communication.)[13]

Fundamental to the method is the contention that knowledge is produced, and so extended, by a *systematic presentation* of existing knowledge, the contents of everyday and other forms of consciousness.[14] The meaning of 'systematic presentation' will be explained in S3. Before this, there follows an intuitive description of that which precedes the actual starting point of the theory – the

---

11 But what we can do is to point at an 'analogy': Hegel's logic is often referred to in this way. But it cannot be 'applied' to social science because that would be alien to its unity of method and content. Whilst we can point out that 'analogy', our method is thus in fact a development from it.

12 For example, Backhaus 1969, Eldred 1984a, Eldred and Hanlon 1981, Eldred, Hanlon, Kleiber and Roth 1982/85. A relevant methodological outline is Bader, Berger, Ganssmann, Hagelstange, Hoffmann, Krätke, Krais, Kürschner and Strehl 1975: 29–114.

13 The terms 'everyday' and 'reflected' consciousness must not be read as judgemental. It is not to be supposed that the recognition of dialectic '... is peculiarly confined to the philosopher. It would be truer to say that Dialectic gives expression to a law which is in fact in all other grades of consciousness, and in general experience.' (Hegel 1817: §81A1)

14 'By the act of reflection something is *altered* in the way in which the fact was originally presented in sensation, perception, or conception. (...) The business of philosophy is only to bring into explicit consciousness what the world in all ages has believed about thought. Philosophy therefore advances nothing new; ...' (Hegel 1817: §22, §22A). In this sense the science (political economy) of the bourgeois *epoch* runs methodologically parallel to that of philosophy. Though for us Aristotle or Augustine may perhaps not be relevant, Smith, Marx and Menger are not a priori less relevant than more recent authors such as Hayek, Robinson or Samuelson.

'context of discovery'. Terms such as 'the holistic object of the theory' (§5), 'necessity and contingency of the object' (§6), 'abstraction' and 'abstract determination' (§7) are introduced initially informally, and subsequently (in Section 3) more formally.

§5. The holistic object-totality

Systematic theory should ideally eschew a priorism, in that there are no phenomena that it excludes from its object: its ideal starting point is all that is perceived (what is called the empirical), that is, the perceived totality. In this sense, it is ideally holistic (and so open), in that it sets itself no restrictions. Though this can be only an ideal, it is not an empty one in that it sets itself the task of locating those phenomena that are not theorised within, or in relation to, the systematic presentation. Within this holistic ideal our social scientific and political-economic concern is the bourgeois epoch, and this we call the 'object-totality' (see S4). Within it there are no a priori restrictions. Perceptions of elements of this totality and conscious conceptualisations of them are *more* or *less* interconnected, that is in consciousness. To the extent that they are *non-connected* they are termed *abstract* (or, equivalently, the *perceived* concrete – cf. Marx 1903: 100).

§6. Necessity and contingency (preliminary introduction)

The objective of science is to set out the precise interconnection of phenomena, that is to determine them (see §9). One key element with respect to the reproduction of the totality is related to the necessity – contingency distinction of phenomena. The totality is an interconnected whole, and what it is is determined by phenomena which are necessary rather than contingent with respect to it.[15]

Given our methodological imperatives an adequate account of the process of conceptualisation must await the systematic presentation itself. However, an illustration may be useful. Assume that a conception of 'capitalism' has been derived, as something different from feudalism and from a Soviet style economy. Assume also that free enterprise investment and state monetary policy have been derived as necessary to it: that is, it has been shown that without these capita-

---

15 'The sole aim of philosophical enquiry is to eliminate the contingent. Contingency is the same as external necessity, that is, a necessity which originates in causes which are themselves no more than external circumstances' (Hegel, 1837: 28; cf. also his 1817: §§143–5). *Our* object (see §§10–11) is not merely to eliminate the contingent. Since ours is a social-scientific rather than a philosophical enquiry, it is concerned to grasp the contingent in the light of the necessary – to identify those elements of the object which are necessary to it, and those which are external to it.

lism could not reproduce itself (as what it is). The policy question may then arise: are either or both of (say) open market operations and credit restrictions *necessary* to the system, or is the one *or* the other policy merely *contingent* (given that some form of monetary policy has already been determined as necessary)? Such a policy may be contingent in that it is determined by the preoccupations of a particular board of the central bank because of particular conjunctural circumstances, because of the ideological complexion of the government in power, or for some other reason. To take this last possibility a little further, with a different government in power the choice of the policy instrument might have been different without changing the essential nature of the system. (Whilst in this schematic example, this mode of argument may appear tautological, in the event it is always open to the counter-argument that such a policy shift *does* entail a fundamental transformation in the essential nature of the system – either on the basis of the same starting point, or on the basis that a different starting point is appropriate.) The point is not that policies may not have different effects, but rather that the choice of policy instrument in this case is not decisive as to whether the system is capitalist or not. What would be being argued is merely that a particular monetary policy does not constitute a differentia specifica of capitalism.

For a different example, consider a very simple theoretical model of investment (I), which is dependent on income (Y), the profit rate (r) and on the ideological complexion of the government in power (B). So we have $I = aY + br + cB$. Suppose this equation is made operational via statistical proxies and so on, and particular values for the parameters a, b and c are estimated (each of which has the same t-value). A relevant question would then be: are these variables and their parameters all equally 'important'? In the usual models, their difference would be only *quantitative*, and it is that which makes them more or less important. But a prior question is: can a *qualitative* order of importance be assigned to these variables? Then at least one such an ascription would be in terms of necessity and contingency. Suppose that (say) the ideological background of the government in power or the level of the profit rate has been determined as contingent. Then their qualitative importance would not be reflected in their quantitative significance. Although the ideology of the government in power may thus quantitatively co-determine the level of investment, the question would be: to what extent does this determine the *concept* of investment – that is, what investment *is* conceived as something that is conceptually interconnected with other phenomena. (In terms of model-building, for a model of a closed economy without government ($I = aY+br$), and one with government $(I = aY + br + cB)$; is there in each case a different conception of investment at work?)

§7. Abstraction and abstract determination: the context of discovery

Having produced an initial intuitive account of 'connection' (§§5–6), the question arises as to *what* it is that connects such phenomena as, for example, employment, the balance of payments, division of labour in the household, criminal law and a particular monetary policy. How can one move beyond phenomena as mere abstractions (events as yet unconnected in consciousness). Connection established only by correlation seems insufficient in the face of the necessity-contingency distinction (§6). One important criterion of connection (others are set ou in §9) is to be sought in the unifying element of phenomena: the element which *unites* them into a totality.

What is it then that unites phenomena and perceptions? Merely to say that they are all *social* phenomena appears to beg the question. Nevertheless it provides the form of an answer, in that particulars are thereby connected, and constituted as universals.[16]

There may already exist more specific notions as to the connection of the phenomena to be grasped, or such notions may be arrived at by theorisation. Criminal law and monetary policy, for example, may both be conceived of as activities of the state (which is to presuppose the existence of the state); employment and the balance of payments may both be conceived of as the result of market exchange (which is to presuppose market exchange); further, it might be argued that the state and exchange both presuppose contract, so that all social phenomena are instances of contract. However, subsuming phenomena under more general phenomena, as species under a genus, is only an *abstract determination*. Though in this way an abstract connection of (say) the balance of payments and criminal law may be provided, this does not constitute their actual interconnection and concrete determination. For this, their *diversity* in unity would have to be systematically shown. The balance of payments, for example, is not determined (as what it is) by its grounding in contract alone; that would require *many determinants*.

16 Of course, to constitute particulars as universals is an act of thought. Hegel (1817: §24A1) puts it like this (in a different context) 'Now, the animal, qua *animal*, cannot be shown; nothing can be pointed out excepting some special animal. Animal, *qua* animal, does not exist: it is merely the universal nature of the individual animals, while each existing animal is a more concretely defined and particularized thing. But to be an animal – the law of kind which is the universal in this case – is the property of the particular animal, and constitutes its definite essence. Take away from the dog its animality, and it becomes impossible to say what it is.'

The move from 'abstract determination' (the starting point of the *presentation*, see also §8) towards 'concrete determination' is what is put forward in this work.

The movement from phenomena and perceptions to abstract determination (for example, from monetary policy to the state and to contract) might be described in terms of 'conjectures' (Popper). From the seventeenth century onwards, moral philosophers or political economists have proposed various such determinations.[17] Our starting point thus derives from reflection upon the various accounts of the nature of the contemporary socioeconomic system. This process of 'digestion' or critical appropriation takes place in what one might call the 'context of discovery' (Popper).[18] In fact the content of the starting point of the presentation (see §§15-17) is relatively familiar within the classical and Marxist tradition, and should not prove unacceptable to other traditions of social science.

SECTION 3   THE METHOD OF DIALECTICAL SYSTEMATIC THEORY

§8. The starting point

The starting point of our social scientific (rather than philosophical) presentation is not merely the highest genus of some hierarchy of

17 As Marx (1903: 100-3) points out, the economists of the seventeenth century in their writings actually set out the path *from* the perceived concrete *to* abstract determination, whereas classical economy took those abstract determinations (wealth creating activity, labour, division of labour, need, exchange value) as their starting point. (Besides Classical Political Economy and Marx, the Austrians and neo-Austrians such as Hayek have also systematically built on such determinations. Because of the claims of these authors (and of Marx in particular) to systematicity, they will be referred to more frequently than the inductive-empirical or axiomatic-deductive model building that economists have produced in this century.) An extensive account of the processes from the perceived concrete to abstract determination and the starting point of the systematic presentation, as well as a related critique of the analytical and the synthetic method, is in Bader *et al.* 1975: 36-60.

18 It may appear here that the starting point is an a priori, whereas it is in fact a result. Marx, confronted with a similar problem, wrote in the Postface to the second edition of *Capital*: 'Of course the method of presentation must differ from that of inquiry. The latter has to appropriate the material in detail, to analyse its different forms of development and to track down their inner connection. Only after this work has been done can the real ('wirkliche') movement be appropriately presented. If this is done successfully, if the life of the subject-matter is now reflected back in the ideas, then it may appear as if we have before us an *a priori* construction' (1867P: 102). (The first sentence reads in German: 'Allerdings muss sich die Darstellungsweise formell von der Forschungsweise unterscheiden.' 1867G: 27.) The starting point is not an axiom. Its validity has to be shown by the presentation itself (see §12).

genus and species. Rather, it is what appears to be the most fundamental moment of the object-totality, which determines (as the argument of the presentation will show) the interconnection of all the necessary moments of the totality. It therefore enables the grasp of these moments in their interconnectedness. (The test of the starting point is thus indeed the success or otherwise of the presentation itself – see §12.)

For the content of our starting point, we draw on and adapt Marx (1859, 1867) (see S4 and Chapter 1). However and more importantly its form derives from the Hegelian opposition of *particularity* and *universality* (§3), along with the notion of *negation* which stresses that thought, the formation of notions, concepts, etc. fundamentally runs in terms of opposites, which thinking then strives to reconcile and transcend. Any starting point is necessarily abstract, in that it cannot immediately grasp its object in its full concrete interconnectedness. The starting point is thus one of *abstract determination*. Universality (the, or a specific universal) may be the starting point ('being' in Hegel's logic), this abstract notion first being given determinateness by its negation (not-being, nothing) and then by some abstract particularising qualification (some determinate being, being there, 'Dasein').[19,20] Thought cannot conceivably make anything of such an abstract notion, other than by thinking its abstract negation and its abstract particularisation. It is in this specific sense that these opposites as applied to the *same* thing or notion are contradictions. In this sense also, to think these things and notions is to articulate their *doubling* (that is, the universal doubles into the universal and its opposite universal, or into universal and particular).

Two further remarks concerning this universal–particular opposition are needed. In the first place, it should be noted that it is precisely the purpose of the presentation to resolve the contradiction from which it starts; it is this process of thought which should render the *comprehension* of reality.[21] The second point is that immediately to subsume single empirical phenomena as particulars under

---

19 Cf. Hegel 1817: §§89–91. (Note that the Wallace translation of 'Dasein' into 'determinate being' is not altogether adequate because the next paragraphs are about the determination ('Bestimmung') of 'Dasein'. Because this 'Bestimmung' is not consequently translated by one term, but by a host of differing approximations, the reader easily gets lost.)

20 Being is the ultimate starting point of philosophy, from which the starting point of our specific object totality (the bourgeois epoch) is to be derived.

21 '... the essence of philosophy consists precisely in resolving the contradiction of the Understanding' (Hegel 1833: 71). 'Comprehension' is our translation of 'Begriff' in its determinate form. Otherwise we use the term 'concept' (as in the Knox translations, rather than Wallace's 'notion'; thus when we use 'notion' this is much less determinate than 'Begriff'. On the problem of translating 'Begriff', see Kainz (1973: 254–5, 263).

universals provides only empty abstractions. Thatcher, for example, is a Minister, a being, for *two* reasons. The first is that (say) a single piece of 'iron' and 'Thatcher' have in *common* that both are 'beings'. This is not only uninteresting but it also provides no clue as to what, if anything, *unites* them. The second reason is that it is the *difference* between phenomena which determines them (Thatcher is a living organic being and iron a dead organic being). But this difference again does not tell what, if anything, *unites* them. As long as no difference *in* unity has been provided we have provided no concrete determination. For example, to try to subsume at this stage credit restrictions (monetary policy) and the nationalisation of an industry (industrial policy) under economic policies (indicating what they have in common), would be ridiculous: not because it might be invalid, but because *as an abstract statement* it does not say anything. It is mere naming, with no indication of in what these notions *differ*, and in what they are *unified*. It is this double determination that systematic dialectical thinking seeks. As Hegel expresses it: 'The truth of the differentiated is its being in unity. And only through this movement is the unity truly concrete', whereas at first, at the starting point: '... difference is still sunk in the unity, not yet set forth as different' (Hegel 1833: 83). The object of the presentation is to grasp the phenomena from which we start in perception as concrete, that is as the 'concentration [Zusammenfassung] of many determinants, hence unity of the diverse' (Marx 1903: 101). But that may be possible only to the extent that these are phenomena necessary to the existent (see §9). Whilst monetary policy or even 'Thatcherism' may be necessary to the existent, credit restrictions or Thatcher may be only contingent to it. In that case, credit restrictions cannot be explained as co-determining the internal *unity* of many determinants, and thus not as a necessary, but only as an *external*, determinant (see §§9–11).

§9. The mode of argument

We now come to the key issue of Part One, the mode of argument of our presentation, in other words, how does the presentation proceed from the starting point to the concrete, the comprehension of the object-totality. The structure of this discussion is as follows. First the mode of argument at a general level is outlined (A). Next its key elements (existence and ground) are further determined (B). Then the necessity–contingency opposition is located within the mode of argument (C). This is followed by a summary (D). In reading the exposition below, it is useful to hold fast to the notion that the argument is *not* based on rules of axiomatic deductive nomological systems. All axioms are eschewed; rather, anything that requires to be assumed, or anything that is posited immediately (such as the starting point) must be *grounded*. But the point is that it should not be grounded merely abstractly (giving the arguments in advance), because this always leads to regression. Rather, that which is posited must ultimately be grounded in the argument itself, in concretising it. It is the intrinsic merits of our presentation – and not some external criterion (§3) – that must convince the reader of the adequacy of the presentation.[22]

A. Generally the presentation is one of gradual transcendence of abstract determination in a movement towards concrete determination, that is of concretisation. The presentation moves forward by the transcendence of contradiction and by providing the ever more concrete *grounds* – the conditions of existence – of the earlier abstract determination. The conditions of existence of earlier abstract determination do not dissolve, but rather transcend the opposition of the *moments* (identity–difference, universal–particular) of the abstract determination. (A moment is an element considered in itself, which can be conceptually isolated, and analysed as such, but which can have no isolated existence.) Their conceptualisation as moments is not negated, but rather transcended in the ground, which provides the unity of the opposed moments. But at the same time it is a further, more concrete, determination of the difference, a difference previously posited, as it now appears, only in itself ('an sich', 'Potentia', potentially, implicitly). So the differences that were previously not set forth as such now come into (abstract) existence. The ground at this new level itself is then an abstract existent showing the contradiction that it cannot exist for itself ('für sich', 'Actu', actually), and so the presentation has to move on in order to ground it in its turn, so as to provide its conditions of existence (Hegel 1817: §§120–4, 1833: 81–3).[23]

22 Of course language is an inter-subjective means of communication which even any axiomatic system must presuppose, in that the system must be explained in terms of language. And of course, language has a logic (rules) of its own; and one may think differently in different languages. Language is in that sense axiomatic for our (as for any) system of thought.

23 The concept of 'grounding' may seem to have two meanings. On the one hand the whole presentation grounds – in the sense of validates – the starting point. On the other, a thing is what it is if it is a necessary aspect of the object-totality because of its interconnectedness within that totality – it is grounded in the totality. Since the starting point (if valid) is the abstract universal determinant of the totality, it may then appear that a more concrete manifestation is grounded in the more abstract, and ultimately in that starting point. This ambiguity is resolved only when the presentation is complete, since it then both grounds concrete phenomena as manifestations of abstract determinants and, at the same time, validates the starting point.

The process continues until the presentation claims (see below) to have reached the stage where it comprehends the existent as actuality ('Wirklichkeit'), in the sense that its conditions of existence have now been determined such that it is indeed actual, and so is concrete self-reproducing or endogeneously determined existence, which requires no external or exogeneous determinants for its systematic reproduction. The presentation is thus a conceptual development. Starting from abstract determination, it seeks gradually to comprehend the initial perceptions (derived in the context of discovery) as interconnected, as difference in unity, as the concentration of many determinants, and so ultimately as concrete.[24]

B. This argument is however premature, because 'existence' and 'ground' first require further determination. *Existence* itself is a universal category, and as such it is abstract. It gains further determination by the *form* of existence, and so it is constituted as *existent*. The existent is then the unity of form and (indeterminate) existence, and as that unity it is essential existence, and appearance.[25] (cf. Hegel 1817: §§124–30. Note that we have rendered Hegel's term 'Ding' (thing) as 'existent' as distinct from 'existence'. Later existence and existent are specified with respect to our object-totality as 'social relation' and 'particular (existent) social relation'.)

24 Marx nowhere set out explicitly his mode of argument. (Unfortunately here the otherwise excellent outline of Bader *et al.* (1975: 92–6) is also somewhat unsatisfactory in that the actual proceeding of the argument is left open.) In the Introduction to the *Grundrisse* Marx does however indicate the stages mentioned here and in §7: initial perceptions – abstract determination – concrete determination (see also Hegel 1817: §48A and 1833: 68–9). 'The concrete is concrete because it is the concentration ['Zusammenfassung'] of many determinants, hence unity of the diverse. It appears ['erscheint'] in the process of thinking, therefore, as a process of concentration, as a result, not as a point of departure, even though it is the point of departure in reality ['der wirkliche Ausgangspunkt'] and hence also the point of departure for observation ['Anschauung'] and conception ['Vorstellung']. Along the first path the full conception was evaporated to yield an abstract determination; along the second, the abstract determinations lead towards a reproduction of the concrete by way of thought ['im Weg des Denkens']' (Marx 1903: 101). (This passage is followed by a critique of Hegel, which seems to us a misreading to the extent that it insufficiently takes account of the fact that Hegel's idealism – at least in his logic – is a transcendental idealism.)

25 The essence of reality is the existent totality comprehended as a totality, that is as an interconnected whole. For us, as for Hegel, there is nothing mysterious about essence and appearance: 'The essence accordingly is not *beyond* or *behind* the appearance, but just because it is the essence which is existent, is the existence appearance' (Hegel 1817: §131, adapted translation). And: 'The appearance shows nothing that is not in the essence, and in the essence there is nothing but what is manifested' (Hegel 1817, §139). To anticipate the presentation, value and surplus value, for example, are not 'essential' categories behind the appearances of prices and profit and interest, as many Marxists would have it.

The *ground*, in providing conditions of existence, gains further determination as the connection of *force* (or 'compulsion') and its *expression*. Considered abstractly (unconnected), a force would seem to be the ground and the existence, as its counterpart, the expression. But because of the essential unity of ground and existence, this connection is one of movement of force (cf. Hegel 1817: §§135–41). The notion of force provides the linkage to the more familiar term for economists (at least for classical and post-classical economists up to J. N. Keynes): *tendency*, which we conceptualise as this 'movement of force' (cf. §2a).

It was pointed out above that the presentation's forward movement is one of gradual transcendence of abstract determination towards concrete determination by providing ever more concrete grounds, and that this movement is recurrent in that these grounds are then themselves abstract existents which have to be grounded, and so on, until the stage of a self-reproducing actual existence is reached. The same recurrence applies to the form of existence and the expression of force which are themselves then (abstract) existent and force (cf. Hegel 1817: §132 and §136A1).

C. Having set out the mode of argument thus far, the notions of *necessity* versus *contingency* (introduced in §6) may now be considered. At first, all phenomena may seem to be contingent (or, as its negation, which is the same, to be externally determined destiny). To derive – by reflection – the existent as existence is to determine its *possibility*; the actual existent is first of all 'possibility', but without further determination it is only that.[26] The contingent and the determinate possibility are then two moments of the actual existent.

The contingency of phenomena does not imply that there is no way of grounding them; the point rather is that the ground of their being is not internal but *external* to them, or exogeneous.[27] In this sense, the contingent and its ground are not *inter*connected. Whilst the outward possibility of the contingent may be indicated, it is not an interconnected possibility, so that the phenomenon could possibly be something else without changing the character of its ground; the force and its expression are thus not essential to each other. In this sense, the contingent as such is non-essential to the totality of the existent (the object); or, to put it the other way around, the totality of the existent is indifferent to the contingent (which could be otherwise

---

26 'Possibility' here should be conceived of as 'plausible' or 'determinate' possibility, *not* as possibility in the sense of an 'assumption', by which anything is possible (as in many economic models) (cf. Hegel 1817: §143, §143A, §145).

27 Compare economic models in which endogeneous variables are ultimately explained only by exogeneous variables or parameters.

without changing the essence of the existent, that is its interconnectedness).

So mere possibility is further determined as *necessity* by the derivation of its interconnectedness within the object totality. Indeed, interconnectedness then amounts to a circle of conditions of existence. It is this difference in unity, this universal interconnectedness (whereby the existent is determined as a necessary moment of the totality of the existent) which constitutes the essence of the existent. This implies, of course, that the presentation cannot be complete before it has determined the internal reproduction of the starting point. It also implies that elements or moments forming a part of the presentation are, properly speaking, determined as necessary only on completion of the presentation.[28] An element or a moment is necessary, then, when it is what it is *through itself*: whilst it is derived, it must contain the antecedent as transcended in itself (cf. Hegel 1817: §§142-9; 1833: 80).

D. In sum, therefore, the starting point of the presentation is abstract in that it is initially taken in *isolation* (a moment) and is posited as universal and ubiquitous, constituting the essential universal form of the object-totality. As an abstract universal, the starting point can be given (abstract) determination only by its doubling into itself and its *negation*. Each of these notions of isolation and negation indicate aspects of one and the same process by which the presentation proceeds. The first is that contradiction cannot remain unresolved, and thus internal contradiction has to be externalised (grounded in its transcendence). Secondly, that which is posited by the abstract concept cannot exist in isolation (if indeed, the object of the theory is a structured coherent whole, which is a prerequisite for systematic knowledge to be possible) and so the contradictions of its existence have to be determined (and so the abstract determination is grounded). The presentation is thus a movement of grounding transcendence in which the elements become ever more particular, concrete, differentiated; they thus become determined as difference in unity. In this way, the object of theory is not presupposed in any postulation of its autonomous existence. Nor is the autonomous existence of the more abstract moments postulated; their conditions of existence are unfolded in

28 Nevertheless, because we also introduce contingencies, we shall use the term 'necessary' determination, etc. in order to differentiate these from the contingent. In doing this, we in fact anticipate the completion of the presentation. Of course, such completion is an unattainable ideal: there will in practice always remain disputes about whether some moments are necessary or contingent. The only practical possibility is to 'close' the presentation at an abstract level, adequate to philosophy – which would be to preclude empirical social science.

providing their ever more particular differentiated grounds. In this grounding transcendence, the interconnectedness of the moments or elements is continuously maintained; and it is this interconnectedness that constitutes the essence of the object determined at that stage, ultimately the essence of the totality. The presentation thus proceeds by way of articulation of the most abstract determinants to the phenomena of the totality comprehended by the most concrete categories in their full interconnectedness.

§10. Actuality in-itself and the actuality of contradiction

In the preceding paragraph, we have to a considerable extent followed Hegel's logic, up to the point where he develops the concept of actuality ('Wirklichkeit'). (In fact, we have used the term 'existent' or incidentally 'actual existent' where Hegel introduces actuality.) Note that Hegel's term 'actuality' (as distinct from reality) refers specifically to that stage in thinking where thought has become *self-conscious thought* ('Begriff', comprehension), which is its essence. Actuality is then the stage where essence and existence have become unity (Hegel 1817: §112 and §142). Thus actuality and thought are not opposed, but thought is, in this unity, actuality.

Indeed this actuality is the resulting process of thought (as 'Geist',[29] not as subjective thought). Thinking thus produces actuality as a process. Now this may usefully be called *transcendental* idealism (which is to be distinguished from ontological idealism). In Hegel's logic the opposition between subject and object vanishes because here thought has itself for its object. Thought realises itself as a process from its being and 'Dasein' to its essence – which is comprehension explicitly posited as such[30] – to its actuality, its essential existence and existential essence.

But, crucially, this actuality is only *actuality in itself* ('an sich', potential) (Hegel 1817: §163). Whilst logic proper may carry on from there, because thought is its object (and this is, of course, what Hegel does in his doctrine of the concept), science cannot reach further than actuality in itself: 'In the other sciences, form and content fall apart, but in philosophy thought is itself its own object; thinking here is preoccupied with itself and is self-determining' (Hegel 1833: 55).

---

29 Neither 'Spirit' nor 'Idea' cover this term very well. Spirit must be read in the sense of 'Spirit of the times', 'Zeitgeist' (e.g. Schumpeter in his History also prefers to use the German). (See also our discussion of inter-subjective conceptualisation in §3).
30 The essence of thought is thus that it comprehends itself as thought, that it is conscious: 'Das Wesen ist der Begriff als *gesetzter* Begriff, . . .' (This is the opening sentence of Hegel, 1817: §112, which has disappeared in the English translation.)

Whilst science may adopt the form of dialectical thought, it cannot reach further than *comprehension* of its object-totality. (And prediction, were it to be possible, would have to be based on comprehension.) This comprehension *in itself* (as science), though it may be a precondition for doing so, does not indeed create actuality for itself (thus scientists do no better than the philosophers of Marx's Theses) (see §13).

From this follows a very important limitation, or rather particularisation, of the application of the Hegelian dialectic in, for example, social science.[31] If this limitation is not grasped then the dialectic of transcendental idealism – also referred to as the 'conceptual dialectic' – threatens to turn into an empirical dialectic (such as that of Hegel in his writings on the philosophy of history and the state), or into the materialism and the empirical dialectic of much Marxism.[32] The point is that contradiction may be a persistent and irreducible characteristic of the actual existent, which generates *continual shifts* in concrete events in pursuit of resolution. (The idealist may be tempted to go beyond this, because reason is capable of doing so: from actuality in itself, reason may *ideally transcend* contradiction – *ideally* moving into the actuality for itself.) The limitation of the Hegelian conceptual dialectic in social science is thus that the content of the actual transcendence of a contradiction may be undetermined. Before this problem is developed, the notion of contradiction requires further elaboration.

1. The first point is that the notion of *dialectical contradiction* is quite different from the notion of 'contradiction' in the formal logical sense – which we will refer to as *formal contradiction*.[33] An initial rather formalistic indication of the distinction is the fact that in dialectical contradiction reconciliation is possible, whilst formal contradictions are irreconcilable because that is their whole meaning. The fact that in dialectics contradictions can be brought together means that they are a different sort of contradiction (Findlay 1973:

---

31 Note that our account of social science and political economy in particular, from within dialectics, is different from Hegel's location of classical political economy *vis-à-vis* his own presentation (see Hegel 1821: §189; cf. Arthur 1988).

32 Transcendental idealism focuses on the unity of consciousness and being; ideal idealism tends to reduce being to consciousness (and materialism reduces consciousness to being). We reject both the idealist and the materialist empirical dialectic (as well as, for that matter, Hegel's pantheism). For a discussion of the empirical dialectic in Hegel see Norman 1976b: 37–42, and 1976a: ch. 6; for a discussion of the materialist empirical dialectic see Norman 1976b: 42–5.

33 There is no intention to cast doubt on the usefulness of formal logic, nor on the crucial significance of the formal law of non-contradiction. Indeed the rules of formal logic cannot be negated on pain of producing nonsense.

68). Further, as already indicated, dialectical contradiction refers to the interdependence of opposed concepts – the unity of opposites; it concerns the distinction between the moments in a *single* concept, and the distinction of these moments tends to make the concept fall apart (and to develop into two opposed concepts). These opposed concepts are not merely applicable to *different* things, but rather 'for the one concept to be applicable, the opposed concept must also be applied to the *same thing*. What is "identical" is also "different", and preserves its identity only in so far as it also becomes different' (Norman 1980: 53). (Examples are the paired concepts universal and particular, cause and effect, contingency and necessity and value and use-value – cf. Chapter 1.) It is necessary to become conscious of the unity of these moments of the concept, and to show *how* the oppsites can coexist within a unity. But note again that with such transcendence the contradiction does not disappear.

2. Secondly, the term '(dialectical) contradiction' must be distinguished from the terms 'conflict' and 'self-contradiction'. *Conflict* (such as that between antagonistic forces) involves contradiction only when the forces in conflict are characterised by interdependent opposed concepts. *Self-contradiction* is the outcome of an internal conflict within the purposive activity of an individual or a social institution (for example, someone holding conflicting beliefs, or saying x but doing y). This kind of inconsistency or irrationality is quite compatible with the 'formal law of non-contradiction' which does not maintain that people (or institutions) never contradict themselves (Norman 1980: 49, 60).

3. Whereas to ascribe conflict and self-contradiction to events, etc. in the world provokes (in general) no objection, to ascribe contradiction to (for example) interdependent opposed forces in the world does (cf. e.g. Colletti 1974). The question then arises: if dialectical contradiction refers to the interdependence of opposed and the unity of opposite *concepts*, may it then be applied to 'the real world of things and events'? This returns us to the status of thought, and the dualism and reductionism rejected in §3. Reality is the active unity of being and consciousness. To admit that human beings (and the relations between them) are real but that contradictions are not would be inconsistent. Neither universals (e.g. human being) nor particulars (e.g., this woman labourer) exist phenomenally as such: it is not written on Thatcher's head, for example, that she is a human being; there can be no sensory acquaintance with 'human being' or 'dog'. It is *thought* via language (which itself is an inheritance from the history of thought) that posits Thatcher as human being (and for that there is no need for a providential tag stuck on her head). This also goes for even more complex concepts such as, for example,

'relation', which also does not exist sensually. In *this* sense there is no reason to exclude contradiction from the world, any more than 'human being' or 'relation'.

We may now return to the limitation of the conceptual dialectic in social science. That the content of the actual transcendence of a contradiction may be underdetermined poses a fundamental problem for dialectical systematic social science (cf. Bader *et al.* 1975: 96-9). As already indicated, its method requires the successive grounding of the starting point by way of derivation of the conditions of existence, in the successive transcendence of contradiction. In principle, phenomena may be grasped only as concrete (as interconnected, as difference in unity) when all contradiction has been transcended and when no external or exogenous determinant is required for the systematic reproduction of the actual existent. Then, and only then, will the starting point have been legitimated. It should not be posited a priori that such a 'final' transcendence of contradiction is a *determinate* one (cf. §9). However, it is the case that if the starting point is not reproduced then the presentation cannot be said to have been completed. On the other hand, one should not be tempted to 'close the system' ideally or wishfully – to conceptualise a contradiction-free object-totality when this is not actual (and this, we contend, is what the empirical dialectic of Hegel, and also the systematic theory of, for example, Eldred *et al.* is eventually drawn into). If it is indeed the case that tendential contradiction is a persistent and irreducible characteristic of the object-totality, then the *continual shifts* in concrete events which attempt to resolve it have to be theorised. This implies that one can never claim to fully have comprehended the actuality of intra-epochal developments, which is actuality in itself (see §13).

Addendum: a. Formal and dialectical contradiction

a. A problem in comparing formal and dialectical contradiction is that the concept of 'opposites' (e.g. 'universal' and 'particular') unlike that of contradictory predicates (e.g. 'red' and 'not-red') cannot be explicated in merely formal terms (Norman 1980: 65-6; the following example and its conclusion follows Norman very closely). The dialectical inter-relationship of opposites 'involves the assertion that "x is F and x is also G, where F and G are opposites" and this, though not equivalent to, at any rate entails "x is F and x is also not-F", which as it stands is formally self-contradictory'. Now the assertion could be reformulated as x-under-aspect-A is F, and x-under-aspect-B is G, which avoids a formal contradiction by predicating the opposites of different logical subjects. 'But what makes it still appropriate to talk about a (non-formal) contradiction is the fact that the different logical subjects are the same *thing* considered under different *aspects*. Thus everything depends on giving some significant content to the concept of a "thing", which is distinct from the concept of a "logical subject" and is not a purely formal concept.' But dialectics must therefore always involve an ontology, because the 'thing' (which includes also entities such as actions and social institutions) has to be constituted more or less concretely (depending on the stage of the presentation). (This should not be misunderstood to imply ontological 'layers' such as in Bhaskar's philosophy of science, and much Marxist essentialist materialism – where, for example, a particular commodity (such as a building) is conceived of as being a real embodiment of labour.)[34] The point is that the dialectic is inseparable from the circular development – for example, 'human being' does not concretely exist; it is an abstraction. Only when the circle has been completed may 'human being' have been given form and content, and then it may be comprehended actually. Only then is the abstract determined as concrete, when also the concrete is determined as abstract; and we may then say that human beings exist.

§11. Theorisation of the contingent

The primary aim of the presentation is to determine the necessary moments of the object-totality (§9) – to find out, ultimately, what phenomena of the actual existent are necessary to it, and what phenomena are contingent (in the sense that they could be otherwise without changing the essence of the object-totality – that is, its interconnectedness). The question is thus whether a specific existent institution or policy (at some place and at some time) is essential. (Of course, the fact that a specific policy is carried out implies that it has *some* ground; the question is whether it is external – perhaps, for example, merely a struggle for power between two ministries – or internal, that is essentially interconnected.)

There are two aspects to the way in which contingency enters into the presentation. The first is related to the problem of continual shifts in concrete events; the second is related to a second aim of the presentation, which is to show how contingency may be theorised within the method.

The first aspect is related to the possibility that the *content* of the transcendence of contradiction may not be determinate (in particular, at later more concrete stages) (cf. §10). (The transcendence as *form* at that particular stage of the presentation must be determinate since contradiction cannot remain unresolved.) The actual content of the transcendence may then be a continually shifting and contingent one. (For example, in Chapter 5, the shift from inflation to economic crisis is an underdetermined trans-

34 See also note 25 on essence and appearance.

cendence.) It should be stressed, however, that contingency does not imply that there can be no stable institutional patterns, albeit temporary ones. The necessary moments and tendencies are always and everywhere the structural framework within which actuality moves, and stable shifts are characteristic of *intra-epochal developments.* The systematic presentation is thus de facto always provisional and incomplete: it must therefore critically grasp accounts of intra-epochal developments in order to incorporate them either as a *necessary transcendence* (necessity of form and content) or as a *contingent transcendence* (necessity of form only); or to identify them as *merely contingent* after all (necessity of neither form nor content). It is thus an internal methodological imperative that the systematic presentation grasps intra-epochal development. The tensions generated within the epoch from the working-out of the necessary moments of the totality continually generate changes in the phenomenal forms in which that totality reproduces itself. Theory can continue to reaffirm its validity only by grasping these changes.

The second aspect arises because we deliberately choose to introduce contingency (at a certain stage). Whilst the previous incorporation of contingency is an internal methodological imperative, the argument for the presentation of contingency here is subsidiary. It is our contention that although the systematic presentation of the necessary moments is of prime importance, there are two reasons for going beyond it. The first is accessibility. To stick to that which is necessary may imply that whilst some parts of the presentation reach the phenomenal concrete in a quite detailed way (because necessity is at that detailed level), other parts remain very general. In the latter case, the phenomenal concrete would have to be grasped from those (perhaps rather inaccessible) general terms. The second reason is that some contingent phenomena may have become very important to (for example) economics or everyday consciousness. Thus even if, for example, a wave of bankruptcies or a monetarist economic policy were to be contingent phenomena, it would be unsatisfactory immediately to grasp these in terms of the tendency of the rate of profit to fall or the necessity to resolve the contradictions of the mixed economy. The presentation thus aims to show *how* it may be possible systematically to provide a link between the necessary and the merely contingent, within a systematic presentation. (It should be stressed that our aim here is primarily a methodological one: to indicate how detailed contingent development may be presented in accordance with the method.)

Addenda: a. Eldred *et al.* and the presentation of the contingent; b. Periodisation in Marxist economics

a. Our insistence on accounting for contingency – intra-epochal contingent transcendence as well as other merely contingent phenomena – differentiates our presentation from authors such as Eldred, Hanlon, Kleiber and Roth, who also work in the field of Hegelian systematic theory, and from whom we have otherwise obtained much inspiration. As against these authors, we do not accept a dichotomy between systematic theory and analysis of the contingent (cf. Eldred and Roth 1978; see also Williams 1984: §30). The value-form analysis of Eldred, Hanlon, Kleiber and Roth (1982/85) and Eldred (1984a) derives from a reconstruction of Marx's fragments of a system together with an extension to those aspects of the object-totality – the state and the private sphere – to which Marx's analysis did not reach. Their reconstruction is based on a reinstatement of the Hegelian dialectic in Marx's work, at the expense of the Ricardian remnants manifest in references to an embodied labour theory of value. The seminal work is Backhaus (1969). In general, our critique of the critical philosophy of these authors is that they tend to carry their idealism beyond transcendental idealism. More specifically, our insistence on the need to theorise intra-epochal developments goes beyond the value-form analysis of these philosophers, for whom such developments are elements of an endless sea of contingency beyond the grasp of systematic theory (for example, Eldred 1984a: 283). However, the methodological imperatives themselves cannot permit the presentation to stop at a point at which it has hypostatised the object-totality as an immutable metaphysical object (see Williams 1984: §45). Whilst we do not dispute the irrelevance of contingent fine grain detail phenomena, nor their inability to be comprehended by a systematic theory, we do dispute the stopping short of the presentation before intra-epochal movement has been accounted for. The contingency of phenomena does not preclude its theorisation, structured description and classification, nor even prediction to within some statistical degree of probability. Indeed, these kinds of intellectual practice are the pragmatic tools of everyday life and political practice, as well as providing the raw (or part-digested) material for systematic thinking, without which it would be tempted to resort to crude description of the untheorised phenomenological world rather than critically appropriating the current most highly developed consciousness of it. (For a critical appraisal of the method of systematic presentation used by Eldred *et al.*, see Williams 1984: §§26–33, §44, §§46–51.)

b. We aim to overcome not only the 'philosophism' of much value-form analytic work, but also the economism of much Marxist economics, which conceives intra-epochal development in terms of an (implicitly) irreversible periodisation into competitive, monopoly-capitalist, imperialist, financial-capitalist and state-monopoly-capitalist historical periods (cf. Eldred 1984a: 123–4).

---

§12. The validity of the theory

Because of the dilemma of epistemology (§3) the presentation itself must rest on its intrinsic merits. This does not imply that there can be no validity principle by which to judge the presentation. It must be judged by the extent to which it manages to provide the grounding of its starting point, not a priori in axioms or assumptions, but in the argument itself. However, if there is a body of systematic theory (cf. §§8–10) then one may of course refer to it and in that sense assume it.[35] We refer, for example, to Hegel's logic for the philosophical grounding of 'the concept'. (And had we been satisfied with, for example, the neoclassical or Marxist theory of value we might, instead of writing Chapter 1, merely have referred to the relevant literature.) The project of dialectical systematic theory means that one can always break into its circle of grounding at any point so as to criticise and improve it. The more substantial and abstract the critique, the more reconstruction work would then be required to reintegrate the theory.[36]

The grounding of the starting point, whilst most important (and, indeed, necessary) to the validity of the theory, is not sufficient. It would be very unsatisfactory to start off (in the context of discovery) from the question as to what determines economic policy and then to end up with only some abstract determination such as the interest of capital, some power block or class relations of the dominant capitalist nation (or any other vulgar versions of Marxism). Even if the starting point has been sufficiently grounded, systematic theory has to be extended to incorporate everyday phenomena and perceptions, including the theorisation of the merely contingent (§11). Validity also requires that the presentation does not stop whilst

35 This is quite another kind of assumption than, for example, that of 'rational economic man' or 'utility maximising individuals' for which economics sometimes refers to psychology. These are *external* assumptions. Even were the reference to psychology correct, economics would still have to ground that starting point in economic theory (whilst 'rational economic man' would have to provide a ground for psychology's starting point). None of this removes the speculative possibility that something like our presentation could indeed ground something like 'rational economic man' as the intermediate starting point for the theorisation of competition subjects (see 6S2). (For an immanent critique of neoclassical economics' lack of systematicity see Reuten 1986.)

36 The critique may be of a specific stage in the presentation, or of the *order* of the presentation. Numerous discussions between the two authors and many rewrites of what is to follow bear witness to the centrality of this latter type of critique. An arbitrary element in the order of discourse is also present in Hegel's logic, which according to Findlay (1973: 69–70) does not necessarily involve a single route: '... I think that the whole of the system is riddled with things that should be differently placed. I don't think that a sound Hegelian criticism would deny this.'

significant moments of the object-totality remain untheorised. 'Significant' is methodologically a very tricky notion; if it should turn out that the concretisation of economic policy at which the presentation arrives is not *connected* with (for example) economic crisis and unemployment (so that these phenomena remain *external* to the presentation), then a 'significant' moment of economic policy would have remained untheorised. In such a case, we might speculate as to the adequacy of the starting point, and/or of some stage of its grounding. The presentation can nevertheless never claim to be complete. If it were to be argued that significant moments have been neglected, then our response would have to be able to indicate where they fitted into our systematic theory, or to go back to it and redevelop the argument. In this sense, systematic theory maintains an endless dialogue with everyday and other forms of reflected consciousness (which is its starting point in the context of discovery – §7).

At the level of the object-totality itself there is, however, one important limitation concerning the question of significance. It is claimed only that the presentation, and, indeed, the method, is appropriate to the *existent* object-totality, which leaves entirely open the question of the appropriate method for any other historical epoch. By the same token, the existent is to be grounded in the existent, so no recourse is taken to historical explanation. Thus although history is significant in explaining why the existent *came* into being, it cannot explain why it is 'what it is', how the existent is *reproduced* as an interconnected whole. Whilst we do not reject the importance of the science of history, we do take issue with all those kinds of historicism (Hegelian, Marxist or whatever) for whom explaining 'emergence' is sufficient for the explanation of 'being' and 'becoming'.[37]

Dialectic systematic theory can thus be seen as successful to the extent that it has provided adequate conditions for the self-reproduction of its starting point in a structured coherent whole which incorporates significant insights from everyday and other forms of reflected consciousness (for us, especially in the fields of orthodox and Marxist economics) in such a way that that

---

37 Of course this is again tricky for a Hegelian; the term 'emergence' is somewhat misleading because it begs the question of 'coming into being'. But history is not the history of the idea (neither as the Absolute, nor that of classes). Rather it is not our object, so that we are not able to provide answers here. But that we do not presuppose, for example, classes (or the individual subject, for that matter) does not imply that these are a priori deemed unimportant, only that their 'significance' would have to be shown by their derivation and that of their conditions of existence.

consciousness can (given adequate reflection and study) come to recognise the antinomies of its conditions of existence *as* that structured totality. This also constitutes the major advance claimed for the present work: that it provides in outline *a method* of grasping the movement of particular sets of phenomena concerned with changes in the apparent macroeconomic state of the world and in economic policy stances towards them, as the temporally and spatially contingent working out of the moments and tendencies of the interconnected existent object-totality (see S4).

§13. Freedom and necessity

Knowledge of what is contingent and what is necessary to the existent would seem to provide an indication of the room for political manoeuvre and the scope for reform. Certainly to try to carry through reforms which challenge that which is necessary to the existent object-totality would necessarily evoke opposing forces in order to resolve the tensions generated thereby. Though even the contingent may be stubborn, it is possible to change, and the actualisation of this possibility requires knowledge of the necessary moments of the existent.

Idealism, in positing the necessary moments of the existent as immutable, would seem to contain certain positivist characteristics (in the Comte–Spencer–Mill sense), even if it goes beyond them in separating out the contingent. Nevertheless Hegel may be turned around (rather than upside down):

> Necessity indeed, qua necessity, is far from being freedom: yet freedom presupposes necessity and contains it as transcended in itself. (1817: §158A, adapted translation)

Freedom, then, first of all presupposes the consciousness of necessity, be it natural or social. Prior to this consciousness the necessary moments of the existent are indeed immutable. Social change can occur only when everyday consciousness comprehends the conditions of its existence – that is, the essence (inter-connectedness) of the existent totality – and consciously wills its transformation. Therefore truth – constituted in the whole – is in itself political. (Conversely, partial truth – which in terms of the whole is false – is also in itself political.) However, even consciously willed transformation is not actual for itself (actuality, 'actu'), since the will itself is socially and naturally constrained:

> Men make their own history, but not of their own free will; not under circumstances they themselves have chosen but under the

given and inherited circumstances with which they are directly confronted. (Marx 1852: 146)

A true grasp of the totality would then have to include a grasp of what could (or could not) be achieved:

> Mankind thus inevitably ['immer', i.e. always] sets itself only such tasks as it is able to solve, since closer examination will always show that the problem itself arises only when the material conditions for its solution are already present or at least in the course of formation ['oder wenigstens im Prozess ihres Werdens begriffen sind']. (Marx 1859: 21; German edn, p. 9).[38]

Truth is in itself politcal, but it may become for itself political – and thus freedom in itself – only if it is comprehended as in itself political.

SECTION 4 VALUE-FORM AND THE STATE: INTRODUCTION

§14. The bourgeois epoch as object-totality of the presentation

The subject-matter of our inquiry is 'the determination of economic policy in capitalist society' (§4). To avoid the existing detailed connotation of the term 'capitalist society' we refer initially to our domain of inquiry as 'the bourgeois epoch'; this is intended to exclude those societies which fall outside the domain (for example, feudal societies). In order to determine economic policy, and conform to the holistic ideal (§5) the domain itself will have to be determined. The object of the presentation is therefore first of all the determination of the necessary moments (§6) of the bourgeois epoch. The reference is to 'presentation' (rather than 'inquiry') for two interrelated reasons. The first stresses that the actual presentation of the argument is indeed a different process from that of an inquiry occurring in the context of discovery (§7). The second reason is a philosophical one. The phrase 'object of inquiry' may have a somewhat dualistic undertone. In discussing the axiom of realism (§3) we argued that, transcendentally, reality is not different from the

---

38 A more 'Hegelian' reading of the sentence after 'or' would be: 'when the material conditions for its solution are already present or (when these are) "at least *comprehended* within the process of their coming into being".' (Note that the citation of Marx is from the famous passage outlining the explanatory materialist version of historical materialism, from which our dialectical presentation stands aside.)

social inter-subjective conception of it. There is therefore no hypostatised 'bourgeois epoch' called up by an observer; rather the presentation itself constitutes the comprehension of the bourgeois epoch.

This Section sketches a brief outline of the course of the argument of Parts Two to Five, concentrating on the starting point and the major transitions. The starting point of Part Two (self-production, dissociation, value-form), is introduced in §§15–16. Part Two (the abstract existence of the capitalist economy) is introduced in §17, and Part Three (discussing the tendencies of accumulation of capital) in §18. §§19–20 then introduce the transition from the presentation of the economy to the presentation of the state and the mixed economy (Part Four). Finally §22 introduces the determination of economic policy and the transition to the presentation of contingent shifts in policy stances of the state and of intra-epochal development of economic policy (Part Five).

§15. From being to the starting point of the presentation: self-production

Humankind is not merely the unity of being and consciousness, it is an *active* unity ('conscious becoming'). Humankind in actively changing its circumstances, changes itself, hence its consciousness of itself and itself as being. Being includes consciousness, and consciousness includes being (§3).

The movement to the starting point of the presentation lies in the notion *self-production*. This movement can be conceived of as a transformation from philosophy to social science. The notion as notion and the concept as concept are presupposed. For their grounding, we refer to Hegel's logic. Hegel's starting point is Being, as negated by Nothing, both of which are for Hegel (1817: §§87–8) empty concepts which do not require much elaboration. From them he moves quickly on to Becoming and 'Dasein' (finite 'determinate' being; being there; which is Becoming posited in one of its moments, Being). One could say that Being and Not-Being are merely the preparatory notions to Becoming and 'Dasein', as the more explicit starting point of his presentation. (For this interpretation see Findlay 1975: xviii.) It is at this very beginning of Hegel's logic that we would locate the movement to our own starting point, though the completion of Hegel's logic as logic (that is as a meta activity at the level of philosophy) is presupposed.

From the preparatory universal and contradictory notions of being and not-being is thus derived *self-production* transcending these contradictory notions, which is further determined as *sociate*

37

being (i.e. social human being).[39] Sociate being is thus self-production posited in the form of one of its moments, being.

The notion of self-production is important because it provides the link from philosophy to the starting point of our political economic presentation. As positing 'the individual' (self), it is contradictory in itself. (This contradiction of the individual – though not conceived of as such – is the starting point of much bourgeois (social) science, for example neoclassical economics.) Self-production conceived of as individual posits self-production in its moment of nothing or not-being, because the human individual is inherently incapable of self-production. Self-production posited in its moment of being is human self-production which is inherently a social activity, *sociation* (Chapter 1).

The notion of self-production also encompasses the activity of the coming into being of consciousness (cf. Hegel's logic). Although there may be a scientific division here in that the notion of self-production is studied under different aspects in philosophy and political economy, they have one and the same root. Both the emergence of reflective thinking – becoming conscious of thinking as thought – and the thinking of the very notion of human *sociate* activity are the negation of the natural mode of life.[40] As this abstract negation, both reflective thought (thought as activity) and the consciousness of activity as human sociate activity are opposed to nature as different from it.[41]

Addendum: a. Hegel on self-production (thought)

a. We have linked Hegel's concepts 'becoming' and 'Dasein' (being there, finite determinate being) to 'self-production' and 'sociation'. In one interesting passage on 'Dasein' Hegel also applies the notion of self-production to thought. (Note that Knox-Miller translate 'Dasein' as 'existence', which is not altogether adequate – though perhaps better than Wallace's 'determinate being' – because in Hegel's logic existence ('Existenz') is used as a further determination of 'Dasein'.)

'Existence in our consciousness or minds we call 'knowing', the thinking Concept. Thus the spirit is this, namely to bring itself into existence, i.e. into consciousness. In consciousness as such I have an object; there is myself and something confronting me. But when I am the object of

---

39 Later on, the related concepts of dissociation and association will be introduced. For coherence of terminology we prefer the neologism 'sociate' to the common term 'social'.

40 For the first connection, reflective thinking as negation of the natural mode of life, see Hegel 1833: 113.

41 Note that without the consciousness of activity as sociate activity, there is no consciousness of nature either (in the dark, all cows are black).

thinking, the spirit is precisely this, to be self-producing, self-objectifying, self-knowing.' (Hegel 1833: 73–4)

(Unfortunately there are some further difficulties in the translation. 'Geist' is first rendered as 'mind' and then as 'spirit'; 'Wissen' is rendered as 'knowing' – note that the equivalent of 'Wissenschaft' is 'science'.):

> 'Das Dasein im Bewusstsein, im Geist nennen wir Wissen, denkenden Begriff. Der Geist ist also dieses, sich zum Dasein, d.h. zum Bewusstsein zu bringen. Als Bewusstsein überhaupt habe ich einen Gegenstand; da bin ich, und das, was mir gegenüber ist. Aber indem das Ich der Gegenstand des Denkens ist, so ist der Geist eben dies: sich zu produzieren, aus sich herauszusetzen, zu wissen, was er ist.' (Hegel 1833, Hoffmeister edn: 104)

§16. Sociation, dissociation and association: the value-form

Self-production and its further determination as sociation are *transhistorical* universals. *In the bourgeois epoch* sociation is negated as *dissociation* in that the units of production are separated from the units of consumption; production and consumption become distinct activities. The activity of self-production is thus contradictorily constituted as sociation and dissociation (1S2).

This dissociation is a *particular* historical *transition*. In this sense, there is a twofold contradiction: dissociation is not only the negation of sociation, it is also a particular form of it! Although this last contradiction is important (because it implies that this dissociation cannot be hypostatised) it is not the concern of our presentation, which is rather the bourgeois epoch. (Henceforth the term 'universal' always denotes universality with respect to the object-totality.) Nevertheless, the bourgeois epoch cannot be posited a priori as eternal. Indeed its historical specificity was a major concern of Marx in his frequent criticism of the classical economists' positing of their concepts as eternal. However, this kind of historical relativity, valid as it may be, does not itself tell us anything about the interconnectedness of existent bourgeois society. What is more, the fact that there has been a particular historical transition – and even that there have been others prior to it – does not say anything about *future* transitions. In any case, determinate transition would require actual comprehension of the conditions of existence of the existent (§13). In these senses historical materialism is not useful for the study of the bourgeois epoch.

The existence of self-production in its negative moment of dissociation (that is, the separation of production and consumption) necessarily requires transition into *association*. The associative transcendence of the sociation–dissociation contradiction lies in the exchange relation (1§4), which is further constituted as *value-form* determined (1§5). The sole existence of value is in *money*. With this transition, the sociative (natural) necessity for the allocation of labour to the production and distribution of useful objects doubles into that of use-value and value (money). This doubling constitutes the useful object as commodity. The doubling of useful objects into use-value (particular) and value (universal) is a contradiction whose grounding transcendence through the economy, society and the state is the guiding thread of our theorisation of the epoch.

Addendum: a. Dissociation and the sphere of households

a. In the bourgeois epoch sociation is negated as dissociation in that the units of production are separated from the units of consumption. Immediately to point out empirical counter-examples – e.g. some specific contemporary community in which this is not the case – is beside the point. The incorporation into the presentation of such specificities would have to await the appropriate stage, when it may be decided whether it is merely *contingent* or not.

Nevertheless, the negation of sociation is in fact incomplete at a high level of abstraction, because within the sphere of households – the units of consumption – there is also 'productive' activity not separated from consumption.[42] A large part of such (usually gender specific) activity is a contingently non-distinct activity (belonging to the more concrete phases of the presentation). However, as will be shown, there is one necessarily gender specific activity in which the non-distinctness of production from consumption is *essential* to the bourgeois epoch, namely the bearing of children. (The apparently appropriate term 'baby-production' appears odd precisely because it is a non-distinct activity.) The point is not so much that in other social formations bearing (as well as rearing) children are also most often gender specific activities, but rather that in the bourgeois epoch this must be a *non-distinct* activity. The point is not the superficial statement that without 'baby-production' the human race would not long persist, but rather that 'production of babies for the market' would be a contradiction that is irresolvable within the bourgeois epoch (see 1§9 and 2§12a). Although not unimportant to the persons concerned it is a secondary point that this non-distinct gender specific activity is the basis of a whole catalogue of others. Although this particularity of women makes them a target of discrimination, it is in principle not irresolvable within the bourgeois epoch.

§17. The value-form and production

Chapter 1 indicates the first, abstract conditions of existence of this contradiction in capitalist production. It is shown how, alongside the doubling of useful objects into use-value and money, labour doubles

---

42 'Productive' has been put in inverted commas because within the household the production–consumption distinction does not apply (see Chapter 1).

into concrete labour (use-value producing labour) and abstract labour (value producing labour), and how these doublings determine the production process as also a twofold one, that of technical and that of abstract labour process (or valorisation process – the process of expansion of value). It is further shown that whilst for the technical labour process three elements of production are required (nature, labour, means of production), only labour is necessary to the valorisation process.

In theoretical terms this part of the presentation attempts to overcome the one-sidedness of the neoclassical utility theory of value as well as the (neo-)Ricardian and Marxist embodied-labour theories of value. It does this by critically appropriating value-form analysis and the abstract-labour theory of value (themselves independent reactions against the labour-embodied theory), and providing a value-form theoretic reconstruction of the abstract-labour theory of value. This enables the presentation to provide the linkage between a market-oriented theory of value (money prices) and production, so that it becomes clear from the outset why the focus is on the allocation of labour. This overcomes one of the key criticisms of Marxist approaches in orthodox economics – that they have no basis for privileging labour over other 'factors of production'.

In Chapter 2, it is first shown how the valorisation of capital necessarily gives rise to the compulsion to accumulate it. Accumulation is next grounded in the credit system (in particular the banking system) and the extended reproduction of labour power. The derivation of the existence of capital as 'many capitals' completes the presentation of the abstract existence of the capitalist economy.

Addendum: a. Everyday consciousness of the dominance of money

a. Whilst the starting point of the presentation is a theoretically mediated one, the introduction of money and the value-form at the earliest stage indicates their dominance in the bourgeois epoch. Everyday consciousness is certainly not devoid of insight concerning the dominance of money; useful things have typically to be bought, and to do this individuals have to control some income source, and so on. And of course a similar insight is also central to orthodox microeconomics in that market mechanisms are perceived as dominant (and – in the apologetic aspects of this discourse – are also posited as eternal and optimal).

---

§18. Accumulation and its tendencies

In Part Three (Chapters 3–5) the expression of the compulsion to accumulate capital is developed. In Chapter 3 the form of existence of accumulation in a tendency to over-accumulation of capital is presented. The expressions of this tendency are in a tendential cyclical development similar, on the one hand, to that analysed in neoclassical and neo-Ricardian theories of labour shortage and on the other, to that analysed in theories of underconsumption (of neo-Marxist and Keynesian varieties). These two (abstract) tendencies of development, which are usually put forward as mutually exclusive, will be presented as interconnected. In Chapter 4, the form of existence of accumulation in a tendency for the composition of capital to increase (capital-using technical development) and a contradictory tendency for the rate of profit to fall are derived. The conditions of existence of this contradiction, as well as its expressions in capital devaluation and restructuring and centralisation of capital, are then derived. Chapter 5 provides an account of the articulation of the tendencies presented in Chapters 3–4. The emphasis will in particular be on shifts in economic development which *contingently transcend* (§11) the tendential contradictions. Economic crises as well as the contingent conditions for overcoming them – in particular the contingent conditions of inflation in the banking system – are introduced. The presentation then approaches what economics perceives as the phenomenal level. In its separation from the political and the private spheres, this is however still one-sided and abstract

---

Addenda: a. Marxist economics; b. The economy, individual subjects and classes

a. The methodology of the whole presentation requires the generation of the conditions of existence of the sociation–dissociation contradiction as transcended in the association of the value-form. In this, it differs not only from orthodox economics but also from Marxist economics, the weakness of which is that much of its theory is fragmented – as revealed in the competing theories not only of value but also of economic development and crisis. Marxists have tended to put forward *one* of the theories mentioned (labour shortage, underconsumption or rise in the composition of capital) rejecting the others as inconsistent with it. Our presentation claims that these theories are systematically connected; it consequently criticises other approaches as being one sided, seemingly forced to neglect certain concrete phenomena.

b. In Parts Two and Three (Chapters 1–5), the market system is presented as the regulator of the economy. The presentation here differs from orthodox as well as Marxist economics, in that it has a fundamentally different starting point. Orthodox economics starts with the individual subject as an (axiomatic) assumption – the individual is assumed as an (atomised) subject of competition deploying an income source (whether property or the capacity to labour) in pursuit of income, in competition with other subjects of competition. In contradistinction to this, our presentation posits valorisation and the derived accumulation of capital as fundamentally a subjectless process, determined neither by the consciously willed activity of individual subjects (pace orthodox economics), nor by any universal social subject (for example, a central planning board), but rather by the value-form grounding of the sociation–dissociation contradiction. Individual willed subjects cannot be assumed but must be developed from within the presentation. Individual subjectivity is thus to be derived from the totality, rather than the totality being understood as the mere aggregation of individual subjectivity.

Our presentation also differs from classical Marxism, which opposes to (atomistic) individualism as the basic unit of analysis economically determined classes, set in an inherently antagonistic class structure. An embodied-labour theory of value is then needed to show the existence of an intrinsically exploited labouring class. Our presentation on the other hand can conceive of class only as a theoretically developed concept. At the level of the economy (Parts Two and Three) classes appear only abstractly as the bearers of the social relations 'commodity producer' and 'controller of valorisation' (labourer and entrepreneur respectively). It is only with the introduction of subjectivity in the presentation of Part Four that they gain further determination.

---

§19. The doubling of competitive society into civil society and the state

In Parts Two and Three (Chapters 1–5) self-production is presented as existing abstractly as value-form determined association. At this level of the presentation subjects are implicit only as subjects without subjectivity – that is, as abstract bearers of economic relations. The contradiction of subjects without subjectivity is the appearance at this level of the contradiction between the abstract value-form and abstract free will.

In Chapter 6, these contradictions are made explicit. They are transcended in *competitive society*, which is the unity of the abstract capitalist *economy* and the abstract social existence of *free will*. We adapt the concept of free will from Hegel (1821), who seems to have been able to relate the economic and the political moments one to the other only externally.[43] We present the internal connections of this relation by developing the abstract bearers of economic relations and the abstract bearers of free will into *competition subjects*, wielding property or the capacity to labour as income sources in the pursuit of self-production in the value-form determined economy.

---

43 See Arthur 1988 for an account of the apparent inconsistency between Hegel's early work on political economy, and the later (and better known) *Philosophy of Right*. (cf. also Plant 1977 and Walton 1984.)

It is argued that the reproduction of competitive society and subjectivity requires the right to property and the right to existence. However, within competitive society these rights cannot exist as social rights, and so they are contradictory. This contradiction is transcended in the doubling of competitive society into *civil society* and the *state*. We are thus able to theorise the state (the political sphere) on the basis of the presentation of the economy as the crucial moment of society – a theoretical task which defeated not only Hegel and Marx but also, we would argue, subsequent attempts in this tradition. The state is shown to be the social subject *vis-à-vis* the social existence of particular subjects in civil society (the reappearance of competitive society with the emergence of the state). However, the contradiction of competitive society reappears in the contradictory relationship between civil society and the state. Bourgeois subjects consent to the existence and activities of the state in the general interest and yet, to maintain the consciousness of free will, must feel themselves subject only to their own will.

As universal social subject the state must hold itself *separate* from the essentially subjectless value-form process of civil society, and yet – in the exercise of its social subjectivity and its management of consent – it must be able to intervene in that society. The relationship between state and civil society is then constituted as a contradictory *separation-in-unity*. The theorisation of the state's activities (Chapters 8–10) consists essentially in the further concretisation of this contradictory relationship and its forms of existence.

§20. Individuals, state and society

Before this, however, Chapter 7 outlines the incorporation into the presentation of the private sphere of the family and personal relations, and the more concrete existence of the state as 'many states'. The relationship between bourgeois subjects and the state has many determinants which are nationally specific, so that the general interest which informs the activities of the state exists more concretely as many particular national interests. The location of this area within the presentation is tentative. We also merely indicate the way towards a value-form theorisation of the private sphere, and relatedly of the development of the bourgeois individual as the contradictory unity of competition subject, citizen and private subject. This is another area which requires considerably more work. In terms of the understanding of the concrete conditions of existence of bourgeois persons it is a vital area for the study in which the dialectic of freedom and necessity (§13) is further grounded.

§21. The mixed economy and economic policy

In Chapter 8, the state as social subject is concretised primarily as maintaining a framework of law, money and social infrastructure. In order to do so, it necessarily re-engages with the economy; consequently the contradictions of separation-in-unity reappear as the contradictions of the *mixed economy* – the contradictory coexistence of value and use-value criteria for resource allocation (cf. §16). This contradictory coexistence is grounded in *economic policy*, and in the state as its agent. Economic policy is the concrete form of existence of the contradictory relationship between state and civil society – separation-in-unity – the contradictions of which are expressed as the antinomies of economic policy.

In Chapter 9, the *welfare* state is derived from the contingency of particular existence in civil society, the inability of the economy to produce one of its own conditions of existence – an adequate supply of labour – and the need for the state to maintain its own legitimation in the consent of bourgeois persons. *Macroeconomic* management is derived from the necessary fiscality of the state and its necessary provision of a monetary framework. The state, in pursuit of its own material reproduction and of its policy objectives deploys these putatively framework components in active economic management; it is constituted centrally as the modification of the value-form determined allocation of resources in the economy by the use-value determined activities of the state. The most direct form of this activity lies in *microeconomic* intervention explicitly aimed at such resource allocation.

As the activities of a sovereign social subject intervening in the basically subjectless processes of the economy embedded in civil society, welfare and economic policy manifest the contradictions of the mixed economy. It is shown how the welfare state conflicts with the value-efficiency of the market reproduction of the economy and, by raising aspirations which it cannot satisfy, threatens to undermine the legitimation of the state. Macroeconomic management similarly tends to mediate the cyclical reproduction of the economy over time, and may confront the state with conflicting demands expressing the contradiction between the right to property (calling for accumulation-oriented policy) and the right to existence (calling for consumption-oriented policy). Most acutely, the interventions of microeconomic policy directly confront the market-reproduction of value criteria with politically and administratively enforced use-value criteria, and thence import the manifestations of this basic contradiction of the bourgeois epoch into the state itself.

§22. The cyclical reproduction of accumulation and policy

The presentation in Chapter 9 (§21) shows the state increasingly intervening in civil society in response to the antinomies which express the contradictions of the mixed economy. Based as it is on the epochal contradiction between value and use-value, the manifestations of the contradictory form of separation-in-unity are not dissolved, but can only be managed in contingently shifting forms of existence (§§10–11). In Chapter 10 it is argued that these are contingently determined by the location of each sovereign state's economy within the world economy. In order to initiate the move towards conjunctural accounts of empirical intra-epochal development the quantitative manifestations of the conflicts of the mixed economy in the threat of economic stagnation and of fiscal crisis of the state are outlined. Two categories of conjunctural settlement – conservative neo-liberalism and social-democratic corporatism – are then presented as currently important contingent groundings of the cyclical course of the intra-epochal development of accumulation and policy.

The presentation thus, in outline, comes full circle to the concrete expression of the systemic attempts to reproduce its starting point – the value-form as the specifically bourgeois mode of association of dissociated individuals incapable of self-production. From our starting point and conceptual development it is shown that the fundamental use-value–value contradiction is not definitively transcended within bourgeois society. The subjectless processes of the economy articulate not only with the necessary activities of the state, but also with the state's contingent and shifting attempt to manage the manifestations of that epochal contradiction. This contingency provides an indication of the room for political manoeuvre and the scope for reform within bourgeois society (§13). If that claim sounds too grandiose, the presentation at least provides a conceptualisation of the current epoch, located in relation to existing conceptualisations, which is open to critique at every step, and which provides the basis for conjunctural analysis, the success or failure of which will also enable the theory to be continually reassessed.

SUMMARY

The object of this book is to present the determinants of economic policy in capitalist society – or, more generally, in the bourgeois epoch. Section 4 provides an outline of the argument of Chapters 1–10; in doing so, we have concentrated on the starting point of the presentation as well as on its major transitions. In §§14–16 we introduced the object of the presentation, the bourgeois epoch. It was shown how this starting point was linked by the concept of self-production to the Hegelian opposites being and nothing, and how it, and the derived sociation are similar to the Hegelian transcendents 'becoming' and the derived 'Dasein'. It was indicated how in the bourgeois epoch sociation is negated as dissociation, and how sociation and dissociation are transcended in the association of the value-form. The next two paragraphs (§§17–18) introduced the presentation of the economy (Chapters 1–5). The transition from the presentation of the economy to that of competitive society, and then the state and economic policy (Chapters 6–10) was introduced in §§19–20. We stress that our presentation of the economy has a different starting point from both orthodox economics (atomistic individuals) and from the classical Marxist economics (classes). It is only at a later stage of our presentation (Chapter 6) that subjects appear – first abstractly as bearers of social economic relations and bearers of free will, then further determined, with the right to property and the right to existence. It is indicated that even these rights can have only an ideal existence in competitive society, so that their condition of existence is the doubling of competitive society into state and civil society, and then the intervention of the state into civil society. This intervention is further concretised in economic policy. §22 introduced the presentation of changing conjunctural policy settlements determined by the articulation of the tendencies of accumulation, and the state's own conditions of existence (notably its legitimation). These are again grounded in the self-reproduction of competitive society. In this way the argument comes full circle – it has returned to its starting point, which should then prove to be a concrete unity in difference.

This book is also very much an essay in methodology. As indicated in the Preliminary Remarks it is our contention that the current state of economic science requires a conscious effort to develop a methodology not only from a transcendental standpoint, but also from within the science itself. Part One has therefore largely been devoted to making our method explicit. Parts Two to Five should be conceived of as a first verification of this method. Section 1 provided an indication of the current state of method in economics, and briefly outlined a critique of the empiricist philosophy of the professed economics methodology from the point of view of the stratification of science. Section 2 gave a preliminary introduction to our method, which is inspired by the logic of Hegel's dialectic. It sets out how thinking fundamentally runs in terms of oppositions, and how reality cannot conceivably be different from the inter-subjective conception of it (§3). These perceptions of the object of inquiry are more or less interconnected in consciousness. Perceptions are abstract to the extent that they are unconnected; it is the object of science to set out the interconnection of phenomena, which determines (and thus explains) them (§§4–6). §7 described the movement in thinking from abstract (unconnected) perception towards abstract determination. In fact such positing of abstract determination is a proposition as to the universality of the object-totality and as to what unites phenomena and perceptions in the abstract. This determination may be cast in terms of conjectures and refutations taking place in the context of discovery.

Section 3 set out our method of dialectical systematic theory proper. The starting point of the presentation – the result of thought in the context of discovery – is abstract, but is not taken axiomatically. The objective of the presentation itself is rather to ground the starting point in the concrete. The starting point is abstract in that it is initially taken in isolation (a moment) and is posited as universal (§8), and thence may at first be given determination only by its doubling into itself and its negation. These notions of isolation and negation each indicate aspects of the same process by which the presentation proceeds. The first is that what is posited in the abstract concept cannot exist in isolation, whence its conditions of existence have to be determined. The second is that contradiction cannot remain unresolved; contradiction has thus to be grounded in its transcendence: in this determination of existence, the abstract concept is being grounded. The presentation is in consequence a movement of grounding transcendence in which the concepts become ever more particular, concrete and differentiated, so that they become determined as unity in difference. The presentation thus proceeds, by way of articulation of the most abstract determinants, to the phenomena of the object-totality ultimately comprehended by the most concrete categories in their (full) interconnectedness. It is this interconnectedness that constitutes the essence of the object-totality (§9).

In §10 we indicated the limitations to the Hegelian dialectic in social science, where in contradistinction to logic actuality may be conceived only as potential ('an sich') actuality: it may not be posited a priori that contradiction is always transcended in moments necessary to the object-totality. Contradiction may rather be persistent in the sense that it is only contingently transcended by way of continual shifts. Next (§11) we expanded on the theorisation of this contingency, as well as of that introduced deliberately into the presentation. It is one of our major aims to show how it may be possible to incorporate an account of the contingent into the method of dialectical systematic presentation. The crucial opposites, *necessity–contingency of the actual, are taken up in §13 in relation to the questions of freedom and social change.*

The question of the validity of the presentation was set out in §12. Methodologically, the presentation should prove its validity first and foremost in the extent to which it indeed manages to provide the concrete grounding of its starting point – that is, the extent to which it manages to transcend all a priori notions. But the method also requires that all significant moments of the object-totality be theorised – as contingent if not as necessary. The third methodological requirement is the opportunity for dialogue. The project of dialectical systematic theory is that one can always and at any point break into its circle of grounding so as to criticise and improve it – provided, of course, that the critic has followed through the argument up to the point where s/he decides to enter into critical dialogue.

Part Two:

The Value-Form and its Reproduction

Chapter one

The Value-Form

PRELIMINARY REMARKS

We have indicated in Part One that it is the aim of this book to theorise the interconnection of empirical phenomena in bourgeois society. The purpose of this chapter is to theorise the character of the connection itself – the character of social relations in bourgeois society. This is, of course, very abstract, and the discourse in this chapter is far removed from the complex content *of those relations.*

Section 1 briefly presents the link from the most abstract logical notions (being and not-being) to the starting point of the presentation of bourgeois society in Section 2. It is a transhistorical account of the material existence of human being: human procreation is existent in sociation, and requires the creation and social allocation of useful objects. This creation and social allocation of useful objects is a naturally necessary condition for human existence. Section 2 presents the dissociative separation of units of production and consumption in bourgeois society, which negates the necessary sociation. The theme of the following Sections is then how this sociation–dissociation contradiction is transcended in capitalism. It is argued that value provides the particular bourgeois form of association. The value-form (expressed in terms of money) then determines the character of interconnection in bourgeois society. Useful objects as well as their creation thus have a contradictory existence: useful objects have the double existence of use-value and money, and the activity of their creation doubles into concrete use-value producing labour, and labour productive of value. In bourgeois society, it is argued, labour and the products of labour are thus socially *recognised as useful only by assuming the form of value: money.*

This conceptualisation of the particular bourgeois form of association is also the basis of our critique of various other value-

53

theoretic approaches. Exclusive focus on the use-value aspect leads to a technicist approach to the capitalist process of production. Production is then considered as a process of production of use-values (as in neoclassical theory), or of embodied-labour values (as in neo-Ricardian and one strand of Marxist theory). These approaches may be appropriate for theorising communal societies, but not for theorising capitalism. Because money is incorporated only – if at all – as an afterthought (as in the classical dichotomy) such approaches are forced to theorise exchange as an 'as if' process, that is as a hypothetical construct within the terms of the theory. Ricardian–Marxist economics thus constructs an 'as if' exchange in terms of embodied-labour values (cf. Himmelweit & Mohun, 1978 and Reuten 1979), whilst neoclassical economics constructs an 'as if' exchange in terms of 'any' good. These constructs inhibit the account of a capitalist economy as an essentially monetary system.

Marx's theory in Capital *(1867, 1885, 1894) may be looked upon as an effort to comprehend the capitalist economy from the point of view of the necessity to manage the value–use-value duality. However, Marx's own theory of value is at least ambiguous, as well as fragmentary in two respects. First, it is not clear to what degree Marx actually distanced himself from the Ricardian labour-embodied theory of value. Though he aims to do so in his writings on value, a great deal of the theory in the three volumes of* Capital *seems to be a retreat to the labour-embodied concept (see §6c). The second ambiguity concerns Marx's derivation of the concepts of exchange value and abstract labour not from capitalist exchange but from commodity exchange in general (and mercantile commodity exchange in particular). The result is that at some point Marx needs to 'transform' his categories so that they suit capitalist exchange and production (see §3a). This second ambiguity has not received much attention (although the 'transformation problem' has). The question of labour-embodied theories of value, however, has been at the centre of the Marxist tradition for the last two decades. Until the 1960s a labour-embodied theory of value dominated entirely, but since then three reactions from within Marxism have developed. The first (led by Steedman, after Sraffa) proposes an approach based on technical coefficients. The second is the 'abstract-labour theory of value' and the third is 'value-form analysis' (see §6c). Each of these strands may find apparent support in Marx's work. In this chapter – whilst implicitly taking the Steedman critique of the labour-embodied theory seriously – we hope to provide a development of the abstract-labour theory of value in the light of value-form analysis. It is central to both of them that capitalism should be theorised simultaneously in terms of use-value and of monetary* relations; or, rather, that the conflict between them should be theorised. The other reason for linking our theory to value-form analysis is of course the similarity of that method to our own (0§4).

The aim is to provide a value-form theoretic reconstruction of the abstract-labour theory of value on the basis of our methodology as set out in 0S3. Apart from systematic and general methodological claims, the presentation in this chapter provides the following new theoretical insights: the conceptual link from Hegel's logic to the starting point of our presentation (Sections 1–2); the derivation of the value-form and abstract labour, not from commodity exchange in general, but from dissociation in capitalism (Section 3); the connection between the commensuration of labour and its products in terms of money in the market, and the ideal pre-commensuration of labour in terms of money in production by which we are able to show how capitalist exchange affects the process of production; the notion that, though there are several factors of production of new useful objects, only labour power can be a factor of production of value-added (Section 5). Though this last point is an integral part of many labour theories of value, it is mostly incorporated only as an axiom or as a common sense notion ('every child knows ...' Marx 1868). Section 4 provides an abstract conceptualisation of money –without taking recourse to commodity money, which thereby differs from most of Marxist economics in this respect.[1]

SECTION 1   SELF-PRODUCTION AND SOCIATION (TRANS-HISTORICAL NOTIONS)

§1. Self-production

The link from the transhistorical universals, being/not-being, to the starting point of our presentation is human self-production. Self-production itself transcends the notion of being and its opposite, not-being or nothing (0§15).

Addendum: a. Abstract link to the starting point

a. 'Self-production' is the abstract link to the starting point of our presentation. It is the result of the process of abstraction initiated within the context of discovery (0§§7–8). Self-production is not an axiom or an assumption but a notion that is grounded in the course of the argument below (0§9). The preparatory notions of self-production are analogous to the

---

1 An earlier version of the main argument of this chapter was presented at the 1986 CSE conference.

preparatory notions of being and nothing in Hegel's logic, which derive the notion 'becoming' (0§15).

§2. Sociation

The notion of self-production (§1) appears contradictory. It is so only if self-production is conceived of as that of an individual. Self-production conceived of as that of an individual posits self-production in its moment of not-being, because the human individual is inherently incapable of self-production. Self-production posited in its moment of being posits it inherently as a social activity – as sociation.

Sociation is further determined as sexual and educational activity, and the activity of creation of useful objects. These activities are naturally necessary for material sustenance. The creation of useful objects – which is a transformation of physical inputs into qualitatively divergent physical outputs – has required to date the use of some combination of three elements: uncultivated and freely available nature; previously created useful objects as instruments (including cultivated nature); and human activity itself. (Hence, to date, this performance of human activity is *one* necessary element for the material reproduction of life.)

Addendum: a. Natural necessity of sociation

a. The natural necessity of the sociate activities is transhistorical. A range of particular useful objects may be created to satisfy the requirement. (The term 'useful object' is used as a transhistorical category. The term use-value is introduced only in §6.) There is no particular necessary organisational form of these activities.

SECTION 2   DISSOCIATION

§3. Dissociation: production and consumption

In the bourgeois epoch, sociate activity (which posits self-production in its moment of being (§§1–2)), is separated into distinct activities of production and consumption of useful objects. This separation articulates *labour* as a distinctive *activity* of production. Not only are these distinct activities, they are themselves *organised* in separate *private independent units*. That the organisation has taken this form is historically specific. In the bourgeois epoch, sociation is thus negated in dissociation, so that self-production is posited in its negative moment. Sociate activity doubles into production and consumption and these again are performed in particular private units, so that labour as a distinctive activity is posited as dissociated labour. However, the sexual and educational activity of procreation (and in particular the gender specific activity of child-bearing) is not separated into productive (labour) and consumption activity.[2] The following three elements of dissociation should be stressed: first, as the units of production are separated from the units of consumption, it is the overall or macro organisation that is one of independent (and in that sense dissociated) labour. Second, the micro organisation of the particular unit of production is not one of free association of labour but one of organisation of labour under a private regime upon which labour is dependent, at least temporarily. In this sense, the micro organisation is also one of dissociation. Labour's dependence at the micro level is the counterpart of its independence at the macro level. Third, a concomitant of both independence and dependence is that the driving force of production is an aim which is *external* to the particular useful objects that are produced (since consumption is separated from production).

Addenda: a. Difference from Marx; b. The private sphere; c. Historical explanation versus necessity.

a. Dissociation is the conceptual starting point of our presentation of the bourgeois epoch. It is unclear where Marx's systematic starting point should be located. He seems to begin with perceptions ('The wealth of those societies in which the capitalist mode of production prevails, presents itself as an immense accumulation of commodities, its unit being a single commodity. Our analysis must therefore begin with the analysis of a commodity' 1867: 43, cf.1859: 27). Backhaus (1969: 100-2) has set out the unsystematic character of the first chapter of *Capital*. It is remarkable that Eldred, Hanlon, Kleiber and Roth, whilst they aim to provide 'a systematic reconstruction of Marx's uncompleted system', and whilst they draw on Backhaus for their critique of Marx, in fact have a similar starting point to Marx's. The difference is that they consider 'single commodity' misleading and start with commodities (Eldred *et al.* 1982/85: 351). However, they seem to sense a methodological problem, as they feel constrained to add: 'At the beginning of the analysis of capitalism, 'the whole' *must* be referred to *but* at the beginning it *can* only be referred to as it appears: capitalist wealth as a

---

2 We owe the insight of the separation of 'activity' into productive and consumption activity to Himmelweit (1984). The separation of the units of production from the units of consumption is also stressed by Weber (1920: 21): 'The modern rational organization of the capitalist enterprise would not have been possible without ... the separation of business from the household, which completely dominates modern economic life, ...' The term 'dissociation' is also used by De Vroey (1981: 176) and by Eldred, Hanlon, Kleiber and Roth (1982/85: 354). Eldred *et al.*, however, link the concept only to the separation of production and consumption.

collection of commodities' (Eldred *et al.* 1982/85: 351, our emphasis). This is indeed a very undialectical 'solution' to a dialectical problem.

The introduction of 'private micro organisation of dissociated labour' at the starting point (§3), is crucial to our presentation. With it we implicitly refer to capitalist production (see also §6a and S5). It overcomes an important ambiguity in Marx's writing on value, an ambiguity that is very well set out by Napoleoni (1973: 6 and ch. 5). Marx (1867) derives the concepts of exchange value and abstract labour (see §6) from the examination of exchange as such. At the point where he does so the reference is not to capitalism but rather to (mercantile) commodity exchange in general. On the other hand, abstract labour comes to be considered as 'labour which is opposed to capital', as wage labour, and then the concept of capitalism cannot be separated from the concept of value (see Napoleoni 1973: 99 and Gleicher 1983). Marx's distinction between mercantilism and capitalism is consequently an ambiguous one. Like Ricardo (but unlike Smith) Marx derives the concept of exchange value from commodity exchange and not from *capitalist* commodity exchange. Therefore like Ricardo, Marx at some point needs to 'transform' his categories so that they suit capitalist exchange (hence forms of exchange-value). The 'transformation problem' is therefore implicit in Marx's derivation of the concepts of value and abstract labour from (mercantile) commodity exchange instead of capitalist exchange, which is necessarily predicated upon capitalist *production*. (See also Cutler, Hindess, Hirst and Hussain, 1977: ch. 1; cf. 6§12e.)

The critique of Marx in this respect also applies to Eldred, Hanlon, Kleiber and Roth (1982/85). Their presentation (e.g. their separation of the capitalist and the labourer (p. 380) and their development of the capital-wage-labour relation *after* the introduction of the commodity) is the more remarkable as they themselves criticise any historical-genetic method of analysis, which might have legitimated such an order of presentation. (Marx's approach was indeed both structural–genetic and historical–genetic – cf. Zelený 1968: 38–9 and Eldred 1984a: xxiv–xxv.)

b. The terms 'private' regime and 'private' organisation have been introduced for want of any better word. They refer to the organisation under the aegis of a firm which will be constituted in Chapter 6 as private property. 'Private' in this sense should be distinguished from the 'private sphere' of the household and personal relations within the bourgeois epoch, which will be introduced briefly in 7S1.

c. To say that the bourgeois organisation of production is historically specific does not imply that it is impossible to explain its coming into being. Particular historical constellations (as described, for example, by Marx) have given rise to it. But such a historical description/'explanation' (however interesting it may be and however much it may contribute to our understanding of the current epoch within history) does not say whether and why something is necessary today (0§§12,16). Smith's (1776) argument (deriving such necessity from human psychological nature) is much more to the point. His effort to provide a basis for the mode of production is, however, not convincing (see Napoleoni 1973: ch. 2, Roll 1938: ch. IV). Neoclassical economics would explain it in terms of efficiency; dissociation then must be conceived of as efficient decentralisation. But this is not sufficient to posit dissociation as necessary: if the argument was that the individual is naturally a utility maximising unit (so that utility maximisation leads to the market because it is efficient), then the market would be part of the utility function. (It is not uninteresting that to counter the argument that 'monopolistic competition' is inefficient, it has been argued that market choice does indeed intrinsically confer utility – see, for example, Hay & Morris 1979: 10–20.)

SECTION 3   ASSOCIATION: THE VALUE-FORM

§4. The exchange relation

In sociation, self-production is posited in its moment of being (§2). The dissociation of labour in the bourgeois epoch negates sociation and posits self-production in its moment of not-being (§3). Dissociation therefore necessarily requires a moment of association, transcending the sociation–dissociation opposition. The dissociation of labour requires a moment recognising the useful objects produced privately as *socially* useful objects, and so the labour performed independently as *social* labour. This necessity is accomplished through the *exchange relation*, which aligns production to consumption and constitutes the private, fragmented, units of production as interdependent. The exchange relation establishes that the dissociated activity of particular labour – producing particular useful objects – becomes associated. The exchange relation thus provides the first condition of existence of dissociation. (This condition is abstract, and neither the form nor the dimension of the exchange relation has been determined.)

Addenda: a. Exchange; b. Exchange and the market; c. Services

a. This concept of exchange is a general one. It includes, for example, the marginal utility school's concept of use-value exchange. As against Marx's (1867) conception, ours does not *immediately* posit the commodity as a form of value.

b. The notion that a dissociated mode of production requires a moment of association is not substantially new. From Adam Smith's (1776) 'invisible hand' to current neoclassical general equilibrium economics, the role of the market has been the central issue of mainstream economic analysis. We do not introduce the market until §6, thus stressing that exchange does not immediately imply it, and that the development of the value-form of products (§5 below) is systematically prior to the prevalence of markets. (However, this systematic argument may not be reversed: the argument does not enable the conclusion that market regulation necessarily implies the dominance of the value-form.)

c. At this stage of the presentation, the notion of 'useful objects' (§2), also includes services. (Below, useful objects, including services, are also referred to as 'products'.) Of course at the abstract level of sociation as social *activity*, it makes no sense to posit services alongside useful objects. The activity of creation of useful objects is itself a 'service' so to speak. (This may provide one clue as to the classical economists' and Marx's difficulty in conceptualising services in their productive/unproductive labour discussions – cf. 10§3.)

§5. The value-form

The organisation of labour for the production of useful objects in private independent units, which is determined externally to the production of particular useful objects (§3), further determines the form and the dimension of the exchange relation (§4). Given that the physical inputs to the process of production qualitatively diverge from the physical outputs (§2), and that such divergence in itself is not the aim of the private process (as might be the case if production and consumption were not separated), the process necessarily requires inputs and outputs to be reduced to a universal, unitary form or common denominator. The necessary exchange relation has therefore to be one of unitary form. *Value* is the *suis generis* of this common denominator; value is thus constituted as *universal*, as opposed to the *particularity* of the physical input and output.

As such, value as a form is the necessary dimension of labour and of the useful objects produced by it in the bourgeois mode of production. It is a *social* dimension and a social universal. It is not an a priori (in Kant's sense) natural–physical dimension and universal (space and continuity), though value is a category as abstract as space and continuity. In social intercourse, the social meaning of value is further constituted, in particular, by the measure of money.[3] Thus the particular products of labour necessarily have to take on a

---

3 The space of an object is further constituted by the measure of length (for which, for example, metres or yards are standards): similarly the value of an object is further constituted by the measure of money – for which, for example, a dollar or a yen are standards. Both length and money are constituted in social intercourse, and as such they are social facts. These remarks are however premature (§7) – the conceptual development of the form or dimension of value is prior to its measure and standards.

social–universal form which is the value-form, for without them being *validated* as such they are socially non-existent.

Concomitantly, *labour power* – the individual's ability to perform labour for a definite period of time – like the outputs and the other inputs of the production process, necessarily has to take on the value-form, namely, the *wage*. The peculiarity of labour power as a necessary input taking the value-form is that it is not produced within the bourgeois mode of production. (It is rather an input from outside, from the private sphere of the household.) Whilst its creation is *not* socially integrated into that mode of production, it thus nevertheless takes the form of the products of that mode.

As both inputs and outputs are necessarily reduced to value as a common denominator, this social–universal form is the external driving force of the enterprise (§3). More precisely, the external driving force is a surplus of value above the value initially laid out (that is, profit).

So the products of labour, as well as labour power in the bourgeois epoch, are entities of a double form. (As we will see later on – §6 – they are entities of a potential double form before the actual exchange has taken place.) They indeed have a double reality. The creation of useful objects is necessary to human self-production (§2), but their dissociative mode of creation in production within the bourgeois epoch demands that they, as well as labour power, necessarily have to take on a social–universal form (value) which is different from their particular form. This mode of production further entails the contradiction that the *social* form is the external determinant of this mode of *private* production. The abstract social–universal form thus dominates over the private-particular such that the private–particular is determined by the abstract social–universal form. As such, the bourgeois mode of production is form determined.

Addenda: a. Abstract free will; b. Abstract labour; c. Labour and labour power; d. The philosophical concept of 'value'; e. Neoclassical economics

a. The value-form is a major moment of association in the bourgeois epoch, but it is one-sided and therefore abstract, as will become clear in the subsequent presentation. Association through the value-form negates the equally abstract moment of *free will* (see 6S1). This association is therefore in itself contradictory. However, without the further development of the grounding of the value-form (which is to constitute the bourgeois economy – §10) this contradiction must remain implicit, that is not yet set forth. Further, sociation (the abstract moment of association) also seems to contain an implicit notion of communality, which the value-form does not express (see 7S1).

b. Up to this point we have not used the concept 'abstract labour'. The form determinancy is prior to this concept.

c. The word 'labour' explicitly refers to the performance of labour, actually or in the past – thus also to the actual or past production of useful objects. Labour may be specified quantitatively in time as its measure. 'Labour power' is the potential to perform labour for a definite period of time, which generally speaking, however, is not specified when referring to labour power, until it is exchanged. Not only is labour itself dissociated (§3 ff.), but so also by implication are the labourers that perform this labour with their labour power.

d. The philosophical concept of 'value' (freedom, love, etc.) was introduced from economics into philosophy by Lotze (see Nauta 1971: 104). Concerning those values there is no (other) socially established unitary form apart from value in terms of money. This distinguishes the economy from other realms of society. For that matter, it also distinguishes economics from other social sciences.

e. A fundamental defect of neoclassical economics is that it studies production and allocation only from the natural necessity aspect of utility (cf. §2). In neglecting the social *form* that useful objects take – namely the form of value or money – it studies the economy from a transhistorical standpoint and thus fails to grasp the specificities of capitalist society. Neoclassical economics theorises the institutions (markets in particular) via which allocation operates, but does so in an abstract (one-sided) way. Peculiarly enough, it tends to analyse the operation of markets in terms of useful objects, whereas the production and allocation of goods and services *only as* useful objects (without taking the form of value, that is without being produced *for* exchange in terms of value) may not require markets at all.

§6. The market: actual abstraction, doubling of useful objects, doubling of labour power, and doubling of labour

The necessary interplay of the exchange relation (§4) and the value-form of labour power and its products (§5) is actually constituted by social intercourse in the market. In exchange in the market, labour power and particular objects are recognised only under the dimension of value in terms of money. Heterogeneous entities are commensurated and as such transformed into money. This transformation is an *actual abstraction* (an abstraction in practice). First, whilst the useful characteristics of labour power and its products may be assessed prior to market exchange, these characteristics are actually abstracted from in the validation as money. The sole purpose of the holder of products is to turn them into money; the initial assessment is merely intended to serve this purpose, and the result is expressed in terms of money. Beyond that, the particular useful characteristics are of no importance to the holder. Secondly, in the exchange process of products in the market, abstraction is being made from both the particular quality and the quantity (time) of the labour that has produced the useful object. This particular labour time is considered only in terms of its ability to create value; money in buying this particular labour actually commensurates it. In this sense particular concrete labour *actually* takes the form of universal *abstract labour*.

The necessary interplay of the exchange relation and the value-form in the market thus actually constitutes the useful object as an entity of *double* form – *use-value and money*. This doubling constitutes the useful object as commodity. It also constitutes labour as an entity of double form – labour as productive of particular use-values (or *particular concrete* labour) and as productive of value (or *universal abstract* labour). This interplay similarly applies to labour power which, commodity-like, is constituted as an entity of double form – as use-value, which is its potential performance of *labour* (particular labour time, specified in the labour contract), and as value (the wage, an amount of money also specified in the labour contract).

With the actual abstraction in market exchange whereby particular heterogeneous use-values are transformed into the social–universal homogeneous form of money, the particular concrete labour performed privately (§3 and §5) is constituted as a definite fraction of the overall social–universal abstract labour of society. That is, it is validated as part of that social aggregate (cf. Aglietta 1976: 38).[4]

Addenda: a. Marx's introduction of the commodity; b. The concept of 'actual abstraction'; c. Value theoretical strands within Marxist theory

a. The presentation diverges in at least one important respect from Marx's theory. The 'commodity' has been introduced here for the first time. The interplay of the exchange relation and the value-form actually constitutes the useful object as an entity of double form, and this *doubling* constitutes the useful object as *commodity*. The useful object is thus identity of identity (use-value) and non-identity (money), and this identity constitutes it as commodity. At first sight this may perhaps seem rather a fine distinction, but it is closely related to our different starting point from Marx's (1859, 1867) as set out in §3a. Marx's presentation is either insufficiently systematic (as Backhaus suggests), above all in that it does not sufficiently separate

---

4 Note that there is no direct correspondence between value-added and abstract labour; the value of means of production is included in this overall abstract labour (cf. 2§16).

discovery (the commodity as it appears, i.e. perception) from the abstract starting point (0§§7-8). Or it is both structural-genetic and also historical-genetic, since Marx starts with commodity exchange (petty commodity production), not with capitalist production (as Napoleoni suggests). From the point of view of our own presentation, the difference would then have to be located in the sociation-dissociation opposition (§3).

b. The transformation of heterogeneous entities in the market is an immanent or actual abstraction (an abstraction in practice). The term 'abstraction' in this respect is also used by Marx (1859: 30): 'This reduction appears to be an abstraction, but it is an abstraction which is made every day in the social process of production' (cf. also Marx 1867[1]: 136-7). Himmelweit & Mohun (1978: 75) use the term 'real abstraction', the disadvantage of which is that one might suppose there could be such thing as an 'unreal abstraction'. All abstractions, including mental abstractions and ideal abstractions (see §8) are real abstractions.

c. The theory here is a value-form theoretic development from the abstract labour theory of value and it marks a clear divergence from the labour-embodied theory of value. Until the 1960s a labour-embodied theory of value dominated much of Marxist economic theory (e.g. Dobb 1937, Robinson 1942, Sweezy 1942, Meek 1956), and against which three reactions from within Marxism have developed. The first is that led by Steedman (1977), based on technical coefficients as derived from Sraffa (1960). The second is the abstract-labour theory of value, which has been developed since the beginning of the 1970s. (See Pilling 1972, Napoleoni 1973, Aglietta 1976, Arthur 1976, Fine and Harris 1976 and 1979, Gerstein 1976, Kay 1976, Himmelweit and Mohun 1978, Elson 1979, De Vroey 1981 and Weeks 1981. Rubin 1928 is an important precursor of this approach.) However, this theory is by no means fully integrated, there being no agreement even on the definition of basic concepts (cf. De Vroey 1982; see also Gleicher 1983, 1985 and Eldred 1984b). The third strand is value-form analysis, which strongly stresses the need for a dialectical methodology, and the importance of which has recently been highlighted by authors such as Eldred, Hanlon, Kleiber and Roth (1982/85) and Hansen, Pedersen and Stenderup (1984), drawing on the seminal work by Backhaus (1969). (It should be noted that Eldred, Hanlon, Kleiber and Roth, in particular, perceive their theory as negating any labour theory of value.) Each of these strands may find support in Marx's work. Though Marx clearly aims, in his writings on value (1859 *Critique*, 1867 *Capital*, ch. One, and various places in the *Grundrisse* and the *Theories of Surplus Value*) to distance himself from the Ricardian labour-embodied theory of value, a large part of the theory in the three volumes of *Capital* seems to be a retreat back to it. This point is taken up at some length by Backhaus (1969), and Eldred, Hanlon, Kleiber and Roth (1982/85). The latter in particular stress the divergence as to value-form analysis between Marx and Engels, the editor of the second and third volume of *Capital*. It may however be noted that an author such as Elson would probably disagree with Eldred *et al.*, since she (1979: 139) stresses that, among other things, the examples that Marx uses in *Capital* 'are always couched in money terms, *never* in terms of hours of labour-time'.

SECTION 4   THE MONEY EXPRESSION OF VALUE

§7. Money as general equivalent

Value is a social universal abstract (§5) the existence of which is concretised in money, which as it appears in the market (§6) is the sole expression of value. There are no pre-market value entities (such as the Ricardian conception of labour-embodied, or the neoclassical utility or marginal rate of substitution). Because value has to commensurate heterogeneous entities, it has to be *measure of value*. If it is to be a systematic measure of value (beyond merely accidental exchange), money necessarily has also to be a fiduciary *store of value*. From the point of view of value-form theory, being the measure of value is thus the first determination of money, and being a store of value its first condition of existence. The second condition of existence of money as measure of value is that it can be a *medium of circulation* (medium of exchange). An entity can be a measure of value because it proves and reproves itself to be the actual medium of circulation. Money as means of circulation reinforces its role as a fiduciary store of value. Because the degree to which sales and purchases synchronise is undetermined, the means of circulation has to bridge, at least temporarily, this non-synchrony. These three determinations of money constitute it as the general equivalent.

Unlike the use-value of a particular commodity, money has no inherent content – neither bullion, nor paper, nor plastic, nor accounting entries. Money is inherently pure form, one dimensional quantity. In this sense money has no value either, only an infinite number of exchange values, one against each commodity (cf. De Vroey 1981: 187). This is the substantial existence of value: pure transcendental form.

Addenda: a. Commodity money; b. Order of the presentation

a. Money is determined at this abstract level as measure of value, fiduciary store of value and medium of circulation. Any further detail of its concrete existence is premature (see 2S2). This presentation does not say anything about the historical emergence of money. From a systematic point of view, measure of value is the most abstract determinant of money, even if historically some entity was an (accidental) medium of exchange before it had become the generalised measure of value.

Our conceptualisation of money diverges from most Marxist as well as Marx's own (1867) grounding of money in the concept of commodity money. (However, in Marx (1867) there is also ample evidence of a form-theoretic line of argument, though he does not push his logic to its conclusion that money is pure quantitative form.) Nevertheless, in Marx (1867) – as well as of course in many other treatises on money – we find the same three determinations (measure of value, store of value, medium of exchange/means of circulation), though often in a different order. (For a good exposition of Marx on money, see De Brunhoff 1973.) A grounding of money in commodity money – even if credit money is given a predominant place – is all the more remarkable with authors such as, for example, Aglietta (1976) who not only have the benefit of hindsight from an era in which money has sloughed off all necessary connection with any commodity, but who also adhere to an abstract-labour theory of value. (Of course within a labour-embodied theory of value commodity money could be consistently theorised.) De Vroey (1984: 382–3) on the other hand – who works within the Aglietta approach – rejects a grounding of money in commodity money: 'Money in its basic determination (i.e., legal money) cannot be considered a commodity'.

b. Section 4 (§7) above logically follows on from Section 3 as does Section 5. Sections 4 and 5 introduce moments that are conceptually on a par. Without loss of content, their order could be changed.

SECTION 5   VALORISATION AND CAPITAL

§8. Capitalist production: ideal pre-commensuration

Products in the bourgeois mode of production necessarily have to take the value-form (§5). Only in the market, however, is the product constituted as a commodity and the labour that produced it constituted as abstract labour in the form of money; only in the market is this labour actually reduced to a definite fraction of the abstract social-aggregate labour (§6). The doubling of products into use-value and money, and of labour into concrete useful labour and abstract labour in the form of money, further determine the form of production as commodity production.

Because exchange in the market is not accidental but systematic, the abstraction of the equation of a product to some definite amount of money can be anticipated in production. Production is production for exchange, so that useful objects are produced *as* commodities, that is, with a view to sale for money. So production is considered as potential money expansion, as *valorisation* (money – production – more money). Before the actual exchange, this is an anticipation. Nevertheless commodities produced ideally represent an amount of value, *ideal money*. In this sense, the actual abstraction in the market is anticipated by an *ideal abstraction*, and the actual commensuration in the market is anticipated by an ideal pre-commensuration.

This anticipation crucially determines the bourgeois process of production, in that it becomes itself form determined. The ideal pre-commensuration of the commodity gives rise to a further ideal abstraction concerning the labour process, which is also pre-commensurated in terms of ideal abstract labour or ideal value. The labour process is then ideally denominated in terms of ideal value, and labour and concrete activity of labour takes on the ideal form of value – labour ideally takes on the form of abstract labour. The labour process then may be calculated in terms of ideal money. *The labour process then ideally takes on a contradictory double form*, that of *technical labour process* (use-value production), and that of *abstract labour process* or *valorisation process*. The external driving force of production, which together with the necessity of exchange necessarily gives rise to the value-form, thus becomes ideally internalised. With this internalisation, the contradiction that the social form (value) is the external determinant of the private production (§5) is transcended: this particular private sphere (bourgeois production) is transcended into the public sphere of *the economy*, determined by the value-form.

With this internalisation, we have also provided a concretisation of the abstract starting point of §3: 'private independent units of production'. To indicate this conceptual development (§§3–8), these will be referred to henceforth as *capital(s)*.

Addenda: a. Capital and firm; b. Ideal abstraction and ideal pre-commensuration

a. The presentation is still at a very high level of abstraction, so that the term 'capital' (and 'capitalist production') does not refer to the fairly concrete level of enterprise and firm. Further, because 'subjects' have not been introduced (see 6§§2–4) of course entrepreneurs, managers and so on cannot be introduced. At this level, there are only 'abstract bearers of social relations'.

b. The concepts of ideal abstraction and ideal pre-commensuration are essential to our theory of value, and together with the determination of valorisation in the next paragraph they are the key contribution to our synthesis of value-form analysis and the abstract-labour theory of value. Although this argument appears to be original, Marx (1867: 78) seems to be making a similar point:

> This division of a product into a useful thing and a value becomes practically important, only when exchange has acquired such an extension that useful articles are produced for the purpose of being exchanged, and their character as values has therefore to be taken into account beforehand, during production. From this moment the labour of the individual producer acquires socially a two-fold character.

In the light of the concept of ideal pre-commensuration we do not agree with De Vroey when he, in an otherwise excellent article, approvingly quotes Gerstein (1976: 250):

> Value is therefore a necessary category because it makes possible the transformation of economic objects, which are heterogeneous realities, into commodities, products of abstract labour. All this is realised through exchange. As Gerstein puts it: 'There is no way to reduce observable concrete labour to social abstract labour in advance, outside the market which actually effects the reduction.' (...) value refers to a measurement whose validity is limited to the point of exchange. (De Vroey, 1981: 178)

To the extent that the quote is meant to be a critique of labour-embodied theories, there is no disagreement.

---

§9. The capitalist production process as valorisation process

The reduction in the market of use-values to a quantity of value – that is, their social validation in terms of money (§6), anticipated in capitalist production as an ideal pre-commensuration – determines the contradictory double form of the labour process (§8). The transcendence of bourgeois private production in the public sphere of the economy (determined by the dominance of the value-form) – whence it is termed capitalist production – does not, however, dissolve this contradictory double character. However much the abstract labour process in fact dominates the technical labour process, the latter (the creation of useful objects) is a necessary moment (§2). Thus although the form (value) determines the content (use-value), form cannot exist without content.

Three elements of production have been distinguished (§2): uncultivated and freely available nature, labour and means of production (including cultivated nature). The contradictory double character of the labour process is further determined by the disparity of the roles played by each of the elements of production in the technical labour process on the one hand, and in the valorisation process on the other. In the production process as technical labour process, *each* of these elements may contribute to the production of new *use-values*. However, in the labour process as *valorisation* process, which determines the production process in its particular capitalist form, the elements of production are dissimilar, first in that not all of them are themselves produced within the capitalist form of production and secondly in that not all of them take the form of value via exchange in the market. Neither labour nor freely available uncultivated nature are produced within the capitalist sphere of production, nor have they been *produced* with a view to sale. Therefore, they do not represent previous value-added. Means of production, on the other hand, have been produced within the capitalist sphere of production, and hence do represent previous value-added. Both labour and means of production are exchanged and valued in the market; however they came into existence, a price label is stuck on them. Freely available and uncultivated nature, on the other hand, does not enter exchange at all (and indeed it is freely available to any capital or to any sphere, and therefore it does not count as value).[5]

It is because labour is the only element that takes on the form of value whilst it is not produced within the capitalist sphere of production that it potentially creates value-added. Thus, again, whilst in the production process as technical labour process each of the elements may be necessary to the production of new use-values, in the production process as valorisation process there is only one socially necessary element of production of value-added, which is labour. This may be briefly expanded upon, taking each of the elements in turn.

A sufficient reason to exclude freely available and uncultivated nature as a factor of production of value-added is that it is not exchanged and valued at all.

Means of production provide no value-added because they have been *produced* previously within a valorisation process, and as such represent previous value-added.[6] Their value is *not* derived from the ideal value of the output of the production process in which they actually figure as means of production, but from the process of production in which *they* were actually produced – that is, their price of production (cf. addendum c).[7]

In contradistinction to means of production, labour is of course not produced previously as it is the activity of production itself. If anything it is labour power that is produced previously. But the key point is that whilst labour power takes on the form of value (the

---

5 This argument is about uncultivated and freely available nature. Of course once it becomes scarce and has been appropriated (6§3) it takes on the value-form (see §11). See also note 7.

6 Nevertheless, it is the *current ideal value* of means of production (as related to the current value of similar means of production, which in them also represents previous value-added) which is in all or in part transmitted in the current production process (see 2§16 and 4§4).

7 If it were argued that their value does derive from the process of production in which they figure, then profits would presumably reduce to zero? It would be difficult to extend this argument beyond a partial analysis. Quite another matter is that the property of, or the command over any (temporarily) absolutely scarce factor of production (land, labour, machines, etc.) may always give rise to rent in the Marshallian sense (1890: 412) (see also §11).

wage), it is not produced within the capitalist sphere of production. The price of labour power has got nothing to do with the 'price of production' of labour power (see addendum b). Labour power is *created* in the private sphere of the household and it is not produced with a view to sale. (Even the production–consumption distinction does not apply here – what is involved is the activity of procreation – §3.) Nor is it produced, like a commodity, by socially validated labour. Labour power thus does not represent previous value-added. The fact that labour power is created outside the capitalist sphere of production is precisely the reason why labour power actually expended *does* potentially create value-added.

The argument that only labour potentially creates value-added should in no way be read to imply that value-added is in some way proportional to labour (for which at this level an aggregative measure is anyway lacking), as a labour-embodied theory of value would have it. It is only the validation of labour and its products in the market that determines where and how much value(-added) is actualised. Labour is the *socially* necessary element of production of value-added (see 2§12b, 2§16 and 4§4).

Addenda: a. Value-added and abstract labour; b. The supply price of labour power; c. Cost accounting and investment appraisal; commodity inputs in education and training; d. Explanation and justification, Smith and Marshall; e. Factors of production in neoclassical theory and the view of Taussig

a. Value-added is linked to abstract labour as a category of the *social* process of validation. But this does not mean that there is no social connection between labour expended in individual processes of production ('labour-embodied' for the sake of argument) and value-added. There is this connection which is precisely abstract labour, the ex-post social allocation of labour (see 2§16).

In Marxist economic theory, labour has traditionally been put forward as a unique element of the process of value creation. (See, for example, Sweezy's (1942: 23–40) 'qualitative proposition'.) With both of the reactions against the labour-embodied theory of value – the abstract-labour theory of value and value-form analysis – this uniqueness of labour seemed to have been lost from the theory. Our value-form theoretic reconstruction of the abstract-labour theory of value shows that the uniqueness of labour may be theorised without any recourse to labour-embodied.

b. The thesis that the price of labour power has got nothing to do with the price of production of labour power, and that these terms are indeed incompatible appears, of course, very un-Marxist. Marx at least seems to have had in mind something like such a price of production, as he conceives the wage related to the reproduction of labour power. The price of labour power (the wage) is determined by supply and demand (cf. 2S3 and Chapter 3), but the supply price contains no value-added whatsoever. To cast this exchange relation in terms of 'unequal exchange' is therefore also beside the point. The issue is rather the contradiction that if one compares labour power and any capitalistically produced commodity, it is intrinsically uncommensurate entities that are commensurated. Whilst the demand price can be further determined within the same dimension (value), the supply price cannot. The analysis of the household as if it were a firm (as both some Chicago monetarists and a particular wing within the feminist movement would have it) is just an hypothetical construct, or it is normative economics.

c. The value of means of production (including previously produced value-added) derives from the process of production in which they were actually produced, not from the ideal value of the output of the production process in which they figure as means of production. Nevertheless (see note 6) it is not their historical value (historical costs) but their *current* value which is relevant (for value-added in particular – see 4§§4–5 and 5§8). At a lower level of abstraction, this is the cost accounting point of view (see also 4§5b). Investment appraisal may involve discounting the net expected value of future revenues, which is an imputation – to use the Austrian phrase – of future ideal value to capital assets (see also §10).

Whilst labour power is created outside the capitalist sphere of production, there can be commodity 'inputs' to the production of specific kinds of skilled labour power, and workers may 'invest' in their education and training (as the 'human capital' approach has it). Such concrete interrelations between the private sphere and the economy cannot be generalised, and they do not impinge on the presentation at this level of abstraction (see also 2§12b).

d. To conceive only labour as potentially creative of value-added has got nothing to do with the question whether profits are or are not necessary – or are 'just', for that matter. The explanation of value-added by labour does not pertain to the question of the necessity of profit, and even less so to its justification. In contradistinction to Marshall (1890) – and many neoclassical economists after him – Smith (1776) seems to have been well aware of this. Whilst he conceives profit as a deduction from the produce of labour,[8] this does not imply for him that profits could be dispensed with, or that they are unjust:

> Thus, the labour of a manufacturer adds, generally to the value of the materials which he works upon, that of his own maintenance, and of his master's profit ... Though the manufacturer has his wages advanced to him by his master, he, in reality costs him no expense, the value of those wages being generally restored, together with a profit in the improved value of the subject upon which his labour is bestowed. (Smith 1776: i, 294–5; see also, for example, pp. 42, 46, 58)

8 Historians of economic thought ranging from Schumpeter (1954) to Blaug (1968) and Rima (1978) produce quite different interpretations of Smith.

For Marshall, however, it seems that explanation and justification have to coincide:

> It is not true that the spinning of yarn in a factory, after allowance has been made for the wear-and-tear of the machinery, is the product of the labour of the operatives. It is the product of their labour, together with that of the employer and subordinate managers, and of the capital employed; and that capital itself is the product of labour and waiting: and therefore the spinning is the product of labour of many kinds and of waiting. If we *admit* that it is the product of labour alone, and not of labour and waiting, we can no doubt be compelled by inexorable logic to admit that there is no *justification* for Interest, the reward of waiting: for the conclusion is implied in the premiss. (Marshall 1890: 587; emphasis added)

Whilst Smith consequently writes about value, and not as Marshall does about physical entities, the context of the Marshall quotation makes it clear that the latter does identify these with values. The point to be stressed is not so much the queer notion of waiting which is somehow physically productive, but that 'justification' should be the reason for providing the argument.

e. In the production process as technical labour process three elements of production have been distinguished. Each of these may contribute to the production of new *use-values*. This view is in conformity with neoclassical theory, from which we depart in considering their analysis one-sided in that it neglects the capitalist form of value. Further, the physical contribution of each of these elements cannot be separated out, contrary to what J. B. Clark thought. Fisher and Taussig – writing in roughly the same tradition – rightly criticised Clark for this notion. Taussig, an early proponent of Austrian type of analysis, puts it like this:

> Tools and machinery, buildings and materials are themselves made by labor, and represent an intermediate stage in the application of labor. Capital as such is not an independent factor in production, and there is no separate productiveness of capital. When, in the following pages, the productivity of capital is spoken of, the language must be taken as elliptic, expressing concisely the result of the capitalist application of labor. (Taussig, 1911: ii, 8)

Thus although capital (i.e. means of production) is no independent factor of production, Taussig seems to ascribe independence to labour in this respect, which is in our view untenable:

> All this analysis of the relation of labor to capital and to saving leads, again, to the proposition that all the operations of capitalists resolve themselves into a succession of advances to the laborers. (...) The laborers as a whole produce more than they receive. Those who borrow, a surplus

and then hire the laborers, can afford to pay back more than they have borrowed. This is the process by which interest on capital used in production comes into existence. (Taussig 1911: ii, 8)

Taussig in the second quotation anyway, seems to slip into a money capital notion of capital. In our view, it is indeed only when it comes to valorisation – which necessarily requires the concept of money value – that such independence may be ascribed to labour.

§10. Capital and the valorisation of capital

Bourgeois production has been constituted as driven by the external force of the pursuit of a surplus over the value initially laid out (§5). Whilst it is only in the market that production may be socially validated (§6), this validation is anticipated during production as an ideal pre-commensuration, so that the production of useful objects ideally doubles into the production of use-values and the production of value – that is, valorisation. These elements determine bourgeois production as capitalist production (§8), in which labour has been derived as the sole and socially necessary element of production of (ideal) value-added, and as such the social determinant of valorisation. With respect to the technical labour process, however, three elements of production may be required (§9). The production of new use-values requires (to date) both means of production and labour power. Because of this necessity of the inputs taking the value-form, and of the necessity double form of the labour process, valorisation takes the contradictory *form valorisation of capital*: that is, capital is contradictorily constituted as the form of self-valorising value. As self-valorising value, capital is contradictorily related to itself. The measure of this relation is the rate of profit on capital laid out: value over value.

Addenda: a. Valorisation of capital; b. Clark's concept of capital

a. Valorisation does not merely *appear* to be the valorisation of capital – as many Marxists would have it – but it does indeed take the form of valorisation of capital. Nevertheless this form is contradictory in that labour has been constituted as the sole and socially necessary element of production of (ideal) value-added, and as such the social determinant of valorisation. In this sense, the capital relation – capital abstractly related to itself as self-valorising value – is a contradictory relation. The playing out of the contradiction of this form is further determined in Chapter 2 and in Part Three, below.

b. The concept of valorisation of capital (or, in everyday language profit-making) has been treated ambivalently in the history of orthodox economic thought. For example, J. B. Clark's concept of capital (see also §9e) seems to refer in a rather uneasy way to the double form of capital as value and use-value. But he then explicitly discards the value component and conceives of capital as some metaphysically homogenised amalgam of use-values (somewhat analogous to the later 'putty', 'leets', 'meccano' or 'jelly' – e.g. Samuelson 1962): 'Capital is this permanent fund of productive goods, the identity of whose component elements is forever changing. Capital goods are the shifting component parts of this permanent aggregate' (Clark 1907: 29). The derived marginal (physical) productivity theory was shown to be in general untenable by the Cambridge–Cambridge controversy ('If all this causes headaches for those nostalgic for the old time parables of neo-classical writing, we must remind ourselves that scholars are not born to live an easy existence' Samuelson 1966: 250). Veblen had already, in his 1908 review of Clark (1907) pointed out the one-sidedness of Clark's concept of capital as capital goods:

> In current usage, in the business community, 'capital' is a pecuniary concept, of course, and is not definable in mechanical terms; but Mr. Clark, true to the hedonistic taxonomy, sticks by the test of mechanical demarcation and draws the lines of his category on physical grounds; whereby it happens that any pecuniary conception of capital is out of the question. (Veblen 1908: 180)

Veblen also showed that in fact Clark implicitly had to have recourse to the 'pecuniary concept of capital' (Veblen 1908: 181–4). Many contemporary texts further muddy the waters. Not only is capital treated as an autonomous factor of production, identified with physical means of production alongside labour (and sometimes land), but 'enterprise' is often added as a fourth factor of production.

§11. Capitalisation and the form of capital-valorisation (rent)

Means of production have been determined as necessarily taking on the value-form (§5). This goes for those reproduced within the economy, but also for non-reproducible inputs (in so far as they can be appropriated – cf. 6§§3–4). The primary category of non-reproducible inputs is land, the value-form of the use of which as means of production is rent. Because valorisation takes on the form of valorisation of capital (as profit – §10), conversely, rent as a value-form tends to be *capitalised*. The alienable element – land – to which it is attached, therefore takes on the form of *capital valorisation*, and with it the alienable element takes on the form of capital, in particular landed capital.

Addendum: a. Industrial and landed capital

a. So far in the presentation, capital has implicitly been restricted to industrial capital, that is capital invested in production (of commodities).

With the introduction of rent and its capitalisation, capital is differentiated into industrial and landed capital. But these are forms of capital in the first place and as such (as capital in general) indifferent as between their investment in industry or in land.

SUMMARY

This chapter has presented a value-form theoretic reconstruction of the abstract-labour theory of value. From the abstract starting point of human self-production has been derived the naturally necessary sociation of procreation and of creation of useful objects (Section 1). The separation, in the bourgeois epoch, of the activity of creation of useful objects into production and consumption, as organised in private independent units, negates sociation as dissociation (Section 2). In the course of this chapter the first and abstract grounding of this contradiction has been provided, in the derivation of the elementary conditions of existence of the sociation–dissociation opposition.

The transcendence of the sociation–dissociation opposition in the bourgeois epoch is in the association of the value-form, the first moment of which is the exchange relation. The second moment is the necessity of the exchange relation taking the value-form. Value as common denominator (in Section 4) further determined as money as the general equivalent), was constituted as the social-universal form that particular labour and the products of labour have to take for these to become socially validated. Concomitantly, labour power also has to take on the value-form. The actual abstraction in the market actualises these commensurations. The interplay of the exchange relation and the value-form in the market constitutes useful objects as entities of double form (use-value and money), and thence as commodities. At the same time labour doubles into particular-concrete labour and universal-abstract labour, and labour power into use–value (potential performance of labour) and value (the wage) (Section 3).

This gives rise to two further determinations which are essential to our contribution to the synthesis of value-form analysis and the abstract-labour theory of value (Section 5). First, because of systematic exchange, production *is considered as potential money expansion or valorisation. Therefore the actual abstraction in the market is anticipated by an ideal abstraction and the actual commensuration in the market is anticipated by an ideal pre-commensuration, whence the production process itself becomes form determined. The labour process ideally takes on the contradictory double form of technical form process (use-value production) and valorisation process. With this doubling the external driving force of production becomes ideally internalised, and the private sphere of production is thereby transcended into the public sphere of the economy determined by the value-form. Second, whilst for the production process as technical labour process three elements of production are required, for the production process as valorisation process labour is the only socially necessary element of production of value-added. The key point of this determination is the fact that labour power is created outside the capitalist sphere of production.*

Because of the double form of the labour process, capital – the necessary value-form of the elements of production as inputs – is constituted as the form of self-valorising value. As self-valorising value, capital is contradictorily related to itself, a relation which is measured by the rate of profit on capital laid out. Capital as self-valorising value then gives rise to the capitalisation of forms of value, even if these do not derive from capital invested in production. The playing out of this contradictory relation will be further determined in the following chapters.

Chapter two

The Extended Reproduction of Capital

PRELIMINARY REMARKS

In Section 1 of this chapter it is argued that the valorisation of capital, presented in Chapter 1, necessarily gives rise to the accumulation of capital. Sections 2 and 3 set out the two major conditions of existence of the accumulation of capital: the existence of credit and the credit system, and the extended reproduction of labour. Whilst the latter is only briefly introduced in order to locate its theorisation within the systematic whole, the presentation of the former goes much further. Consequent upon our value-form theoretic reconstruction of the abstract labour theory of value, credit money and the credit system are presented without taking recourse to commodity money. In this, the theory is different from most Marxist monetary theory. Not only is a foundation of credit money in commodity money unnecessary, it would also be invalid from the point of view of our method. A reconsideration of the Marxist theory of money is also demanded by the theorisation since the second half of the 1970s, of the postwar development of capitalist monetary institutions (see the work of the French Marxist monetary school, stemming from De Brunhoff and Cartelier 1974, De Brunhoff 1976 and Aglietta 1976; for a more recent treatment, see Lipietz 1983; in the U. K. the work of, for example, Ergas and Fishman 1975, Harris 1976, Innes 1981, Coakley and Harris 1982; Evans 1985 can be mentioned). Though these authors stress the major importance of credit money – and many of them conceive it to be the *capitalist money par excellence – this is not reflected in their abstract theorisation of money. The way this anomaly is usually addressed is by introducing credit money via a historical development from commodity money; there is nothing wrong with such a historical description in itself but it cannot be a substitute for abstract theory. What is more, historical order of appearance need not correspond to logical order of presentation.*

Section 4 introduces the concept of 'many capitals'. The interaction of capitals is presented at an abstract level, and the term 'many capitals' stands for that abstract determination. From it is derived the concept of 'capital stratification' which is the key to the theory of Chapter 4. The determinants of Sections 1–4 provide a first, abstract, concretisation of the value-form of useful objects and labour introduced in Chapter 1. These interconnections are presented in Section 5, when we introduce the concept 'money expression of labour'.

The presentation in this chapter does not, of course, start from scratch. In particular, the theorisation of money and credit (Section 2) has a history longer than any other subject in economics. Many of the issues in themselves will consequently be familiar. But for these, as for any other less familiar issues, it is the order of their presentation and their particular interconnections by which they are to be comprehended.

SECTION 1 THE ACCUMULATION OF CAPITAL

§1. The extended valorisation of capital

Value has been determined as the internalised external driving force of production, which thereby ideally takes on the double form of technical labour process and abstract labour or valorisation process (1§8). Whilst labour is the only socially necessary element of ideal valorisation (1§9), it is because of the necessary double form of the production process that valorisation takes on the contradictory form of valorisation of capital. Profit becomes the internalised measure of the external driving force of production (1§10). Valorisation is the expansion of capital (M–M'). As it is not consumption but profit which is its driving force, the logic of this expansion is more profit and further expansion (M–M'–M"). Production is then geared towards continual increase of profit, achieved first by an increase in control over the labour process by capital (§2), and second by accumulation of capital (§3). The inherent limits of these are overcome in technical change (§4).

§2. Increased control over the labour process by capital

Control over the labour process by capital is implicit in the valorisation process. That this process is geared to the increase in profits implies that capital is continually driven to increase control, with the effect of decreasing costs per unit of physical output and increasing the rate of profit.

Addenda: a. References; b. Limits to intensity of labour

a. Related to control over the labour process is the variation of the working time. Almost half of Marx's 1867 (Parts III–V) deals with the analysis of absolute and relative surplus value. Since the beginning of the 1970s there has been a renewed interest by Marxist-oriented scholars in the study of the labour process. See, for example, Gorz 1971, Braverman 1974, Marglin 1974, Palloix 1976, Brighton Labour Process Group 1977; for a collection of documents on nineteenth-century Britain see Berg 1979. See also Eldred 1984a: §55, and 6§4 below.

b. One aspect of the control over the labour process is the increase in the intensity of labour, to which there are not only physiological but also social and moral limits. The moral element, in particular, does not belong to this level of abstraction (see 6§5 for the related right to existence). With a decrease in the length of the working day, the possibilities of an increase in intensity of labour per hour increase. There is therefore a trade-off – depending on the technique of production – between intensive use of labour and the degree of utilisation of capacity of means of production.

§3. Accumulation of capital

There are clearly limits to cost reduction via increase in control over the labour process (§2). For a given length of the working day and technique of production, the intensity of labour cannot be increased indefinitely. Capital is enlarged (to be reproduced on an extended scale) via investment of profit, thereby extending the valorisation of capital (its self-expansion) to the accumulation of capital, and thence to the potential self-expanding valorisation of capital. The accumulation of capital follows logically from the necessity of the value-form and of valorisation of capital, in which it is implicit that the internalised external driving force should be carried to the extreme of continuously expanding valorisation of capital via its accumulation.

Addenda: a. Borrowing and lending; b. Investment of profit

a. At this level of abstraction, our concern is capital in general: individual capital in the perspective of total capital. Investment may of course also be effected via the détour of borrowing and lending profit. Money capital and credit is introduced in the next section.

b. That the fully developed logic of the value-form of production entails that profit be invested does not exclude consumption out of profit. The enforcement of the investment of profit will be further concretised with the introduction of 'many capitals' and competition (S4). Our determination of accumulation at this level of abstraction is similar to Marx's. Thus in

Capital, Vol. I he posits the drive towards the accumulation of capital along with the growth of consumption expenditure out of profit:

> ... the expenditure of the capitalist ... grows with his accumulation, without the one necessity restricting the other. At the same time, however, there develops in the breast of the capitalist a Faustian conflict between the passion for accumulation and the desire for enjoyment. (Marx 1867P: 741)

§4. Accumulation of capital, technical change and technology

The extension of valorisation is limited by the possible increase in the intensity of labour (§2), which therefore also limits the extent of accumulation of capital (§3). The investment of capital in new techniques of production overcomes these limits. A new process technique may both itself reduce unit costs and create the possibility for new organisational techniques to increase the intensity of labour, and thereby further decrease unit costs. With its introduction, not only (potential) profits but also the rate of (potential) profit on the newly accumulated capital tends to increase. Capital then tends to be invested not only in technically advanced plant and equipment but also in the search for new techniques of production – that is, in technology. The production of knowledge leading to innovatable inventions then also takes on the value-form. This leads to the development of particular technology and the search for particular techniques which are expected to increase profits and therefore further enhance the accumulation of capital (see Chapter 4).

Addendum: a. References

a. For the concepts of organisational technique and process technique, see van Santen, 1970; see also Eldred, Hanlon, Kleiber and Roth 1982/85: §19 and Eldred and Roth 1978: Appendix. Our concepts technological and technical change are broadly analogous to the concepts 'invention' and 'innovation' respectively (cf. Freeman 1974: 7; see further 4§1b). For an overview of economic theories of technological change, see Roobeek 1987.

§5. Accumulation and the expansion of the circuit of capital (introduction)

For capital to be continually constituted as self-valorising value it has to take on the double form of value and use-value in different guises: of exchange of money capital (M) against commodity capital (C) in the guise of inputs of means of production (MP) and labour power (LP); of production (P) – as technical labour process and as valorisation process; and of exchange of potential commodities (C') against valorised money capital (M'). Thus we have

$$M \rightarrow C\{MP;LP\} \ldots P \ldots C' \rightarrow M' \text{ etc.}$$

In short $M \rightarrow M'$ and so on. Were all surplus value (M' minus M) to be consumed unproductively then the 'circuit' would merely be reproduced. The continuous expansion of the circuit, $M \rightarrow M' \rightarrow M''$ and so on via the accumulation of surplus value requires growth of the labour power input – from outside the circuit itself. (Means of production are produced within the circuit.) It also requires the expansion in some way of money. To carry the circuit metaphor through, the expansion of the circuit has to be fed from outside. In order to expand, it requires to be opened in two ways: via the extended reproduction of money (S2) and the extended reproduction of labour power (S3).

Addendum: a. References

a. There are many different (metaphorical) representations of the circuit of capital (e.g. Sweezy 1942, Fine 1975, Desai 1979). Marx introduces the circuit of capital in his 1885 (Part One); he elaborates at length how different schools of thought must have different conceptions of the circuit of capital.

SECTION 2   THE CREDIT SYSTEM: REPRODUCTION OF MONEY AND MONEY CAPITAL

§6. Money and the expansion of the circuit of capital

In 1§7, three determinations of money as the expression of value were presented: it must be a measure of value, which is conditioned by it being a store of value and a medium of circulation. Money has no essential content, being pure form or one dimensional quantity. The grounding of the accumulation of capital – in particular the expansion of the circuit of capital (S1) – further concretises the concept of money. In the absence of credit, the validation of commodities produced requires the actual presence of money. Accumulation and the expansion of the circuit of capital therefore further quantitatively determine money.

Addendum: a. Money and credit

a. To say that 'in the absence of credit' validation requires the presence of money is somewhat dubious. Money must already be fiduciary general equivalent. Implicitly, it is indeed generalised credit. Therefore 'credit money' (§8) is almost a tautology. To the same extent that money-in-general has to be present to validate commodities, so also must credit money. However, conceptually credit-in-general (§7) is prior to credit money.

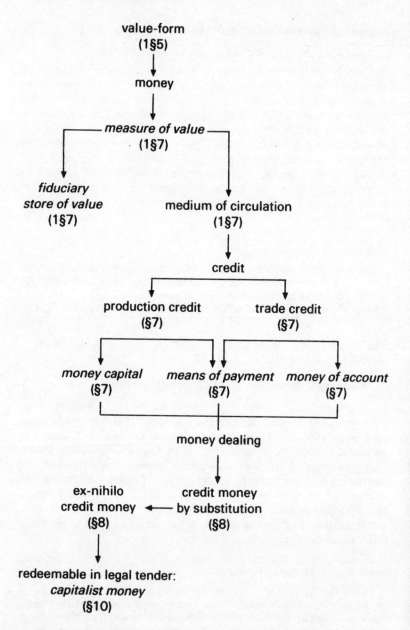

Figure 2.1 The interconnection of money and the credit system.

§7. Credit: money of account, means of payment and money capital

The circulation of commodities does not require the actual presence of money. Similarly, the circulation of money does not require the actual presence (or even the prior production) of commodities. Each of those forms of circulation may involve instead a different form of credit: trade credit and production credit respectively. With *trade credit*, commodities are sold and delivered but the payment is deferred by contract (bill of exchange). Payment, however, is not necessary to settle each contract, since chains of credit may arise. Money as a medium of circulation then doubles into *money of account* and *means of payment*. Only when credits and debits do not balance is it necessary that money actually be present as means of payment. With *production credit*, commodities are sold and paid for but delivery is deferred until the commodities are produced. In effect money capital is thus lent out (by the buyer) against a share in the future profit (as interest). Money as a medium of circulation then doubles into *money* (or finance) *capital* and *means of payment* (see Figure 2.1).

The important similarity between these forms of credit is that they are both based on past production and on an *accumulation* – of commodity capital (in the case of trade credit) and of money capital (in the case of production credit). No money circulates which is not the result of previous production and valorisation. On an aggregate level both these forms of credit are thus based on a *closed* circuit of money (cf., however, De Brunhoff 1973: 80–1, 94n who seems to suggest otherwise). Each is thus merely the transfer of the title to capital from one holder to another. Conversely, it is clear that credit is implict in every act of market exchange: trade credit if a commodity is handed over first; production credit if money is. In either case, the oral or written contract adopts the role of medium of circulation within a private relationship.

§8. Banks and the issue of credit money: private pre-validation

The non-synchrony of sales and purchases, the clearing of chains of trade credit and the bringing together of the demand for and supply of money capital generate the activity of money dealing (financial intermediation) by banks. As a potentially profitable activity, money dealing itself takes on the value-form whereby it is constituted as money dealing capital. Whilst other institutions than banks participate in this intermediation, the latter are not merely credit brokers but also issue *credit money*, which is accepted as a medium of circulation beyond the private credit relation between contractants (§7). Banks' credit money is necessary to resolve the limit to the expansion of capital, which would otherwise be imposed by those private credit relations and by some quantity of money. The existence of credit money is predicated upon the doubling of the medium of circulation into money of account, means of payment and money capital. Its acceptance as medium of circulation is based upon it being an at least temporary fiduciary store of value (1§7). Whilst credit money originates also in a private relationship between bank and client, it subsequently acquires a social character, by circulation as a representative of the general equivalent (Aglietta 1976: 335).

Credit money is either issued by depositing general equivalent money with the bank, or it is issued against a new loan, that is created *ex-nihilo*. Whereas the former is merely an act of money dealing which *substitutes* credit money in circulation for money which *has* validated previous production, ex nihilo created credit money in circulation is an *anticipation of production and realisation* in the future. The bank which advances this form of credit money on the basis of a loan performs a *private pre-validation* of production, which is socially validated when the anticipated production is realised (De Brunhoff 1976: 46; see also Aglietta 1976: 332–5). Whilst this kind of credit also anticipates production, unlike production credit it is not based on a compensatory withdrawal of money from circulation. Thus its circuit is not closed (cf. De Brunhoff 1973: 94 and De Vroey 1984: 385). It can therefore act to facilitate the overall expansion of accumulation.

Addendum: a. The credit system and costs

a. Very often the existence of the credit system is conceived of as merely a matter of *costs*, rather than as a necessary condition of existence of the expansion of capital accumulation in a developed capitalist system. (For example, Ergas and Fishman (1975: 7). the costs of 'servicing the stock of the money-commodity' are 'reduced by the centralisation – in the government and the banks – of the tasks to which they correspond'.)

---

§9. The social expression of private pre-validation

In pre-validating future production of a capital by ex nihilo creation of credit money, the bank of course anticipates the success of the borrowing capital, expecting that the pre-validation will be followed by production and actual *social* validation (i.e. sale) of commodities. Then the credit money would return to the bank (together with interest), cancelling the credit. The ex nihilo created credit money thus manages in the event to close the circuit which it opens initially by the influx of the credit money. The point is that the pre-validation of the production of a capital, anticipating expansion, has to be confirmed at some stage by the actual expansion of *other* capitals. Expansion indeed can be validated only by expansion. Other capitals must accumulate (say) the value equivalent of the credit money that they received from the pre-validated capital in payment for example for means of production or, indirectly, for consumer goods out of wages. They must thus generate extra effective demand. The credit money is then indeed a successful medium of circulation.

If, however, the borrowing capital is not successful, the bank suffers a loss in that it foregoes the principal as well as the interest agreed upon which affects its solvency. There are then three possibilities. *First*, though the borrowing capital fails other capitals nevertheless accumulate and expand, and the credit money that they receive from the borrowing capital keeps on circulating in an *expansionary* manner. In this situation, the bank's liquidity position is not affected. The *second* possibility is that the credit money keeps on circulating, but in an *inflationary* manner. Then the expansion of other capitals (and of the capital circuit as a whole) is 'fictitious'. The equivalent of the bank's loss (the principal) is then socialised in that it affects all holders of money (as well as creditors and debtors). Again, the bank's liquidity is not affected. The *third* possibility is that other capitals do *not* expand in a compensating way, but withdraw from circulation the money received (directly or indirectly) in payment from the borrowing capital. That money then must act as store of value (unless with it other capitals cancel their own credit with their own bank), which would mean that credit money had to be a permanent and not merely a temporary store of value. The bank's creditors may thus withdraw money, the effective general equivalent, from the bank. Should the bank's liquidity be insufficient then this may provoke chain reactions, eventually to the extent of bankruptcy. Because of this continuous underlying threat to a fragmented banking system there is a tendency for banks to extend their domain of operation and to collaborate in inter-bank credit; the banks thus become bankers' banks.

Addenda: a. Pre-validation and inflation; b. Commercial networks

a. From a purely monetary point of view, it could be argued that with full capacity utilisation even one initial pre-validation always has an inflationary effect. However, this is compensated for by a concomitant deflation when the additional (pre-validated) production is performed and realised, and when on the basis of this expansion the production is continued. This may be illustrated with a simple example. A bank provides production credit to some enterprise x. The credit is used to buy additional labour power (with the income from which the labourer then buys consumer goods) and means of production. This drives up prices and profits of y (the aggregate of all other enterprises). If this price and profit increase does not stimulate (extra) capital expansion of y, prices remain at the increased level. But the production of capital x (or its equivalent) would not then be realised, and money would be withdrawn from circulation. Only if the price and profit increase of y stimulates extra expansion would the extra production of (say) enterprise x be realised. It may then cancel its credit and be left (if successful) with a profit. Next period's capital x (which now requires less credit) meets the expanded production of y, and so y's prices may decrease again.

b. At a lower level of abstraction, the interactive expansion of capitals determines banks as centres of commercial networks. Thus the bank's granting of credit to capitals may be conditioned by binding it to purchases with other clients of the bank: directly so, or indirectly via the influence of banks in the company's board of directors (cf. Fennema 1982).

§10. The Central Bank and pseudo-social validation: the fully developed credit system

Expansion of money as medium of circulation is necessary for the ongoing expansion of capital and its validation (§§6–7). A fragmented banking system issuing credit money against debts provides the necessary means of circulation. However, as long as credit money is not accepted as a permanent store of value it cannot function as full money, so that it may lose its medium of circulation function (§§8–9). The reproduction of money as general equivalent and its conditions (existent as measure of value, means of circulation and store of value – 1§7) is therefore further concretised as *Central Bank money*. The Central Bank's position derives not only from its being a dominant banker's bank (§9) but also from its legally enforced status granted by the state (see 8§4; cf. De Brunhoff 1976: 40–8 and Evans 1985: 103). Within its domain, Central Bank money functions potentially as full money because it is the legally *enforced* currency. It is a store of value because it is enforced means of payment – legal tender.

The Central Bank has the discretion whether to attempt to prevent bank crises or not, but if it does so it sustains the private pre-validation of the banks. This then reinforces credit money as a fiduciary representative of the general equivalent on a par with Central Bank money. To the extent that the Central Bank guarantees that credit money is redeemable in Central Bank money the banking system is then a fully developed credit system.[1] Credit money then

---

[1] This guarantee may apply only to those banks that conform to the rules set by the Central Bank.

develops into a full store of value, and hoarding is expressed in a decrease in current accounts (credit cancelling), or an increase in deposit accounts, resulting in an increase in the banks' reserve ratio. With this guarantee of redeemability the Central Bank shifts the frictions inherent in the private pre-validation by banks (§9) to the social aggregate sphere (see 5S3).

It has been indicated that, when private pre-validation by a bank through the ex nihilo creation of credit money is not turned into actual production, or when it is not realised in the market, the bank makes a loss. If this loss is covered by the Central Bank through the provision of its money against a loan to the bank, the private loss (whilst remaining a private loss) is matched by a social loss. Non-realisation is then expressed in devaluation of the currency and inflation, so that the private loss is socialised – equally shifted to all holders of (credit) money. The initial rupture of the circuit by pre-validation – which has not been closed by the integration of extra production – is now closed by a decrease in the purchasing power of each unit of money. The additional money issued by the Central Bank socially validates the private pre-validation; but because it does not operate as a realisation of private labour and the commodities produced by it, it is only a '*pseudo-social validation*' (De Brunhoff & Cartelier 1974, Aglietta 1976: 350, De Brunhoff 1976: 46–7). The conditions of existence of money (that it is measure of value, medium of circulation *and* store of value) are then eroded. The association of private labour through the value-form then comes into conflict with its socially enforced mode of regulation. This conflict and the contradictions to which it gives rise is played out in the articulation of the accumulation tendencies and state economic policy (Part Five).

Addendum: a. Redeemability of credit money

a. Not only is commodity money merely a historically *contingent* guise of money (and so cannot be the basis of its abstract determination), it is also incompatible with the concept of a fully developed credit system. Uncompromising pseudo-social validation by Central Banks is not possible when Central Bank money is redeemable legal tender, only when money is stripped of all connection with any commodity. On the other hand, such pseudo-social validation also implies that credit money gains (legal) redeemability *into* Central Bank money, which is a condition of existence of a fully developed credit system. (In this context De Vroey (1984: 383) refers to 'all bank money being unified by Central Bank money'.) This condition need not be established in a formal institutional relation between banks and Central Banks; its concretisation (including the rules the former have to obey for this guarantee to be met) is contingent.

Indeed, the redeemability of Central Bank money into yet another entity does not fit a fully developed credit system, and so fully developed money, and so also a fully developed capitalist system. (From that perspective such a system did not exist prior to the 1930s or, internationally, prior to the 1970s.) All money, including Central Bank money, is fiduciary (cf. Hicks 1967: 59). The Central Bank provides money with a certificate so to say, which for what it is worth depends on confidence in the Central Bank.

§11. Banks, money capital and the rate of interest

With the banking system as a fully developed credit system, credit money is constituted as the capitalist money par excellence, in that it overcomes the monetary limits to the accumulation of capital. With respect to accumulation, no sensible borderline can be drawn between money and capital (cf. §7) – the expression of both lies in bank accounts and their transfers. First, Central Bank money tends to be deposited with banks, and the circulation of money typically takes the form of current account transfers. Withdrawing money from circulation ('hoarding') is typically expressed in increasing deposit accounts (or also in credit cancelling). It implies an increase in the bank's reserve ratio, and thence in its ability to supply credit, generating a downward pressure on the interest rate. (Expansion of money in circulation generates a converse sequence.) Secondly, lending and borrowing of money *capital* between non-banking capitals is reflected in current account transfers. Bank intermediation has the same effect: it is reflected first in substitution of current accounts for deposit accounts (by the lending capital) and next by increasing current accounts (for capital borrowing against a loan). Withdrawal of money capital from investment also increases the banks' reserve ratios (expressed in a disparity of deposit accounts and lending) and thence exerts a downward pressure on the interest rate (and vice versa).

The interest rate is thus determined by the banks' reserve ratios via its effect on the supply of credit. But that ratio is itself determined by the *demand* for money (as well as by monetary policy – see 9§4), itself derived from the rate of accumulation and of profit on industrial capital. Fundamentally, then, the rate of interest and the amount of money in circulation are demand determined. Ultimately non-banking money capital and banks can decide only whether *to lend or not*, at any rate of interest.

Addendum: a. References

a. This abstract determination of the rate of interest does not of course consider the full complexity of money and capital markets. As Harris (1976:

145) notes, the category of interest has received little attention from Marxist economists, whilst Marx's writings on the matter 'are confused and at times appear contradictory' (p. 149). Marx denied the existence of a price (value) of money capital 'around which the market rate fluctuates and which equals the market rate when supply and demand "coincide"'. In contrast to later neoclassical theory, he rejected any 'natural' rate of interest (Harris 1976: 147; cf. 145–55). Our approach (see also De Vroey 1984: 387) questions the usefulness of a borderline between money and money capital in this context (cf. the different account of Harris 1976: 153–5). The thesis that the rate of interest is fundamentally demand determined appears to be in agreement with Harris's account (cf. p. 153), and the view that money creation is demand determined is also stressed by De Vroey (p. 385) and by post-Keynesians such as Kaldor. (However – cf. §9 – in contrast to Kaldor, the argument that the quantity of money is demand determined does not preclude the possibility of inflation being generated via the quantity of money – De Vroey 1984: 388; see also 5§8.)

More fundamentally, the term 'supply' of money (or credit or loanable funds) may be misleading (and this also applies to land and labour power) since money, although it is traded like a commodity, cannot be produced as one in the twofold private labour process of use-value production and valorisation (1§9). It has no value, and its use-value is socially determined (1§7).

SECTION 3   EXTENDED REPRODUCTION OF LABOUR POWER

§12. Extended reproduction of labour power

The first and most abstract condition of existence of the accumulation of capital is the credit system (S2). The second is the extended reproduction of labour power (§5). Its first determinant is a wage rate adequate to the procreation of labour power. Prior to the presentation of the state (Chapter 6), a wage rate adequate to the procreation of labour cannot be grounded. The wage rate and rate of accumulation are therefore mutually dependent as theorised in the 'population doctrines' of classical political economy.[2] The second determinant is the dissolution of areas of non-capitalist or semi-capitalist production, concomitant on the accumulation of capital, which feeds the reserve of labour available for further accumulation.

---

2 Whilst Malthus's account is best known, there are many forerunners (see Schumpeter 1954: 250–8). The interconnection of accumulation and the wage rate is further determined in 3S2 and 5S1 (see also Kay 1988). The interconnection of the wage rate, the right to existence and labour law is introduced in 8§3.

Addendum: a. Procreation and the private sphere

a. The capitalist mode of production necessarily requires labour power to be created and recreated *outside* the circuit of capital (within the private sphere and the state – cf. Part Four) (1§9). As well as being the site of procreation, the household is the most significant non-capitalist area of creation of useful objects. Mostly this has been a gender specific activity (which has generated gender particularity in and beyond the market). The difficulty for capital in taking this over is that household activity needs relatively few means of production (so that their property is not at issue) and that the character of this activity is such that relatively little efficiency gain is to be obtained from larger scale organisation. It is true that capitalist production of means of production for the household as commodities has partially replaced household activities (laundries, convenience foods, dishwashers, etc.), so that a *potential* labour reserve for capital has been created. (What is more, households have had actually to supply this labour power in order to be able to afford these convenience commodities.) However, child-bearing and early rearing has been one area where this kind of substitution is largely absent. Nevertheless early upbringing remains to date a labour-intensive job with relatively moderate efficiency gains to be obtained from large scale production. At issue is not only efficiency, but also moral factors relating to the separation of the private from the economic and the public spheres (7S1). These appear most acute with respect to the actual creation of babies, which to date has been the (natural) monopoly of the household. Nevertheless Huxley's (1932) story is no longer mere fiction. It is technically possible to produce babies in a capitalist production process. Speculation as to the possible extension of capitalist production to this sphere probably belongs to a lower level of abstraction, but mass production of people under capitalist relations would also pose a contradiction at an abstract level. With the annexation of its source, value-added as an economic category would disappear. This contradiction would seem to be irresolvable within the bourgeois epoch. A *self-contained* circuit would be constructed in which it costs *less* then one hour of labour to produce one hour of labour. Such a circuit might expand indefinitely, except as limited by natural resource depletion. The value of labour would be reduced to zero and concomitantly the value of the products of that labour. The only remaining value category would be 'rent' on the *property* of the stock of all *natural* resources that can and have been appropriated. Such a situation is even gloomier than the 'crumbling walls' predicted by Schumpeter (1943: ch. XII). Capitalism, rather than completing the progressive course of history as predicted by Marx, would return to the darkest of its wombs. All this is speculation, but the prevention of that which is technically possible and initially profitable by mere moral sanction would be unique in history.

SECTION 4   MANY CAPITALS: CAPITAL STRATIFICATION

§13. Inter-branch interaction: the tendency to equalisation of rates of profit

All determinations presented so far have been at the level of social capital as capital in general. The dominance in the production process of valorisation over the technical labour process ensures that capitalist production is *indifferent* to the particular use-values produced (1§5). This indifference is the counterpart of valorisation taking the form of valorisation of capital whereby accumulation takes the form of accumulation of capital in general (as universal). Capital is however also many particular capitals, subsumed under capital in general, which whilst invested in particular branches of use-value production are nevertheless merely units of one and the same thing. The interaction of many capitals is therefore simultaneously 'the relation of capital to itself as another capital' (Marx 1939/41: 650).

This interaction is first determined as inter-branch interaction of capitals. Capital can via the mediation of money capital flows be accumulated and concentrated in *any* branch of production. Value, the internalised external driving force of capital, determines that capital valorised and validated in the one branch may flow to be accumulated in another, in pursuit of a higher rate of profit. Inter-branch interaction and accumulation of capital thus establish a *tendency* of equalisation of average rates of profit (TERP) as between branches. The TERP is a concretisation of the association through the value-form (1§5) of the organisation of labour for the production of useful objects in private independent units in the bourgeois epoch (1§3).

Addenda: a. Abstract notion of competion; b. Tendencies; c. The TERP

a. The interaction of many capitals provides an abstract determination of competition at the level where agents, enterprises, etc. have not yet been introduced (see Chapter 6). At the current level there is no fundamental difference between parts of capital and capital in general. (By analogy, parts of capital within one enterprise – e.g., plants or other units – may be considered as many capitals.) But even at a lower level of abstraction, competition cannot be reduced to an empirical question of the number of units. Weeks (1981: 153) has aptly called such a view 'the quantity theory of competition'.

The abstract notion of competition as 'many capitals' derives from Rosdolsky's (1968: 41–50) interpretation of Marx's *Grundrisse*. We would however agree with Mandel (1983: 90–1) that it goes too far to suggest (as Rosdolsky does) that even the concept of 'many capitals' is not required up until the kind of analysis we find in the third volume of *Capital*. (For a further critique of Rosdolsky's interpretation see Bader *et al.* 1975: 101–6 and Heinrich 1986.) A good summary statement of the concept of competition at the current level of abstraction is provided by Marx, 1939:

> Competition merely *expresses* as real, posits as an external necessity, that which lies within the nature of capital; competition is nothing more than the way in which the many capitals force the inherent determinants of capital upon one another and upon themselves. (p. 651)

b. Methodologically all tendencies are abstract moments (0§9). To what extent they are actualised (for example, the extent to which rates of profit are indeed equalised) can never be established at the level of abstraction at which they have been derived. Rather, tendencies determine the more complex moments which ground them.

c. A more extended analysis of the tendency of equalisation of rates of profit (TERP) is given in Reuten (1978). Besides the fact that the value-theoretical foundations are there insufficient, the equality of rates of surplus value in and between branches of production was merely posited. That analysis shows that the TERP is not necessarily predicated upon market price movements in the branches from and to which capital flows. Rather, the technical structure and labour productivity in the relevant branches will be affected.

---

§14. Intra-branch interaction: the tendency to uniform prices

The first determination of the associative interaction of capitals is inter-branch interaction (§13), the second is intra-branch interaction. Valorisation of capital forces cost reduction and increase in the productivity of labour (§2), however many capitals there are in a branch or industry. This also applies to the accumulation of capital and technical change (§§3–4). The (intra-branch) interaction of capitals in product markets is determined by the compulsion *continuously* to realise the ideal value produced. This, together with the generally temporary character of sales and purchase contracts[3] establishes a tendency towards uniform prices in a market. This tendency applies also to labour power; it is again predicated on the temporary character of sales and purchase contracts (for labour power) whereby the competition among capitals for labour

---

3 In general, contractual sales above the average market price in one period would have the effect of repelling buyers in the next. Note that our concept of capital interaction presented in this Section does not specify particular forms of competition.

establishes a tendency for wages, and the intensity of similar labour, to become uniform across capitals. The articulation of these tendencies ensures that the profits of any one capital come to depend on the technique of production adopted. The interaction of capitals therefore reinforces and reproduces more concretely the compulsion to the accumulation of capital in new techniques of production (§4).

§15. Capital stratification

Accumulation of capital in new and cost reducing techniques of production applies to inter- as well as intra-branch investment of capital (§§13–14). In both cases the initiating capital secures an extra profit. The consequent threat of price competition and the necessity for continuous valorisation compels competitors to follow suit. However, each capital is burdened with the fixed costs of its already accumulated capital, and in order to preserve the existing capital value it will thus scrap old plants only when a new technique offers net profits greater than the gross profits on its existing plant. Since, therefore, plants embodying new technology will in general not be immediately adopted by all capitals, each branch of production tends to be composed of a *stratification* of capitals dated according to cost of production, and concomitant rate of profit differences.

With the determination of interaction of capital, dissociated units of production (1§3) have been grounded in the existence of capital in the form of many capitals and capital stratification.

Addendum: a. Stratification and vintage models

a. The concept of capital stratification will be expanded upon in 4§4. There are certain similarities between it and that of capital vintages posited by some modern neoclassical theories (see 4§4a and the references given there). Conventional neoclassical and some Marxist theories, on the other hand, posit 'small' *homogeneous* plants, or firms, engaged in atomistic competition. It is hard to understand what would then keep competition going. Indeed that conception of competition is highly ambiguous. As every unit is a perfect copy of every other, no more than comparative static states (differing from each other only to the extent that *exogenous* variables differ) can be described. Such a conception may be traced back to the lack of differentiation between homogeneous capital as value and the heterogeneous embodiment of capital in a technical sense – that is, the double form of capitalist production.

SECTION 5   THE ARTICULATION OF THE MOMENTS PRESENTED IN PART TWO

§16. The money expression of labour and abstract labour

The actual abstraction of particular labour, particular useful objects and particular labour power into the abstract universal form of value (1S3) has been further concretised, first by money as the expression of value (1S4) and secondly by valorisation, taking the form of valorisation of capital (1S5). From valorisation, the accumulation of capital, the credit system, the extended reproduction of labour power and the concepts of many capitals and capital stratification were derived (2SS1–4). The interplay of these determinations constitutes the prices of labour and of commodities – the quantitative expression in terms money of the value of labour, of the commodities produced by it and of labour power. Prices constituted in the market provide the actual moment of association of dissociated production: with the validation of dissociated labour in quantities of money it is constituted as abstract labour, and as such as part of the social circuit of capital.

The moments presented so far determine the money expression of labour, which further explicates the interconnection of the fundamental determinations of Part Two.

1. The association necessary because of the dissociated organisation of production and consumption in bourgeois society (1S2) appears to be manifest in the interaction of many capitals.

2. *Inter*-branch interaction of capitals generates flows of capital, mediated by money capital, between branches – the tendency to equalisation of rates of profit. This tendency, as well as the tendential compulsion to accumulate capital whilst preserving the existing capital value, constitutes a tendency for branches of production to be composed of a stratification of capitals, dated according to technique and concomitant rate of profit differences. *Intra*-branch interaction of capitals establishes a tendency towards uniform wages and intensity of labour for similar specific labour, as well as a tendency towards uniform prices for similar specific commodities (2S4).

3. Whilst valorisation takes on the form of valorisation of capital, the capitalist production process is necessarily a twofold process dominated by the value-form. The uniform prices established in the market have therefore to be anticipated, so that the labour process is ideally pre-commensurated in terms of the ideal output price (1S5). Because of the articulation of the tendencies of stratification and uniform prices, the ideal value, m, of the labour time in each unit of

capital (plant) i generally differs. If the ideal value of the *average* labour used up in some branch (k) is m_k then, in general, because of the stratification of capital, ideal values will differ *within* each branch:

$$m_i \neq m_j \tag{2.1}$$

Across branches, ideal values will in general also differ

$$m_k \neq m_l \tag{2.2}$$

4. These ideal pre-commensurations are however not actual commensurations. It is only in the market that the commodity is constituted as an entity of double form (use-value and money) and that the particular private labour is validated as a definite fraction of the abstract social labour (1S3). *Prices* are first determined, not by the labour used up in some particular private plant according to the technique adopted in that plant but as a recursive process by the labour used up in that plant in comparison to that required by the socially necessary technique (conceived for the moment as the average technique). In this particular sense, the price of a commodity is *determined* by socially necessary labour, and our presentation thus here encompasses the abstract-labour theory of value. The ideal pre-commensuration m_i may thus (contingently) diverge from the actual validation ('realisation'):

$$m_i \lessgtr \mathbf{m}_i \; ; \; m_k \lessgtr \mathbf{m}_k \tag{2.3}$$

where $\mathbf{m}_i$ and $\mathbf{m}_k$ are the realised *money expressions of labour*. Then $\mathbf{m}_i l_i$ is the expression for *abstract labour* of plant i. Summing the labour realised in each plant (or branch), *abstract labour* is

$$\Sigma \, \mathbf{m}_i l_i \equiv \mathbf{ml} \equiv \mathbf{Y} \; ; \; \mathbf{ml} \gtrless ml \gtrless \mathbf{ml} \tag{2.4}$$

(where l_i and l are, respectively the private and social aggregate labour expended, and $\mathbf{Y}$ is the social aggregate value-added).

5. Through the validation in the market, the commodity is then integrated into the (expanding) social circuit of capital as determined by the compulsion to accumulate (2S1).

6. Accumulation and expansion of the circuit of capital is, however, first conditioned by the mediation of commercial trade and production credit giving rise to money capital (2S2§§6–7). Credit increases the money income velocity of circulation (v). The consequent change in the aggregate *production* of *ideal* pre-commensurated value-added, Δml, is brought about by a change, Δv, in a closed money circuit

$$\Delta(ml) = \Delta Y = M^c \Delta v \tag{2.5}$$

(where M^c is money in circulation).

7. The aggregate expansion of the circuit of capital is next conditioned by the ex nihilo creation of credit money, privately pre-validating future production (2S2§8). This shows up as an increase of M^c in equation (2.5), uncompensated by changes in v. This introduces a one sided opening of the circuit $(\Delta M^c v)$, which has to be matched first by production, so that ΔM^c already circulates to buy means of production and labour-power,

$$\Delta(ml) = (\Delta M^c)v \tag{2.6}$$

and then by the social validation of this production:

$$m(\Delta l) = \Delta M^c v \; ; \; m(\Delta l) \equiv \Delta Y \tag{2.7}$$

whence the ΔM^c may (temporarily) return to the bank.

8. However, if the social validation (2.7) does not take place (so that the bank's solvency is eroded), this typically gives rise to inflation (2S2§9) of the money expression of labour (**m**),

$$(\Delta m)l = \Delta M^c v \; ; \; (\Delta m)l = \Delta Y \tag{2.8}$$

Thus in the absence of inflation (or deflation), changes in the social aggregate value added are predicated upon changes in the incorporation of labour into the circuit of capital, and the monetary expression of labour (**m**) is constant. With inflation (or deflation) the monetary expression changes, and so the value added. Value-added is thus no measure of the use-value purchasing power. Even in the absence of inflation and with value added constant, that purchasing power may increase because prices decrease.[4] But whilst the social aggregate **m** is constant in the absence of inflation (or deflation), branch monetary expressions (m_k), or plant monetary expressions (m_i) may change due to relative changes in labour productivity or, temporarily, due to structural changes in demand from the one branch to the other.

9. This possibility of inflation becomes structural when Central Banks (in order to prevent bank crises) guarantee the redeemability of credit money into Central Bank money, and when private losses of banks are overcome by 'pseudo-social validation' (2S2§10). With the concomitant erosion of money as store of value, the contradictory character of the double form of labour and its products in bourgeois society is transcended into the contradictory interplay of the forces of accumulation of capital (Part Three) and the necessity of the state and economic policy (Parts Four and Five).

---

4 Thus in our presentation inflation or deflation are monetary concepts, and they are not identified with changes in the general price level (see 5S3).

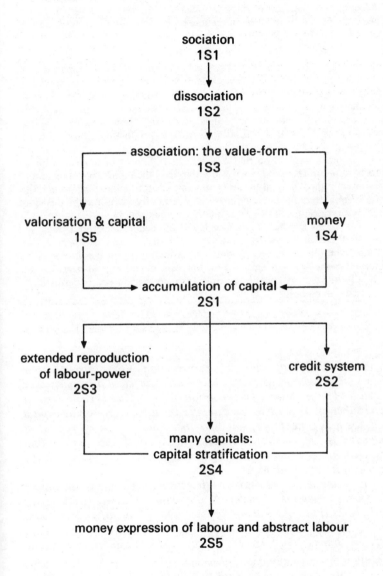

Figure 2.2 The value-form and its reproduction (Part Two).

Addenda: a. Aglietta's 'monetary expression of the working hour'; b. Schematic presentation of the interconnection of the moments derived in Part Two, (see Figure 2.2)

a. Our concept of 'money expression of labour' (m and m_i), constituting the concepts of 'abstract labour' (ml and $m_i l_i$) and of 'ideal pre-commensurated money expression of labour' (m_i), differs from Aglietta's 'money expression of the working hour' (1976: 43; see also De Brunhoff, 1976: 39) which we shall denote by m^*. In the first place, the latter is used by Aglietta only at the macroeconomic level. Secondly, it is predicated upon what he calls 'the monetary constraint' that realisation is equal to production. Thus Aglietta's

$$m^* = Y/l$$

is the monetary condition that $Y = Y$. The fulfilment of this condition of course implies that at the macroeconomic level the monetary expression of labour embodied is equal to the expression of abstract labour. Though this may be attractive for heuristic reasons, it is hardly useful for the theory of capitalism, since it is in fact an equilibrium condition.

Lipietz in his excellent book (1983: 139–86) denotes abstract labour by l and l_i (rather than our ml and $m_i l_i$). Whilst this may preserve a clearer link to Marx's concept of abstract labour it risks giving rise to labour-embodied interpretations (though this is not Lipietz's intention). Abstract labour (actually or ideal) is constituted only through the market, in terms of its expression in money.

SUMMARY

From the value-form theoretic reconstruction of the abstract-labour theory of value and from the valorisation of capital in particular (Chapter 1), the extended valorisation of capital has been derived. It determines an increase in control over the labour process by capital and the investment of profit, so that valorisation of capital is extended to capital accumulation. The limits to these are at first resolved in technical change, reducing costs and increasing the productivity of labour (Section 1).

The accumulation of capital is first grounded in the credit system (Section 2). From the two forms of commercial credit (trade credit and production credit) money of account, means of payment and money capital have been developed (§§6–7). From these again were derived banks and credit money. Most important to the accumulation of capital is the unity of ex nihilo created credit money and production credit, that is the private pre-validation of labour by banks. It has been argued that the concomitant break in the circuit of capital has to be closed by production and social validation of that production if it is not to generate inflation, together with a decrease in the solvency of banks. Insolvency and eventual bankruptcy threaten this necessary pre-validation (§§8–9). This determines the grounding of the banking system in the existence of the Central Bank as banker's bank, which reinforces credit money as fiduciary money. Thus whilst the Central Bank provides the conditions of existence of continuous pre-validation, its loans to banks in case the social validation of the bank's pre-validation fails take the form of a pseudo-social validation. Generalised inflation results, which erodes money as a store of value (§10). Pre-validation by banks is reflected in their reserve ratio. In a fully developed credit system, no sensible borderline can be drawn between money capital and money (which are both typically bank accounts), and 'hoarding' (withdrawing money from circulation) is expressed in an increase in the banks reserve ratio, and hence a downward pressure on the rate of interest. Whilst the reserve ratio determines the interest rate, it is itself determined by the demand for money as derived from the rate of accumulation and the rate of profit of industrial capital. Ultimately non-banking money capital and banks may decide only whether to lend or not, at the going rate of interest (§10).

Next to the credit system, the extended reproduction of labour power is a major condition of existence of the accumulation of capital. This has been very briefly indicated in Section 3. The further concretisation of this condition is taken up in Chapter 3.

The concept of interaction of 'many capitals', which is 'competition' conceived abstractly, was presented in Section 4. Inter-branch interaction generates the tendency towards equalisation of rates of profit, and intra-branch interaction generates the tendency towards uniform wages and prices in any one market. These tendencies, together with the compulsion to invest capital in cost-reducing and labour-productivity increasing techniques of production (§5), establish that each branch of production tends to be composed of a stratification of capitals, dated according to cost of production, and concomitant rate of profit differences. The concept of stratification of capitals is further concretised in Chapter 4.

This stratification of capital entails that particular production processes will be ideally pre-commensurated (1S5) against different ideal values of labour. Prices are thus not determined by the labour used up in some particular plant according to the technique adopted in that plant, but as a recursive process by the labour used up in any plant, in comparison to that appropriate to the socially necessary technique. From these determinations has been derived the concept 'money expression of labour', which links the determinations presented in Chapters 1 and 2. It thus provides a concretisation of the value-form of labour and useful objects (Section 5).

Part Three:

Tendencies of Accumulation of Capital

Chapter three

The Tendency to Over-accumulation of Capital: Labour-shortage Profit Squeeze and Underconsumption

PRELIMINARY REMARKS

In this chapter, two familiar theories explaining stagnation of accumulation of capital will be briefly integrated into the systematic presentation: the labour-shortage theory of the profit squeeze (§3), and underconsumption theory (§4). In our view, these theories cannot be applied immediately to complex phenomena such as economic crises. The issues on which these theories are based further ground the conditions of existence of the accumulation of capital and are introduced into our presentation at a much more abstract level than is common (Section 1). The two theories would appear to be mutually exclusive: in the first case (labour-shortage profit squeeze) recession or stagnation is explained by wages increasing too much, in the second (underconsumption) by deficient wages (and/or unproductive state expenditure). Here (Section 2) each is presented as a particular expression of the tendency to over-accumulation of capital, *revealing different aspects of it – costs and production in the first case, and production and demand in the second. To establish this last point is the main purpose of this chapter; therefore the two theories will be introduced only briefly.*

In Chapter 2S1, technical change has been introduced along with the accumulation of capital, but so far no change in the value composition of capital (the ratio of the value of means of production to the wage sum) has been discussed. Implicitly either a decreasing, a constant or an increasing value composition of capital is possible, and indeed the account in the current chapter is indifferent to which occurs. This issue will be taken up in Chapter 4. For expositional purposes, however, it is useful to assume the value composition of capital (insofar as it is determined by the technical composition and not by distribution) constant.

SECTION 1 THE TENDENCY TO OVER-ACCUMULATION OF CAPITAL

§1. Accumulation, the tendency for the rate of surplus value to rise and the validation of extended production

From the valorisation of capital has been derived its extended valorisation and accumulation (2S1), grounded most abstractly in the credit system (2S2), and then in the extended reproduction of labour power (2S3). The following propositions are entailed by the presentation so far:

(1) Accumulation of capital generates an increasing amount of ideal surplus value s (2S1), defined as $s = (m-w)l$ (where m is the ideal money expression of labour, w the wage rate and l social aggregate labour – cf. 2§16). (The term 'ideal' refers to as yet unvalidated entities – 1§8).

(2) Accumulation of capital, and the technical change concomitant on it, tend to give rise to increasing intensity and productivity of labour (2S1). Concomitantly the *rate* of ideal surplus value ($s' = (m-w)/w$) tends to increase. Abundant labour reserve is a condition of existence of this tendency (cf. 2S3). (Labour scarcity, conversely, counteracts this tendency – see §2.)

(3) The notion of accumulation of capital and technical change – derived so far – does not entail a particular change one way or the other in the value composition of capital. (The value composition of capital (ß) is defined as the ratio of the value of means of production (K) and the wage sum (wl), so $ß = K/wl$.) For purely pragmatic reasons we assume the value composition of capital (insofar as it is determined by the technical composition and not by distribution) constant here (Chapters 4–5 deal with changes in the technical and value composition).

(4) From propositions 1–3 above, it follows that the rate of ideal profit, r (defined as ideal surplus value produced, s, over capital accumulated, K+wl, so $r = s/(K+wl)$) tends to increase.

From these, the following propositions may be developed:

(5) If all wages are consumed and if all realised surplus value, s, is accumulated, z (so $s = z$) then the validation or realisation of all production (so that $ml = ml$ – 2§16) would require the intended accumulation of all ideal surplus value $s = z$, so that r would then be equal to $z/(K+wl)$.

(6) The social validation of extended production concomitant on accumultion would then require the equality of rate of profit and rate of accumulation (defined as $z' = z/(K+wl)$, so $r = z'$). Given

proposition 4, this would require *an increasing rate of accumulation.* (7) Such a rate of accumulation would again require a concomitant rate of integration of labour power over time, l', into the circuit of capital, so that once any unemployed labour is absorbed, the rate of growth of the labour force N', must be greater than or equal to that rate of integration of labour power, so that $z' = l' \leqq N'$.

In the way propositions 5–7 have been formulated, they are of course analytical, merely serving as a frame of reference for the account of the tendency to over-accumulation of capital in §2, and its expressions presented in §§3–4. Proposition 5, the validation of production ml = ml and its requirement that over time s = z is of course very stringent. The reproduction of association through the value-form does not require this equality, but it does require that some level of validation be anticipated. In general, if we define production as $X = \delta K + ml$ (where δ is the rate of depreciation) production validated X and thence ml is determined by expectations as to profit and the rate of profit (cf. Keynes 1936: ch. 12), for which the development of the realised rate of profit itself is a major determinant.

Addenda: a. Rate of investment; b. Harrod-Domar and Cambridge growth models

a. With the capital composition constant, an increasing rate of accumulation of capital also implies an increasing rate of investment. 'Investment' is commonly taken to refer to investment in means of production only (i.e., excluding a wage fund) a practice that we shall follow for expositional reasons.

b. That not all ideal value-added is in the event realised (ml is not necessarily equal to ml) is a common theme in Austrian economics, whilst neoclassical general equilibrium economics tends to neglect it. The relationships between rates of accumulation, of growth of the labour force and of output growth, have been extensively analysed in the 'dynamic Keynesian' Harrod-Domar models, in terms of the rate of growth of capital stock warranted by entrepreneurial expectations, the so called 'natural' rate of growth, and the actual rate of growth, respectively. (The seminal references are Harrod 1939 and Domar 1946.) These models rely ultimately on external (contingent) determinations in the shape of constraints on the 'natural' rate of growth and entrepreneurial expectations. The relationship between rates of accumulation and rates of profit, required for 'golden age' growth, have been extensively analysed in the Cambridge growth models (see, for example, Kaldor 1957; Pasinetti 1961/62; see also §4d).

---

§2. The tendency to over-accumulation of capital

With increasing control over the labour-process and intensity of labour, via the introduction of new techniques of production, the rate of surplus value tends to rise (2S1). This is reflected in a tendency for the rate of accumulation to increase, an ultimate condition of existence of which is a relatively abundant labour force. Labour abundance may prevent increasing labour intensity being reflected in wage increase, and facilitates the reflection in wage decrease of price decreases concomitant on any decrease in unit costs. Ultimately, however, the accumulation of an increasing mass of surplus value must deplete the reserve of labour, which (via an upward pressure on wages) counteracts the increase in the rate of surplus value, eventually causing it to decrease, leading to a decrease in the rate of accumulation of capital. Accumulation therefore tends to take the form of relative *over-accumulation of capital*: it is extended up to the point where capital becomes abundant relative to labour, because of excessive valorisation.

Addenda: a. Forward reference; b. Equilibrium growth

a. The tendency to over-accumulation of capital is one form of existence of accumulation. The other is the tendency for the composition of capital to rise, and along with it the tendency of the rate of profit to fall (Chapter 4). In the next paragraphs, the two expressions of the tendency to over-accumulation – labour-shortage profit squeeze (§3) and underconsumption (§4) – will be derived.

b. Formally, one cannot of course exclude the (indeterminate) possibility of a rate of surplus value such that the rate of capital accumulation will indeed be reduced to the growth rate of labour supply (for a Marxist account of this state, roughly comparable to our current level of abstraction, see Glombowski 1983: 378–81).

SECTION 2   EXPRESSIONS OF THE TENDENCY TO OVER-ACCUMULATION OF CAPITAL

§3. Over-accumulation of capital and labour-shortage profit squeeze

Increasing accumulation of capital tends towards over-accumulation in that ultimately the concomitant depletion of the reserve of labour gives rise to a downward pressure on the rate of surplus value (§2). One expression of this tendency to over-accumulation of capital is its effect on labour costs and production, whence it takes on the form of labour-shortage profit squeeze. Once valorisation and accumulation of capital have been extended up to the point where labour becomes scarce, competition between capitals for labour tends to generate increasing wages (or wages decreasing less than prices), thus squeezing profits and reducing the rate of increase of accumulation. If the rate of accumulation drops below the rate of increase of the labour force, unemployment increases, competition for labour decreases and the wage rate tends to decrease. These interactions may give rise to a cyclical pattern of profits, accumulation and unemployment. But such a cyclical pattern is contingent; if it occurs it need not be regular in length or amplitude. (Note also that we use the term 'cycle' in the sense of fluctuation in general, without any specification as to duration.)

Addenda: a. Marx and the Marxist theory of the profit squeeze; b. Diffusion of wage rate increase; c. Factors affecting the reserve of labour power; d. The indeterminacy of wages.

a. The substance of §3 is part and parcel of almost every strand in economic theory, though there are important differences as to the reactions to wage increase that are theorised: for example, substitution in neoclassical theories, so called vertical maladjustments (i.e. between the investment goods sectors and the consumer goods sectors) and inflation in Austrian oriented theories, and quantity adaption in post-Keynesian theories (including the cumulative displacement of the warranted from the actual rate of growth initiated by the natural rate of growth in Harrod-Domar models – cf. §1b). The theory may be traced back to Smith (1776: i. 61,316), for whom the rate of accumulation determines the change in the wage rate as a long run determinant. In Ricardo (1817: ch. xxi) the theory is used to explain short term adaptations (that is before the longer term changes in population growth as a result of real wage changes occur). Marx presents a similar theory in ch. 25 of *Capital* (1867 and 1867P; ch. 23 in 1867G) not only as a determinant of cycles in general, but also as a concrete historical, regular cycle of 10 years (the period tending to decline over time). From the point of view of our method, the reference to empirical facts here is illegitimate, the explanation of such concrete phenomena as 'the' cycle requiring many more mediations.

Within the Marxist tradition (not excluding more Ricardian-oriented authors) the theory has been developed at various levels of abstraction and from various methodological perspectives into what is labelled the 'theory of the profit squeeze'. In general, the focus in this theory is on class struggle over the distribution of income and its effect on accumulation and employment. The (initially) more empirically oriented work derives from Glyn and Sutcliffe (1971, 1972) and Boddy and Crotty (1975). (For a short taxonomy see Olin Wright 1977: 216–17; see also more recently Glyn and Harrison 1980 and Armstrong, Glyn and Harrison 1984.) Model-analytic work derives in particular from Goodwin 1967. (For a short taxonomy and additional references see Glombowski 1982: 21–2 and 1984: 74–5.) Goodwin stipulates that profits and expansion force wages up and profits down: 'This is because of the tendency of capital, though not capitalists, to breed excessively'. 'The improved profitability carries the seed of its own destruction by engendering a too vigorous expansion of output and employment, thus destroying the reserve army of labour and strengthening labour's bargaining power' (p. 449). Recently Goodwin's model has been extended so as to incorporate, inter alia, capacity utilisation and various forms of technical development, as well as welfare state institutions such as unemployment payments (for example, Glombowski and Krüger 1984, 1986 and Thio 1987). Notwithstanding the importance of such analysis, it seems hard within such an approach to theorise a hierarchy of conceptual determination (see 0§6). Nevertheless they are indeed essential to the discovery of the detailed links in that systematic qualitative order. As Glombowski writes: 'My plea for mathematical model-analysis concerns the context of discovery ('Forschungsprozess'), not the presentation ('Darstellung') ...' and: 'The use of mathematical models would be problematical if they were to be applied in a mechanical and reductionist way, that is if historical contingencies were suppressed and if only those non-economic elements that can be derived from economic processes, were incorporated' (Glombowski 1984: 67–8, our translation).

b. Scarcity of labour in relation to accumulation need not be general for wages to increase. Depending on the particular contingent forms of wage bargaining, the wage increase of scarce sections of the labour force may be diffused to other segments in which labour may still be relatively abundant. Unemployment may thus temporarily coexist with labour scarcity. Empirical analysis of this phenomenon has been in terms of the so called 'Unemployment–Vacancy' analysis (see, for example, Driehuis 1978 and the references given there). Another aspect of the complexity of the labour market, much stressed by Keynes and the Keynesians, is that even if labour is abundant, wages may be sticky downwards.

c. The reserve of labour power is determined not only directly and indirectly by accumulation, but also by demographic and social-demographic factors, influenced by medical care, technical possibilities of birth control, children as old-age care insurance, legislation on compulsory education and retirement, required education related to the state of technological development, migration, and so on. The dissolution of areas of non-capitalist production has already been argued to be indirectly affected by the accumulation of capital (2§12). Though each of these affects the potential accumulation of capital, each is differently affected by it. Whilst they are all endogenous to the system, their further determination belongs to a more concrete level than that of the present book.

d. The presentation in §3 has been couched in terms of directions of change of the wage rate, but in general the exact effect of accumulation and the reserve of labour on the wage rate and the wage level is indeterminate.

Economic theory has provided three approaches to the determination of the wage rate. In some Marxist theory the wage rate is made dependent on class struggle, which is clearly only a nominal solution as long as there is no fully constructed theory of class struggle. Another Marxian variant relates the size of the reserve army to historically specific possibilities of its overflow into non capitalist or semi-capitalist modes of production (see, for example, Mandel 1970). In neoclassical theory the wage rate is made dependent on the marginal physical productivity of labour and factor substitution. Quite apart from all the problems with the concept of marginal productivity, as revealed, for example, in the Cambridge–Cambridge 'capital controversy', it remains unclear what would happen if the wage rate decreases below the level at which labour power is reproduced. Classical theory has focused on the growth of the labouring population (2§12), but the classical economists themselves were well aware of the fact that the level of the subsistence ('the natural price of labour') is not itself a given (see, for example, Ricardo 1817: 54–5), so that only directions (not magnitudes) of change may be established.

§4. Over-accumulation of capital and underconsumption

One expression of the over-accumulation of capital (§2) is in the effect of labour scarcity *on* wages and profits and so on the *rate of accumulation* (§3). Another is in the effect of labour scarcity on production and its validation. The validation of extended accumulation itself requires an increasing rate of growth of accumulation which itself ultimately requires an abundant labour force (§1). The negation of this last condition operates not only on the wage rate but also on the validation of production via consumption out of wages. Labour scarcity may cause the wage rate to increase and the profit rate to decrease: however, there is no force to ensure that the wage rate *increase* is *sufficient* to validate production. If it is not, the tendency towards over-accumulation of capital takes the form of underconsumption.

In general, accumulation in the previous period determines capacity in the current one. An increasing rate of growth of accumulation and of employment of labour power can be realised only if the production of production capacity (in the investment goods sector) accommodates it. However, if the rate of growth of the labour force (N'), and so of employment of labour power (l') is insufficient with respect to the rate of accumulation, then *over-capacity* builds up. Depending on the degree of over-capacity, only part (or even none) of the surplus value realised will be accumulated. The rate of integration of labour, constrained eventually by the rate of growth of the labour force then becomes less than the rate of the accumulation, which itself thus falls below the ideal rate of profit $N' = l' < z' < r$ (cf. §1, propositions 6–7). Thus when over-capacity starts appearing, accumulation slows down, generating further over-capacity and so on. In the context of two departments of production, assuming the decrease in the rate of growth of labour integration to be equally distributed over the economy, the decreasing rate of growth of consumption generated by this decrease of the rate of growth of the labour force ($C' = wl'$ – assuming no savings out of wage income) will first hit department II (producing means of consumption). To the extent that the output in this department was already restricted by the decreasing rate of growth of the labour force, there is initially no reason for lay-offs (because there is only over-capacity). It is only accumulation that stagnates so that part of surplus value realised is not accumulated within department II. In department I (producing means of production), production has also been restricted because of the decrease in the growth of the labour force (and so there is also over-capacity here). But on top of this, part of production does not get realised because the demand from department II has slackened. There is then over-production to the extent of the difference between surplus value realised and that accumulated in department II. This may give rise to either of two reactions. Prices may decrease (possibly to the extent that they no longer cover costs of the plants low in the stratification of capitals – 2§15), which will eventually lead to labour lay-offs. Alternatively labour may be laid off immediately in department I, decreasing demand (and in the next period employment in department II). These interacting price and quantity adjustments may set up a downward spiral.

It may seem paradoxical that the *scarcity* of labour leads to *unemployment*, and then stagnation of accumulation and even de-accumulation, *because wages have not risen sufficiently* (cf. §3) (or because there has been insufficient unproductive consumption on the part of capital – see addendum a). However a presentation encompassing both production and realisation through the two-sided nature of labour (as both the sole necessary element of valorisation and as the major source of effective demand required to realise ideal value produced) reveals that there is no paradox, only a series of interconnected processes. If competition between capitals generates sufficient wage increase at an early stage, over-production does not come into play and investment does not lag behind the surplus value realised.

Addenda: a. Underconsumptionism; b. Unproductive expenditure; c. Underconsumption and disproportionality; d. Equilibrium growth models; e. Models of growth and accumulation; f. Empirical comparison of profit squeeze and underconsumption theories

a. Underconsumption in §4 has been presented as merely one expression of accumulation (rather than as a one-sided general underconsumptionist thesis) which shows similarities with the theories of the cycle put forward by Lederer (1925) and Preiser (1933), cf. Haberler (1937: 133–4, 137–41). Most other theories of underconsumption implicitly or explicitly posit a tendency towards *stagnation* in general. A history of such theories is provided by Bleaney (1976). Shorter characterisations are given by Haberler (1937: 118–41) and (of the Marxist type only) by Olin Wright (1977: 210–16). Bleaney (1976: ch. 6) provides evidence why Marx – contrary to Sweezy's (1942) opinion – should not be considered as an underconsumptionist. Whilst Bleaney (1976: ch. 1, 6, 9) devotes considerable attention to Luxemburg (1913) and Sweezy (1942), he does not mention authors such as Bauer (1936), upon whom Sweezy (1942: 186) bases himself.

Best known within the Marxist type of (stagnationist) underconsumptionism is Sweezy (1942: ch. X), together with Baran and Sweezy (1966). (However, as Glombowski (1984: 69) indicates, there is in principle no difference between these – and Bauer's (1936) – Marxist analyses, and Domar's (1946) Keynesian analysis.) Before explaining our disagreement with a *general* underconsumptionist theory (as exemplified in Sweezy) we shall summarise it, making use of the notation introduced in §1. This theory is predicated upon the general relation of the rate of accumulation to the rate of growth of consumption, without the growth of the labour force (i.e. potential labour power) being a binding constraint. It is based on the following set of propositions:

(1) Ongoing accumulation of capital causes the amount of (ideal) surplus value to increase over time.
$$ds/dt > 0 \tag{3.1}$$
(2) Because of increases in the intensity of labour, labour productivity increases over time. Though the real wage may increase over time, labour *abundance* prevents it keeping up with productivity increase. The rate of (ideal) surplus value (s') therefore increases over time:
$$ds'/dt > 0 \tag{3.2}$$
(3) The value composition of capital ($ß = K/(wl)$) remains constant over time (either by assumption, or by reference to some alleged 'stylised facts'):
$$dß/dt = 0 \tag{3.3}$$
(Note that in the usual treatments of the underconsumption theory technical change is not excluded, but it plays *no* determining role; it is anyway usually assumed that technical change does *not* alter the value composition of capital over time – cf., for example, Sweezy 1942: 182. Technical change is thus neutral with respect to changes in ß.)
(4) It follows trivially from propositions 1–3 that the rate of ideal profit increases over time:

$$dr/dt > 0 \tag{3.4}$$

The underconsumption thesis is then that there is a tendency for the economy to run into stagnation – eventually via economic crises – because of realisation problem. If all wages are consumed, then surplus value must be either accumulated (z) or unproductively consumed (u). The realisation of all production thus requires:

$$s = z + u \tag{3.5}$$

Dividing through by (K + wl) we have (cf. Olin Wright 1977: 213) the ideal rate of profit:

$$s/(K + wl) = z/(K + wl) + u/(K + wl) \quad \text{or} \quad r = z' + u' \tag{3.6}$$

Over time, then:

$$dr/dt = dz'/dt + du'/dt \tag{3.7}$$

For ideal profits to be realised, proposition 4 then requires the rate of accumulation (z'), and/or the rate of unproductive consumption (u') to *increase* over time. Underconsumptionism excludes $dz'/dt > 0$ (by assuming a constant relation between capital stock and consumption), because a secularly increasing rate of growth is excluded, at least for advanced capitalism (cf. Sweezy 1942: 189). In this case, then, to prevent deficient realisation, the rate of unproductive expenditure would have to increase over time. However, the underconsumptionist thesis is that – as Olin Wright (1977: 213–14) puts it in his comment – in capitalism there are no tendencies 'that guarantee that the rate of unproductive demand will grow sufficiently fast to fill the gap between the rate of accumulation and the rate of potential profit. The demand for unproductive, wasteful consumption does not grow spontaneously in the same way that demand directly derived from accumulation grows automatically with economic growth'.

We disagree on two issues with the generalisation of this theory. The first is the proposition as to wages and surplus value in relation to the labour force, and the second is the proposition as to the composition of capital. First, if there is an abundant labour force in relation to labour power required, then wages indeed may not keep up with productivity increase, and so the rate of surplus value will rise. But if the labour force is indeed abundant, then there is no reason why an increasing rate of growth of accumulation (along with an increasing rate of growth of labour power employed) should be impossible. (Sweezy on the contrary, seems to take at face value that it is impossible in mature capitalist countries: 'It is quite possible that national income should grow at an increasing rate in a 'young' capitalist country where manpower is abundant or rapidly increasing ... But in an 'old' capitalist country ... national income is almost certain to be growing at a declining rate' (1942: 189). An increasing rate of growth of accumulation would be inhibited only if it outran the rate of growth of the labour force. Now we agree that in this case if wages do not rise sufficiently (or if there is no compensating unproductive consumption) there will be underconsumption (§4), but this thesis cannot be generalised. Indeed when labour power is relatively scarce, increasing wages due to capitals' competition for labour (§3) cannot be excluded. Secondly, the proposition as to the rate of accumulation in relation to the (constant) composition of capital requires further development. Reference to an empirical study of a restricted period of time (Sweezy 1942: 182) is insufficient (see Chapter 4). Even if the value composition of capital were to be constant for a period of time, this does not say anything about the rate of accumulation. (Conversely, from a more or less constant rate of accumulation one cannot derive a thesis as to the value composition of capital. The processes of technical development, accelerated depreciation and inflation/deflation further complicate the issue – see Chapters 4–5.) Underconsumption is thus a systematic possibility (but *one* expression of the over-accumulation of capital), and we disagree with its immediate application to the concrete.

b. Tendencies of 'unproductive expenditure growth' have been analysed in Baran and Sweezy (1966) which is still the standard treatment in this respect (cf. 10§3). The presentation of the subsequent chapters may show that the premature abandonment of the theorisation of accumulation – in particular in relation to technical development (as in Baran and Sweezy 1966) may over-stress the systematic importance of underconsumption and unproductive expenditure as resolutions to contradictions, rather than expressions of them. This should not be taken as an underestimation of Baran and Sweezy, but their work needs to be incorporated into a systematic structure.

c. Underconsumption is manifested in a disproportionality between the sectors producing means of production and those producing consumer goods. This disproportionality, however, is not the cause of non-validation. Indeed any non-validation spreading over the economy may be cast in terms of disproportionality and reproduction schemes, and this would have to be done explicitly for any analysis of the stages of non-validation. (It may incidentally be mentioned that according to Moggeridge (1976: 104) Keynes used Marx's conceptualisation of realisation in his lectures.) Some Marxists (in the tradition of Tugan-Baranowski and Hilferding – cf. Sweezy 1942: 158–62) see disproportionality as a general cause of economic crisis, and certain variations of this theory are also mentioned in treatises on the business cycle (for example, Haberler 1937: 84). We agree with Mandel that disproportionality cannot be a cause of economic crisis: 'The anarchy of capitalist production therefore cannot be regarded as a cause in itself, independent in particular of the contradiction between production and consumption which is a distinctive feature of capitalism' (Mandel 1962: 367). But since the existence of the contradiction posited by the dissociative separation of production and consumption is grounded in the dominance of the value-form over resource allocation, it cannot be accurately characterised as anarchic, although it may be reproduced by anarchic processes.

d. In terms of post-Keynesian growth models, over-accumulation in the form of underconsumption related to labour scarcity (§4) shows some similarities with Robinson's cases of 'restrained golden age' and 'creeping platinum age'. (But in her models rising demand for credit induces the interest rate to go up, which checks accumulation – Robinson 1962: 135–9.) There is of course one case – that rate of (increase of) growth of accumulation and that particular wage rate in between wages being too high and wages being too low – in which extended accumulation would not seem to give rise to over-accumulation. This 'golden age' case is however merely an abstract possibility. ('I used the phrase "a golden age" to describe smooth, steady growth with full employment (intending thereby to indicate its mythical nature).' Robinson 1962: 133) There are no systemic forces keeping the rate of accumulation and the wage rate on that particular path; on the contrary, the tendency for the rate of surplus value to rise seems to divert them from this path. (However, such a contingent 'golden age' like state of the economy cannot be excluded. For an analysis of its conditions from within Marxist economics, see Glombowski and Krüger 1984, cases 1 and 2.)

e. The cumulative spiral interaction between growth paths – such that the natural rate of growth (to maintain unemployment constant) constrains the actual rate of growth so that it is forced below the rate of growth warranted by the 'optimal' level of capacity utilisation, generating demand deficiency motivated decisions which generate further over-capacity – has been rigorously modelled in variations of the Harrod-Domar model (§1b). The advantage of our presentation is that it integrates this closed model into a presentation of over-accumulation, labour-scarcity, profits squeeze and underconsumption. What is more, this presentation is linked to our theory of the value-form, and also (see Chapter 4) integrates the tendency of the rate of profit to fall predicated upon competition-induced technical change. Though they claim to be a 'dynamic' extension of Keynes to disequilibrium cases, Harrod-Domar models are in fact of a 'moving equilibrium', steady-state growth variety, not qualitatively different from comparative static models, except that they are not generally devised to be stable. Although we have not done it here, the development of our approach enables a conceptual structure which can simultaneously incorporate the insight of post-Keynesian, Harrod-Domar and neoclassical models of growth and accumulation.

f. At the much more concrete level of empirical phenomena, in both labour-shortage profit squeeze and labour-shortage underconsumption theories, wages may increase due to competition between capitals for labour. But if this is insufficient, the effect is on accumulation via realisation and production, rather than via costs and surplus value. However, in both cases there is a correlation between wage increase on the one hand and profit and accumulation decrease on the other. Superficially, then, it may seem plausible to argue in *both* cases that excessive wage increase causes stagnation.

SUMMARY

This chapter has presented the tendency to over-accumulation of capital. With increase in the composition of capital blended out (see

Chapter 4), the validation of extended accumulation of capital requires an increasing rate of accumulation, which requires an abundant labour force. However, the forces increasing the rate of surplus value, and the accumulation of surplus value, generate depletion of the reserve of labour, and so valorisation and accumulation tend to be extended up to the point where capital is abundant relative to labour (Section 1). The expression of this tendency to over-accumulation of capital is in labour-scarcity profit squeeze, or in labour-scarcity underconsumption (Section 2). The first is generated when the extension of valorisation and accumulation up to the point where labour becomes scarce leads to increasing wages. Increasing production costs then squeeze profits, giving rise to a reduction in the rate of accumulation and to relative abundance of labour once again. Labour-scarcity underconsumption occurs when insufficient wage increase is generated, and so the tendency to over-accumulation of capital is manifested in underconsumption, and accumulation stagnates. Labour scarcity, via a total wage sum insufficient to realise production, gives rise to unemployment and thence further reduction of the wage sum.

The two theories of accumulation (profit squeeze and underconsumption) which are usually put forward as mutually exclusive have now been presented as interconnected. They are only different expressions of the contradiction that the accumulation of capital is extended up to its negation in over-accumulation.

Chapter four

The Tendency of the Rate of Profit to Fall: Devalorisation, Devaluation, Restructuring and Centralisation of Capital

PRELIMINARY REMARKS

The tendency to over-accumulation of capital is expressed in labour-shortage profit squeeze and underconsumption (Chapter 3), and is one form of existence of the accumulation of capital, predicated on the necessary incorporation of labour into the circuit of capital. In this chapter, we present the other major tendency of accumulation: the 'tendency of the rate of profit to fall', deriving from increasing labour productivity, technical change and increase in the composition of capital. These forms of existence of accumulation each derive independently, but at the same level of abstraction, from the compulsion to accumulate. Their articulation is theorised in Chapter 5.

The theory of the tendency of the rate of profit to fall (TRPF) was a substantial part of almost all economic theories from Adam Smith until the end of the nineteenth century. For Jevons, for example, there is no doubt as to the existence of the tendency: 'There are sufficient statistical facts, too, to confirm this conclusion historically. The only question that can arise is as to the actual cause of this tendency' (Jevons 1871: 246). In more recent times, however, TRPF theory has been confined almost entirely to Marxist or Marxist inspired work (see, however, the references in Harris 1983), where the tendency is related to the increase in the composition of capital concomitant on labour-expelling technical change. However, even here the issue remains controversial, due partly to the fact that there is little agreement as to the appropriate level of abstraction. Some authors interpret the tendency as an empirical trend of either short run cyclical or long run secular development. It will become clear that this is not our view. A tendency is a concept belonging to a specific level of abstraction, and so is quite different from the concept of an empirical trend. Another important controversy relates to the question of how technical change could ever produce a fall in the rate of profit when new techniques are presumably introduced only in order to secure increases in the rate of profit. Thus, it is argued, rate of profit decreasing technical change will just not come about. If the rate of profit is to decrease, it must be for reasons other than changes in the composition of capital brought about by technical change. Because of this apparent falsification, many authors (drawing in this respect on the seminal papers by Okishio 1961 and Himmelweit 1974) conceive the TRPF as being insufficiently grounded. (The TRPF is alleged to lack a microeconomic foundation, as Roemer (1979) expresses it.)

These controversies are expanded in addenda §1a and §3a. We shall argue that, besides the fact that authors such as Okishio (1961), Himmelweit (1974) and Roemer (1979) cast their analysis in one sided physical (use-value) terms, their analysis is also inadequate in that it is comparative-static. Once the theory is cast in dynamic terms, conditions of existence (or, appropriate 'microeconomic foundations') for the TRPF can indeed be provided, and the analysis of the 'Okishians' reduces to a special case. Our own account derives from the requirements of their systematic presentation. In Section 1 the tendency of the rate of profit to fall is presented as one form of existence of the compulsion to accumulate capital. Section 2 shows that it is a contradictory tendency, which has elsewhere been insufficiently grounded. The further concretisation of the concept of capital stratification (Chapter 2) provides the conditions of existence of this contradiction. From it, the expressions of the TRPF in devaluation of capital and, contingently, restructuring and centralisation of capital will be derived (Section 3).

SECTION 1 THE TENDENCY TO RELATIVE EXPULSION OF LABOUR

§1. The tendency for the composition of capital to rise

The accumulation of capital in new techniques of production overcomes the constraint to increasing valorisation of capital imposed by the inherent limits to increase in labour intensity. The compulsion to introduce new techniques of production – reproduced by the existence of many capitals – ensures that not only the design of technical change, but also technological change itself, takes on the value form, and that they are incorporated into capitalist enterprises (2§4). The expression of this process is first in the continual change of the process of production, typically in the form of continual increase in labour productivity. This implies that in use-value terms, a unit of labour tends to work up an increasing mass of means of production (raw materials and depreciating fixed means of production), so that the technical composition of capital (TCC) tends to increase. It also implies that at the *point in time* when a TCC increasing technique is introduced, the composition of capital in terms of the prices at that point in time increases (that is the value composition of capital (VCC) – the ratio of the value of the means of production to the value of labour – power increases). Of any unit of profit accumulated an increasing share tends therefore to be invested in means of production, and a decreasing share in the wage fund. There is thus a tendency towards relative expulsion of labour. (Whether this expulsion actually decreases employment depends also on the mass of profit.)

The tendency for the composition of capital to increase thus counteracts the extended incorporation of labour into the circuit of capital and the derived tendency to over-accumulation of capital. On the one hand, it retards (or even prevents) the eventual scarcity of labour and the concomitant upward pressure on wages (3§3). On the other, accumulation in an increasing share of means of production (generating a relative increase in the rate of growth of the means of production producing department) counteracts underconsumption (3§4). However, both labour using accumulation (Chapter 3) and its negation in relative labour expelling accumulation derive independently from the accumulation of capital (2S1), and are therefore to be theorised first as moments (0§9), before their articulation in Chapter 5.

Addenda: a. The law of the tendency of the rate of profit to fall and the order of presentation; b. Technology, technique and the technical, organic and value compositions of capital (TCC, OCC and VCC).

a. The tendency for the composition of capital to increase is an integral part of 'the law of the tendency of the rate of profit to fall' (TRPF). Along with the theory of value (and the so called 'transformation problem') the 'law of the TRPF' is the most controversial issue within Marxist economics. The controversies around the TRPF may be classified into four groups. The *first* concerns the question as to whether or not the composition of capital may empirically be seen to be rising. This does not bear upon the theoretical issue at this level of abstraction. Although empirical investigation is useful to concrete analysis it cannot refute abstract theory. (This is agreed by many participants in the debate who, on other grounds, object to the theory; see, for example, Roemer 1979: 380.)

The second controversy concerns the argument as to why the composition of capital should be rising. Some years ago this issue was taken up again by Shaikh (1978) in critique of the position taken by Dobb (1937), and commented upon by various authors in the *Cambridge Journal of*

Economics (1980). For Dobb, the eventual increase in real wages (one expression of the over-accumulation of capital in our conceptualisation) *gives rise* to the introduction of labour-saving techniques, and thence increase in the composition of capital. Shaikh, on the other hand, posits the tendency of the composition of capital to increase as fundamental, whilst it is unclear how he relates it to over-accumulation. Marx, to whom Shaikh refers for support, does not provide the answer as to the relation of the two tendencies. The tendency towards relative expulsion of labour (concomitant on the tendency of the composition of capital to increase, and giving rise to the TRPF) is certainly an important law of tendency in Marx's *Capital* – 'in every respect the most important law of modern political economy'. Although according to Fine (1982: 118) the law of the TRPF as such – without the counteracting tendencies – 'could well have been presented at the end of Volume I' (and indeed, according to Rosdolsky (1968: ch. 2) Marx originally intended to do so) it is in fact presented in Volume III, whilst theoretical priority (Volume I) is given to over-accumulation ('The General Law of Capitalist Accumulation'). In our presentation the tendency for the composition of capital to rise is on a par with the tendency to over-accumulation. We would conceive of Dobb's account as being at a lower level of abstraction.

The third controversy concerns the question of the ambiguous role of the rate of surplus value, in particular in relation to wage decrease. This is taken up in §2. The fourth controversy of objections – whilst adopting the initial conditions of the increase in the composition of capital and the independence of real wages – is addressed to the lack of microeconomic foundation of the tendency. It is argued that the criteria determining decisions over the introduction of new techniques would exclude a fall in the rate of profit (see §§3–4, and §5). The resolution of these questions hinges on a systematic order of presentation of rigorously separated out levels of abstraction.

Finally, there is the question as to the status of the law of the TRPF itself in relation to empirical trends. As we have indicated in Part One, though tendencies cannot be taken to be empirical statements in the sense that their effects can be directly observed, they do affect the concrete. Contrary to some Marxist theorisations the TRPF cannot be interpreted as a trend (Weeks 1981: 205; cf. also Cutler, Hindess, Hirst and Hussain 1977: Vol. 1, ch. 6). Before the theory can be confronted with the empirical, the articulation of these tendencies (see Chapter 5), and their interconnection with economic policy (see Part Four) has to be theorised. Further concretisation may then have to take account of contingencies that require detailed historical and conjunctural examination.

b. Freeman (1974: 7) defines the pair of concepts invention and innovation (initially introduced by Schumpeter 1934) as follows:

> An *invention* is an idea, a sketch or model for new or improved device, product, process or system. . . . they do not necessarily lead to technical *innovations*. . . . An innovation in the economic sense is accomplished only with the first *commercial* transaction involving the new product, process, system or device, although the word is used to describe the whole process.

Our 'technological change' and 'technical change' are broadly analogous. By a state of technology we mean a state of knowledge concerning techniques of production that are technically feasible. By a change of technique we mean the actual implementation of technology in production with reference in particular to changes in the ratio of the means of production to labour. In a physical (technical) sense, the term 'technical change' is operational only if the bundles of inputs and the bundles of outputs remain homogeneous, whilst their compositions do not change (the 'corn' parable). Indeed the market (value) provides a measure, but then technical progress gets identified with cost decrease – or even increase in the rate of profit. Indeed, given that input and output mixes do change, there is no other way in economics to conceive of technical progress (though see Solow 1957).

The same problem arises with the concept of technical composition of capital. Though it may have an intuitive meaning, there can be no social measure of it. Marx uses three concepts of the composition of capital: the technical (TCC) the organic (OCC) and the value composition (VCC). As his definitions of the OCC and the VCC in Volumes I and III of *Capital* (Marx 1867: 574; 1894: 145–6, 154) are inconsistent, Marxists often use the terms interchangeably. A useful interpretation of the difference between them is given by Fine & Harris (1976 and 1979: 58–61). However our concept of the composition of capital (CC) in general differs from theirs in two respects: for us the CC always includes fixed capital; and we do *not* measure the denominator in wage goods but rather in terms of wages. (To incorporate wage goods or the value of wage goods in the CC is a Ricardian hangover: the value of labour power – the wage sum – is directly relevant to capital.) It follows from this that the TCC may indeed be given an intuitive meaning only as the ratio of the mass of means of production to the mass of labour power used up. The *OCC* is then this same ratio measured in values at the point in time when means of production and labour power have been bought. It is an historical costs measure: the ratio of constant capital (the value of means of production, taking account of the turnover time of its circulating component) to variable capital (the wage sum, taking account of turnover time) in historical prices. The *VCC* is this same ratio in *current* prices.

Our concept of the *instantaneous* VCC, reflecting changes in the TCC, is akin to the OCC, and the differences between it and the OCC on the one hand, and the VCC on the other hand is that the VCC takes into account changes in prices which are *the result of* the change in the TCC. Because the increase in labour productivity associated with a rise in the TCC typically tends to decrease prices of both means of production and – under particular conditions – labour power, a rising TCC need not be reflected in the VCC. These conceptual distinctions are crucial if the presentation is not to be restricted to static equilibrium analysis, and if the dynamics of capitalist development are to be taken into account. The concept of instantaneous VCC (unlike the OCC as defined by Fine and Harris) is not restricted to their level of analysis of *production*. (Our structure of levels of abstraction is quite different. Relatedly Fine and Harris retain pre-market value categories as distinct from money prices throughout their analysis.) (This has been implicitly criticised by Himmelweit and Mohun 1978; see also their 1981: 249, note 37.) The distinction between pre-market values and money values is an insufficiently grounded Ricardian remnant (in both Marx and Fine and Harris), and dynamic theory needs no such pre-monetary concept (Chapter 1). Both VCCs are monetary concepts. It is sufficient to differentiate between historical costs – real outlays of capital – and current prices affecting devaluation and revaluation of capital. It is this last aspect (see §5) which is crucial to the 'law of the tendency of the rate of profit to fall'. In reference to the 'composition of capital', the dimension is always monetary.

§2. The tendency of the rate of profit to fall (TRPF)

The rate of profit **r** is the ratio of profit (value added, **m**l minus wages, wl) to capital laid out (K + wl):

$$r = \{(m - w)l\} / \{K + wl\} = \{(m - w)/w)\} / \{K/(wl) + 1\}$$

(where K is capital invested in fixed and circulating means of production; w is the money wage rate; **m** is the money expression of labour; and l is labour (measured in time); K/(wl) is then the composition of capital).

The tendency for the composition of capital to rise (§1), generates a tendential decrease in the rate of profit, leading to a tendency for the rate of accumulation of capital to decrease. The tendency for the rate of profit to fall is one form of existence of accumulation of capital (the other being the tendency to over-accumulation of capital – 3§2).

Formally, a tendential fall in the rate of profit may be offset by a sufficient rise in the rate of surplus value **(m–w)/w**. It is however important to re-establish that **m** (the money expression of social labour) and w (the average money wage rate) are macroeconomic categories and that their determination does not directly derive from instantaneous changes in the composition of capital. Let us briefly expand on each of the components (w and **m**) of the rate of surplus value. First, in the absence of inflation, an increase in the value composition of capital and the social use-value productivity of labour tends (in the absence of quantity rationing – see §4) to be accompanied by decreasing commodity prices. But this does not immediately lead to changes in the wage rate, though the purchasing power of the wage is affected by it.[1] Changes in the wage rate are determined rather by the articulation of changes in the intensity and organisation of the labour process and unemployment (3§2, see 5S1).

Secondly, given the conception of inflation (deflation) as an increase (decrease) in the money expression of labour, **m**, and the

1 However, such price decrease does affect the composition of capital through its means of production component (see §5).

tendency for the effect of increases in labour productivity on m to be offset by concomitant price falls, an increase in the *social average use value* productivity of labour need have no effect on social income ml, since the effect of the increased number of use-values will tend to be just offset by a decrease in the general price level ($2\S16$; see 5S3).[2] But even when m is constant, value added ($ml \equiv \Sigma\, m_i l_i$) need of course not be, if l may change. Furthermore, the micro counterpart of m, m_i may not be constant since it is a function of the deviation of the micro *value* productivity of labour from the social average value productivity of labour m. Relative changes in micro *use-value* productivity of labour may change relative prices and may affect m_i, without affecting m. Similarly, to the extent that unit costs decrease an increase in the average use-value productivity of labour in some branch k tends to be expressed in price decrease. But even then value-added in this branch, $m_k l_k$ might remain constant or even increase, since it depends not only on the relative productivity increase measured by m_k, but also on the size of the branch as measured by l_k.

Because the TRPF does not by itself immediately affect the macroeconomic categories m and w, at *this* level of abstraction, the rate of surplus value may be kept constant (see 5S1 for the articulation of the TRPF and changes in the rate of surplus value). It does however immediately affect the micro and branch-level categories m_i and m_k, and the concomitant rates of surplus value (see §4).

SECTION 2 THE CONTRADICTION OF THE TENDENCY FOR THE RATE OF PROFIT TO FALL

§3. Contradiction of the TRPF (introduction)

Valorisation of capital has been shown to be predicated upon the *integration* of labour into the circuit, since the latter is the sole socially necessary element of production of potential value added, and so also of potential profit (1S5). Further, accumulation of capital has been conceptualised as being geared towards *increase* in profit and the rate of profit – that is, to increasing valorisation and rate of valorisation of capital (2S1). These determinations contradict the conceptualisation of accumulation derived in §§1–2: the

---

2 Our concept of inflation derives from Aglietta (see 5§7). Thus we do not treat an increase in the general price level as identical to inflation. (Nor do we treat deflation as identical to a decrease in the general price level – or to a downward spiral in expenditure, for that matter.)

tendential increase in the (instantaneous) value composition of capital and the relative *expulsion* of labour, and the tendency of the rate of profit to *fall*.

Indeed, it is this contradiction which is grasped by the law of the TRPF. The further concretisation of the law reveals how this contradiction is transcended. (Reference to the *law* of the TRPF, rather than just to the TRPF (§2), is intended to refer to this concretisation in its complexity.) In §4, the existence of this contradiction is grounded, presenting the conditions in which it is indeed transcended. In particular, it shows how the contradiction of a tendential *increase* in profit and the rate of profit along with the accumulation of capital in new plants (2§4), and the tendency of the rate of profit to *fall* (§2), is transcended in a concretisation of the concept of capital stratification (2§15), and in the devalorisation of capital. The more concrete *expression* of this contradictory form of accumulation in capital devaluation (§5) and in restructuring and centralisation of capital (§6) is then determined.

Addendum: a. The critique of the TRPF by Okishio, Himmelweit and Roemer

a. The contradiction of increase in the rate of profit along with accumulation of capital in new plants and the tendency of the ra te of profit to fall has led authors such as Okishio (1961) and Himmelweit (1974) to reject the TRPF. A more general statement of the Okishio and Himmelweit critique (extending to a model including fixed capital) was provided by Roemer (1979).[3] The critique of these authors is usually considered to be the most telling and, although their framework of analysis is quite different, their critique is to some extent relevant to the current level of our presentation. They agree with us that: (1) The empirical discussion of whether or not the composition of capital is rising and the rate of profit falling does not bear upon the theoretical argument ('The empirical investigations, then, are certainly necessary, but they cannot provide refutation of a theory.' – Roemer 1979: 380); (2) An eventual refutation of the theory does not depend on a change in the rate of surplus value (consequently the part of their argument relevant to this is couched in terms of the maximum rate of profit, with wages approaching zero).

Basically, their critique is that the TRPF lacks a microeconomic foundation.[4] As capitals are impelled to increase profit and the rate of profit they will introduce only new techniques that are cost-reducing (2§4) so, the

---

3 Himmelweit's contribution was written independently of Okishio's. In the literature authors within this type of approach are sometimes referred to as 'Okishians'.

4 The type of problem is of course well known in neoclassical and Keynesian macroeconomics (see, for example, Dow 1985: ch. 4).

argument goes, the average rate of profit cannot decrease.[5] Typically, the average rate of profit will increase in terms both of old and of new equilibrium prices.[6] As it stands, all this is quite correct.[7] The crucial question is, however, to what extent this comparative static equilibrium account in Sraffian terms adequately deals with the dynamic problem of the TRPF (cf. also Fine 1982: 112–5). Within the 'Okishian' account, all new least-cost techniques are adopted by *all* capitals. Whilst this 'procedure' may seem intuitively adequate when all capital is conceived of as circulating capital (as with Okishio and Himmelweit) it is not adequate when fixed capital is taken into account (as with Roemer, challenged to do so by Shaikh 1978). Capitals will not in general adopt a new technique when its expected increase in revenue and the rate of profit does not compensate for the early obsolescence of the fixed capital of the old technique (see §§4–5). But Roemer evades the dynamic problem of the TRPF because of his odd conceptualisation of fixed capital. In one of his models he assumes that all fixed capital lasts forever, and proposes that 'if the rate of profit can be shown to rise as a consequence of technical innovation in a model when fixed capital lasts forever, *a fortiori* it should rise when fixed capital wears out, ...' (1979: 385). The static conception is shown here very clearly – in this conception, fixed capital does not need to be *replaced*. All capitals within a sector of production are homogeneous, so the problem of eventual devaluation of fixed capital (when prices decrease) which affects different capitals unevenly according to their state of amortisation, is defined away.[8] The same goes for his Von Neumann type model where he assumes that only those processes are operating 'which produce a maximum profit rate'.

However, this critique of the 'Okishians' does not preclude the possibility that they are correct in arguing that the 'microfoundations' of the TRPF are indeed inadequate or even lacking altogether (see §4). (However, for our method the notion of 'microfoundations' is in fact misleading. The competitive interaction of individual agents implied by the term constitutes

5 This part of the argument was also provided by Samuelson (1974).

6 When the constant real wage is conceived of as a commodity input (Roemer 1979: 381–2) then the rate of profit always increases if the input–output matrix is indecomposable; if it is decomposable the rate of profit might remain the same.

7 Shaikh's (1978) critique of Okishio and Himmelweit – to which Roemer (1979) also replies – is that capitalists are forced (microeconomically) to reduce cost prices whence indeed according to the Okishio theorem the profit margin on costs increases; at the same time, however, the profit rate might decrease. We find this very unconvincing, because it seems to imply that some fixed capital costs are not part of cost prices. What is more, we would argue that the profit rate is the first criterion from which the other two follow. See also the comments on Shaikh by Steedman (1980), Nakatani (1980), Bleaney (1980) and Fine (1982: 125–7), as well as the reply to the first three by Shaikh (1980).

8 This is all the more remarkable because Roemer (rightly) accuses Shaikh (1978) of neglecting amortisation of fixed capital. It may be noted that this problem would remain even if technical changes could be perfectly foreseen (pp. 387–8), unless of course capitalists were, because of foreseen technical changes, to decide not to invest at all.

only the relatively concrete condition of reproduction (Chapter 6) of the more abstract fundamental moments of the value-form, valorisation and accumulation (Chapters 1–2) and the (macro) tendencies from them.)

§4. The conditions of existence of the contradiction of the TRPF: stratification and devalorisation

The contradiction of the tendency of the overall rate of profit to fall (§2) and the tendential increase in profit and the rate of profit along with the accumulation of capital in new plants (2§4) is grounded in the further determination of the concept of capital stratification (2§15). Capital tends to be stratified because, whilst valorisation is a continuous process, the accumulation of capital in means of production is a discrete 'lumpy' process, as is entry to a new branch of production. The capital embodied in plants is therefore dated differently. But as techniques and labour productivity change continually over time, dated stratification is characterised according to these factors. And as there is a tendency to uniform prices in a market (2§14), this dated stratification is also a stratification of different rates of profit.[9]

The prevalence of this stratification is derived from the compulsion to valorisation, accumulation and preservation of capital (2§15). Therefore, when new techniques of production are available (with higher calculated plant rates of profit) preservation of *capital* already accumulated may prevent immediate moves towards investment in new-technique and maximum rate of profit *plants*.[10] Scrapping of plants is enforced only when prices no longer cover prime costs. Before that, the scrapping of plants in favour of investment in new ones is determined first by the difference in rates of profit on the investment in an already existing plant, and on that

9 See also §2. If rates of profit are calculated over the lifetime of an asset and if there is perfect foresight, calculated rates of profit might be equal. This does not however affect the argument (see also note 16 below). Our presentation highlights that the state of the economy conceptualised is not one of equilibrium, nor of perfect competition.

10 We are drawn into this way of presentation by the static equilibrium analysis of this matter, where the rate of profit is identified with the plant's 'physical' rate of profit. The rate of profit of any one capital is of course the weighted average of the investments of that capital in several plants. Note again that competition is conceived to be 'heterogeneous' or 'oligopolistic' rather than 'perfect'. Salter (1960) has shown that in case of perfect competition capital would always immediately move to the new technique plant.

in a new plant (inclusive of capital foregone because of scrapping); and secondly by the availability of means of finance (out of amortisation and/or out of additional credit).[11]

Capital invested in a new plant and added to the stratification operates thus with up-to-date techniques of production – those with the highest composition of capital, maximal productivity of labour and minimal unit costs of production. Prior to scrapping of plants, this investment increases the branch (or economy) production capacity,[12] which induces one of two effects (or a combination of them). The first is that plants in the branch operate at over-capacity as compared with the previous period; the second is that prices are driven downwards. In either case plants at the bottom of the stratification that no longer cover prime costs will have to be scrapped.[13] Thus when plant $(n+1)$ is added to the stratification $(1, \ldots, n)$, and when (h) plants are scrapped, the previous stratification $(1, \ldots, n)$ becomes $(1+h, \ldots n, n+1)$. We shall pursue the alternative of price decrease (the over-capacity alternative has the same result).[14] Because of price decrease, the revenue of the remaining part of the previous stratification $(1+h, \ldots, n)$ decreases, whereas the revenue of the new stratification $(1 + h, \ldots, n, n + 1)$ typically increases with the average rate of growth.[15] The decreased revenue of the capitals in the previous stratification reflects their *devalorisation*, which is thus due to the labour productivity of any

11 This implies that a maximum rate of profit can be gained only by fully amortised capitals. Our conceptualisation here and in the remainder of this paragraph differs from neoclassical vintage models (see addendum a).

12 Whilst the reference here is to a branch the argument typically holds for the economy as a whole.

13 The new plant capital may initiate this price decrease because it operates at minimal costs. It then functions as price leader. Subsequent scrapping is the typical process. Of course plants at the bottom of the stratification may be scrapped pre-emptively. The expected price decrease – or alternatively the expected over-capacity – will be taken into account by the capital considering the new plant prior to the investment. In general, the initiation of price decrease by this capital, in order to induce scrapping of plants at the bottom of the stratification so that the new plant can operate at near to full capacity, may be advantageous to it (see the Appendix). Although we think that it is important to conceptualise the processes of adaptation (price decrease and scrapping) our argument here does not rely on it. In principle, the argument (price decrease in particular) could also be cast in terms of a Sraffian equilibrium model with joint production.

14 It has the same result in terms of the current argument. It has, however, different effects with respect to employment of labour and effective demand.

15 Of course in case of (macroeconomic or branch) stagnation the revenue may remain constant or decrease. On the other hand, one branch may of course grow above average. This does not, however, affect the general argument (see also the Appendix).

one capital in some period, relative to the average, lagging behind that in the previous period.[16]

Thus, because investments and costs are unaffected whilst revenue decreases, the rate of profit of the capital accumulated in the remaining part of the previous stratification $(1 + h, \ldots, n)$ decreases. That of the capital invested in the new plant $(n+1)$ tends, at the new price to increase as compared with the average rate of profit $(1, \ldots, n)$ at the previous price, or with the rate of profit of the plant just below it in the stratification (n) at the previous price.[17] Since the new plant $(n + 1)$ operates at lower production costs than the previous plant (n), then in any case the rate of profit of the new plant capital at the new price is above both that of the nth and the average rate of profit. (This is in fact sufficient for the argument.) Because with the additional plant the *average* composition of capital tends to increase (§1), the *average* rate of profit tends to decrease.[18] But it is because of the relatively greater labour productivity of the capital added to the stratification $(n+1)$ that its comparative profitability increases, since the value productivity of labour in the $(1 + h, \ldots, n)$ plants thereby decreases (typically by a decrease in output prices). Therefore also, not only is the money expression of labour, m_i, stratified increasingly from $(1, \ldots, i, \ldots, n)$, but it also tends to decrease (devalorisation) for all i when the stratification is extended. (A formal treatment of the argument is presented in the Appendix to this chapter.)

Thus, whilst the rate of profit on newly invested capital – previously invested in another branch or previously invested lower in the stratification – tends to *increase*, the average rate of profit in a branch or in the economy as a whole tends to *decrease*. The contradiction of the tendency of the aggregate rate of profit to fall, and the increase in the rate of profit along with the accumulation of

16 Devalorisation of capital – to be sure – goes beyond any normal wear and tear. It might be argued that to the extent devalorisation is foreseen at the point of investment, it is incorporated in calculating the 'marginal efficiency of capital'. But even if there were perfect foresight in this the argument is unaffected. It cannot prevent devalorisation, and even with devalorisation net profits over the lifetime of the asset may still be positive and optimal.

17 Within the 'Okishian' argument it is even sufficient that the $(n+1)$ composition of capital and the $(n+1)$ rate of profit at the *old* prices is just above that of (n) at the old prices. So if the $(n+1)$ rate of profit is only just above that of (n) and if the $(1 + h, \ldots, n)$ rate of profit decreases at the new prices or the new capacity utilisation, then the Okishian argument is falsified for all plausible cases (those in which there is indeed accumulation of capital – see also §6).

18 Price decrease of course affects capital outlay on circulating constant capital (raw materials, etc.). It does, however, not affect previous capital outlay on fixed constant capital. The effect of the related devaluation of fixed capital is taken up in the next paragraph.

capitals in new plants, is an abstract contradiction which has been resolved – at this level of the presentation – in its grounding in the stratification of capitals.

Addenda: a. Capital stratification, scrapping and vintage models; b. Capital stratification and 'transformation'

a. The processes of scrapping and investment have been introduced here at the elementary level required by our presentation of the TRPF. (For an overview of more sophisticated descriptions of these, as well as the discussion relating to optimal innovation decisions and processes of diffusion of techniques, see, for example, Hay and Morris 1979.)

Our conceptualisation of capital stratification is not restricted to the tendency for the composition of capital to increase. Rather, it is the typical form of existence of capital and therefore it constitutes also the conditions for the reproduction of the tendency of the rate of profit to fall. (However, the effect of this form of existence on the average rate of profit will increase along with the increase of the relative share of fixed capital.)

As already indicated, our concept of 'stratification' is different from the more orthodox concept of vintages (see Solow 1970: ch. 3; the seminal references are Johansen 1959, Salter 1960, Kaldor and Mirrlees 1961/62, Solow, Tobin, von Weizsäcker and Yaari 1966, Cass and Stiglitz 1969). In the neoclassical conception obsolescence of plants is determined by the real wage (wage costs exceeding the average labour productivity on a plant) rather than by the addition of plants to the stratification, introducing new cost-reducing techniques of production and the resulting price decrease and/or over-capacity. The notion of the extra profits gained by the capitals at the top of the stratification is closely related to Schumpeter's notion of temporary monopoly profits accruing to the first capital to innovate, which are then gradually eroded as the innovation diffuses through the industry and even the economy (see, for example, his 1942).

b. To the extent that it makes sense at all to use the term 'transformation' within value-form theory, the reference must be to the crucial transformation in the market when commodities are turned into money. This actual commensuration gives rise to an ideal pre-commensuration in production (1§8). The process of devalorisation when the stratification of capitals is extended, shows however certain similarities to what is often seen to be at stake in the conventional transformation analysis (see, for example, Fine and Harris 1979: 21–34). In fact, the conceptual framework presented here was first developed when studying the significance of the alleged transformation (see Reuten 1978: 19–26). The one author who has developed a conceptualisation of the TRPF similar to ours in this respect is Weeks (1981: 204–8).

SECTION 3   EXPRESSIONS OF THE TENDENCY FOR THE RATE OF PROFIT TO FALL

§5. The TRPF and devaluation of capital

Along with the tendency towards increasing productivity of labour, the technical composition of capital and thereby the instantaneous value composition of capital tend to increase (§1). The consequent tendency for the rate of profit to fall (§2) means that increasing valorisation of capital produces with it a decreasing rate of valorisation (§3). This contradiction is transcended in the concretisation of capital stratification (§4). But in this transcendence the contradictions of the TRPF find further expression. One expression is the tendential negation of the stratification of capital (see §6). The other is that the price decrease typically concomitant on this form of existence of accumulation, since it also affects input prices, may prevent the increasing technical composition of capital (TCC) being translated into an increasing value composition of capital (VCC).[19] However, this price decrease affects the fixed capital outlay only of *new* plants, so decreasing the VCC when the top of the stratification TCC is replicated. Thus, as far as fixed capital outlay is concerned, this counteracting tendential price decrease does not affect the fall in the rate of profit of the prevailing capital, which is the effect of *devalorisation of capital* – that is, a relative decrease in valorisation of the previous stratification of capitals (§4). *Input* price decrease affects rather the *value* of the capital outlay of the previous stratification, and this *devaluation of capital* tends to be carried into effect by *output* price decrease. So when input prices decrease – affecting new plant investments – and when this is translated into output prices, it again decreases the revenue of the previous stratification of capital. Therefore there are two ways (depending on the contingent accounting practice – see addendum b) in which devaluation of capital may be manifest. One is in a further decrease in the rate of profit, the other is in the immediate writing-off of capital when prices of means of production decrease. In both cases the sum of depreciation allowances and surplus value (i.e. the cash flow) decreases.

From a one-sided physicalist (use-value) approach it might seem that such devaluation of capital does not affect its reproduction; in particular when (in case of current cost accounting) capital is

---

19 This effect depends upon the procedural blending out of changes in the money wage rate, so that price decreases affect the value composition of capital (even if the price decrease were to be similar in all branches of the economy) rather than the rate of profit. (See further addendum a and 5§3.)

devalued immediately so that the level of the profit rate is restored to that just prior to devaluation. Indeed physical reproduction (that is, the number of units of output of a plant) need not be affected by the input price decrease because new means of production can be brought at the lower price. But this does not take away the fact that because of devaluation the valorisation potential has decreased. This becomes obvious when a plant is wholly financed by credit; then the amortisation fund may be sufficient to buy a new plant, but not to cancel the credit.

One expression of increasing labour productivity, TCC and instantaneous VCC, is thus devaluation of existing capital. Macroeconomically, devaluation of capital is the counterpart of the price decrease that counteracts the translation of the increase in the TCC into an increase in the VCC.

Addenda: a. Price changes and the TRPF; b. Devaluation and devalorisation

a. Changes in the money wage rate are determined by the rate of unemployment, and so they cannot be seen to be determined immediately by changes in prices consequent upon the TRPF (for their articulation with the TRPF, see 5S1). Price decrease affects the VCC $(K/(wl))$ directly in the case of new investments, and indirectly through devaluation for previous investments. There is one common exposition of the law (most treatments in terms of labour embodied, but also Fine & Harris) in which this does not happen. Then the 'real' wage rate in the denominator of the capital composition is treated as a constant. With price changes affecting all branches of production uniformly, and in the absence of fixed capital (or in equilibrium) price decrease does not affect the VCC as a ratio. Rather price decrease affects the realised rate of profit, r, thus counteracting its initial fall.

In our presentation, as well as in both Fine and Harris 1976, 1979, and Weeks 1981, value changes do affect the composition of capital, but the way this happens is different. These authors define the organic composition of capital (OCC) as directly reflecting the TCC (§1b) and what typically happens in the Fine and Harris conception is that one capital introduces a new technique which raises its TCC and OCC. At the prevailing prices this raises the rate of profit of this capital. Because of this other capitals also adopt the new technique.[20] This establishes new prices and so the rate of profit for all capitals in the branch (including the initiating one) decreases.[21] Subsequently the price decrease works through the economy, and so all

---

20 It is in particular this bit of the argument which we would consider a comparative static hangover. It would appear that Weeks' conception lies in between ours and that of Fine and Harris.

21 Why prices decrease (only) when other capitals adopt the new technique is not explained. In our conception, price decrease is related to over-capacity.

relevant prices typically decrease. Now the composition of capital at the new set of prices is the VCC. But because of the price decrease, capital has been *devalued* (according to, say, the difference between OCC value and VCC value). Within their argument, this capital devaluation (which is effected via reorganisation of capital, whether in economic crisis or not) again raises the rate of profit.

b. It could be argued that in our concept of capital stratification (§4) devaluation of capital also occurs, though only latently, when new techniques are introduced (prior to any input price decrease). This latent devaluation would become manifest when plants are scrapped and capital is reinvested in new plants. However, we prefer to call this 'devalorisation of capital', as the effect of technical change and productivity change (giving rise to devalorisation) and the effect of input price decrease (giving rise to devaluation) are predicated upon different processes. Because of the different compositions of capital and the different labour productivities, the money expression of labour in each plant in the stratification is different (2§16); output price changes affect the profit calculation but not the cost calculation for each plant, as in the historical (dated) cost accounting convention. The other major accounting practice (current costs, present value or replacement value accounting)[22] could also be applied to technical change. Devalorisation would then be directly expressed in the price calculation, so that the ideal price calculations (ex ante) are identical for all plants. In this case, the (latent) decrease in the value of capital is manifest, though the ex ante price calculations do not reveal it. However, with either practice it is possible to have at the same time different asset appraisals from that expressed in the balance sheet, the accounting basis of which may be current (present) value, which may or may not be directly expressed in the value of the assets.

Thus depending on the accounting practice *devalorisation* may be manifest either in a decreasing money expression of labour (m_i), *or* in a reduction of the value of capital. In the first case valorisation decreases in comparison with anticipated valorisation; in the second previous valorisation is in part annihilated. The net effect is of course the same. For expositional purposes we refer (unless otherwise indicated) to the first manifestation.

§6. The TRPF and the restructuring and centralisation of capital

The more rapid and sustained the productivity increase, the more it has the effect of wiping out the mass of profit of unamortised capitals, as expressed in both decrease in the rate of profit along with devalorisation and scrapping of plants (§§3–4), and in devaluation of capital (§5). The speed of this productivity increase is contingent. Should it accelerate, then the rate of liquidation of the least efficient

22 This accounting method was originally set out by Kovero in 1912 and by Schmidt in 1921; cf. Polak (1940: 15–16).

plants will also do so. Prices established in the market then approach the level of prices implied by the most efficient plants, which further devalues capital. With an accelerating rate of liquidation the forces giving rise to the TRPF tend to be expressed in the *restructuring of capital*, one form of which is the bankruptcy of capitals and the possible repurchase of liquidated assets by other capitals at near to scrap value. Another form (which may prevent such bankruptcy) is that of mergers, takeovers and participations – that is, the *centralisation of capital*. Restructuring and centralisation *reduce* the *range* of the stratification of capital, though not necessarily to the same extent as that of plants. Because stratification is a condition of existence of the TRPF, range reduction is a further expression of the contradiction of the law.

Centralisation of capital counteracts the tendency for the composition of capital to rise; it tends to retard technical change, the implementation of which would require the building of new plants. Stratification proceeds by the temporary creation of over-capacity and price reduction such that the least efficient plants are expelled from the stratification. This is feasible (without a considerable reduction in profit and the rate of profit for the initiating capital) only with a sufficiently large difference in productivity of labour and unit costs of production between the top and the bottom plant. With the reduction in the range of the stratification because of centralisation, it is exactly this *difference* in costs which is reduced. Price decrease may then not lead to scrapping of plants, so that additional plants then tend to increase over-capacity.

However, innovation in new techniques and its implementation in additional plants may still be profitable if it creates sufficient cost difference. This may require that technological and technical knowledge be built up, so that technical change then tends to come in waves. During such a build-up, scrapping of plants will stagnate, but once sufficient technical knowledge has accumulated, the stratification will be extended again, etc., ultimately giving rise to renewed devaluation and centralisation.

The contingent expression of the forces generating the TRPF, in centralisation of capital, thus counteracts the existence of the TRPF in capital stratification. So the rise of the composition of capital (§1) itself is counteracted. Because this has a wave like character the TRPF is manifest in the form of cycles of centralisation. (Note again that we use the term 'cycle' in the sense of fluctuation in general, without any specification as to duration or regularity.)

Addenda: a. Restructuring, centralisation and waves; b. Relation between Chapters 3 and 4

a. Our conception of the process of 'restructuring of capital' does not in general diverge from the mainstream Marxist tradition, so that it has been presented only briefly. Fine and Harris in particular (1979: 83–7) link the process of restructuring to the TRPF. An excellent treatment in this respect is given by Weeks (1981: 208–13). Our notion of 'centralisation of capital', on the other hand, does differ from that of the mainstream, in particular in the way it theorises the contingent wave-like expression of the TRPF. The notion that technical change comes in waves is akin to Schumpeter's conception (see, for example, his 1942), but he offers no account of why it is that inventions are produced during the slump and implemented at the beginning of and during the upturn. Our argument is that inventions are produced all along, but that their implementation in the slump would not pay, not just because there is a slump (since, as presumably over-capacity has been cured via restructuring, slack demand cannot be the problem), but because the centralisation of capital produces a decrease in the range of stratification and so in fact competition between capitals remains only latent.

b. The tendency towards over-accumulation of capital (Chapter 3) and the TRPF are tendencies at the same level of abstraction. If we blend out their systematic interrelation then they would both give rise to a tendential decline in the rate of accumulation, and generate counteracting forces. Both also reveal, in their different ways, the contradictory nature of capitalism. The forces of valorisation and accumulation of capital which are generated by association through the value-form are expressed in forms which appear to contradict their existence. We have indicated how the necessity of the valorisation of capital tendentially gives rise to its decrease (expressed in labour-shortage profit squeeze or underconsumption) (Chapter 3). Similarly the drive to increase the profit rate of the individual capitals tendentially gives rise to a decrease in the rate of profit of capital as a whole (expressed in devaluation, restructuring and centralisation of capital). The articulation of these tendencies is taken up in Chapter 5.

SUMMARY

This chapter has derived the tendency towards increase in the value composition of capital (VCC) and the tendency of the rate of profit to fall (TRPF), as one form of existence of accumulation of capital (Section 1), which is produced along with that presented in Chapter 3. The TRPF contradicts the tendential increase in profit and the rate of profit concomitant on the accumulation of capital in new plants as derived in Chapter 2 (§3). This contradiction has usually been conceived rather as an inconsistency, and so authors such as Okishio, Himmelweit and Roemer have rejected the TRPF because of its lack of 'microeconomic foundations'. The dialectical systematic presentation has revealed that the TRPF may be adequately grounded if the comparative static analysis of these authors is replaced by a dynamic conceptualisation, incorporating fixed capital, thus rejecting any alleged inconsistency.

The contradiction is transcended in the existence of stratification of capital. When new VCC-increasing techniques of production are available (with higher productivity of labour and lower unit costs of production), preservation of capital already accumulated prevents immediate moves towards investment in plants embodying such techniques, and so capital tends to be stratified in a range of different compositions of capital, money expressions of labour and concomitant rates of profit. When additional capital is accumulated in new plants, the concomitant capacity increase produces either price decrease or over-capacity. Because of the resulting revenue decrease, sub-marginal plants at the bottom of the stratification will have to be scrapped. Because of the higher productivity of new plant capital, relative to the previous stratification, its comparative profitability increases, along with comparative profitability decrease (devalorisation) of the rest of the stratification. Therefore whilst the rate of profit of newly accumulated capital may increase relative to the capital just below it in the stratification (even if its value composition is higher) the average rate of profit of the stratification decreases because of the average increase in the value composition of capital. Thus whilst the average rate of profit decreases, profit is 'redistributed' from the bottom to the top of the stratification (Section 2).

In Section 3 the price decrease typically concomitant on the TRPF was shown to counteract the VCC increase of newly accumulated capital but at the same time that price decrease produces devaluation of capital previously accumulated in fixed means of production. This reduces the reproduction of accumulation. (General over-capacity instead of price decrease produces a similar result, although the VCC increase is then not counteracted.) A further, but contingent, expression of the TRPF lies in the restructuring and centralisation of capital. The more rapid and sustained the productivity increase, the more it has the effect that plants will have to be scrapped before the capital invested has been amortised. With accelerating liquidation of the least efficient plants, the forces giving rise to the TRPF are expressed in the restructuring of capital, one form of which is the centralisation of capital. The range of the stratification of capital is thereby reduced, counteracting the gradual increase in the VCC. Technical knowledge then tends to be implemented in waves, and therefore in this expression the TRPF is manifest cyclically.

Appendix to Chapter 4: A Model of Capital Stratification

This Appendix outlines a model of the process of interaction between stratified capitals, in the face of an increasing composition of capital (see 4§4). The presentation is both formal and abstract, and cannot give support to a view that the actual rate of profit must decline. In the face of the kinds of critique that have been directed against the TRPF we make use of an analytical model, which should be interpreted as the analysis of a moment, itself embedded in a systematic context, so that the crucial assumptions are endogenously interconnected with the whole. Simplifying assumptions are appropriate only if in principle these could be dispensed with in an extended model.

Let any one branch of production at time t be composed of a set of $(g \ldots, i, \ldots, n)$ plants $\qquad$ (A4.1)
Each plant has K_i value of means of production invested, consisting of fixed constant capital (F_i) and circulating constant capital (A_i):
$$K_i \equiv F_i + A_i \qquad \text{(A4.2)}$$
In each production period a planned fraction δ_i^f of fixed capital is used up. Accordingly a fraction δ_i of the value of constant capital is used up every period:
$$\delta_i K_i \equiv \delta_i^f F_i + A_i \qquad \text{(A4.3)}$$
The amount of labour (in hours) employed in the production period is l_i. Wages are paid at the beginning of the period at a rate w, which is uniform for the branch. Therefore wl_i is variable capital. (For simplicity, turnover times are assumed to be equal for each plant so that rates of profit are readily comparable.) The ideal money expression of the labour in plant i is m_i. Therefore ideal surplus value (ideal profit, neglecting interest payments, etc.) is:
$$R_i \equiv (m_i - w)l_i \qquad \text{(A4.4)}$$
So the ideal value of production (X_i) in the period is:
$$X_i \equiv \delta_i K_i + m_i l_i \equiv \delta_i K_i + wl_i + R_i \qquad \text{(A4.5)}$$
And the rate of ideal profit (r_i) is:
$$r_i \equiv \{(m_i - w)l_i\}/\{K_i + wl_i\} \equiv \{(m_i - w)/w\}/\{(K_i/(wl_i)) + 1\} \qquad \text{(A4.6)}$$
where $(m-w)/w$ is the rate of ideal surplus value and K_i/wl_i is the value composition of capital.

The branch average rate of ideal profit, r, is (deleting branch subscripts):
$$r \equiv \{(m - w)l\}/\{K + wl\} \qquad \text{(A.7)}$$
where $K = \Sigma K_i$ and $ml = \Sigma m_i l_i$

Plants are stratified from $g \ldots, i, \ldots, n$ such that: (a) unit costs of production are stratified decreasingly:
$$\{\delta_i K_i + wl_i\}/\{u_i\} \geqq \{\delta_{i+1} K_{i+1} + wl_{i+1}\}/\{u_{i+1}\} \qquad \text{(A4.8)}$$

135

(where u_i is the use-value output of plant i in appropriate units), and (b) the value composition of capitals is stratified increasingly:

$$[K_i]/\{wl_i\} < \{K_{i+1}\}/\{wl_{i+1}\} \qquad (A4.9)$$

Branch sales revenue (ΣX_i) grows over time at the average rate of profit

$$\Sigma X_{i(t)} = (1 + r) \Sigma X_{i(t-1)} \qquad (A4.10)$$

Alternatively branch revenue (ΣX_i) is exogenous to the model, leaving open the possibility of dynamic changes between branches:

$$\Sigma X_i = \Sigma X_i^* \qquad (A4.10a)$$

For simplicity, it is assumed that demand is iso-elastic with respect to price. The transitory market price (p) is (initially) set according to some expected change, based, for example, on changes in the past. In the absence of anticipated price changes, these ideal production prices are merely equal to the prices realised in the previous production period:

$$p = \gamma p_{t-1} \qquad (A4.11)$$

(A4.10) and (A4.11) leave open the possibility of non-realisation of use-value produced. Use-values realised (Σu_i) are equal to:

$$\Sigma u_i = \Sigma X_i / p \qquad (A4.12)$$

For simplicity, unrealised use-values produced (or alternatively capacity under-utilisation) ($u_i - \mathbf{u}_i$) are assumed to be distributed over the branch in proportion to the use-value output (or capacity) of each plant:

$$\mathbf{u}_i = u_i (\Sigma u_i / \Sigma u_i) \qquad (A4.13)$$

(where u_i is the number of use-values produced (or the capacity) and $\mathbf{u}_i$ is the number of use-values realised in the market). Alternatively to equation (A4.11), in an oligopolistic setting, the price may be set by the capital at the top of the stratification – which operates as price-leader – such that it maximises profit. In a setting of collusion, more specifically, this would involve the price being set such that some (estimated) upper segment of the stratification (j,...,n) maximises the realisation of their use-values produced (or optimises capacity utilisation). Equation (A4.11) then becomes:

$$p = \sum_1^n X_i / \sum_j^n \mathbf{u}_i \qquad (A4.11a)$$

(where $\sum_j^n \mathbf{u}_i \rightarrow \sum_j^n u_i$ or where $\sum_j^n \mathbf{u}_i$ optimises capacity utilisation of j, ... n.)

Plants necessarily have to be scrapped when prime costs ($A_i + wl_i$) are not covered. So for each plant in use we have:

$$p\mathbf{u}_i \geqq A_i + wl_i \qquad (A4.14)$$

Earlier scrapping may occur in the light of strategic market considerations.

For simplicity, it is assumed that plants are closed down (but not immediately scrapped) when production costs are no longer covered. Thus we have for all plants in use:

$$\mathbf{pu}_i \geqq \delta_i K_i + wl_i \qquad (A4.15)$$

(since $\delta_i K_i = \delta_i^f F_i + A_i$ – see equation A4.3).

It is assumed that plants for which equation (A4.15) does not hold are not immediately scrapped. (This assumption affects the price setting behaviour of the price leader, since in effect there is always latent over-capacity in a branch, and the price leader has to compete it away. This assumption provides a foundation for the alternative equation (A4.11a).)

It follows from this model of stratification that when capital is accumulated in new plants, extending the stratification to $n+1$ and then to $n+2, \ldots, n+s$, either prices have to fall (in line with average branch unit costs) or realisation of use-values will be deficient so that all plants will operate below capacity.[1] In either case the proceeds of all existing plants$_n$ decrease, concomitant on the addition of plant $n+1$ ($p\sum \mathbf{u}_i$ decreases). *Therefore* both the profit ($\sum_n^n \mathbf{R}_i$) and the average rate of profit of the capital accumulated in these plants $(g, \ldots, n)$ decreases.[2] This profit decrease in capitals $g, \ldots, n$ is due to their relative decrease in productivity. (Previously, when the stratification was composed of $g, \ldots, n$, they on aggregate, of course produced at average productivity. The addition of plant $n+1$ decreases the $g, \ldots, n$, productivity as part of the average $g, \ldots, n, n+1$.) And this $g, \ldots, n$, comparative profit decrease is concomitant on the $n+1$ comparative profit increase. But because of the addition of plant $n+1$ the average capital outlay increases, so the average $(g, \ldots, n+1)$ rate of profit decreases in comparison to the previous average $(g, \ldots, n)$ rate of profit. The model of capital stratification thus shows that increase in the rate of profit along with the accumulation of capital in *new* plants is quite compatible with a decrease in the average rate of profit. It thus shows

---

1 Of course the model is not one of perfect foresight in which capitals accumulate exactly according to the demand there is ·to be realised. Rather they compete in order to increase their market shares. If they manage to cut production costs sufficiently their rate of profit increases whilst other capitals are expelled. If they don't manage competitors remain in the market with a lower rate of profit all round.
2 The money wage does not decrease merely because of price decrease itself, so w is taken to be constant. Previous fixed capital investment may devalue because of price decrease (§5), but this does not do away with the previous capital outlay itself which is relevant for the rate of profit. The outlay of circulating constant capital (A) is however affected by the price decrease and this counteracts the rate of profit decrease.

that the Okishio type of argument describes a special case which may not be generalised.

We may now have a closer look at the deviation in profitability of plants from the branch average, which may be expressed as:

$$\mathbf{R}_i \equiv (\mathbf{m}_i - w)l_i = (m_i - w)l_i + \mathbf{pu}_i - X_i$$
$$= (m_i - w)l_i + (\Sigma X_i / \Sigma u_i)\mathbf{u}_i - X_i \qquad (A4.16)$$

(Where bold characters, as always denote realised entities.)

It follows that the money expressions of the labour in each plant (m_i) are stratified increasingly from (g, ..., n, ..., n+s) at each point in time. But for each individual plant in operation m_i decreases over time when the stratification is extended; we call this *devalorisation*. (Properly speaking, it is only the macroeconomic m which remains unaffected when there is no inflation or deflation, whilst branch m's, because of inter-branch changes, might vary (2§16). Excluding such changes, the absence of inflation implies the constancy of the branch m – though of course not the constancy of each m_i within the branch.) For the branch as a whole we have at each point in time:

$$\mathbf{R} \equiv \Sigma \mathbf{R}_i \equiv (\mathbf{m} - w)l = (m - w)l + (X/u)\mathbf{u} - X \qquad (A4.17)$$

which leaves open the possibility of over-capacity ($u > \mathbf{u}$).

The case where $u = \mathbf{u}$, is in our framework feasible when the price leader sets the price so as to expel competitors from the stratification. Equation (A4.17) then reduces to:

$$\mathbf{R} \equiv (\mathbf{m} - w)l = (m - w)l \qquad (A4.17a)$$

However equation (A4.16) is not reduced:

$$\mathbf{R}_i \equiv (\mathbf{m}_i - w)l_i = (m_i - w)l_i + \mathbf{pu}_i - X_i \qquad (A4.16a = A4.16)$$

where now $\mathbf{u}_i = u_i$.

The term $(\mathbf{pu}_i - X_i)/l_i$ expresses the deviation of $\mathbf{m}_i$ from the branch average $\mathbf{m}$. These equations A4.16a and A4.17a mark our conceptual divergence from the Okishio type of comparative statics, in which all capitals are average plant capitals, so that $\mathbf{pu}_i = X_i$. (Which is plausible when it is *assumed* that there is no fixed capital – as is the case with Okishio 1961 and Himmelweit 1974, but not with Roemer 1979.)

Chapter five

Articulation of the Tendencies of Accumulation and Inflation

PRELIMINARY REMARKS

Chapters 3 and 4 have derived the two major tendencies of accumulation of capital: the tendency to over-accumulation of capital (TOC) and the tendency of the rate of profit to fall (TRPF). These tendencies are moments at the same level of abstraction. Section 1 of this chapter theorises their articulation. In particular, it will be shown how the TRPF and the TOC mutually interact on the rate of surplus value.

Chapter 2 derived the requirement of credit money, pre-validating production as a condition of existence of the expansion of capital. In Section 2, it is argued that such pre-validation, together with an actual squeeze on profits produced by the interactive effects of the TOC and the TRPF, introduces elements of potential financial crisis into the system. The actuality of such crisis is underdetermined, being contingent mainly upon the degree of collaboration between banks (eventually under the umbrella of the Central Bank). Whilst expansion of accumulation must necessarily alternate with contraction, this may well be a gradual rather than a crisis-ridden process. It is not our purpose to provide accounts of the processes of economic crises, details of which are determined by many contingent circumstances, but merely to locate the possibility of economic crisis within the presentation, and to indicate some important aspects of it.

Section 3 theorises the inflationary reproduction of accumulation, and shows how inflation may modify the extent to which the shift from expansion to contraction of accumulation takes the form of economic crisis. Inflation is presented as counteracting the TRPF, and as protracting the TOC. It is shown that this counteraction reveals an antagonism between industrial and money capital. Thus whilst generalised inflation seems to overcome the contradictions of the accumulation of capital, the playing out of this conflict, as well as the erosion by inflation of money as the general equivalent, shows that these contradictions are irreconcilable.

In the course of this chapter we shall gradually depart from the necessary moments *of the reproduction of the capitalist economy*. To some extent, elements of contingency are introduced in Section 1, when the articulation of the TOC and the TRPF is theorised. That articulation itself is a necessary moment, and though it can be shown how these tendencies articulate, only the systematic possibility of the effects is determined. In Section 2, the shift from expansion to contraction of accumulation is in itself shown to be necessary, but whether this is manifest gradually or via crisis is contingent. Nevertheless a number of factors determined at that level of the presentation make the economy vulnerable to economic crisis. Section 3 shows how inflation, whilst it is not necessary to the reproduction of the economy, tends to overcome economic crisis; nor is it necessarily the only possible process that could be generated from within the economy to do so. It is thus shown how it is possible within a systematic presentation to proceed beyond the theorisation of necessary moments.

Sections 1–2 set out the implications of Chapters 1–4 from the point of view of our method. To a considerable extent, the problem in them is that encountered in that literature on the TRPF concerned with the effect of changes in the rate of surplus value. (Usually this is considered to be an effect internal to the TRPF, whereas in our presentation it concerns the articulation of the TOC and the TRPF.) The first paragraph of the section on inflation, relating it to obsolescence, is inspired by the monetary theory of the French Marxist regulation school, and in particular by Aglietta (1976) and De Vroey (1981, 1984). The combination of their theory (explaining the emergence of inflation), and ours in Chapter 4 (in particular, the concept of 'range of stratification of capitals'), enables us not only to extend the account of the emergence of inflation, but also to theorise its slowing down. Further, their theory can be extended to account for the shift from inflation to deflation (§8 and §10) when the conflict between industrial and money capital, as well as its effect on the position of banks, is theorised.

SECTION 1   THE ARTICULATION OF THE TENDENCIES TO OVER-ACCUMULATION OF CAPITAL AND FOR THE RATE OF PROFIT TO FALL

§1. The TOC and the TRPF (introduction)

The tendency to over-accumulation of capital (TOC) and the tendency of the rate of profit to fall (TRPF) (Chapters 3–4) have

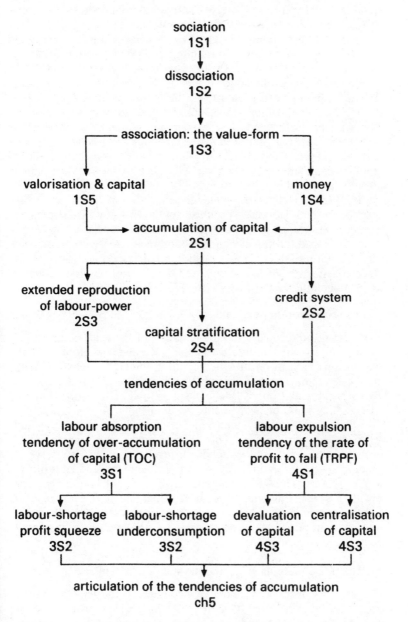

Figure 5.1 Interconnection of the value-form, its reproduction, and the tendencies of accumulation of capital.

each been derived from the valorisation and accumulation of capital (Chapters 1–2). As such they are moments at the same level of abstraction (See Figure 5.1) The TOC is produced by an increasing rate of valorisation and accumulation and of absorption of labour into the circuit of capital (3S1). The expressions of the TOC in labour-shortage profit squeeze and underconsumption counteract the increase in valorisation and accumulation, either by pushing up wages and so pushing down the rate of surplus value, or by constraining wages and so constraining validation of production (3S2). The TRPF is produced by the tendency for the composition of capital to rise, from increasing labour productivity and relative expulsion of labour (4S1); it has existence in the form of capital stratification and devalorisation (4S2). The expressions of the TRPF in devaluation, restructuring and centralisation of capital annihilate previous accumulation and produce, contingently, cyclical implementation of new techniques (4S3). Each of the tendencies by itself thus finds expression in forces counteracting the increase in valorisation and accumulation, but they also mutually interact. The TRPF counteracts the TOC (§2 below), and the effect of this counteraction tends to counteract the TRPF itself (§3 below).

§2. The composition of capital

The TRPF, predicated upon the tendency of the value composition of capital to rise, counteracts the TOC and therefore also its expressions both in profit squeeze and in underconsumption. With the value composition of capital (VCC) in so far as it is determined by the technical composition of capital (and not by distribution) rising – any mass of profit being accumulated absorbs less labour into the circuit (and buys more means of production) as compared with a constant VCC. This slows down the approach of accumulation to the ceiling at which there is no available reserve of labour power, and reduces the growth in the mass of ideal profit at any wage rate. Over-accumulation in the form of labour-shortage profit squeeze is thus counteracted. Any increase in VCC also causes capital deepening, so that over-accumulation in the form of underconsumption is counteracted by the resulting increased demand for capital goods.

§3. The rate of surplus value and devaluation of capital

The tendency of the VCC to increase counteracts the depletion of the reserve of labour by the TOC (§2). As long as the articulation of these tendencies maintains an effective reserve of labour, it enables the rate of surplus value to be pushed up, because the price decrease made possible by the increasing labour productivity concomitant on the TRPF (4§4) enables the wage rate to be depressed. The increase in the rate of surplus value counteracts the *devalorisation* of stratified capitals, the condition of existence of the TRPF (4§4), however, it does not affect the *devaluation* of fixed capital, which is the expression of the TRPF (4§5).[1] The decrease in the wage rate (for which an effective reserve of labour is a condition) and devaluation of capital are both generated by price decrease (and the higher the composition of capital the more important is the effect on devaluation of capital). Thus not only do the TOC and the TRPF by themselves generate forces counteracting the increase in valorisation and accumulation (§1) but in their articulation they also tend to undermine the dynamic of accumulation. Whilst the rate of surplus value may keep on increasing because of the joint effect of an effective reserve of labour (§2) and price decrease, that price decrease also generates devaluation of capital.

Addendum: a. Rate of surplus value and devaluation

a. The increase in the rate of surplus value generated by the tendency of the VCC to increase is generally considered to be a major counteracting force to a tendential fall in the rate of profit (4§1a, 4§3a). For the 'Okishians', an increasing wage rate is indeed the only factor that could generate a fall in the rate of profit. Chapter 4 emphasises the dynamic character of the TRPF and stresses the crucial role of fixed capital, as revealed in the devaluation which is a major expression of the TRPF (4§5). Whilst an increase in the rate of surplus value because of wage decrease (concomitant on price decreases together with an effective reserve of labour) may compensate for the initial fall in the rate of profit, this only affects profits, not the value of the capital previously accumulated, which is devalued because of the price decrease generated by the tendency of the VCC to increase.

SECTION 2   FLUCTUATIONS IN THE RATE OF ACCUMULATION OF CAPITAL

§4. Gradual expansion and contraction

Valorisation and accumulation of capital have been shown tendentially to undermine themselves in that they are counteracted

---

1 Whilst 'devalorisation' (a relative decrease in the money expression of labour of capital invested) is one element of the conditions of existence of the TRPF, 'devaluation' (a decrease in the value of fixed capital due to decrease in prices of assets) is an expression of the TRPF (4§5 and 4§5b). In order to follow the argument in this chapter, the interconnection of the concepts developed in the main paragraphs 4§§4–6 should be borne in mind.

by devalorisation and devaluation. To the extent that the TOC and the TRPF each by themselves give rise to a cyclical course of accumulation, their articulation modifies this cyclical movement. In particular the increasing VCC leading to the TRPF has the effect of slowing down the rate of absorption of labour into the circuit of capital, and concomitantly reducing the upward pressure on wage rates (§2). The cyclical effects implied by the TOC are thus modified by the TRPF. Further, the increasing labour productivity and decreasing prices underlying the TRPF tend to facilitate a downward pressure on wages. The resultant increase in the rate of surplus value (partly) compensates for the devalorisation of capital concomitant on the TRPF (§3), tending to modify the cyclical effects implied by it. The articulation of the TOC and the TRPF thus appears to produce in particular an extension of the length of the cycle, whilst it does not eliminate the alternation of expansion and contraction. However, whether the articulation gives rise to more or less gradual alternation, or to crises of expansion and contraction, is indeterminate.

Addendum: a. Character of alternation of expansion and contraction

a. Because gradual alternation of expansion and contraction, as well as alternation via eruptions of crisis are systematic possibilities, the presentation stands apart from much of Marxist economic theory (in which accumulation of capital necessarily gives rise to crises), and from most of neoclassical theory (in which crises could – if at all – occur only as a result of shocks external to the system).

---

§5. Credit and the acceleration of expansion and contraction

Accumulation of capital requires an accommodating credit system (2§6). Production and realisation are anticipated via the ex nihilo creation of credit money by banks, so that production is pre-validated against a share in future profits, in the form of interest (2§8). Although this initially overcomes the limits to the expansion of the circuit of capital – and may even accelerate it – any eventual contraction also tends to accelerate (so the amplitude of a cycle would increase). Such acceleration is caused by the interest which has to be paid out of surplus value. With increasing surplus value and increasing rates of profit, the payment of interest is no hindrance to further investment and credit. A squeeze on surplus value and the rate of profit, on the other hand, is intensified by the burden of interest payments.

The extent of the need for accommodation by banks in the expansion phase is increased by decreases in growth of the cash flow due to increased obsolescence of plants related to prolonged technical change. In general, the TRPF exists in devalorisation of capital, but at a rate which is indeterminate. However, with *increasing* obsolescence and devalorisation (in addition to a squeeze on (the rate of growth of) surplus value) the share of banks' interest in industrial cash flow tends to rise, and so industrial profits are squeezed. (The average risks of banks then increase so that they become more reluctant to provide further credits, hampering the further accumulation of capital.)

§6. The systematic possibility of economic crisis

The expression of the alternation of expansion and contraction of accumulation is indeterminate (§4), economic crises being merely one manifestation. Economic crises are indeterminate not only in that they are not necessary but also, conversely, in that there are no institutions within the economy which prevent the development of the articulation of the TOC and the TRPF from being crisis-prone. Economic crisis is, however, a systematic possibility (0§9). The system is vulnerable because of the *combination* of, firstly, the possible cumulative expulsion of labour from the circuit of capital related to the articulation of the TOC and the TRPF and, secondly, the credit system.

First: the necessary association of dissociated production and consumption in bourgeois society is established through the value-form, which has been grounded in the valorisation and accumulation of capital (1S3, 1S5, 2S1), the continuity of which reproduces the system. Ruptures in that continuity cannot persist if the system is to survive. The TOC and the TRPF are indeed contradictory moments of accumulation in that they impinge on the continuity of valorisation, which is threatened by the expulsion of labour from the circuit of capital arising from the decrease in the rate of accumulation predicated upon the TOC or the TRPF. That such expulsion is a threat follows immediately from the necessity of labour to the valorisation of capital (1S5), but in addition a decrease in the general wage bill, due to any rupture in the circuit followed by labour lay-offs, reduces the demand for consumption goods, and so undermines valorisation. Further lay-offs may then have a cumulative effect on the effective demand for consumer goods; the subsequent decrease in accumulation is multiplied, and so on.

Second: since the expansion of accumulation is being accommodated by credit from the banking system, a disruption in that accommodation may also have cumulative effects on valorisation and accumulation. Should bankruptcy of unsuccessful capitals affect the liquidity of banks (2§9), and thus lending to other capitals, it then multiplies both to other capitals and to the banking system. In particular, when losses on lending are distributed unevenly within the banking system itself (perhaps from specialisation of banks), bankruptcy of banks may be avoided only by inter-bank credits and/or takeovers.

Whilst devalorisation and devaluation of capital are endemic, the extent to which particular capitals are able fully to amortise fixed capital depends on the range of differences in productivity of the capital stratification. Should amortisation fall short of the financial needs of renewed investment then capitals merely fail and are extinguished from the social circuit. However, devalorisation and devaluation become acute when production is pre-validated by banks. The losses of bankrupt industrial capital are then transmitted to money capital and, unless compensated for by the interest on other debts (or by the Central Bank socialising the loss – see S3), credit expansion is hampered on a social scale. Local breaks in the circuit of capital then multiply into the disruption of the social circuit. Through further bankruptcies, the devaluation of capital which was latent in previous price decrease becomes manifest, as the fixed capital of bankrupt capitals is forced to circulate in its entirety as assets are liquidated. This process then gives rise to restructuring of capital (4§6) as well as to wage decrease due to unemployment, which may cumulatively generate a new wave of bankruptcies and restructuring. In this way, restructuring related to centralisation counteracts the introduction of composition of capital increasing techniques of production and the concomitant devalorisation and devaluation. As argued in 4§6, this is due to the decrease in the range of stratification produced by the centralisation of capital. Because of range decrease, price decrease is not an effective means of curing over-capacity when new technique plants are added to the stratification; so centralisation-related range decrease tends to generate 'hoarding' of technology in the period of contraction following economic crisis, so that technical change comes in waves (4§6).

Overall then, decrease in valorisation in conjunction with credit-accommodated accumulation potentially gives rise to cumulative processes of bankruptcies, restructuring of capital, expulsion of labour and wage decrease. Bank credit therefore makes the system vulnerable to economic crisis. The counterpart of credit accommodated expansion is the accommodation of contraction, both of which are determined by the actual contingent make-up of the banking system. The course of gradual expansion and contraction of accumulation produces valorisation, devalorisation and devaluation alongside each other. (Branches or sectors of the economy, however, may go through phases of major restructuring of capital, producing merely local breaks in the circuit of capital.) But with expansion and contraction via economic crisis, valorisation, devalorisation and devaluation become manifest in a sequential order, and on a social scale. The key links in this sequence are the credit system and the centralisation of capital, giving rise to a decrease in the range of stratification of capitals, and again to stagnation in the introduction of new techniques and a new boom of valorisation.

Addenda: a. Economic policy; b. The presentation of inflation

a. The result that economic crises are a possible manifestation of the contradictions of the capital relation, not the necessary form of the alternation of expansion and contraction of accumulation, provides the possibility of economic policy being able to avoid them (see Part Four). But the result that economic crises are one expression of the contradictions of the capital relation provides an indication of the limits and the tensions of such policy. Even if economic crises are avoided by economic policy, it appears that it cannot eliminate the contradiction of which they are an expression.

b. The presentation up to and including Section 2 may now be considered complete, in that all the necessary moments reproducing the economy that can be theorised from within it appear to have been theorised. Nevertheless in the next Section inflation is introduced as a moment that is merely contingent with respect to the reproduction of the economy, in order to show how contingent phenomena may be grasped from the point of view of our method. To choose inflation here is of course challenging in the light of the presentation so far. From 4S2 onwards price *decrease* has been the recurrent theme. Nevertheless, over the last 50 years increasing prices have outweighed any price decrease implied by increasing productivity. Of course, even if inflation proved to be empirically persistent, this would not make it less or more contingent, since the prevalence or absence of inflation does not negate the essential nature of the capitalist economy. This methodical insistence on, for example, inflation as continent, does not at all, however, mean that it is unimportant to what is actually happening in the economy, merely that it requires theorisation at a lower level of abstraction so that the contingent and actual can be grasped in the light of the necessary moments (0§11).

SECTION 3   CONFLICTS OF THE INFLATIONARY REPRODUCTION OF ACCUMULATION

§7. Industrial capital and banks: devalorisation, credit and inflation

The valorisation of capital has been concretised in two major tendencies of accumulation, the TOC and the TRPF (Chapters 3-4), the articulation of which has been further concretised in the oppositions of valorisation and devalorisation, and of accumulation and devaluation of capital which determine the course of economic development. Economic crisis has been presented as a possible manifestation of the contradictions of the capital–labour relation, which may be actualised through the contingent combination of the particular form of the credit system and cumulative expulsion of labour from the circuit of capital, related to the articulation of the TOC and the TRPF (§6).

One crucial element effecting the crisis-proneness of this course of development is the degree of devalorisation and devaluation, and the degree to which it is enforced and so becomes manifest in the bankruptcy of capitals. Banks which have granted credits to devalorised and devalued capitals are confronted with the problem of whether to accept the loss, or to provide those capitals with *new credits* so as to recover (part of) it in the future. The extension of such renewed credit is predicated upon an integrated banking system (2§§8–10). Whilst new credit money pre-validates production, its exact destination is not determined. Credit money representing credit which has not been cancelled returns to the banking system as a deposit or circulates in an expansionary or an inflationary way (2§9). The 'extra money' (De Vroey 1984: 384–9) thus does not necessarily generate inflation, but is merely its contingent monetary condition.

Inflation – conceptualised as an increase in the money expression of social labour, m, (2§16) – requires in addition an upward move of prices relative to labour-productivity change.[2] The concept of inflation is thus not identical to the concept of (even continuous) price increase. It is quite compatible with insufficient *price decrease* in the face of productivity increase (Aglietta 1976: 366–7). On the other hand, general price increase does not necessarily require an increase in the quantity of money (De Vroey 1984: 390–2). Increasing capital composition, devalorisation, devaluation, bankruptcy and restructuring of capital have been shown to give rise to a decrease in the range of stratification of capital, and so technical change stagnates, giving rise to cyclical development (4§6, 5§6). *Renewed* pre-validation by way of credit modifies this development. Whilst obsolescence and devalorisation continues, its manifestation in bankruptcies is counteracted. And because it is production with new

---

2 With the money expression of labour (m) constant – thus in the absence of inflation – the micro (m_i) or branch (m_k) money expressions may increase or decrease due to change in *relative* labour-productivity (cf. 2§16 and 4§4). With inflation the micro expression m_i may similarly deviate from the macro expression m.

techniques that is being pre-validated, technique change is initially protracted. However, this modification also (§6) decreases the range of stratification. First, because of renewed pre-validation, more capital tends to be concentrated within the advanced layer of the stratification. Secondly, because technique change is protracted, the rate of anticipated obsolescence increases. In other words the expected economic lifetime of means of production decreases.[3]

This particular form of range decrease gives rise to an upward bias in prices. First, increases in anticipated obsolescence are reflected in output prices (cf. Aglietta 1976: 369; see addendum c), requiring additional credit for the buyers of producer goods and to pay any consequent additional wages.[4] Both of these tend to have spiral effects. Secondly, range decrease reduces the scope for overcoming over-capacity by price decrease (4§6, 5§6). The combination of these two forces produces continual inflation.

However, range decrease tends to slow down the rate of obsolescence and the rate of the introduction of new techniques. (The degree of credit renewal thus also tends to slow down.) As with the manifestation of accumulation in contraction via economic crisis (§6), technology is 'hoarded' and tends to be implemented in waves. Its conditions of existence are, however, quite different. In the absence of inflation a wave of new techniques was preceded by a phase of restructuring (including restructuring of the credit relations). With the inflationary reproduction of accumulation, decrease in the range of stratification and the concomitant waves of new techniques' introduction are imposed on the old structure of capitals.

Addenda: a. §6 and §7 compared; b. Fractioning logic and centralisation logic; c. Aglietta on anticipated obsolescence

a. The most important similarity between the presentation in §7 and that in §6 is the change of the range of stratification and the related acceleration and deceleration in the introduction of new techniques (cf. Schumpeter's waves of implementation of new techniques). The most important difference is that obsolescence and devalorisation are not manifest in crisis but in the

---

3 A simple example may illustrate this. Assume 10 plants in a branch of production, with a physical lifetime of 10 years each, and an evenly distributed end of lifetime of each plant, so that there are no reinvestment cycles. Then if technical change occurs steadily, there is a 'technical gap' of 10 years between plants 1 and 10. If the economic lifetime reduces to 5 years (ceteris paribus, in particular technical change is to occur at the same speed as before) the technical gap – and so the gap in production costs per unit of ouput between plants 1 and 10 – is only 5 years.

4 If wages did not rise, the 'real' wage would have decreased.

increasing *indebtedness* of capitals, and relatedly in *inflation*. The losses of capitals are in fact socialised (cf. 2§10).

b. The possibility of providing devalorised capitals with new credits on a large scale so as to rescue part of them is predicated upon an integrated banking system. The alternative for banks is either to place the sanction of losses on the particular capitals *or* to consolidate debts, thus providing the condition for inflation and socialisation of the loss. Aglietta and Orléan (1982: ch. 2–3) have called these alternatives the 'fractioning' as opposed to the 'centralisation logic' (see De Vroey 1984: 386–7). Credit renewal does not imply that banks provide a 'carte blanche' to industrial capitals, which would have to present well structured projects to the bank, and the chances of getting new credit will be improved if future obsolescence is anticipated.

c. The explanation of the process of creeping inflation by anticipated obsolescence originated with Aglietta (1976: 313–15 and 365–70), who stresses that 'it is not the process of cumulative inflation that is hard to understand, but rather the permanent existence of creeping inflation'. However, the systematic context of Aglietta's theory is different from ours in §7. Over-accumulation of capital, rather than being predicated upon accumulation in relation to the reserve of labour – cf. Chapter 3 – is related to a structure of departmental disproportionality which is introduced quite haphazardly in relation to the tendency of the rate of profit to fall (1976: 353–6).

There tends to be an upward bias to prices from the increase in anticipated obsolescence reflected in prices, and from range decrease. As to the *first*, the question is how credit would *pre*-validate production, since accommodating credit is not provided to the producers anticipating the obsolescence, but gradually to the purchasers of their output. With anticipated obsolescence, producers increase (ideal) prices on account of the concomitantly planned increased rate of depreciation. This price increase applies to both departments of production so that (if the purchasing power of the wage were to be maintained) money wages would also need to increase gradually, which has again to be financed by bank credit. This appears to be what Aglietta is hinting at when he writes:

> We showed that relative surplus-value depends on an integration of the two departments of production which spreads the transformations in the forces of production of Department I in such a way as to develop the social norm of mass consumption. This linkage between the two departments involves a permanent devalorization of fixed capital. This is realized by the creation of a depreciation allowance obviously advanced on credit since it is incorporated into current expenditure, which does not correspond to the realization of any past labour, since the corresponding elements of constant capital are devalorized by obsolescence. But this depreciation allowance enters the circuit of income to purchase newly created means of production. (Aglietta 1976: 369)

Aglietta's language is, however, ambiguous. From our point of view, the purchase of newly created means of consumption should also be included in the last sentence.

The *second* way in which price increase is established, related to the decrease in the range of stratification of capitals, is our extension of Aglietta's theory, the attraction of which is that changes in the range of stratification may also provide an explanation for deflation (see §10).

§8. Inflation and devalorisation: the conflict between industrial and non-bank money capital

Pre-validation of production by banks together with obsolescence and devalorisation of capital, give rise to inflation, mitigating the crisis-proneness of economic development (§7). Once inflation becomes self-perpetuating it counteracts not only the devaluation, but also the devalorisation of capital. Devaluation is counteracted if prices of (fixed) means of production no longer decrease, or do not do so in proportion to productivity increase. However, if prices actually increase, then the *revaluation* of (fixed) capital may compensate (or even over-compensate) for devalorisation (see addendum a).[5] At the same time, however, for accumulation to go on, industrial capital must increase its indebtedness (because of the credit-renewal required due to obsolescence and ongoing inflation). This increasing indebtedness is the counterpart of revaluation of capital. The implied decrease in the rate of profit (TRPF) is now imposed increasingly on money capital, including banks, as its purchasing power is continuously reduced.[6] The industrial capital gain is thus the equivalent of the money capital loss, so that inflation reveals a potential conflict between them.[7] (Nevertheless, the position of banks is different from the position of non-banking money capital. To the extent that banks maintain an adequate fit between short term and long term borrowing and lending (maturity matching), it is the banks' creditors that suffer from inflation – see addendum b.)

Money capital is necessary to industrial capital to finance accumulation (2§§6–7), and the requirement for credit determines

---

5 The account is in terms of money, the capitalist measure of value, and not in 'physical' terms. The presentation here mirrors that of the TRPF in 4§§4–5, and is in fact concerned with forces counteracting the TRPF. Thus in as much as devaluation of capital concomitant on price decrease need not (but may in case of debts) affect 'physical' reproduction, revaluation of capital concomitant on price increase could well do so.

6 This is not immediately and simply reflected in the interest rate so as to keep the so-called 'real interest rate' constant (see below).

7 The manifestation of this potential conflict is also contingent upon the extent to which industrial and money capital are institutionally integrated.

the rate of interest in relation to the rate of profit. For money capital the only alternative is to *not* lend (2§11) and this alternative determines its power base. Only from within a partial analysis (taking the point of view of an 'individual money capital agent' (cf. Chapter 6) rather than that of money capital as a whole) could it be argued that money capital has the alternative of investing in unproductive assets (precious metals, works of art, real estate, and so on). However, this is not *lending* money capital but buying property. Relatedly, this merely *shifts* the money capital title to the previous property owners. Therefore if money capital refrains from lending to industrial capital (as well as from consuming), the money gets hoarded, ultimately in the form of increase in bank reserves (2§11). That money capital's power base is determined by the only alternative being to not lend is not affected by inflation. The 'real' interest rate then, is a *result* rather than a determinant of the interest rate; lending at a negative 'real' interest rate may be preferred to having no interest at all.[8] Nevertheless, and quite independent of the level of the 'real' interest rate, the money interest rate tends to be pushed up because of the increasing demand for credit by industrial capital.

The effects of the articulation of these factors (industrial capital's capital gain, redistribution between industrial and money capital, increasing indebtedness of industrial capital, interest rate increase), especially the sequential order and the size of the effects, are contingent. (1) In order to be able to recontract credits at a higher interest rate, banks increasingly substitute short term for long term lending, tending to put a strain on industrial capital. (2) When contracts expire, non-banking money capital tends to withdraw fixed interest assets (such as bonds) from industrial investment. Alternative investment in existing shares, real estate, and so on drives up their prices. However, money capital so invested ultimately gets deposited with banks, or takes the form of near-banking call money. Industrial capital then has to further rely on short-term credit provided by banks to keep accumulation going.[9] (3) The progressive increase in demand for extra credit because of inflation causes the share of interest in surplus value progressively to increase. (4) To the

---

8 The implication of the 'real interest rate' argument would be that with *deflation*, money interest rates at some point would have to become negative. ('Real interest rate' is of course a theoretical construct. 'Money' interest rates are real so that the proper term for such a construct would be 'indexed interest rate' – cf. Adarkar 1934 and Robertson 1934: 70–1.)

9 This part of the argument applies to the substitution of investment in existing shares and real estate, etc. for fixed interest assets. Money capital will also be invested in newly issued shares.

extent that the share of non-banking money capital in industrial investment declines, the risk for banks increases. In the absence of sufficient security, they will then require a risk-premium on top of normal interest, and further credit will tend to be conditional on increasing bank's influence in the management, even to the extent of engendering restructuring.

The devalorisation of capital associated with the TRPF thus tends to be counteracted by inflation to the detriment of money capital. With the substitution of˙short-term bank credit for long-term finance, the effect of inflation is then reimposed on industrial capital.

Addenda: a. Revaluation of capital (example); b. Inflation and the interests of money and industrial capital

a. The revaluation of capital is most transparent when we consider the case in which an asset is wholly financed by way of credit, and this may be illustrated by an example. When a sum of money, £q, is borrowed to buy a fixed capital asset (such as a machine) at a price £q, which is calculated linearly to depreciate in n years' time, then each year amortisation, included in the output price, will be £q/n. At a steady rate of inflationary general price increase of z per cent per year, the new value of the asset (as bought by competitors) will also rise at z per cent per year, and so current amortisation will (ceteris paribus) also increase at z per cent per year. At the end of the life cycle of the asset, the sinking fund will therefore exceed the initial £q, and after cancelling the debt an inflationary capital gain remains. Of course, to the lender the purchasing power of £q will have decreased, and of course the purchase of a new asset requires an increase in indebtedness.

b. Inflation reveals a potential conflict between industrial and non-banking money capital. In general (and contrary to much of the Monetarist argument in this respect), inflation is in the interest of industrial capital (whilst central bank stabilisation of the value of the currency is in the interest of money capital). This is true only as long as lending is not indexed, but that is not an easy matter. Lending could be indexed to the general price level. Then the interest rate could be 2 per cent, or whatever rate agreed upon, plus the percentage of change in the general price level. From the point of view of money capital this would seem fine as long as prices increase. But when prices decrease by an amount near to that rate, they might refuse to lend.

Banks play a crucial role in the accommodation of inflation, but to the extent that they maintain an adequate match between short- and long-term assets and liabilities, they do not in the main suffer from inflation, except via the devaluation of their monetary reserves. This loss may well be compensated for by increasing the share of short term lending (which can be more easily inflation-proofed) over long term borrowing. It is then rather the banks' depositors that suffer. Apart from the 'hoarded' deposits of money capital, these deposits also include savings out of wages. The heterogeneity of money capital (including pension funds, insurance companies, etc.), further complicates the examination of the conflict posited in §8 (see, for example, Harris 1976), which in any case – extending to the personal distribution of income as it does – belongs to a lower level of abstraction.

§9. Inflation and the TOC

Whilst inflation tends to counteract the effects of devalorisation of capital associated with the TRPF (§§7–8), it tends rather to reinforce the effects of the tendency to over-accumulation of capital (TOC). Obsolescence and the introduction of new techniques boosts employment in the production of means of production, even those which are themselves labour saving, whose long run net effect is expulsion of labour. As long as anticipated obsolescence is continuously pre-validated by banks, major breaks in the circuit of capital via bankruptcies are prevented. Obsolescence itself then produces an upward growth trend, upon which the cyclical manifestation of the TOC then tends to be imposed. The articulation of inflation and the TOC therefore produces inflation along with both upswings and downswings (stagflation). The relative decrease in average rates of unemployment associated with the upward growth trend inhibits the regular disciplining of the labour force, which not only affects the level of the wage but also the intensity of labour, and so the rate of surplus value comes under pressure. So inflation not only tends to weaken the disciplining force of the market as between capitals, but also the actual subordination of labour.

§10. From inflation to deflation

Banks have been shown to play a major accommodating role in the process of accumulation of capital. Nevertheless this accommodation cannot overcome the contradictions inherent in the valorisation of capital. It cannot overcome the conflict between industrial and money capital, and even less so that between capital and labour. Inflation accommodated by the banking system permits accumulation to continue. Therefore, along with the relative expulsion of labour, predicated upon the rise of the capital composition associated with the TRPF, the rate of employment may in fact increase. This generates a further decrease in the rate of surplus value associated with relative labour shortage (§9). At the same time continuous inflation creates a drain on the industrial rate of profit, because banks themselves attempt to make lending inflation proof via rates of interest, and so short term lending is substituted for long term lending (§8). At the same time, the withdrawal of money capital from industrial investment increases banks' risk, and continual inflation decreases the banks' reserve ratio, further increasing this risk in terms of their survival. This increase in risk, together with the drain on the rate of profit of industrial capital, causes the rate of pre-validation by banks to slow down. Therefore both the rate of increase of accumulation and the rate of potential inflation slow down.

As long as the banking system co-operates (either by inter-bank credits or by takeovers) to prevent bank failure, the process of decrease in the rate of pre-validation may be accomplished gradually and without financial crisis. Such co-operation, which is enhanced by ties to central banks as well as by co-operation between them, is however contingent. The course of this process of *gradually* decreasing the rate of pre-validation will typically involve selective pre-validation: credits being allowed to the strong (less risky) capitals at the old rate, whilst weak capitals are merely sustained without increases in the rate of pre-validation or any major new credits. (Of importance in this respect is the extent to which banks' clients are clustered so that eventual bankruptcies have positive feedback effects within the cluster. Keeping one capital going (with dubious prospects) may prevent other capitals, in the same cluster, and to which that bank has also provided credit, from being drawn into loss positions.) So whilst the average rate of pre-validation decreases, increased pre-validation to the strong layers of capital proceeds. Therefore, whilst weaker capital cannot advance up the technical stratification, the stronger keep on advancing at the top.

Selective pre-validation creates a differentiated structure of capital (with an efficient and an inefficient stratum), and relatedly the range of stratification increases. This enhances the efficacy of retardation of price increase after the introduction of new techniques of production as a means of curing over-capacity by enforcing the obsolescence of capitals at the bottom of the range. The ultimate outcome of this process is indeterminate. To some extent, it depends on the relative size of the efficient and the inefficient capital strata. When the inefficient stratum is relatively small, a short period of restructuring of capital (with the rate of inflation slowing down) may be followed again by a new inflationary boost, and so on. When the inefficient stratum is relatively large, the extinguishing of inefficient capitals may be cumulative so as to give rise to a spiral of increasing unemployment, decreasing wages and demand-deficient over-capacity. Retardation of price increase, or a price decrease, then further enforces restructuring of capital.

However, such moderated inflation, or even deflation, restores the tensions and conflicts that inflation helped to overcome. On the one hand it may make investment in industry again attractive to non-banking money capital. Whilst this reduces the extent of the banks' risk (and thus may encourage a renewed boost of credit), decreasing prices both restore money capital's power base, and annihilate industrial capital's gain from revaluation of capital (§8). On the other hand, decreasing prices bring with them the well-known difficulty (Keynes 1936: ch. 19) that wages may not decrease along with prices.

§11. Inflation, the TOC and the TRPF

Inflation (§§7–10) has been shown to modify the articulation of the tendencies of accumulation (S1). In particular, it modifies the expression of the contradictory character of these tendencies in gradual contraction, or in economic crises (S2). The actual course of the inflationary reproduction of the articulation of the TRPF and the TOC is indeterminate. The period over which it may persist is dependent on contingent aspects of the banking system as well as of the make-up of the stratification of capital. Inflation may postpone and mitigate economic crises, and the banking system may even prevent the financial crises related to it. But inflation provides only a temporary form of existence of the contradiction that valorisation and accumulation of capital are necessarily counteracted in devalorisation and devaluation. Inflation cannot abolish this counter-action; it can postpone it *vis à vis* industrial capital, and it can protract its effects.

The more inflation does this, the more actual functioning money (£, $, yen, etc.) comes into conflict with its grounding (2S2) of the existence of the association of dissociated production and consumption in the value-form (1SS1–3). Money has been deter-mined as an at least temporary fiducial store of value to the contingent extent that the circuit of capital is non-synchronous (1S4). When actual money is no longer fiduciary in this respect then it stops functioning as means of circulation and general equivalent, and so another guise of value necessarily has to appear. The under-mining of this fiduciary aspect cannot be pinned down to a particular rate of inflation, and indeed is also a function of the stability of that rate. However, increasing inflation and the concomitant search for stores of value other than money undermine the role of banks, diverting investment away from productive areas which require continuous bank intermediation.[10] The production of other stores of value also distorts the associative function of the money expression of value, in that it reallocates productive resources (with concomitant disproportionality effects) towards them. It is exactly because such

10 Quite another issue is that, for compensation, banks may enter those other markets as intermediaries.

stores are not only means of circulation that the associative function of the money expression of value threatens to break down. But along with this, the valorisation of capital increasingly appears as a mere phantom of itself: a perpetuum mobile based on a book-keeping-like act of price increase.

Therefore, and quite independently of the threat to the natural necessity for material sustenance (1S1, cf. also 6§§5–6) associated with the allocation of resources toward mere stores of value, continuously increasing inflation cannot persist. Inflation cannot overcome but can only modify the manifestations of the contradiction of the valorisation and accumulation of capital.

Addendum: a. Consciousness of the oppositions of valorisation and devalorisation, and of accumulation and devaluation of capital

a. Allegorically speaking, capitalism may be characterised as an Homeric Sisyphean labour. According to Camus (1942: 143) the hero is a tragic one because he is conscious of his tortuous labour. Unfortunately, though the bearers of the capital relation may be heroes, they do not always seem to be tragic in *this* respect.

SUMMARY

This chapter provides an account of the articulation of the tendencies of accumulative derived in Chapter 3 (the TOC) and in Chapter 4 (the TRPF). In Section 1 the effects of the articulation of the TOC and the TRPF were presented. The TRPF counteracts the expression of the TOC in labour-shortage profit squeeze and under-consumption. First, the VCC increase concomitant on the TRPF slows down the rate of integration of labour into the circuit of capital, which slows down the increase in the wage rate implied by the TOC. The increasing demand for means of production generated by an increasing VCC also counteracts the expression of the TOC in underconsumption (§2). Secondly, the increasing labour productivity and decreasing price concomitant on the TRPF affect the use-value purchasing power of the wage. The effect of this on the level of the wage rate is dependent on the reserve of labour. In a state of labour abundance there will be a downward pressure on the wage, such that the form of existence of the TRPF in devalorisation is counteracted by the positive effect of an increasing rate of surplus value on the rate of profit. In a state of labour scarcity the wage tends not to be affected by price decrease, and so a double squeeze operates on the rate of profit (§3).

The articulation of the TOC and TRPF modifies the course of cyclical accumulation implied by each considered in isolation. In particular, the cycle of expansion and contraction of accumulation tends to be extended. In Section 2 it was argued that the exact character of the alternation is indeterminate: a gradual course of alternation without disruptive economic crisis is compatible with the presentation up to that point (§4). Nevertheless, the combination of the credit system (which tends to increase the amplitude of cycles –§5), and the eventual cumulative expulsion of labour from the circuit of capital related to the articulation of the TOC and TRPF, tends to make the economy vulnerable to economic crises, one important characteristic of which is enforced devalorisation and devaluation and the restructuring and centralisation of capital. The decrease in the range of the stratification of capitals, and the concomitant retardation in the introduction of new techniques related to it, together with the disciplining effect of the crisis on the labour force, forms the basis of a new phase of expansion of accumulation. As a corollary to our presentation then, waves of implementation of new techniques (Schumpeter) may be explained endogenously (§6).

In Section 3 the (contingent) inflationary reproduction of accumulation has been presented. Inflation is merely one possible process generated within the economy to overcome economic crisis (which in itself is merely one possible manifestation of the contradictions of valorisation and accumulation). The contingent monetary condition of inflation is related to obsolescence and devalorisation of capital, in combination with continued pre-validation of production by banks even when fixed capitals have not been fully amortised. Rising (or insufficiently decreasing) prices are related in particular to the decrease in the range of capital stratification concomitant on continuous pre-validation by banks. Whilst the inflationary reproduction of accumulation appears to overcome the alternation of expansion and contraction via crisis, it gives rise to waves in the implementation of new techniques analogous to those in the absence of generalised inflation (§7). The revaluation of capital produced by inflation provides a compensation for the devalorisation of capital in the form of capital gains. But its counterpart is a loss in the purchasing power of the non-banking money capital lent to industrial capital, causing its gradual withdrawal from industry, and so the latter has to rely increasingly on short-term bank credit. This gives rise to an increasing share of interest in surplus value, and so the inflationary compensation for the devalorisation of capital is reduced (§8). A further effect of protracted inflation is the enforcement of the cyclical manifestation *of the TOC, which however tends to be imposed on an upward growth trend. The relative decrease in average rates of unemployment associated with it inhibits the regular disciplining of the labour force. This not only affects the level of the wage but also the intensity of labour, and so the rate of surplus value comes under pressure (§9).*

It was then argued that because of the withdrawal of non-banking money capital from industry, and because of the reinforcement of the TOC, a drain on the rate of profit tends to be created. This causes banks to slow down the increase in lending to industry which, depending on the structure of the banking system, may be accomplished gradually by a process of selective lending, generating a dual structure of strong and weak capitals. The concomitant increase in the range of stratification of capitals tends to slow down price increase (or even to decrease prices). A resulting deflation, however, restores the tensions and conflicts that inflation was to overcome (§10). In §11, the articulation of the TRPF and the TOC with inflation has been related back to the starting point of the presentation. It was argued that because protracted inflation undermines money as the store of value not only is the position of banks within the circuit of capital undermined, but so is the associative function of the money expression of value. Continuously increasing inflation therefore cannot persist. Inflation cannot overcome but can only modify the manifestations of the contradictions of the valorisation and accumulation of capital.

Part Four:

The State and the Mixed Economy

Chapter six

From Competitive Society to the State and Civil Society

PRELIMINARY REMARKS

The value-form, and its reproduction as the specifically bourgeois mode of association (1S3) has been presented so far with subjects and subjectivity blended out. Their introduction in this chapter makes it explicit that the bourgeois economy (Chapters 1–5) is not itself adequate to the reproduction of subjects – nor, therefore, of itself.

For much economic theory the state is a beneficent autocrat or a group of Platonic guardians or of competitively elected power-holders, responding automatically to the best available advice as to what constitutes social welfare and how to achieve it. Even economic theories of the state which escape this 'black box' mentality tend to be economistic in the sense of basing their analyses of the state upon the notion of atomistic agents maximising subject to constraints. Analysis of the state then differs from analysis of the market only in the arguments of the objective functions and the constraints (see Whynes and Bowles 1981 for a recent synthesis of economic theories of the state). Marxist theories of the state have tended to be reductionist – reducing the state to an instrument of some pre-existent capitalist class or to the functionalist epiphenomenon of the 'needs of capital (accumulation)'. (For a critical survey, see Jessop 1982.) Whilst economic (and, more generally, social-scientific) theories can be grasped as reflections (however unconscious) of the logic of the processes of the value-form in competitive society, they lack an integrated conceptualisation of society. What is missing in particular from both mainstream and Marxist theories is the conceptual development of 'society' between the account of the economy and that of the state (S2).

Starting with the value-form as the specifically bourgeois mode of association necessitated by the dissociation of individuals incapable of self-reproduction, Part Two has developed capital, valorisation and the extended reproduction of capital. Part Three has then presented the tendencies of accumulation, their forms of existence, and the expression of their contradictions. However, the implications of these concretisations for the association of non-self-reproducing individuals have not been drawn out. This chapter explicates these implications, presenting the contradiction between the value-form and abstract free will. Thus it starts in the economic core determined by the universal value-form, which is negated in abstract free will. From this contradiction is derived the society of competing subjects deploying income sources (which are forms of value) in order to survive. Whilst the existence of these 'competition subjects' is grounded in the rights to private property and, ideally to existence, such rights cannot be reproduced within competitive society. This contradiction is grounded in the doubling of competitive society into civil society and the state. Competitive society thus mediates between the economy and the state, which is a necessary condition of existence of the bourgeois totality. The state is an alienated expression of the demands of a persistent communality implicit in the concepts of sociation and association, manifest in the inadequacies of the value-form determined economy to the reproduction of the non-self-reproducing concrete particular individuals for which it was to be the specifically bourgeois mode of association. (In Chapter 7 this implicit communality is further particularised as many national communalities manifest in national civil societies.)

SECTION 1   ABSTRACT FREE WILL

§1. Value-form, abstract free will and subjectivity

The reproduction of the value-form, valorisation and capital accumulation have been presented (Parts Two and Three) as structurally determined – that is, as subjectless processes. They are determined neither by any individual will nor by the will of any overarching social subject. Nevertheless the value-form is the specifically bourgeois mode of association, and association inherently concerns dissociated individual subjects incapable of self-production (1S1). Subjects have been only implicit in the presentation so far, as subjects without subjectivity, that is as mere *bearers of economic relations*. But subjects without subjectivity are contradictory. This contradiction derives from the (abstract) existence of *free will* which contradicts the *structural* determination of association through the value form (see addendum a). (Free will without any such determination is also contradictory since that would imply subjectivity without subjects: there would be mere bearers of free will.) At this level of abstraction the bourgeois subject thus enjoys free will, but only abstractly, that is as constrained by its conditions of existence within the capitalist economy: it would seem that particular free will can exist only in communality. But because of the negation of sociate activity (and the communality implicit in it) into dissociation – in particular the separation of production and consumption (1§3) – communality seems to become explicit only, if at all, in the private sphere of bourgeois society (0§15; see 7S1). Though the value-form determined association of the economy cannot be indifferent to the reproduction of labour power, it is in the event in itself indifferent to the reproduction of subjects. Because a subject's free will is in fact determined by its conditions of existence, free will can, within the bourgeois economy, be only abstract. The contradiction between the value-form and free will cannot consequently be resolved within that economy.

Addenda: a. Abstract free will; b. Liberal individualism

a. Abstract free will is a Hegelian concept (Hegel 1821: §§4 and 5). The will is abstract in being universal yet consisting of determinate aims (Hegel 1821: §§34–5). The abstract right to exercise free will, as the universal set of rules governing the exercise of the rights of property and person (S2), is to be contrasted with morality ('Sittlichkeit'), which is concerned essentially with disinterested conduct (see Pelczynski 1984a: 8). It is also to be distinguished from substantial right – which rests on substantial ties such as those of kinship and personal relations (in the private sphere) or of political life (in the sphere of the state – but also, for Hegel, in the corporations of civil society).

b. The concept of abstract free will is reflected in liberal individualism's discussions of negative versus positive conceptions of liberty (Berlin 1958). The conclusion of these analyses is that liberals must content themselves with 'negative' forms of liberty (freedom from constraint), since positive conceptions lead to inevitable socialistic (and market-mechanism undermining) threats to liberty by requiring measures to enforce substantial equal access to liberty. However, these results are already implicit in their starting point in the postulation of atomistic, undetermined individuals.

SECTION 2 COMPETITIVE SOCIETY

§2. Competition subjects and income forms

The contradiction of the value-form and free will and the derived contradictions of subjects without subjectivity and subjectivity without subjects (§1) is transcended in the *competitive society* of

165

competition subjects. Within society, the bearers of abstract free will exist more concretely as competition subjects, determined by capitalist economic relations (Parts Two and Three). Competitive society is thus the unity of the abstract capitalist economy and the abstract social existence of free will, and the competition subject is the unity of the bearer of abstract economic relations and of abstract free will. At the level of abstraction of Parts Two and Three, labour and capital have been determined as the abstract bearers of the economic relations constitutive of capital as self-valorising value (1S5). From the valorisation of capital have been derived the concepts of landed, money and industrial capital (1§11, 2§7). The distributional relations implicit in capitalist production are further particularised as the *value-forms of income* – wages, rent, interest and profits respectively. These are value-forms in that they are sums of money quantitatively determined by the processes of generalised capitalist production and exchange.

Labour and capital exist more concretely as the *income sources* of competition subjects, who are subjects (in contrast to the mere bearers of economic relations) just because they have the abstract free will to deploy their income sources in pursuit of income in competition with other competition subjects.

Addenda: a. The 'state-derivation' debate; b. Character-mask

a. The intermediate step in the derivation of the state (S3) from the value-form–free will contradiction, transcended in competitive society, differentiates our account from the German capital-logic and state-derivation approach (see Holloway and Picciotto (eds) 1978). In this way, the alleged functionalism of these approaches is to be avoided, without falling into instrumentalism. The forms of the state and its policies are not simply to be derived as epiphenomena of the logic of capital, nor is the state conceived as some pre-existent entity in the hands of capitalists (see Jessop 1977 and 1982 for critical surveys of theories of the capitalist state; for an earlier, rather functionalist, attempt by one of us to derive economic policy direct from the needs of capital, see Williams 1982).

b. The transition from mere bearer of economic relations – what Marx called the 'character-mask' ('Charaktermaske') (Marx 1867: 82, 89; 1867G: 100; 1867P: 179) – to the competition subject with abstract free will is an important step in the conceptual development from the starting point in dissociation and the value-form to the state. At the level of Parts Two and Three, the necessary moments of the economy could be discussed in abstraction from social and political moments, and concomitantly in abstraction from willed subjects. The systematic presentation in §§1–2 enables us to come to grips with the interplay of agency and structure which runs through much social science, and to which Marx's solution is contained in the famous dictum about people making history, but not in conditions of their own choosing (Marx 1852: 146; cf. 0§13).

§3. Income sources and right to property

The abstract free will of competition subjects to deploy income sources in pursuit of income, to own and alienate money and commodities, and to deploy money income for the purchase of commodities – whether for consumption or production or as a loan – is grounded in the bourgeois *right to property*. The right to property is a universal right: even competition subjects that have no property in an income source have property right over the money received in wages, and in whatever commodities may be bought with it. The right to property is the expression of the competition subjects' abstract freedom to compete for income.

§4. Property and the capacity to labour

Competition subjects' income sources are not congruent with each other. First of all there are the three forms of income (interest, rent and profits) that derive from property in an income source (money capital, landed capital and industrial capital respectively). There are thus three property owning categories of competition subject: money capitalist, landed capitalist and entrepreneur.

The wage as a form of income, however, does not derive from *property* in an income source but rather from a universal *capacity* inseparable from the labourer. Free wage labourers are a particular category of competition subject because their income source (labour power) is not a property in the sense of money or a commodity which can be held or alienated. Labour power is the income source of last resort at the level of competitive society for those who do not own (sufficient) property income sources. Inseparability and this last-resort income role of labour power is the basis of other-direction and alienation within the labour process.

The differentiation of income sources into property and labour forms is the expression in competitive society of the contradictory unity of capital and labour in the capital relation (1S5). As an element of production also, labour power is inseparable from the labourer, a subject with free will. Prior to the formal equality of competition subjects is the inequality of capital and labour as character masks (2§2), which reappears in competitive society as the difference between property owning subjects and those who must rely on their capacity to labour. Capital's control of the labour process thus requires mechanisms of real subordination in a hierarchical structure of managerial control. The entrepreneur as manager thereby receives a further determination as bearer of a specific kind of labour.

The incongruence of income sources expresses, at the level at which subjectivity has been introduced, the existence of classes with the necessary antagonism one to the other derived from the capital relation. Each of these classes has its own implicit subjectivity, restricted by market forces, which is the particular existence of their abstract free will. The labourer must sell their labour power; the landed-capitalist must rent their land and the money capitalist must invest their money capital. The entrepreneur must obtain and deploy these elements of production so as to produce and sell commodities.

The right to own and alienate money and commodities in the shape of private property (§3) is thus intrinsic to the processes of competitive society: the bourgeois right to property is a concrete condition of existence of the value-form. The processes of competitive society are the appearance at the level of subjective economic activity of the processes of valorisation.

Addenda: a. Labour and property; b. Entrepreneurship; c. Class

a. The wage is a categorically different income form from property incomes. Surplus value can be reaped precisely because the labourer, unlike the capitalist, does not receive a 'rate of return' proportional to the value of any element of production advanced in which they have property (because labour power has no such value!), but rather receives a contractually fixed wage. In this respect, Eldred (1984a) does not advance beyond Locke (1690: section 26), where he conceives every man as having 'property in his own person'. Hegel, on the other hand, makes the invalidity of property right over persons (in the bourgeois epoch) quite clear: 'Objectively considered, a right arising from a contract is never a right over a person, but only a right over something external to a person or something which he can alienate, always a right over a thing' (Hegel 1821: §40a). (Cf. the critique of Eldred 1984a in Williams 1984: §§40–1.)

b. The term 'entrepreneur' is adapted from the Austrian literature. (It is usually associated with Schumpeter – for example, his 1934 – although he is on the margins of the Austrian school proper. A comprehensive account of the more mainstream contemporary Austrian position is given in Kirzner 1973, based on the seminal work of von Mises 1949. Their difference from Schumpeter, for whom entrepreneurs periodically appear from outside the market and stir it up by their innovative activity, lies in their perception of entrepreneurship rather as an essentially *equilibrating* aspect of the market process itself, consisting of the spotting of opportunities to appropriate profit from arbitrage in a world of intrinsically imperfect information.) For the Austrians 'pure' entrepreneurship does not depend on property in capital, 'knowledge' nor in some fourth 'factor of production' (in addition to land, labour and capital) such as 'entrepreneurship' (see Kirzner 1973: ch. 2).

In our development of the concept we conceive the entrepreneur at this level of abstraction as implicitly endowed with property in functioning capital, entitling them to the residual surplus (after paying off debt service and dividends to other – non-entrepreneurial – shareholders). Without this property relation, any entrepreneurial profits remain only, in Marx's terminology 'profit upon alienation', which must in the aggregate be zero. We can agree, then, that profits of enterprise arise (proximately) from entrepreneurial activity, but in order to appropriate them the entrepreneur must have property in functioning capital, that is in the firm (see Marx 1894; Ch. XXIII). Our critique of this mystifying source of 'new profits' is thus to conceive it as the *unity* of property in capital and a particular kind of managerial (*viz.* entrepreneurial) labour. It is the development of the character mask 'industrial capital' with the introduction of subjectivity – the active, willed capitalist who having spotted the market opportunity brings together capital (their own, borrowed or that of shareholders) and labour to the production of a commodity to meet it (cf. Mises 1949: 253; and Kirzner 1973: 69, for the entrepreneur as the 'ultimate hirer' of other factors of production). It is for this reason that, unlike Marx, we use the term 'entrepreneur' for the developed form of 'industrial capitalist'. Liberal ideology aside, entrepreneurship might be exercised by a person or by a collective institutional agent; at this high level of abstraction the issue as to which does not arise. (Cf. Mises 1949: 253–4, where he characterises enterpreneurship abstractly as a 'function', whose embodiment in a person is a 'methodological makeshift'.) The neoclassical critique of the Austrian concept, on the other hand, is based on the apparent assumption of perfect (money) capital markets, as only then will anyone who spots a market opportunity, whatever their means, be able to raise capital at a rate reflecting the expected returns adjusted for risk. Our critique, which is more fundamental, is rather that 'entrepreneurship' can be separated from capital (see, for example, Kirzner 1973: 49) only by having an inadequate conception of the latter. For us, capital beyond a mere character mask is the active element of production and exchange – the unity of control of money capital, managerial labour and entrepreneurship. Without the first, the last could not reap the reward of its percipient activity. The entrepreneur is the subjectively active industrial capitalist. (For more on the Austrians, as a component of the 'systematic liberal' view of the state–society relation, see 8§1 addendum a, §4 addendum c, §10 addendum a and §14 addendum c.; 9§4 addendum b, §8 addendum a and §12 addendum a; 10§5 addendum b and §6 addendum a.)

c. Our conceptualisation of class would differ from both orthodox and Marxist social science. It would start from the four categories of forms of income as value-forms. Marxism tends to an economic determinism in which classes are read off directly at the level of the economy from ownership-control of (versus separation from) the means of production. We see the intervening development of competitive society as a necessary step for the development, at a lower level of abstraction, of the concept of class. For orthodox social science, class is either theorised in terms of pre-existent individuals engaging in atomistic, game-playing optimisation (which is also the view taken by 'analytical Marxism' – see, for example, Roemer 1982), sometimes resulting in coalitions; or it makes do with merely descriptive taxonomies based on income levels, job classification, social status, and so on. Although a prime mover in the rediscovery of the abstract-labour approach, Himmelweit (1977) offers only the standard differentiation of Marxist from mainstream economics on the basis of the substitution of class for individual as the 'basic unit of analysis'.

§5. The right to existence

Bearers of value-form determined social relations have been transcended in competition subjects. Whilst the deployment of income and income sources by competition subjects has been grounded in the bourgeois right to property, the wage as income source is derived rather from the universal capacity to labour (§§3–4).

Subjectivity – the abstract free will to deploy income sources as property and the capacity to labour in competitive society – has its existence in particular competition subjects. If competition subjects are to have the right to deploy income sources and own property – the manifestation of the specifically bourgeois mode of association in the face of the contradictions of self-production (0§15; 1S1; and §§2–3 above) – they must also have the *right to existence*.

The bourgeois subject is then the economic character mask with abstract free will and the abstract right to existence. However, bourgeois subjects by themselves, as the bearers of abstract economic relations and free will cannot make concretely actual the rights to existence and property – just because their free will is abstract, that is, contradicted by their structural economic conditions of existence in competitive society. Subjects live by deploying income sources in pursuit of income. Whilst the right to property (in valorised and accumulated capital) is reproduced, albeit abstractly, within competitive society, the capacity to labour is not. Whilst labour power is bought and sold as a commodity on generalised markets, it is not a commodity, not being produced within a capitalist firm nor with a view to being sold. The reproduction of labour power entails the reproduction of subjects which cannot be guaranteed within the abstract logic of competitive society (1§5 and 1§9, 2 §12).

Addenda: a. Right to existence in Marx and Hegel; b. The starting point of microeconomics

a. Critics of bourgeois society often object to the notion that it involves even such an abstract right to existence. But it is precisely the fragmented individualism of competitive society which makes individual social being so precarious that it has to be expressed in the specifically bourgeois form of *right*. The development of right to existence which cannot be guaranteed at the level of competitive society is both a reconstruction and an extension of Marx. Marx (1844b), in the context of a polemic against Bauer's notion of the emancipation of the Jews, makes quite clear that rights cannot be made social in the bourgeois epoch, but can have only a formal existence, as state-enforced political rights (cf. §9). For Hegel, the precariousness of existence in a civil society (S3) isolated by excessive *laissez-faire* is not a matter merely of the contingency of material success. Rather it generates forms of consciousness and conduct inimical to human self-realisation. Competition subjects thus tend to live for momentary satisfactions since it is difficult to live one's life by design in an environment not subject to self-conscious social control (see Walton 1984: 252).

b. With the introduction of subjectivity the presentation has arrived at the starting point which is merely postulated by economics – agents freely competing on product and factor markets. For the classical economists, this is expressed as a natural human propensity to truck and barter (Smith 1776: i, 12). For modern microeconomics it is expressed either as a matter of convenience, to be verified by confronting the derived conclusions with empirical data (for example, Friedman 1953: 218) or as the axiomatic 'rationality postulate' (see, Caldwell 1982: 147–64). One general result of this postulation is the inability of mainstream economics to grasp the specificity of the epoch, its discourse falling into two parts. On the one hand, the rationalist models of general equilibrium analysis, inapplicable to existing societies (or even their economic aspects); and on the other, contingent or partial equilibrium and policy analysis, unable to ground its conclusions in any conceptualisation of the totality in which the detailed processes described are embedded. In contrast, value-form theory derives competitive society as a necessary form of appearance of the process of social production in the bourgeois epoch. By the development of the subjects of competition from the basic value categories – and back from the abstractly willed activities of the former to the reproduction of the latter – it grounds its account of society in the form determined totality (0§§9, 14). It is thus able to offer a critique of that everyday consciousness which sees bourgeois society as the incarnation of inalienable natural rights to property, existence, freedom, equality, etc., by pointing out the specificity of right to the bourgeois epoch, and its merely abstract nature.

---

§6. The subjective reproduction of value-form association

Competitive society comprises the totality of competition subjects competing within the opportunities offered by the value-form determined economy. The success of competition subjects in deploying their income sources constitutes at the same time their own reproduction and the reproduction of the economy, which is not consciously directed by any social subject, being rather reproduced 'behind the backs' of particular subjects, regulated only by the 'invisible hand' of market forces (1§6). This regulation reproduces the value-form determined whole, but only by processes in which particular companies come and go, particular property owners prosper and fail, and particular labourers are more or less successful in selling their capacity to labour. Competition subjects as abstract bearers of the value-form determined economic relations of the economy are indifferent to the particular existence of their competitors. The use-value composition of output, and how it is produced and distributed, are subordinated to valorisation: value, not use-value criteria dominate the social allocation of resources.

However, it is a necessary condition of the continued existence of competitive society that adequate labour power be reproduced (2§12). Since labour power is inseparable from the labourer, whose existence cannot be ensured by the abstract universality of the valorisation processes, competitive society at this stage of the presentation cannot guarantee the reproduction of its own conditions of existence (cf. 0§9). At the level of competitive society considered abstrctly, right to existence can be at best only an ideal, in the shape of an eternal human right. The point is that the right to exist (and lower order corollaries such as the right to a job and to an adequate income) is inherently *concrete and particular*, whilst the *abstract and universal* principles of competitive society – the valorisation of value and abstract free will – are indifferent to the concrete and particular existence of specific subjects. The logic of the economy demands that income be received only in exchange for contribution to valorisation. The principle 'to each according to their contribution to valorisation as determined by contracts freely struck in accordance with market-enforced commercial criteria' does not contain within it the principle 'to each according to their need on use-value criteria'. The reproduction of particular existence appears as external to the driving force of the economy. Whilst the value-form as the specifically bourgeois mode of appropriation transcends the separation of units of production by recognising commodities produced as socially useful, the systemic criterion of social usefulness is value and valorisation, not appropriateness (on use-value criteria) to the social reproduction of particular subjects (1S3).

SECTION 3   CIVIL SOCIETY AND THE STATE

§7. The doubling of competitive society

Competitive society is the form of existence of the contradiction of the value-form and free will (S1). The competition subject has been grounded in the universal right to property together with an abstract right to existence (S2). Right cannot subsist as a social right, affecting the operation of society grasped only abstractly as competitive society (§§5–6). Right at this level of abstraction is then both necessary and impossible – it is contradictory.

The ideal abstract right to existence is continually under threat contingent upon the opportunities made available by the workings of competitive society, and by the quantitative levels of contracts struck between competition subjects. Not only is the value-form economy indifferent to the existence of particular competition subjects but there are also systemic tendencies of accumulation articulated in cyclical crises which make even more precarious the existence of particular subjects (Part Three). Subjects with the ideal right to existence are thus continually under threat from the contingencies and crisis-ridden nature of the subjectless reproduction of the whole. A crucial site of the threat to particular existence is the conflict between property and existence rights within the wage–labour relation (§4). Property owners, through the entrepreneur, seek to buy labour power as cheaply as possible, and to deploy it as intensively as possible, without regard to a living wage or safe working conditions for the labourer. Conversely, labourers seek to optimise their standard of living and working conditions in selling their labour power.

Within competitive society, predicated upon the competition of each against all and the universal principles of valorisation and free will, the right to existence can be no more than a morally inspired striving after some perceived eternal human ideal against the market-enforced dictates of valorisation. The abstractness of the right to existence contradicts its inherent concrete particularity. It can thus have no existence at the level of competitive society in abstraction. This contradiction is grounded in the transcendence of competitive society in the *doubling of competitive society into civil society and the state*.

Addenda: a. Doubling; b. 'Civil society' in Marx and Hegel; c. Classics of European political philosophy

a. The doubling of competitive society into civil society and the state is a crucial step in the understanding of how the systematic presentation is the argument as to the essential interconnectedness of the socioeconomic system (0§§8, 9, 12). The presentation so far has come to a fundamental contradiction. Further development therefore requires that the object of theory be expanded: the entity theorised so far (competitive society) is to be transcended by a more extensive, concrete entity – bourgeois society, consisting of civil society and the state. Civil society is the reappearance of competitive society *vis-à-vis* the state. This procedure is conceptual; there is no suggestion that competitive society (generalised capitalist commodity production and exchange together with the existence of abstract free will) is some historically pre-existent phase of development (cf. 0§12). The procedure allows the internal arguments themselves to drive the presentation forward: if the presentation of the totality is to be complete and internally coherent, it clearly cannot stop at the stage at which it has derived a necessary impossibility – a contradiction: 'in dialectic it is the insufficiency of the premises that leads to the more sufficient conclusion' (Findlay 1975: xiii).

b. The development of the state from the value-form is based upon a reconstruction (Williams 1984: §§10–18) of Eldred (1984a: especially §§71–121). It provides a rectification of Hegel's seminal work (1821), and involves the conceptualisation of civil society, the state and (only provisionally) the private sphere (7§2) as co-existent moments of bourgeois society, derived from the sociation–dissociation contradiction grounded in the value-form. This is in contrast to Hegel's conceptualisation of phases in the historical working out of the Idea through family, civil society and the state (Kortian 1970: 198; cf. Hegel 1821: §181). Civil society is the development of competitive society with the appearance of the state. As Marx put it: 'Civil society embraces the whole material intercourse of individuals within a definite stage of development of productive forces. It embraces the whole commercial and industrial life of a given stage' (Marx and Engels 1902/3: 57). Hegel's characterisation is perhaps even more to the point: 'civil society is the battlefield where everyone's individual private interest meets everyone else's (Hegel 1821: §289A – the German 'alle gegen alle' seems to be a direct reference to Hobbes's famous phrase); and 'In civil society each member is his own end, everything else is nothing to him. But except in contact with others he cannot attain the whole compass of his ends, and therefore these others are means to the ends of the particular member' (Hegel 1821: §182A). The well-known passages in Marx on the English Factory Acts make the point of the indifference of the valorisation processes to the individual existence of particular labourers (Marx 1867: Ch. X). Hegel also argues that existence is necessarily continually under threat in competitive society (even when crisis-free reproduction occurs), and that such reproduction is prone to cyclical crises of over-production, exacerbating the precariousness of existence (Hegel 1821: §243–5; see also the discussion in Plant 1984: 232; and 5§6 above).

c. The object of theory in §7 also bears some similarity to the classics of European political philosophy in both the 'social contract' and 'natural rights' traditions. With hindsight, it is possible to see that these approaches share a basic methodological inadequacy in the postulation (either as an historical fact or as a thought experiment) of some kind of pre-social 'state of nature' from which can be identified eternal natural human rights which are paradoxically under threat in the unrelenting atomistic competition of that natural world. The state is then either derived directly from these natural rights or it is conceived as arising (in history or in its intellectual legitimation) from a rationally entered social contract by which perfectly self-conscious denizens of the state of nature agree to subject themselves to the authority of a superior social subject (see Hobbes 1651; Locke 1690; Rousseau 1762). The major advance of the value-form theoretic approach is that it is concerned to grasp the state from the competitive economic core of civil society. Of course, no developed bourgeois social system was available to classical political philosophy, so it is a mark of their genius that the more competitive versions of the classical state of nature bear an uncanny resemblance to competitive society. Specifically, value-form theory grounds property and ideal existence right in the existing socioeconomic system, rather than in some postulated pre-social state of nature.

§8. Subjectless regulation and the state as social subject

With the transcendence of competitive society into civil society and the state the object of theory has been expanded to grasp bourgeois society divided along an axis between competition-dominated civil society and the state. Right cannot be reproduced within competitive society and therefore it is contradictory. The doubling of competitive society into state and civil society provides the form of existence of this contradiction.

Civil society is determined by the *subjectless* economic processes of valorisation and accumulation, reproduced by the generalised structures of commodity production and exchange and the income seeking activities of competition subjects in competitive society regulated by the market. The state is particularised as the *social subject* legitimated to intervene in, and thence negate, the subjectless processes of civil society in pursuit of what it conceives as the general interest. The existence of the state is grounded first by its positing right as law (§9), and secondly by its legitimation in the will of its citizens (§10).

Addenda: a. The universality of the state-form; b. The price system

a. It is crucial that the state as a form is universal. This is how it must appear to the consciousness of bourgeois subjects if it is to maintain its legitimation (§10) by their consent (via the inner state – see §12). Contrary to Hegel for whom the state was the *concrete* universal (Hegel 1821), for us its universality remains abstract, maintaining its existence only in separation from civil society (§11). The emergence of the state (conceptually) does not resolve the conflict between value-form processes and the particular wellbeing of persons. To do so would involve some new organic *unity* in which the particular and the universal were reconciled. Instead questions of general wellbeing are relegated to a *separate* entity, the state. In Marx's (albeit historical) account, within the bourgeois epoch 'Political emancipation was at the same time the emancipation of civil society from politics, from even the *appearance* of a universal content.' So civil society was left with 'the *unbridled* movement of the spiritual and material elements which form the content of his [egoistical man's] life'. Hence 'He was not freed from property – he received the freedom of property. He was not freed from the egoism of trade – he received the freedom to engage in trade.' (Marx 1844b: 233). In other words, the freedom of property and to trade became, in principle, universalised.

In contrast to the universality of rights and their expression in the form concretised in the existence of the state, the moment by which isolated, dissociated particular needs and labour are made social (associated: 1S3) in civil society is an abstract universal, maintaining the fragmentation whilst mediating it (Hegel 1821: §192). For Hegel, civil society is subjectless in that it is 'an association of members as self-subsistent individuals in a universality which, because of their self-subsistence, is only abstract' (Hegel 1821: §157). And so there arises the need for the state, a political and administrative power representing the universal and public interest (cf. Kortian 1970: 205).

b. It should be emphasised that market forces do indeed regulate the economy. The particular size of any specific money price or income agreed upon has an element of contingency, nor can any particular competition subject be sure of success in deploying their income source. It is nevertheless the case that the tendential reproduction of valorisation (see the account of pre-commensuration in 1§8 and of the articulation of the tendencies of accumulation in Chapter 5) also thereby allocates resources to the production of use-values as commodities for the (however inadequate) satisfaction of consumers' and producers' wants. However, the price system, to use the conventional economic terminology, is inadequate not only to the production and distribution of use-values but also – and in principle – to the reproduction of the system at the level of value: the systemic tendencies of accumulation may threaten the reproduction of the valorisation processes (Part Three). To the extent that orthodox economics theorises market failures intrinsic to the system, to which the state must address itself (see, for example, Baumol 1952) it also recognises this state of affairs (for a rigorous but non-technical overview see Hahn 1982).

---

§9. Right and law

The state as social subject is further particularised as universal defender of individual right and sanctioner of individual wrong. The sanctioning of wrong invariably involves interference with the rights of the wrongdoer, something which no *particular* individual subject could rightfully do. It must therefore fall to the state as the *universal* social subject. The state then is the bourgeois state insofar as it acts to maintain the forms of competitive freedom, which it does by *positing right as law*. The state is the definer, identifier, arbiter and punisher of wrong and the arbiter of conflicting claims to right. It is the concretisation of right at the level of the state and civil society (see 8§§2 and 3). The state protects and upholds right from outside civil society.

§10. Legitimation and the citizen

The state is next grounded in its legitimation by the will of subjects to submit to it, since it universally protects their rights.

The state's activities are legitimate to the extent first that they are within the form of law (§9), and secondly that they derive ultimately from the will of competition subjects. The legitimation of the state in the will of subjects is a concrete expression of the existence of abstract free will (§1). Concomitantly the bourgeois subject gains a further determination as a *citizen* of the state.

The state exists to defend subjects' rights to property and existence against wrong, into which the conditions of competitive society will tempt them. Nevertheless the state's activities should not subvert the conditions for the working of market mechanisms, since these provide the context in which freedom of property and the pursuit of income can reproduce the processes of valorisation to which the needs of particular existence are subordinate. This means that the state is, in its fundamental determination, concerned with the protection of private property and the facilitation of its unhindered deployment in pursuit of rightful income. Yet the state must also be concerned to determine what constitutes the legitimate ways in which it can seek to actualise the otherwise only ideal right to existence, in order to maintain its legitimation by the consent of citizens.

§11. State–society separation and political versus social reproduction of right

The intrinsically concrete determination of abstract right as particular right to existence, to which the value-form processes are in themselves indifferent can be only formally satisfied as a political right enforced by the state. The conflict between the value-form and the particular right to existence is not overcome in their grounding, but rather *concretely separated*: value-form processes are confined to civil society whilst the actualisation of right is delegated to the separate state. The processes of valorisation proceed in civil society, within the context (see 8S1) set by the state including the defence of property and existence rights and arbitration between conflicting rights. Civil society embodies a mechanism by which competition subjects are regulated, namely the invisible hand of market forces; those aspects of the totality not adequately coped with by this mechanism fall to the (sometimes conscious) regulation of political and administrative mechanisms within the state.

The state stands above and outside opposing particular interests to provide the context within which unconsciously regulated competition can proceed. It must then impose itself as a separate social subject wielding power over subjects; it confronts them and demands loyalty and obedience on pain of sanction. The implicit co-operative and communal aspects of personal relations find only this alienated expression in the state (see also 7S1). The state satisfies these aspects as if it were external to civil society, in the form of politics. For the bourgeois subject there is no emancipation from the force of valorisation and from bourgeois right – no social emancipation – rather, co-operative and communal demands find their expression only in an alienated form of existence – the form of political emancipation.

Addenda: a. Separation in classical political philosophy; b. Marx on separation; c. Separation and market forces; d. Separation and abstract right

a. The argument that the form of separation is necessary to bourgeois society is common to many classical political philosophers. For example, Locke (1690) argues that the emergent competitively individualistic society required an impartial arbiter in the form of the state, which is to defend individual liberty by guaranteeing private property. The value-form theoretic approach shows how the defence of property right does indeed reproduce bourgeois civil society with its fragmented individualism and market domination, with communal aspects of social relations hived off to the, necessarily separate, state. Modern liberalism sometimes tends to collapse any distinction between state and civil society, conceiving them as a unitary legal and institutional framework within which individuals pursue their self-interest (cf. Pelczynski 1984a: 7).

b. For an account of this form of separation in Marx's early writings, see Marx and Engels (1902). For example: 'Through the emancipation of private property from the community, the State has become a separate entity, beside and outside civil society' (Marx and Engels 1902: 80). That Marx and Engels considered that the contradictions of competitive society give rise to the emergence of the separate state is also clear: 'And out of this very contradiction between the interest of the individual and that of the community the latter takes an independent form as the *State*, divorced from the real interests of individual and community, and at the same time as an illusory communal life' (Marx and Engels 1902: 53). (The term 'illusory' here should be read with care in English: the forms of consciousness in which the state is grasped may leave everyday consciousness in oblivion of their connection with value-form processes, nevertheless they affect social processes.)

c. The form of separation is derived by Holloway and Picciotto (1977) directly from the needs of capital accumulation, in a manner which we have described as (economistic) functionalism. Eldred (1984a) is the first author to derive the state–civil society relationship from the value-form determined processes of valorisation. One of the authors (Williams 1982 and 1985a) has earlier characterised the functional division between market and state regulation in terms redolent of welfare economics. The state is seen to step in to arbitrate those conflicting interests which cannot be, or in fact are not, harmonised by the market. Apart from the functionalism of this approach, it rests on the assumption that markets do indeed harmonise conflicting interests. Sen (1983) has argued persuasively that markets function effectively only where there is already some perceived communality of interest, conflicts always requiring some external mediation. To maintain them as the immutable conditions of existence of humankind, the economic laws of civil society must be kept separate from the broader aspects of human aspirations, which must therefore be located in the separate sphere of the state and/or the private sphere (7§2; cf. Ilting 1977b: 222).

d. The necessity of the form of separation is already implicit in the concept of abstract right (§1a): 'The legitimation function of forms of abstract right in Hegel's *Philosophy of Right* is thus twofold: they serve as the philosophical foundations of the rule of law in the modern state, and they justify practices of exchange in the market places' (Benhabib 1984: 160). The 'market place' alone is not adequate once the existence of subjects has been recognised in the presentation because 'That which is intrinsically non-alienable, first and foremost the public right of individuals to be recognised as persons, and all that personality entails, cannot be subject of contract' (Benhabib 1984: 163). The contradiction between subjective particularity and objective universality is transcended in the doubling of competitive society into civil society and the state. With it, the contradiction is not eliminated, rather it is resolved into a form in which it can exist – the form of separation (Hegel 1821: §184; cf. also Kortian 1970: 199).

§12. Separation-in-unity: the outer and the inner state

Subjects, in their abstract free will, will the state as the protector of their property and existence (§10). This legitimates the state to intervene in the subjectless process of valorisation and accumulation as universal social subject (§8). However, whilst subjects will the state, the latter's activities are nevertheless experienced as an externally imposed power, conflicting with their freedoms of property and person (§10). It is a condition of the legitimation of the state that as the social subject it stands outside the individual competitive struggles of civil society. The absence of any social subject within civil society is also a condition of existence of the dominance of the value-form and its reproduction via subjectless market mechanisms. Both the legitimation of the state and the acceptance of economic forces as immutable laws thus have as a condition of their existence the form of *separation between state and civil society*.

It is a condition of the legitimation of the state that it be perceived, in all its institutions and activities, as the manifestation of the will of people. For consciousness of free will to be maintained subjects must feel themselves subject, ultimately, only to the dictates of their own will, however mediated. Whilst the egoism of civil society leads citizens to will the *imposition* of state regulation in the name of the general interest, at the same time their self-interest as competition subjects leads them to will that these impositions impact elsewhere than on themselves. The relationship between the state and civil society is thus one both of necessary separation and of necessary *unity*.

This contradiction is grounded in the doubling of the state into the *outer state* (that which has been presented hitherto) and the *inner state*, by which the consent of the people to legitimate interventions is to be reproduced without subverting the necessary form of separation. With this doubling the existence of the state takes the form of *separation-in-unity*.

The necessary particularisations of the legitimate outer state in the bourgeois epoch are that it confront its citizens as universal social subject (§8), reproducing right as law (§9) whilst maintaining separation-in-unity. The specific concretisation of the inner state is contingent. One such concretisation is bourgeois constitutional democracy, with its separation of powers, system of representation without mandation and professional, rule-bound, neutral civil service. The universal nature of the outer state as social subject, legitimated by the will of bourgeois subjects that it uphold their rights of property and existence, is then manifested institutionally in the inner state by the separation of powers of the legislative, executive and judicial branches. The *legislature* frames and enacts laws which are the outcome of parliamentary debate couched in terms of what is to be deemed to be in the general interest. The *executive* carries out the provisions of these laws, whilst the *judiciary* identifies and adjudicates on any alleged breach of them by citizens, within and without the apparatuses of the state.

It is important that this particularisation of the inner state as bourgeois democracy is contingent. The systemic necessity lies in the form of separation-in-unity, so that whilst separation is maintained, citizens have formally to consent *in some way* to the state. The necessity for this consent does seem to have the most obvious affects on the state's activities and structures in the case of bourgeois democracy. It is also the case that the formal equality of competition subjects before the 'economic laws' reproducing the value-form is most clearly reflected in an inner state structure embodying the formal equality of citizens before the law and as enfranchised voters. Subsequent reference to *contingent* aspects of separation-in-unity will therefore be to the bourgeois democratic form.

Addenda: a. Hegel; b. Marx; c. Consent and democracy; d. Bourgeois democracy; e. Von Flatow and Huisken

a. Hegel is the seminal reference for the relation between outer and inner state (Hegel 1821: §§183, 230ff). Knox (Translator's foreword to Hegel 1821: xi) summarises succinctly the necessary separateness of the outer state and the role of the inner state in constructing a consciousness of identity: 'In civil society, the law which defends the security of property and enforces contracts is regarded as an external force; in the state the law receives its content from parliament and so is the law of the citizens themselves.'

b. The manifestation of the form of separation-in-unity in the democratic mechanisms of the inner state is expressed thus by Marx:

> The deputies of civil society are constituted into an 'assembly' and only in this assembly does the *political existence and will* of civil society become *real*. The separation of the political state from civil society takes the form of separation of the deputies from their electors. (Marx 1927: 193)

And: Modern philosophy

> considers the state as the great organism in which must be realised juridical, moral and political freedom and where the individual citizen, in obeying the laws of the state, only obeys the natural laws of his own reason, of human reason. (Marx, in Easton and Guddat (eds) 1967: 130, amended translation)

Marx in his critique of Hegel (for example, Marx 1927 and 1844) also argued that particular (capitalist) interests are presented 'as if' they were the general interest. Whilst we do not disagree with the substance of this critique, our methodological imperative not to separate being and consciousness (0§5) would lead us to characterise this formulation of it as only an *external* critique. An internal critique would show how capitalist interests – or, more abstractly, the value-form – are reproduced via the state as the general interest.

c. A somewhat less academic source emphasises the ultimate consent required for the actions of even the least democratic modern state: 'Nations won't change their national policies unless and until people change their private policies. All governments, even Hitler's, even Stalin's, even Mussolini's are representative' (Huxley 1936: 155).

d. The phenomenal expressions of the bourgeois inner state and the fine detail of the related state–civil society relation are diverse. Typically, voters (equal as enfranchised citizens, just as competition subjects are before the law and in their equal rights as persons) periodically cast votes to choose between competing manifestos as to what is perceived to constitute the universal interest. The political party, alliance, coalition or presidential candidate which wins this electoral competition then forms a government to direct the institutions of the state to put into practice its perceived vision of the general interest by legislation, administration and regulation. There also exist constitutional and procedural checks and balances, degrees of relative autonomy between branches of the state, written and unwritten codes of practice and mechanisms of management control and accountability designed to minimise the divergence between particular and general interests (cf. Chapter 10).

e. Contrary to von Flatow and Huisken (1973), for value-form theory subsumed interests in common between all subjects do not of themselves constitute a general interest (Eldred 1984a: §74d). Since the state appears as the universal form, the general interest is what the state says it is, provided only that it maintains its own legitimation by winning support so that that which it acts upon and articulates as the general interest has sufficient (as determined by the specificities of the inner state) support from citizens in terms of their perceived common interest. However, if the state is merely concerned with the management of perceived and agreed common interests of citizens (as von Flatow and Huisken would have it) then there can be no necessary expression of the contradictions of the capitalist economy at the level of the state's concrete practice. Nor can the intrinsic limitations to the state's attempted transcendence of the antinomies of competitive society for particular existence imposed by the form of abstract right be theorised. Von Flatow and Huisken cannot provide conceptual mediations, basing the contradiction between state form (separation-in-unity) and state activities (Chapters 8–9) on the fundamental contradictions between the value-form and the natural imperatives of production/consumption of useful objects (cf. Blanke, Jürgens and Kastendiek 1974; Hirsch 1974). For value-form theory the constraints imposed on the state by the needs of capital are *internal*. They are to be grounded in particular policy objectives which the state may set itself from time to time as universal social subject, upholding the rights of property and existence.

Only at the level of subjectivity can 'interest' be introduced, so that revenue forms, and thus the interests associated with them, provide the link from the level of the bearers of economic relations (character-masks) to that of subjectivity (from which the state can be developed). This differs fundamentally from von Flatow and Huisken in arguing that the necessary form of the state has to be derived from a more fundamental level of abstraction than the 'surface' of bourgeois society at which they start (if by 'surface' is meant concretised everyday perceptions or 'forms of appearance'). In fact, the 'surface' metaphor is inappropriate in terms of the methodological imperatives of form theory, which involves a systematisation of perceptions (everyday consciousness and fragments of more mediated consciousness) rather than some kind of archaeology of hidden moments and tendencies underlying the surface of everyday life. The point, then, is that what is determined by the abstract moments of the totality are the necessary forms of consciousness of the persons of the bourgeois epoch (cf. Eldred 1984a: §74c). Without this mediation von Flatow and Huisken are reduced to 'adding on' subjectivity to character masks, reducing the latter from social relations in all their interconnectedness, to objects which can be owned (cf. Eldred 1984a: §74d; and Reichelt 1974). The antagonistic distributional interests of property and labour are not merely part of the concrete surface of bourgeois society. They are rather an aspect of *competitive society* in which the fundamental distinction between property and labour as income sources emerges on the basis of the prior doubling of the production process into valorisation and technical labour processes. Competitive society is not the (concrete) surface of the bourgeois totality, rather it exists at an abstract level. (Here, of course, we disagree with Marx, also – cf. Marx 1894: Part VIII.)

A frequent, justified, criticism of von Flatow and Huisken in the literature is that, despite their attempt to distance themselves from the 'simple commodity production' approach, they are unable to theorise the fundamentally different and antagonistic interests of holders of income sources. In then trying to theorise the contradictions between the value-form and the natural imperatives of production/consumption of useful objects, von Flatow and Huisken come close to reverting to the errors of economistic capital-logic, since they can mediate the surface interests of revenue holders with the logic of the bourgeois epoch only *externally* by asserting that, in the end, the common (and thence, for them, general) interests are constrained by the needs of capital, and so by the interests of capitalists (cf. Jessop 1982: 120–1). As von Flatow and Huisken themselves point out 'simple commodity production' cannot be the point from which the conceptualisation of the bourgeois state is to be developed, precisely because that notion cannot capture the antagonistic class structure of the capital relation. Bourgeois society is not characterised by the communality of interest characteristic of a social system in which each trades only the products of their own labour. Such a conceptualisation obscures the fundamental difference between property-income sources and the labour-income source (§4). Systematic presentation enables the presentation of the most basic moments of the totality first, but without positing any possibility of their autonomous existence. There is no suggestion that competitive society (generalised capitalist commodity production and exchange together with the existence of abstract free will) is some historically pre-existent phase of development.

SUMMARY

In the presentation of the economy (Chapters 1–5), subjects have had only an implicit and contradictory existence as the bearers of economic relations – subjects without subjectivity. In this chapter, it has been argued that the structural determination of association through the value-form in the bourgeois economy is in contradiction with the existence of free will and subjectivity, since the value-form is indifferent to the reproduction of particular subjects. This contradiction is transcended in competitive society, the unity of the abstract capitalist economy and the abstract social existence of free will. The bearers of economic relations and of abstract free will are concretised as competition subjects. These are subjects with the abstract free will to deploy their income sources in pursuit of income within the constraints of the opportunities offered by the value-form determined economy. There are two (nominal) classes of competition subjects: subjects of property-income sources and those of labour–income sources. These classes are the expression at the level of competitive society of the categories determined in the capital relation. The specificities of labour as an element of valorisation and production are manifest here as the peculiarities of labour power as the income source of last resort inseparable from the subject (§4).

The existence of the competitive society of competition subjects has been grounded in the rights to property (§3 and *4) and to existence (§5), whereby the competition subject is determined as bourgeois subject. However, at this level of abstraction the bourgeois subject has only an abstract (ideal) right to existence: existence is continually under threat both from the indifference of valorisation and accumulation to particular subjective existence and from the internal antinomies of those processes (§6). The right to existence is contradictory at the level of competitive society. The transcendence of this contradiction lies in the doubling of competitive society into civil society and the (outer) state (§7).

Civil society is determined by the subjectless economic processes of valorisation and by the income-seeking activities of competition subjects, in the context of the separate existence of the state. The state is determined as the universal social subject which upholds the universal rights of property and existence (§8). The existence of the state is grounded first in its positing of right as law (§9), and secondly in its legitimation by the will of bourgeois subjects whose consent depends upon their perception that the state is upholding their rights as constitutive of the general interest – i.e., in universal forms (§10). Nevertheless, the right to existence is still only a formal political, not a substantive social right (which would be to transform the epoch from one based on the value-form to one based on some kind of reconciliation of self-production and dissociation within society). In order to maintain its universal form and yet cope with the intrinsically particular nature of existence right, the state must maintain itself separate from civil society, hence the formal nature of the reproduction of existence as a political right. The value-form is the specifically bourgeois mode of association which is to overcome the contradictions of self-production; but the right to existence has

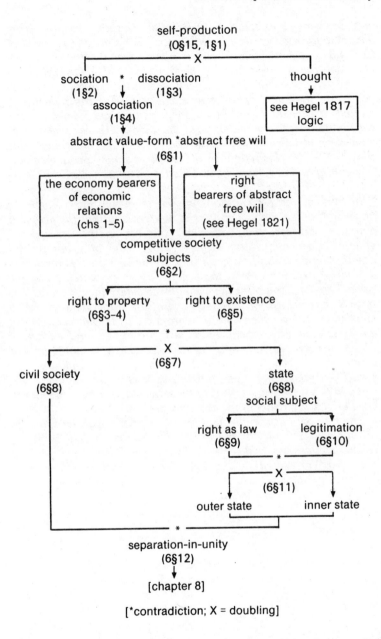

Figure 6.1 Explication of the contradiction between the abstract value-form and abstract free will: separation-in-unity.

only an alienated existence at the level of the state, separated from the value-form processes of civil society. For the consciousness of free will to be maintained, subjects must feel themselves subject ultimately only to the dictates of their own free will. Yet the egoism of civil society leads bourgeois subjects to will the imposition of state activity in the name of the general interest. This contradiction is grounded in the doubling of the state into outer and inner state, and concomitantly the determination of the state–civil society relation as separation-in-unity (§12). The mechanisms of the inner state may contingently be concretised in the shape of bourgeois democracy. The conceptual development of Chapter 6 is summarised in Figure 6.1.

In outline, the presentation now encompasses society and the (inner and outer) state. The state is bourgeois in that the people it represents are essentially bourgeois subjects, in their two determinations as competition subject (with rights of property and negative existence) and citizen. This basis for the state ensures that in defending private property, the negative right to existence and the value-form, it is reproducing value-form determined society. The state is thus the form determined expression of people's will. At a more concrete level, the totality is reproduced by the market forces of the system of generalised commodity production and exchange. Those aspects of relations which necessarily cannot be, or contingently are not, reproduced in civil society – which are not reducible to the cash nexus – fall, at this level of abstraction, to the state. In this way the legitimacy of the state and the apparent natural-law like characteristics of the economy are reproduced.

The foundations are now laid for the further particularisation of the subject, civil society and the state (Chapter 7) and further to concretise the state–civil society relation. The form of the state has been here presented at the most general and therefore most universally valid level, which is then to be concretised in the forms of policy initiated in Chapter 8.

Chapter seven

Particular Subjects, State and Society: the Private Sphere and Many States

PRELIMINARY REMARKS

The reproduction of labour is necessarily separate from production in the economy (Chapter 1). Further concretisation of this activity has been only implicit in the presentation so far, in which bourgeois society has been conceptualised as constituting (and constituted by) the public social relations of the economy, civil society and the state; the focus has been rather on the material reproduction of bourgeois society. The notion of individuality has been only implicit, in the contradictory notion of self-production (Chapter 1), which has so far been transcended only by social activity and the existence of society (Chapter 6). It is made more explicit in this chapter, but it is not concretised and therefore we have no criteria adequate to the method to judge the accuracy of its location at this point in the systematic presentation.

The starting point of much bourgeois social science in the mere positing of empirical individuals, with no attempt to query their conditions of existence, has been implicitly (and explicitly – 6§5a) criticised. There is an apparent conflict in a society conceived of merely as the aggregation of given atomised individuals, yet in which individuality – surely in part at least the product of socialisation – is supposed to be possible. Our introduction of individuality here can only be abstract, the presentation making no pretence to grasp the concrete individual in all its (inherently) concrete complexity. The contradictory existence of individuality within the private sphere stems on the one hand from its material existence, and on the other from the consciousness of free will (the empirical existence of which is presupposed in most bourgeois social science).

The state and civil society are also further contingently particularised in their existence as a multiplicity of states, and concomitantly of national civil societies. There exists no developed

Marxist theory of nation, nationality and nationalism, and we do not attempt to provide one here. Rather we attempt only to articulate the intrinsically world-wide value-form processes with the de facto existence of the state only as many states. Since there is no world state – and, notwithstanding such institutions as the United Nations, the World Bank and the International Monetary Fund, apparently no other effective world-wide social subject – states are potentially conflicting. Since there is no apparent world-wide general interest, nation-states have to define and defend their own national interests. Yet this is all within the context of the universal scope of the value-form which is imposed on states both by world-wide market forces and by bilateral and multilateral agreements orientated around free trade.

SECTION 1   THE PRIVATE SPHERE AND INDIVIDUALITY

§1. Particular subjects and individuality

The bourgeois subject is the concretisation of the abstract bearer of socioeconomic relations and the bearer of abstract free will (6§§1–2), endowed with the particular rights of property and existence (6§§3–5). With the introduction of the state the bourgeois subject is further particularised as the (alienated) citizen, necessarily separate from its existence within civil society (6§§9–11). It is now provisionally proposed that the particular subject is endowed not only with subjectivity but also with (abstract) *individuality*. This individuality derives from the consciousness of free will (cf. Hegel 1821: §37), which is 'the will of the subject as a single individual aware of himself' (Hegel 1821: §106).[1]

§2. The private sphere

The introduction of individuality also provides a concretisation of the notion of *communality*, so far only implicit in sociation (1§2) and association (1S3; 6§1), and thus also a concretisation of dissociation (1§3) within bourgeois society (6§2). Individuality can have no concrete existence in the public spheres of civil society and the state. Since particular subjects' individuality derives from free will (6§1),

---

1 The introduction of individuality here is no more than a provisional proposal intended to fill out the presentation of bourgeois society. Note that we use the terms subject, person and individual quite differently from Hegel. We rely on Hegel without any guarantee that his insights have been adequately grasped in the presentation.

one moment of the existence of individuality is in what may be called the *private sphere*. Cf. Hegel's account of 'the family':

> The family, as the immediate relationship of mind, is specifically characterized by love, which is mind's feeling of its own unity. Hence in a family, one's frame of mind is to have self-consciousness of one's individuality within this unity as the absolute essence of oneself, with the result that one is in it not as an independent person but as a member. (Hegel 1821: §158)

The private sphere, which is necessarily separate from the bourgeois economy (1§9; 2§10b), is the site of the consumption of commodities in pursuit of the reproduction of particular subjects on a daily and inter-generational basis (1§3). The bourgeois economy and the private sphere are thus interdependent for their material reproduction (though even the private and economic spheres together are still not adequate to the existence of particular subjects – 6§7). There is thus an element of value-form determination of the private sphere.[2]

The existence of individuality in the private sphere thus has two contradictory determinations – abstract freedom of will and the value-form – deriving from different moments of the totality. Their transcendence will consequently be highly complex. Provisionally it may be taken to be both inherently concrete and contingent, involving an account of the interconnections of the perceptions of everyday private life, such as family, friendship, love relations, procreation, child-rearing, housework, leisure, recreation, as well as their gender-specific divisions.[3]

Addenda: a. Separateness of the private sphere; b. Marx on the three moments of the object-totality

a. It should be noted that it is a characteristic specific to the bourgeois epoch that the private sphere, which in earlier epochs might have been an integral part of civil society, partaking in commercial and industrial life, is separated off as an area of social life.

b. For Marx, the state, civil society and the 'private sphere' constitute a totality since 'the political state cannot exist without the natural basis of the family and the artificial basis of civil society' (Marx 1844a: quoted in Ilting

---

2 It is this 'economic' determination which is one-sidedly stressed by the 'human-capital' approach of orthodox economics.
3 Value-form theorisations of the private sphere can be found in Hanlon 1983 and forthcoming PhD; and Kleiber 1981.

1984: 106). However, equally within the bourgeois epoch the private sphere cannot exist without the state and civil society, nor the latter without the two former.

§3. Society and individuality

The diremption of the social whole into three spheres – civil society, the state and the private sphere – has its counterpart at the level of individuality. The bourgeois subject (whatever its income source) is fragmented into competition subject, citizen and private subject. The bourgeois *person* is this (fragmented) unity.

The competition subject partakes in the economic core of civil society, competitive society. It is driven by egoism and economic calculation in competition to deploy its income source successfully. That success is measured along a single dimension – value. In the face of the value-form determined processes of competitive society, each competitive subject equally partakes of the abstract free will of the sphere. Relations between competitive subjects are reduced to the abstract universality of the cash nexus. This is the bourgeois person in its 'sensuous, individual and immediate existence' (Marx 1844b: 234).

The citizen partakes in the attributes of abstract, alienated communality – politics – and non-arbitrary rationality of the state. The citizen is driven by the striving for the satisfaction of the communal and co-operative aspects of itself neglected in civil society, to bring about its version of the general interest and to defend its property and its person. Success is measured along multidimensional aspects of communality, but only in the alienated form of politics. In the face of the state as arbiter and enforcer of the general interest, all citizens are typically equal before the law and as enfranchised voters. The relations between citizens are not substantively communal, but rather formally political in that citizens relate to each other only through the political processes of the state. Their communal interests are imposed as the general interest, by the state. This is the bourgeois person as 'political man ... simply abstract artificial man, man as an allegorical, moral person' (Marx 1844b: 234).

The private subject partakes in the search for personal, interactive, co-operative, altruistic and multidimensional relations in the private sphere. It is driven by the attempt to reproduce itself in all its individuality – to overcome the lived antinomy between communality in the alienated form of politics and the value-form determined association of civil society. Given the objectively fragmented basis of the bourgeois person there can be no success in this pursuit – only tenuous, momentary solace from the demands of civil society and the state in the residual subjectivity of the private sphere. This is because the individual must venture out of the private sphere into civil society as competition subject in order to gain incomes and buy commodities; and into the state in order to attempt to realise its social nature and to defend its property and person. Relations between private subjects are overlaid with the multiple dimensions which find no place in civil society and the bid to overcome the alienation of communality in the state, and with the doomed striving to overcome the forcible sundering and alienation of individuality and communality into civil society and the state respectively.

These three major determinations of the person in the bourgeois epoch constitute only a provisional proposal for a substantive theory of the existential conditions of concrete individuals. That theory itself is beyond the scope of this book.

Addendum: a. Marx and Hegel

a. The reflection of the separation of state and civil society in the alienation within the individual of the communal from the existential aspects of its being is made clear in Marx's discussion of religion:

> the spirit of the *state* where man behaves – although in a limited way, in a particular form and a particular sphere – as a species-being, in community with other men ... has become the spirit of *civil society*, the sphere of egoism and of the *bellum omnium contra omnes*. It is no longer the essence of *community*; but the essence of *difference*. It has become the expression of the *separation* of man from his *community*, from himself and from other men (Marx 1844b: 221; cf. 1927: 149).

> Just because individuals seek *only* their particular interest, which for them does not coincide with their communal interest ... the latter will be imposed on them as an interest 'alien' to them, and 'independent' of them as in its turn a particular, peculiar 'general' interest ... On the other hand, too, the *practical* struggle of these particular interests, which constantly *really* run counter to the communal and illusory communal interests, makes *practical* intervention and control necessary through the illusory 'general' interest in the form of the State. (Marx and Engels 1902: 53–4)

These two moments of the person are forcibly torn apart, 'Actual man is acknowledged only in the form of the *egoistic* individual and *true* man only in the form of the *abstract citizen*' (Marx 1844b: 234). So that:

> Where the political state has attained its full degree of development man ... lives in the *political community*, where he regards himself as a *communal being*, and in *civil society*, where he is active as a *private individual*, regards other men as means, debases himself to a means and become a plaything of alien powers. (Marx 1844: 220)

Relatedly, as Pelczynski 1984b: 270) argues, Marx insists that the so-called natural rights of man were in actuality the rights of fragmented, egoistic competition subjects, which can be conceived as 'natural' only if the essence of humankind is reduced to the moment of its existence in competitive society. Here alienation's basis in private property (which Marx had at this time not yet traced back to its foundation in the value-form) is also explicated:

> private property is the material sensuous expression of *estranged human life* ... The positive supersession of *private property*, as the appropriation of *human* life, is therefore the positive supersession of all estrangement, and the return of man from religion, the family, the state, etc., to his *human*, i.e. *social* existence. ... economic estrangement is that of *real life*. (Marx 1932: 349)

Marx's fragmentary insights on these matters clearly owe a lot to Hegel for whom, in the family, the individual self-consciousness is of self only as part of a unity; in civil society, particularity triumphs over universality and the self is conscious of itself only as a separate, independent, selfish agent; and in the state self-consciousness is to regulate nature and society in accordance with the rational pursuit of self-determination. Nevertheless for Hegel, the individual limited to private interests will necessarily perceive the state as an external imposition whilst it also guarantees the existence of civil society in which these interests find their expression (cf. Ilting 1977a: 105).

SECTION 2   THE EXISTENCE OF THE STATE AS PARTICULAR STATES

§4. National civil society and the state

The contradiction of abstract value-form and abstract free will (6S1) has been transcended in competitive society (6S2) and its doubling into civil society and the state (6S3), whose interrelationship is grounded in separation-in-unity (6§12). Bearers of economic relations and of free will have concomitantly been developed into bourgeois persons – the unity of competition subject, citizen and private subject.

Bourgeois society can be further concretised by its de facto existence only as many particular *national* bourgeois societies, determined by characteristics of a geographical, ethnic, linguistic, traditional, religious, ethical and psychological nature. The particular legal, historical and political constellation of these characteristics determines the particular existence of civil society as *national civil society* and respective state. This determination is based on the one hand on the universal value-form processes of valorisation and accumulation (implicitly world-wide in scope), and on the other on particular national forms of free will, right to existence and individuality. It is thus the particular nation which is a focus of loyalty and unity for the bourgeois person, whose will thus legitimates their particular state.

Whilst value-form processes are implicitly world-wide, seeming to require a single world state, the concrete condition of existence of the reproduction of the monodimensional value-form determined totality lies only in the multidimensional *complex of many states*.[4] Abstractly, the value-form is indifferent to national boundaries. More concretely, it is nation-states which reproduce the social context (Chapter 8) in which the value-form determined totality can be reproduced. The world economy is fragmented into many economies embedded in national civil societies within which particular states have jurisdiction. These multidimensional aspects of national civil society and national state restrict the existence of the universal social subject (6§8) to that of one of a number of potentially conflicting social subjects.

Addendum: a. Marx and nationalism

a. When nation and state coincide nationalism can act as a cohesive moment for the state. Conversely, when they do not, nationalism can become a disruptive force *vis-à-vis* the state. It has been argued that for Marx nationalism was an existent political force which had to be taken into account in political practice as a potent focus of revolutionary struggle against foreign domination, and that such liberation was seen as a precondition of economic, social and political development. It was not, however, something that should or could be grasped in terms of the value-form (Pelczynski 1984b: 277-8). It has been speculated that as an enlightenment thinker Marx perceived that the progressive effects of rationalism, even in the alienated forms of liberalism and free competition, would eventually disperse nationalistic loyalties and conflicts (Berlin 1972: cited in Pelczynski 1984b: 262). Relatedly, Marx adopted from Hegel the notion of civil society as an essentially universalising and cosmopolitan influence which would overcome nationalistic rivalries. The concrete existence of bourgeois society only as particular nations has been incorporated into our systematic presentation. A provisional proposal for the theorisation of nationalism along the same lines might seek to derive it from the conflict between civil society and the private sphere, since it is within the latter that the bourgeois person seeks solace from the one-

---

4 Notwithstanding that these are mediated by some shadowy fragments of world-state entities such as various United Nations agencies, the International Monetary Fund (IMF) and World Bank, the European Economic Community and the General Agreement on Tariffs and Trades.

dimensionality of the former so that the multidimensionality of individuality and the private sphere is reflected in the determinants of nation.

§5. The state and the national interest

Given the existence of civil society as a multiplicity of civil societies (§4), the general interest in accordance with which the state acts (6§12) must appear in the form of many *national interests*, each of which confronts each other as a means and potential obstacle to its own realisation. Competition subjects will the realisation of their own rights by the actions of their own state in accordance with its own definition of the national interest. Money-capitalists and entrepreneurs typically expect their state ultimately to defend their interest against the activities of other states. Labourers look to their own nation state for the defence of their rights as persons against any infringement by other states.[5]

Addendum: a. State and many social subjects

a. The presentation of the state as many states occurs at a more concrete level of abstraction than the derivation of the state from value-form determined competitive society, which is indifferent to the multiple determinants of nationality. Civil society thus:

> has ... a homogenizing tendency. It creates a social world in which national, cultural and historical considerations are secondary or irrelevant, where 'abstract universality' reigns supreme, a world theoretically epitomised by the rational economic man of the classical political economists and happiness-maximizing individual of the Benthamite utilitarians, as well as the burgher or member of civil society as Hegel portrays him in his *Philosophy of Right* [Hegel 1821]. (Pelczynski 1984b: 264)

So that:

> modern man is not only a member of the abstractly universal civil society of producers and consumers or contracting legal persons [competitive society] but also a member of a specific, ... national community existing within a political framework. He is also a member of the 'concrete universal' of a political community and in one way or another participates in (as Hegel [1821] puts it) 'the concrete life of the state'. (Pelczynski 1984b: 265)

So the transition which is being outlined in this section concerns that from the state which arises along with 'The conception of civil society ...

5 Different national interests are the different, politically successful conceptions of how the rights of the different national citizens are to be actualised, defined (amongst other things) by the different norms of what constitutes an adequate rate of reward for the deployment of labour (cf. Marx 1867: 524).

grounded in a universalistic, cosmopolitan and rather abstract view of man and society ... without reference to national factors', to the recognition that 'state power is generally a product of a ... nation, and that it often serves as an instrument for the protection of national values or of national self-assertion' (Pelczynski 1984b: 276).

§6. The lack of a world-wide social subject

Not only is the world-system of nation-states and national civil societies not subordinate to any superior world-level social subject, it is the only concrete manifestation of such a subject, required as a condition of existence of the world-wide value-form process. Particular states in their relations to each other are in a situation analogous to particular competition subjects in abstraction from the superior social subject, the state. That is to say their relations are based upon negotiations between subjects on the basis of agreed communality of interest and of the construction of a perception of mutual benefit, leading to bilateral and multilateral contracts of various sorts, including those substantiating mutual recognition. Like competition subjects, states operate within the abstract universal value-form processes reproduced by world market forces which determine the forms of their mutual interactions. But unlike competition subjects, there is for the states no superior social subject in the form of a world-state. Each state is in principle a *sovereign* state – there is no transcendence of these sovereign wills in a world-wide social subject. Without a world social subject there can be no concrete expression of any general interest transcending the national interests of the many states (§5). Without a world-wide social subject, with the legitimate (that is, consciously willed) monopoly of force to sanction their contracts, treaties, agreements and understandings, the relationships between nation-states are characterised only by the indeterminacies of evasion, cheating, lying, manipulation, bullying – in a word, wrong – so that these relations are continually threatened by conflict and ultimately war.

A state's ability to reproduce (and even extend) the scope of its national interest in this 'state of nature' is crucially dependent upon its relative – ultimately military – strength. In turn, this depends upon the economic strength of that segment of the world economy over which it exercises control. This economic strength then becomes a weapon in itself for the defence and extension of its national interest.

Addendum: a. Hegel and inter-state relations

a. The indeterminacy of inter-state as opposed to inter-personal relations arises for Hegel from the absence of a world-wide social subject over and above the many states: 'since there is no power in existence which decides in face of the state what is right in principle and actualises this decision, it follows that so far as international relations are concerned we can never get beyond an "ought"' (Hegel 1821: §330A; cf. §333), so that 'what is absolute in it retains the form of an ought-to-be, since its actuality depends on different wills each of which is sovereign' (Hegel 1821: §330). Hegel also makes the analogy with competition subjects (Hegel 1821: §332), whilst pointing out that, unlike a contracting person, 'autonomous states are principally wholes whose needs are met within their own borders' (Hegel 1821: §332). The autonomy of nation states is still conditioned less by the increasing economic interdependence of modern states as they become more and more integrated into the world-market, than by relative strength. Consequently, 'It is as particular entities that states enter into relations with one another. Hence their relations are on the largest scale a maelstrom of external contingency and the inner particularity of passions, private interests and selfish ends, abilities and virtues, vices, force, and wrong.' (Hegel 1821: §340; cf. §339).

An account of the historical development of the state might emphasise warfare rather than welfare as the primary determinant of the national state. Any value-form theoretic account of the 'warfare state' would start here, with the interplay of the indifference of the world-wide value-form processes to the reproduction of particular individual existence in particular geographical locations on the one hand, and the existence of many states on the other. The utility of appealing to alien threats in order to bolster the self-perception of national sovereignty is a cliché of attempts by governments to bolster their legitimation. Hegel grounds this kind of consciousness in the conditions for the existence of the state as an autonomous social subject (Hegel 1821: §322). As another commentator put it: 'Hegel's conception of nationality ... made an essentially political factor – sovereignty or independence – the central feature of nationhood' (Pelczynski 1984b: 276). Hegel also comes close to deriving the necessity of a supranational world-state but, being Hegel, he contents himself with a world-mind: 'The state in its actuality is essentially an individual state ... is a moment in the very Idea of the state, ... States as such are independent of one another, and therefore their relation to one another can only be an external one, so that there must be a third thing standing above them to bind them together.' (Hegel 1821: §259A).

SECTION 3   SOVEREIGNTY, INTERNATIONAL COMPETITION AND MONEY

§7. International competition

The value-form, and the implicitly world-wide compulsions of valorisation and accumulation, are reproduced at a more concrete level by market competition (cf. 1§6, 2S4). Entrepreneurs and money-capitalists compete within world-wide markets, as to a lesser extent do all competition subjects. Nevertheless, the existence of national economies with national levels of development constitutes a series of obstacles to the world-wide formation of market prices (cf. 2S4), and therefore to the world-wide opportunities for pursuit of income (6§2).

Each state's ability to further its national interest and protect its citizens' rights are subject to the constraints and opportunities of the world-market enforced value processes. The different national economies are differentially integrated into the world economy. Within many national economies money capital tends to be more orientated towards world-wide value processes than industrial capital, which in itself is physically located within a national territory (not necessarily its own). The qualitative and quantitative extent to which national economies are integrated into the world economy affects the ability of the state to pursue its national interest over and against that of other states.

The existence of a structure of nation-states within a world-wide system of value-form determined processes paradoxically serves to enforce the imperatives of valorisation and accumulation upon national economies embedded in national civil societies, by reinforcing the intrinsic economic competition of the world markets with political rivalry between states competing for power and autonomy *vis-à-vis* one another.

Addenda: a. Competition or inter-state conflict; b. International value commensuration; c. International competition

a. For an attempt to introduce many states in a value-form theoretic account of the bourgeois state see Eldred (1984a: §§90–93). For a critique, see Williams (1984). It is a category mistake arising from the use of the same word to equate, as Eldred does, the rivalry between states for power and influence (or even for economic hegemony) with the competition between competition subjects (particularly capitalists) in pursuit of successful income source deployment. In contradistinction, our presentation does not conceptualise states competing on world markets but rather capitals, which may be based in one state and operate within another. The extent to which either the home base or the host state will support capitals based or operating within its territory will depend on that state's perception of its own national interest, which of course may have ramifications beyond its geographical boundaries (cf. Williams 1984).

b. The insight that national social and political relations form obstacles to the concretisation of the in-principle world-wide value-form processes is initiated in Williams (1979). As Marx put it in reference to money: 'The different national uniforms worn at home ... indicate the separation between the internal or national spheres of the circulation of commodities and their universal sphere' (Marx 1867: 125). And again in reference to national difference in the productivity of labour: 'The average intensity of labour changes from country to country; here it is greater, there less ... The more intense national labour, therefore, as compared with the less intense, produces in the same time more value, which expresses itself in more money' (Marx 1867: 525). Though this begs the question as to how these different values might be commensurated since they will be expressed in different currencies, that merely technical problem has now been resolved by the device of 'purchasing power parities'. Nevertheless these parities are still in part determined by the relationship between different currencies' exchange-rates, contingently determined by the overall relationship between national economies, modified by speculative activity and states' specific attitudes towards the international value of their currency. The translation between currencies at the official exchange rates need thus bear no systematic relationship to the relative values of any two commodities to be exchanged between the two economies. This is illustrated by the fact that the exchange ratio between any two commodities might be quite different if the exchange-rate transformations were carried out via a third currency. This indicates that such transformations appear not to be transitive – the market reproduction of world-wide value forms are interrupted at national boundaries (cf. Marx 1867: 525).

c. The insight that international competition exacerbates the excesses of capitalist competition over the production and sale of commodities is also initially Marx's: 'But as soon as people ... are drawn into the whirlpool of an international market dominated by the capitalistic mode of production, the sale of their products for export becoming their principle interest, the civilised horrors of over-work are grafted on the barbaric horrors of slavery, serfdom, etc.' (Marx 1867: 226).

§8. The lack of a world money

The form of existence of the state as many states modifies the scope of money from that of the universal general equivalent to that of a particular national general equivalent. Gold can act as an international means of payment but, since the quantitative extent to which such payment is achieved is contingent upon the price of gold in each of the two currencies mutually agreed by the payer and the payee and since value is purely quantitative form, gold is by no means an absolute universal equivalent (cf. 1S4, 2S2). Since there is no world state nor even a world monetary authority, gold as world money is contingent upon universally agreed principles for gold parity, if not upon a set of parities tied to the price of gold. These principles and parities, like other relations between states, are ultimately conditioned by negotiated contracts, agreements and treaties and are therefore subject to all the multiple determinants of the 'state-of-nature'-like inter-state relations (§5). The structure of the world monetary system thence depends on the ability of a state or group of states to maintain hegemony over, or the community of states to maintain agreement on, such a structure of parities and gold prices.

Addenda: a. Marx and international money; b. Historical versus conceptual development of money; c. Hayek and international currency; d. Nation and national currencies

a. Here we disagree with Marx when he says: 'When money leaves the home sphere of circulation, it ... returns to its original form of bullion' (Marx 1867: 141). In fact, this is a manifestation of a wider disagreement as to the basis of money in the bourgeois epoch. Where Marx seems to derive it historically from commodity money, we do so from the value-form (1S4). If money is conceived of as commodity money and concomitantly value as embodied labour, then it is possible to theorise a self-regulating economy. If money is conceived of as essentially the form of value, then the presentation is forced to proceed to the introduction of the state as monetary authority if it is to theorise a holistic, self-subsistent object-totality. Similarly, we cannot agree with Marx when he asserts that 'In the trade between the markets of the world, the value of commodities is expressed so as to be universally recognised.' Nor, *a fortiori*, that 'Its real mode of existence in this sphere adequately corresponds to its ideal concept' (Marx 1867: 141), since this 'ideal concept' would entail a world-state (or at the very least a world monetary authority). Indeed, in a footnote to this last statement Marx elaborates the grounds of our disagreement by referring to the necessary interventions of the state in the working of any bullion standard. He mentions Sir Robert Peel's Bank Act of 1844, imposing regulations on the Bank of England, and notes that those regulations were based on 'The value of silver ... estimated at its price in the London market' (Marx 1867: 141n), a contingent quantitative determination in relation to money as the general equivalent. No doubt the extent to which England dominated the then existent bourgeois world may have made sterling a temporary world-money in effect, and the sterling price of gold and silver the determinant one but, as subsequent developments indicated, this was a passing contingency. Of course, it was the strength of the British economy which underlay sterling's world position, but that does not quantitatively determine the exchange ratios between commodities in any universally commensurable manner.

It can be argued that historically Marx saw the evolution of money and the evolution of national state power as related developments (De Brunhoff 1973: 45-6; cf. Marx 1859: 150), so that 'As soon as the precious metals become objects of commerce, the universal equivalent of everything, they also become the measure of power between nations' (Steuart, quoted in Marx 1859: 150). However illuminating such historical arguments, for the value-form approach the determinants of the bourgeois totality are to be conceptually not historically derived.

b. An appeal to history, as not being methodologically decisive, offers no support for a conception of the world economy as a self-regulating regime based on commodity money. Gold (and later silver as well) certainly emerged as an international means of circulation along with expansion of commodity exchange in Western Europe from the fifteenth to the nineteenth centuries. Certainly, also, the emergent national currencies of the emerging network of states and city-states were partly convertible. But intra-nationally they had from the beginning a fiduciary element, and inter-nationally their parities were the subject of inter-state rivalry, negotiation and agreements (cf. Marx 1939/41: 130–1, 133; De Brunhoff and Bruini 1973: 125; Edwards 1985: 168–9). In the nineteenth century, the sterling gold standard which evolved was by no means an automatic regulator of world economic relations. Rather, it was dominant from its basis in the credit transactions of the City of London, backed by the power of the British state (Edwards 1985: 169). From 1922 onwards the (US) dollar gold standard was similarly dependent on the international dominance of the US economy and the US state (Edwards 1985: 170). During this period, even the fetishised form of appearance of any absolute standard of value was gradually eroded by the removal of the pound's convertibility in 1931, the Bretton-Woods agreement in 1944, the postwar expansion of foreign holdings of US dollars by private banks, the collapse of the Bretton-Woods parities in 1971 when dollar-convertibility was suspended, the short-lived (14 months) Smithsonian agreement on new and more flexible parities, the declining hegemony of the dollar as reserve currency in the face of the yen and the Deutschmark, the further expansion of unregulated Eurodollar (and other 'offshore' currency) markets in the 1970s, the declining influence of national central banks' (and of the IMF's) influence over the world monetary system and the concomitant increase in international flows of footloose money capital, destabilising exchange rates and relative interest rate structures (cf. de Brunhoff 1976: 48).

The lack of a world-wide social subject in the face of the essential need for such a subject to back a world money means that the world monetary system is still prey to the contingencies of the conflictual relation between states (De Brunhoff 1976: 49). With parities and gold prices subject to market forces within macro-currency markets plus national-policy determined interventions mediated only by ad hoc and occasional bilateral and multilateral agreements, there can be no systematic international commensuration of commodities, only intra-national commensuration and contingent external relations internationally. For perceptive remarks on the analytical history of money, see de Brunhoff (1976: 38–60).

c. Even the radical liberal Hayek has to conclude that neither gold nor any autonomous working of international currency markets can provide automatic regulation of the world economy: the gold standard's 'operation rested on its being an international standard, and if, for example, the United States today returned to gold, it would chiefly mean that the United States policy would determine the value of gold and not necessarily that gold would determine the value of the dollar' (Hayek 1960: 335). Even if bullion and currency markets could be totally liberalised, 'the control of the value of this standard would still be in the hands of the authorities of the biggest countries participating in it' (Hayek 1960: 522).

d. National currencies cannot be comprehended as only economic phenomena. Like the nation itself they are determined by historical, traditional, geographical, ethnic, linguistic, religious, ethical, psychological, legal and political factors which complicate the analysis of national policy towards the currency. Regimes of 'dirty floats', cross-cut with partial treaty and other agreements are an aspect of a period of increased atomistic conflict between nations in a time of recession in the world economy. The absence of world money has even, on occasion, resulted in reversion to barter between nations (De Brunhoff 1976: 52). The crux of the matter is that any such world money will be an arbitrary and transient thing in the continued absence of a world monetary authority, backed by the power of a world state. The (always imperfect) bearer of the role of world-money is arbitrary, not because it has no historical cause, not even because such cause is not economically based, but because it depends ultimately on the conflicting sovereign wills of the world's nation-states.

SUMMARY

The particularity of the subject (Chapter 6) has been provisionally concretised with the proposed introduction of individuality, deriving from the consciousness of free will. The private sphere is then contradictorily determined by, on the one hand, the material reproduction of particular subjects, necessarily separate from the bourgeois economy and, on the other, by the existence in it of individuality. The bourgeois subject has thus been constituted as the fragmented unity of private subject, competition subject and citizen, reflecting the diremption of bourgeois society into the private sphere and the public spheres of civil society and the state.

Bourgeois society has been further concretised in its particular existence as national civil society and respective nation-state, determined by a complex of characteristics. Individual subjects seek to express the communal aspects of their being both in their retreat into the private sphere and in these specific national characteristics. The state is the universal social subject, but that social subjectivity has existence only in the particular restricted sovereignty of each of a multiplicity of potentially conflicting states. Whilst the value-form is intrinsically world-wide, its social and political conditions have existence only in this fragmented form. Separation-in-unity thus receives further determination from international competition within

201

the world economy, and from the existence of the universal general equivalent, not in the form of a world money (which would require a world state), but only as a multiplicity of national currencies.

Chapter eight

The Mixed Economy and Economic Policy

PRELIMINARY REMARKS

As well as being partial and local, analyses of the state's economic activities to date have focused on the content of such activity and neglected its forms. None of them seems able to theorise adequately state activities in the interests of society as a whole, which are resisted as much by the leaders of industry and commerce as by the labour movement, which often seem incapable of resolving economic problems, and yet which do appear to achieve (or at least not destroy) the reproduction of the value-form determined totality (cf. Holloway and Picciotto 1978: 2). The central methodological problem which has dogged Marxist attempts to theorise economic policy has been their inability to incorporate coherently the economic 'needs of capital', the existence of many capitals, the apparent consent of workers to their continued exploitation, the doctrine of the antagonistic class structure and the universalist forms of the state. (See Williams 1982, where all these objects of analysis are identified, but not synthesised into a systematic theory.)

The value-form theoretic way forward is to focus on the contradictory form of separation-in-unity (6§12), derived from the contradictory unity of value and use-value in the commodity (Parts Two and Three). Indeed, the guiding thread of the remainder of the presentation is the attempt to present the, ever-more interventionist, forms of the state–civil society relationship. Economic policy is a key moment of the contradictory unity of civil society – dominated by value-criteria, and the state – with its rights-based concern to ensure, in principle, universally adequate use-value criteria in bourgeois society. Chapters 8–10 indicate the outline of a systematic, general theory of the economic, social and political determinants of economic policy in the bourgeois epoch. They ground the value-form processes theorised in Part Three and the necessary state forms

203

outlined in Chapters 6–7, each of which is itself derived from the account of the value-form in Part Two. The aim is to provide the conceptual basis for fleshing out the state forms with an account of the institutions, actions and policy stances by which the state attempts to actualise the imperatives of the value-form and its own status as the rights-based state.

The political form of the inner state in which the contradictions of separation-in-unity are grounded has been argued to be contingent (6§12 and addenda c and d). One typical, widespread and appropriate form is bourgeois democracy, which is also that political form in which the necessary concern of the state with the rights of its citizens is most overtly expressed. Whilst we have by no means derived bourgeois democracy as the necessary grounding of the value-form through the capitalist economy, competitive society and separation-in-unity, we have indicated that it is one possible grounding. In the course of the following chapters the presentation of the more concrete contingent *conditions of existence of the bourgeois epoch will refer to the kinds of policies which are more overtly typical of bourgeois democratic states (or those with aspirations in that direction). Nevertheless, it is implicitly the claim of our presentation that the concrete expression of those moments presented as* necessary *conditions of existence of the bourgeois epoch are indeed effective in other political forms for bourgeois society: that the states of such societies – however undemocratic, repressive and authoritarian – are confronted with the need continually to manage the manifestations of the antinomies of the mixed economy, including their neglect of the rights-based imperatives of the bourgeois state. Repression is, of course, a mode of management, however unstable. Whether this implicit contention that bourgeois societies of all political forms face similar antinomies – the manifestation of the necessary conditions of existence of the value-form – is correct, can be assessed only by a value-form theoretic conjunctural examination of such a society (see Part Six for an indication of how this might proceed).*

The state's existence is derived from its grounding the rights of property and person in competitive society. It has already been shown that the economy is not self-sufficient. The contradiction of the universal social subject necessarily separated from that which is subject to it (and in addition determined by its existence as but one of many states embedded in the world economy – 7SS2–3; see 10§§1 and 2) is transcended in the social context for the economy (S1). As separate, universal social subject the state is able in principle to uphold right and sanction wrong, and to uphold the conditions for the market reproduction of the economy within which persons as

*competition subjects seek, in the first instance, the reproduction of
their existence by deploying their income sources. However, even as
a mere social context the state requires material reproduction, for
which it is dependent upon civil society, since it is itself in principle
separated from the production of value. This dependence is
ultimately expressed in taxation (S2). In providing the social context,
the state cannot maintain itself separate from civil society. The transcendence of this contradiction is in the concretisation of separation-
in-unity as the mixed economy (S3). But the contradictions of the
mixed economy – of law and labour law, of money and of infrastructure – have themselves to be grounded in policy and in the state
as its agent (S4).*

*There is one rival approach to our systematic theory of the mixed
economy which deserves special mention, and that is the systematic
liberalism typified by Hayek (1960, 1944; for other accounts see also
Nozick 1974; Friedman 1962 and Niskanen 1973). Unlike that of
more pragmatic, middle-of-the-road analysts of economic policy,
Hayek's account is well located in a coherent conception of the
totality of the liberal society, based upon a free-market economy. In
its most adequate versions systematic liberalism is based upon the
single abstract postulate of the moral primacy of negative individual
liberty over all the moral imperatives. From this is developed the
necessity of free markets, and a concomitant preference for
minimisation of the purview of the state. The strength of this
approach is that it does not hesitate to integrate moral imperatives
into its holistic logical grasp of the nature of society. However, value-
form theory is able to show that this systematic liberalism neglects
the essential interconnection of the putatively transhistorical
imperative of political individualism and the value-form within the
historically specific bourgeois epoch. It is blind to the threats to
effective individual liberty from the value-form determined processes
of the capitalist market economy, which are at least as significant as
those from the impositions of the liberal democratic state.*

SECTION 1   THE SOCIAL CONTEXT FOR THE ECONOMY

§1. Subjectless regulation and the state as social subject

The economic kernel of civil society is subjectlessly regulated by the
invisible hand of the market, reproducing the value-form (6§8). The
state is the social subject standing necessarily outside civil society, yet
legitimated by the will of citizens to intervene in these subjectless
processes in pursuit of what it conceives as the general interest
(6§10). Since the state has existence only as many states embedded in

the world economy (7S2), its universal social subjectivity is restricted to that of a particular sovereign (7S3).

The contradiction of a universal social subject which has to remain separate from that over which it is to exercise its subjectivity (and which is concretised only as a particular sovereign) is transcended in the first concretisation of separation-in-unity (6§12) – the constitution by the state of a *social context* of institutions and practices, within which subjectless regulation by the economic forces of the ubiquitous structure of markets can operate. This is particularised in the forms of law (§§2–3), the constitution of money as legal tender (§4), and infrastructure (§5).

Addendum: a. Hayek and the state

a. The great liberal theoreticians, and particularly the Austrian school of pro-market economists, have a very clear notion as to which state activities are compatible with the logic of liberal capitalism, and which are potentially threatening to it. The former include the contextual activities of government which provide, but do not impose – beyond those impositions within the rule of law (§2) – the necessary framework for the market to function adequately (see, for example, Hayek 1960: 222–3).

---

§2. From right to the rule of law

The state in the bourgeois epoch is grounded in the will of bourgeois persons that their rights as property holder and person be upheld (6§10). In the competitive struggle of civil society persons are tempted into the violation of the rights of others – that is into wrong (6§9). The state as upholder of right must therefore enact, promulgate and enforce rules in accordance with its view of how best to prevent wrong. Right as determined in competitive society is enforced in civil society concretely by the state, in the first instance in the form of law. The prevention and sanctioning of wrong is primarily a question for criminal law. However, the law of contract, which substantiates the right to hold and deploy property by regulating the processes by which it is alienated in exchange (typically by buying and selling for money), may be enforced by processes either of criminal or of civil law.

In the event of conflict of right the market forces of competitive society may be unable to operate. At the level of competitive society (civil society in abstraction from the state) as between equal right ultimately only force can decide. Within the bourgeois totality the state as the universal social subject (6§8) must have a monopoly of the legitimate use of force, and therefore has the role of arbitrating and ultimately deciding in case of conflict of right. As well as the civil law generally, within which the courts operate to arbitrate between conflicts of right, there may also be quasi-legal and sub-legal institutions for arbitration and settlement of claims. Administrative bodies concerned to regulate economic activitiy in such areas as safety and consumer protection are also determined primarily as arbitrators between conflicts of right not resolved by market mechanisms. The relations of civil society may also leave it unclear as to where right or obligation (the necessity to act so as to respect others' rights implicit in the universality of the form of right) in fact lie. The legal and arbitrational activities of the state must thus provide for the clarification of right.

The state provides a detailed context in which right can be legitimately exercised. Hence as a *framework* the content of the law must be oriented round the reproduction of private property and of the negative right not to have one's property or existence usurped by the deliberate or negligent action of any other particular person. Persons as property-owners will the state as the promulgator and enforcer of the rule of law, which is itself in accordance with the forms of right in that it is rational, universally enforced and treats all persons as equal before the law. In competitive society competition subjects were formally equal as income source holders and bearers of the rights of person and property. This formal equality reappears at the level of the state as the equality of all citizens before the law – the rule of law.

Addenda: a. Right and law. b. Equality and the rule of Law; c. Law and policy; d. Property and liberty; e. Historical versus conceptual development of the state

a. The transformation from right to law is expressed thus by Knox: 'Universal and particular, form and content, appear in civil society to fall apart ... but none the less the pursuit of private ends here turns out to be conditioned by universal laws. These are implicit to start with (as the laws of economics), but they become explicit later as a system of laws and institutions for the protection of private property and as barriers against private selfishness' (Knox 1942: 353).

b. 'Equality before the Law' is not the usual defining characteristic of the rule of law, which is rather characterised as the absence of constraint of citizens other than in accordance with non-arbitrary and non-discretionary existing regulations (laws). However, equality before the law can easily be shown to be equivalent to the rule of law in this sense. Freedom from arbitrary, discretionary constraint by the legitimate force of the state implies that citizens are equal before the law in the sense that they are equally subject to existing law. That is, the extent to which the law may be invoked to sanction their behaviour depends only on the extent to which they fall under the pre-existent universal categories to which particular laws apply. Equality before the law does not, of course, entail that citizens are concretely all equally subject to the sanctions of every law. This exactly reflects the formal equality of competition subjects, which precisely does not entail concrete economic, let alone social equality (cf. 6§11).

Contemporary political science and legal theory also utilise a notion of separation in order to maintain formal equality of citizens in the face of social inequality (see, for example, Kahn-Freund 1968 and 1972). The abstract equality of citizens before the law is real in terms of their abstract equality as competition subjects before the value-form. The strength of the law is that it reflects that real equality and reproduces it. Its weakness is that it is blind (necessarily) to the real social inequalities concomitant to the regulation of economic activity by the value-form.

c. The legal and the policy (S4) aspects of the state cannot be totally disentangled – as witness the economics-law literature in such areas as (de-) regulation and industrial relations (see, for example, *The Journal of Law and Economics*, various issues). Our purpose here is to show the close link between the rights of property and person (based on the economic level – competitive society), and the rule of law (as an aspect of the rights-based state). Systematic liberal theorists make it quite clear that the consciousness of individual right is at base an assertion of the need for individualistic economic freedom: 'The classical argument for freedom in economic affairs rests on the tacit postulate that the rule of law should govern policy in this as in all other spheres' (Hayek 1960: 220). The guiding thread of Chapters 8–10 is the attempt to present the ever-more interventionist forms of the state/civil society relation, which increasingly tend to diverge from the rights-based state's subjection to the rule of law (cf. Hayek 1960: 222). The basic contradiction between state and civil society re-emerges at this more concrete level as the tension between the rights-based rule of law and economic freedom of competitive subjects on the one hand, and economic policy on the other. Unlike with Hayek, however, the principle of individual economic freedom as the highest good is not postulated but rather has been derived from the value-form determined nature of contemporary society and grounded in its conditions of existence.

d. The radical transcendence of liberal conceptions of the relationship between property and personal liberty implied by the presentation should be noted. For liberal theories the right to property is a defence of the right to personal liberty (negatively conceived) against the encroachment of the state. For the value-form account the right to property and the right to existence (negative) of such subjects are derived from the value-form, yet are in contradiction with it, so calling into being the state. No doubt the liberal concept was efficacious in the democratic struggles against the absolutist state, but in the bourgeois epoch the ideal right to existence is at least as much under threat from the value-form determined processes of the economy in civil society. Where classical liberalism derives property rights from some pre-existent human or natural right, value-form theory is concerned with the grounding of these rights in their concrete conditions of existence. Nevertheless radical, pro-market liberalism provides the clearest accounts of the necessity of the form of the rule of law for the reproduction of the value-form system by market forces (for example, Hayek 1960: 229). Whilst both social-democrats and 'one-nation' conservatives may see radical liberalism as a fetishisation of market forces, value-form theory shows that that fetishisation is not an aspect merely of one particular (radical-liberal) ideology, but is rather a form of consciousness of the logic of the value-form determined totality of bourgeois society.

e. The presentation here should not be confused with either the history of the simultaneous evolution of market relations and of the rule of law in the transition to the bourgeois epoch or the political-philosophic thought experiment whereby the state is justified as the outcome of some actual or hypothetical social contract between citizens (cf. 6§7c). Rather, from the standpoint of contemporary everyday consciousness, the state is continuously reaffirmed as the universal social subject by the will of persons. Hegel (1802–3), in his early writings, outlines the relation in history between the 'spread of formal, legal norms in social life and the emergence of market relations' (Benhabib 1984: 161). But, as Benhabib points out, the mature Hegel is concerned with the conceptual development of the forms of the state: 'When values like the security of property, the satisfaction of needs and the enjoyment of goods are universalised, relations in the ethical community come to be defined by the legal norms of formal equality among individuals' (Benhabib 1984: 161). Benhabib does not discuss the determination of the universalisation of these values by the value-form, being mainly concerned to differentiate the Hegelian account of the state from the social contract theories of such philosophers as Hobbes, Locke, Rousseau, Hume, Kant and Fichte. Like Hegel and Hume, we do not posit a real or hypothetical state of nature nor any real or hypothetical contract resulting in the legitimate state (cf. 6§7c). Rather, the state and the rule of law are developed from the conceptualisation of competitive society, and their notions are thus not dependent on the historical mode of their coming into being, however illuminating an account of that process might be.

§3. The capital relation and labour law

The capital relation, manifested in the contractual relation between capital and labour over the exchange of labour power (1§6; 2§10) is the site of endemic conflict of right derived from the conflict between the right to property and the right to existence, specifically that of those who, having insufficient property that can function as an income source, must rely on their universal capacity to labour (2§10; 6§4). This conflict is reflected in the body of labour law concerned with the legitimate conditions of employment, working conditions, restrictions on wages, the regulation of trades unions and the arbitration of industrial disputes. The specificity of labour as an element of production (1§9) and as universal income source of last resort (6§4), and thus the specificity of labour taking the value-form, reappears in the specificity of labour law.

§4. Money and the state

Money is the central motif of the bourgeois epoch, and yet cannot be reproduced within competitive society alone. It is the sole independent form of actualisation of value (1§7). This actual reduction of the multiple forms of use-values to a single dimension (1§5) is the sine qua non of the form-determined processes of valorisation (1S5) and accumulation (2S1). The all-pervasive nature of money is the actualisation of the form-domination which characterises the bourgeois epoch (0§14). Money as a value-form separate from use-value (or usefulness) makes valorisation and accumulation a possible and rational drive for bourgeois persons. Money, and the universal command of commodities that it endows, means further that labour ceases to legitimate any necessary title to property in the product of that labour: labour takes on the value-form of wage-labour (1§6) – of labour power sold as an income source for money (6§4).

The substantial bearer of the value-form is an historical contingency. For example, gold has acted as money only because it exhibited various convenient physical qualities, as well as having acquired over historical time certain mystical attributes which make it contingently suitable to be grasped by the essential money-form. Money is not a commodity, because its essential characteristics cannot be reproduced by capitals regulated by market forces. Whatever physical characteristics may be built into a commodity to make it suitable to act as money, they cannot ensure its essentially *social* reproduction as the universal equivalent form of value. Within competitive society the socialising moment is money-regulated generalised commodity production and exchange, but the reproduction per se requires a social subject – the state.

Clearly the physical production of notes and coin is not an essential role for the state. Rather the state is to enforce the framework of money as legal tender. All competition subjects are legally obliged to accept money in payment of debts, for the sale of commodities, and as income. More generally, the state must ensure that money can act as the general equivalent form of commodities, which entails that it attempts to ensure an orderly relationship between money and the generality of commodities (cf. 9§4). The state reproduces the monetary framework primarily through the 'bankers' bank' – the national central bank and its legally enforced status

(2§10), as well as through financial regulatory agencies. It will be concerned to reproduce the supply of money necessary for expanding circuits of capital (2§6) and for the financing of its own material reproduction (S2), and to prevent cumulative bank failures by ensuring that action is taken to cope with banks and other financial institutions threatened with illiquidity and insolvency (5§§6–10; see also 2§9, and 9§§4 and 9).

Addenda: a. Marx on money; b. De Brunhoff on money; c. Hayek on money

a. In spite of his false, commodity money starting point (1§7a), Marx locates the necessity of the state to the reproduction of money in the contradictions of (commodity) money itself (Marx 1939/41: 150): 'Since the standard of money is on the one hand purely conventional, and must on the other hand find general acceptance, it is in the end regulated by law' (Marx 1867: 102, 125). Whilst he appears to conceive paper money as a mere symbol of bullion, it becomes clear that the 'law peculiar to the circulation of paper money' relates the quantity of paper money to the quantity and prices of commodities available for circulation – that is, the total quantity of value – which is quite independent of any gold standard (Marx 1867: 128). Marx's further argument against those (like Fullarton) who wished to argue that state-enforced paper was as efficacious as gold in fact consists of an account of the potentially inflationary consequences of over-expansion of the quantity of money (for our account of inflation, see 5S3), regardless of its physical shape. It is, of course true that if people believe that money should be bullion-backed, then the rate at which bullion can be imported and ultimately extracted from the ground may act as some constraint on the possibilities for states to undermine their currency by undisciplined monetary management. But that does not constitute commodity money as the essence of money (Marx 1867: 128–30). Marx himself concedes that, within a state's jurisdiction: 'this token [paper money] must have an objective social validity of its own, and this the paper symbol acquires by its forced currency. This compulsory action of the State can take effect only within that inner sphere of circulation which is coterminous with territories of the community' (Marx 1867: 129–30).

b. De Brunhoff (1976: 37) argues for the necessity of the state to the reproduction of money since '[t]he political and social effects of money are dependent on its economic nature as an expression of the division of society into autonomous economic individuals' (De Brunhoff 1976: 47). The state's management of money as the general equivalent involves the management of the articulation between the three moments of the 'monetary pyramid' (De Brunhoff 1976: 40–3): private credit money, constituted by the relation between industrial capital and money capital (2S2; 5§§7, 8); national currency, constituted within the jurisdiction of the state by the relations between private banks and the central bank, which issues such money (or at least regulates such issues) (2§8); and international money, constituted – however fragilely and contingently – by relations between central banks (more or less subordinated to states), and mediated in part by international institutions such as the International Monetary Fund (7§8). In addition to the limits on the state's monetary power imposed by the social power of money (Marx 1867: 132; cf. De Brunhoff 1973: 47) and by the monetary power of other states, there is also the specific power of the banking system of money-dealing capital (Marx 1894: 404; cf. De Brunhoff 1973: 121). As social subject, the state has reason to establish a hoard, which is quantitatively of a much higher order than the hoard of even the largest capitalist (Marx 1859: 150; cf. De Brunhoff 1973: 46).

c. Even Hayek, notwithstanding his rejection of a state monopoly in fiduciary issue, perceives the necessity of a state (controlled) bank to manage money and credit systems, determine what is to be legal tender, etc. (Hayek 1960: 324–5, 520–1). The reason given by Hayek for the state's management of the monetary framework is, like Marx's, implicitly based on the notion of money as at best a 'peculiar' commodity: 'changes in the relative supply of money are ... much more disturbing than changes in any of the other circumstances that effect prices and production' because 'money, unlike ordinary commodities, serves not by being used up but by being handed on' so that 'the effects of a change in the supply of money (or in the demand for it) do not directly lead to a new equilibrium' (Hayek 1960: 325). 'Exactly the same applies if any part of the stock of money is destroyed, or even if people start holding larger or smaller amounts of cash in relation to their receipts and outlay, than they normally do' (Hayek 1960: 325–6). The point is that such changes in what Keynesians have termed liquidity preference are likely to be frequent, rapid and unpredictable and so may need to be countered by changes in the aggregate money supply. Under developed credit conditions 'not only will the supply of money not adjust itself to such changes in demand, but it will tend to change in the opposite direction', because 'the same considerations which will make people want to hold more money by lending produce fewer such claims, and vice versa' (Hayek 1960: 326).

§5. Infrastructure

The third particularisation of the state's constitution of the necessary social context for the economy is that of the infrastructural framework. There are elements of the (physical) framework needed by capitalist commodity production which cannot be – or contingently are not – reproduced in the value-form because they cannot be (or are not) sold at a price which will cover the costs of producing them together with the normal rate of profit. Relatedly there may be such elements which can be reproduced at a lower cost collectively than they can be competitively.

There are areas of state activity abstractly grounded in bourgeois right which, at a more concrete level, have an infrastructural determination with respect to the economy. The crucial use-values which are ubiquitous to capitalist industry and commerce but which are not adequately reproduced in the value-form fall into two groups: those which are determined at a more abstract level and have intrinsic non-commodity determinants, such as the pseudo-commodities money (§4) and labour power (Chapter 9; cf. 2§10); and those which are not so determined such as communications, transportation, utilities and energy. The determination of a use-value as infrastructural does not per se necessitate state intervention, nor does it determine the manner of that intervention. Such infrastructural elements may therefore be reproduced in the competitive economic sphere or by the state. Their production and distribution may be regulated or subsidised by the state, or the state may merely purchase them as commodities and redistribute them in a non-commodity form. Nevertheless, the category of infrastructure has real effects: unlike the generality of use-values, those which are infrastructural cannot be allowed to cease production without jeopardising the reproduction of the economy, and yet are peculiarly likely to be inadequately supplied (even purely on value criteria) because of some 'public good' or 'externality' characteristic.

Addenda: a. Public expenditure and infrastructure; b. Hegel and infrastructure

a. Economic analysis of public expenditure and the public sector is based to a large extent on a one-sided discussion of infrastructural items, analysed in terms of the commodity-form threatening categories of 'public goods', 'externalities', 'natural monopoly' and 'positional goods' (see Williams 1985b: 5). Classical political economy was also concerned with infrastructurally significant use values which could not be profitably reproduced in the competitive sector (see, for example, Smith 1776: ii, 180–1).

b. Hegel recognised that, as the principle of self-interest came to pervade society and as society became more complex, the need for state provision of infrastructural goods and services 'factors which are a common interest ... contrivances and organizations which may be of use to the community as a whole ... universal activities and organizations of general utility call for the oversight and care of the public authority' (Hegel 1821: §235).

SECTION 2   THE MATERIAL REPRODUCTION OF THE STATE

§6. Taxation

The condition of the state's existence as social subject constituting a social context within which the subjectless regulation by economic forces can operate (S1) lies in its material reproduction. Since the state is necessarily separated in principle from the processes of material reproduction located in the economic core of civil society (6§11), it must appropriate the means for its material existence from civil society by taxation, borrowing or charging for the services it provides. Sale by the state of its services as commodities conflicts with its form determination, and state borrowing must eventually be serviced from tax revenues. The contingency of these moments of the state's revenue raising determines the necessary existence of the state as the *tax state*. Taxation overrides individual property right. As the universal social subject the state may exact taxation, provided only that it does so legitimately in the name of the general interest (6§10). It is in keeping with the value-form that bourgeois state exacts tribute from its citizens largely in the money form of taxation rather than in the form of specific use-values or services.

Addendum: a. Hegel and money-form of taxation

a. Hegel argued that it is only if the services to be exacted 'are reduced to terms of money, the really existent and universal value of both things and services, that they can be fixed justly and at the same time in such a way that any particular tasks and services which an individual may perform come to be mediated through his own arbitrary will' (Hegel 1821: §299, cf. 299A). He also argues that resistance to the tax state is endemic in the everyday consciousness of the bourgeois person 'as injurious to their particular interest, as something inimical and obstructive of their own ends. Yet ... particular ends cannot be attained without the help of the universal' (Hegel 1821: §184A).

---

§7. The state as competition subject

To reproduce itself physically the state will trade commodities with civil society (cf. §6). In these trading activities the state acts not as the social subject per se but rather as a simple competition subject. Nevertheless its disproportionate size in commodity and money markets and the peculiar characteristics of infrastructural use-values mean that as competition subject the state will have a qualitatively different impact on civil society from that of ordinary competition subjects.

SECTION 3   CONTRADICTIONS OF THE MIXED ECONOMY

§8. The mixed economy

The relation between the state and civil society in the bourgeois epoch necessarily takes the form of separation-in-unity (6§12), so that the state must provide the social context for the economy (S1). The state exists, but is separated from the production of value so it must raise revenue by taxation (S2). The right to income derived from property and from the universal capacity to labour (6S2) is therefore diluted by the requirement for the material reproduction of the state. Rights of property upon which the functioning of civil society rests are modified by the state. It also follows that the reproduction of any particular state depends on the success of its economy (see 9§§3 and 9). With the grounding of the state as provider of the social context for the economy, separation-in-unity has contradictory existence as the *mixed economy*, which is further particularised in the conflicts of the rule of law (§9), of the monetary framework (§10) and of infrastructure (§11). The economy is 'mixed' in that it has been now constituted systematically by two conflicting principles – primarily market reproduced value-criteria, and use-value criteria reproduced primarily by political and administrative mechanisms.

Addenda: a. The state as sovereign; b. Offe and the mixed economy; c. Economics and the mixed economy

a. The contradiction of the value-form and state activities grounded in framework activities are inevitable consequences of the nature of the state as the universal social subject above which there exists no superior subject. For the state to be effective as an agent of policy (see S4 and Chapter 9), it must be vested with power and legitimacy which could threaten the dominance of the value-form. It should be noted, however, that the state can also be called to account not by some superordinate entity (since there is no world state) but by its own citizens on the basis of the alleged failure of the state to deliberate, decide and act in accordance with the universalistic principles adequate to its concept.

b. The writings of Claus Offe (for a recent collection in English see Offe 1984) on the manifest conflicts of the mixed economy are important here, and they draw together and synthesise a very broad range of work on the state. However, from a value-form theoretic standpoint, his method seems to be that of model-building, based on a fusion of Marxist sociology and systems theory. His argument is historicist and his apparent holism is structural-functionalist. What is offered is a definition of a model of a system which is a structure of three pre-existing sub-systems, which have to be articulated *externally* (0§5) in various relations of dominance, etc. on the basis of their functional efficacy in reproducing the whole system. What is more, the three sub-systems he offers are categorically different: the 'exchange system' and the 'state system' seem to be categorically on a par, but the 'normative system' cannot be confined to the 'family'. Even in purely functional terms the private sphere interpenetrates the other two systems. For these reasons, Offe's so-called 'contradictions' of the mixed economy-welfare state would very often be more appropriately termed 'conflicts' or 'tensions', since they are not located in a systematic conceptual structure (cf. 0§10). There also appears to be a conceptual divorce between the value-form and commodity-form so that the former pre-exists the latter. It is crucial that value is created in the process of generalised capitalist commodity production and exchange, expressing the conflict between the qualitative use-value aspect of the commmodity and its purely quantitative value aspect (Chapter 1) (see especially Offe and Ronge 1976: 119-29). The result of these conceptual inadequacies are a number of historicisms – assertions about contingent historical developments which ascribe to them necessity. However, it is not our intention to deny the insights of such work but rather to locate it within an account of the bourgeois totality. Offe's essays contain many thought-provoking descriptions and classifications of the tensions of the welfare state which came to a head in the 1970s, including many of the contradictions of the mere existence of the mixed economy in terms of the distinctive effects of taxation (as well as of intervention) (see, for example, Offe 1981: 149). In its detailed descriptions of some of the interrelationships between state and society and in its ingenious attempts to construct empirically testable predictions Offe's work is complemented, not negated, by ours.

c. In neoclassical economics the conflicts of the mixed economy are played out largely as the distortions of the trade-offs facing economic agents. As the exhaustive formalisations of welfare economics have demonstrated (for a seminal account directed at the implications for understanding the state, see Baumol 1952; for a more recent account see Levacic 1987: ch. 6), even the minimal existence of the state with the concomitant necessity for taxation will distort the trade-offs in whichever markets – capital, labour or goods and services – feel the ultimate incidence of taxes. There can be no such thing as a 'neutral lump-sum tax'. This has, of course, been recognised since the time of the classical political economists: 'there are no taxes which have not a tendency to lessen the power to accumulate' (Ricardo 1817: 95). '[I]f it do not act on profit, or other sources of income, it must act on expenditure' (Ricardo 1817: 106; cf. De Brunhoff 1976: 105).

§9. Conflicts of the rule of law: property right and the labour contract

The first particularisation of the contradictory existence of the mixed economy concerns the conflicts of the rule of law for civil society, which derive from the state as the universal social subject which can thus in principle introduce any content into the form of law that it can get through the apparatuses of the inner state (6§12). Although in itself the law is the adequate form of state activity *vis-à-vis* civil society, the state may, in pursuit of welfare, economic and other policy objectives (see Chapter 9), legislate against the logic of the value-form processes as long as it can pass such legislation off as being in the general interest. The law's tension with the value-form becomes most acute where it has to arbitrate between conflicting rights. Such conflict is centred around the capital relation – the site of the basic conflict between the capitalist's right of property and the labourer's right to existence – and thence is manifest in industrial relations, employment, labour and trades union legislation.

Labour power is not a commodity, although it is allocated as if it were (1§6, 2§10, 6§4). Being a peculiar 'commodity', labour power is a peculiar subject for a legally enforced contract. Contracts in general enable the ex ante fixing of a mutually agreed market price for the sale of a commodity by competition subjects, enforceable ex post by law. In the labour contract, labour law stipulates *in advance* conditions on the price and on the exact nature of what is sold,[1] enforceable ex post. Labour law places constraints upon the content of contracts, such as explicit or implicit minimum wages, requirements on the health, safety and other provisions of the working environment, and restrictions on capital's control over the labour and over the hiring and firing processes. Indeed there is controversy as to the extent to which such contracts should be legally enforced at all. In the contract between labourer and capitalist, control over the former's person is alienated to the latter, albeit for a fixed period. What is more, the labourer is systematically bound to enter such contracts in order to gain an income. The upshot is that the law is very often not in fact enforcing a contract between individual competition subjects, but rather providing the ground rules for a struggle between labour collectively and capital collectively. These rules constitute an impediment to valorisation without overcoming for labour the antinomies of the inadequacy of its income source. The contradictions of the right to existence (6§5) are displaced into the conflicts of the labour contract. The perceived neutrality of the law, and thus the legitimacy of the state, is subverted to the extent that it is perceived as treating inadequately either the rights of labour (predicated on existence) or those of capital (predicated on property).

1 Consumer and environmental protection legislation may act similarly in markets other than labour markets, but such laws do not, as far as we can see, have the same necessary value-form determinations – they are contingent.

The form of law cannot overcome the conflict between property and existence right, which is based ultimately on the contradiction between value and use-value. It can only pragmatically manage it. Periodically the rule of law is brought into question – and thus also the legitimation of the state – when the law appears to everyday consciousness to favour either capital or labour too overtly. The principle of both the value-form and the rule of law is concerned with the relations between abstractly equal individuals – competition subjects and citizens respectively. Labour law is concerned with conflict between concretely unequal collectivities – capital and labour. Labour law is therefore a contradictory form within the bourgeois epoch.

Addendum: a. Common and labour law

a. Just as the capital relation provides the crucial site of conflicting right so labour law, with its recognition of the right to combine, of collective legal subjects and of the existential import of the level of wages over and above their function as a market price, is in conflict with the rule of law and with the operation of the value-form determined market system. The theory of labour law is crucially concerned with the conflicts between the individual right to compete and the right to combine, reflected in the conflict between the provisions of labour law and the general principles of the rule of law: 'the common law knows nothing of a balance of collective forces. It is (and this is its strength and its weakness) inspired by the belief in the equality (real or fictitious) of individuals and it operates between individuals and not otherwise' (Kahn-Freund 1972; 2). Of course, the common law does not exhaust the law and does not play the same role in all bourgeois states as it does in the United Kingdom. What is more, statute law is perfectly capable of defining legally constituted agents which do not coincide with concrete human individuals. Nevertheless the conflict to which Kahn-Freund refers here may then reappear, for example, when an individual trade unionist goes to law to defend the right to work in opposition to the activities of the collective legal agent, the Union. The outcome of such a case will depend on the principle of the rule of law – non-arbitrary and non-discretionary imposition of legal sanction against each individual.

---

§10. Conflicts of the monetary context

Money, the sole autonomous manifestation of value, is essentially a social entity which cannot be adequately reproduced within competitive society. The state must therefore incorporate a central monetary authority (2§8). The state is concerned with monetary flows in two ways: it must provide the monetary framework for the market (§4) and it must manage its own finances (§6).

The state reproduces itself physically by necessarily monetary appropriations from civil society (S2). There are (underdetermined) limits to what the state can appropriate directly via taxation, but the state will enter financial markets as a relatively very large and powerful competition subject. Such massive appropriations of money by the state provide an alternative investment for money that would otherwise have remained within the circuits of capital, one in which it typically acts as mere revenue for the employing of labour unproductive of surplus value. This appearance of the state in the guise of capital is a threat to its separation from civil society. The state also has the power to expand the quantity of money ex nihilo (2§§7 and 8), either directly or via the monetary authority and the banking system, which may either socially validate successful private production (one of the bases of successful Keynesian multiplier processes – 9§3), or it may only pseudo-validate production, and so be inflationary (5S3). The exact impact of these monetary actions of the state depends, amongst other things, on how they are funded (as well as the state's explicit monetary policy – 9§4), but they may be expected to modify the cyclical fluctuations of the economy (5S2). The state is necessary to the reproduction of money as the general equivalent form of value, but the state as monetary authority is inextricably linked with the state as revenue raiser. In its role as monetary authority, reproducing money as the general equivalent, the state must act as lender of last resort, and at the same time attempt to manage the macroeconomic balance between monetary and industrial circuits of capital. The former role and the management of credit creation required by the latter may come into conflict. What is more, the pressures on state finance may tempt the state into monetary behaviour which undermines both the acceptability of money as the general equivalent and relatedly the control of credit creation. Facing such conflicting demands, the state's management of money is a source of threats to its legitimation by this or that group of competition subjects. To the extent that it acts largely to maintain 'sound money' it may be perceived by domestic industrial capital and the competition subjects dependent on it as neglecting their interests at the behest of internationally-orientated money capital (cf. 5S3). To the extent that it allows such demands to undermine the currency (through inflation and devaluation) the state may stand accused of disrupting the processes of wealth creation upon which it and all its activities depend. However much the state may attempt to disengage itself from civil society, monetary flows constitute an indissoluble nexus between the market regulated capitalist economy and the politically and administratively regulated state, which it is thereby condemned to manage as best it can.

Addendum: a. The neo-liberal view of state money

a. Hayek (1960: 336, 520–1) argues that the basis of the state's power to regulate money in circulation depends ultimately on the threat not to supply money, which it nevertheless has a duty to do as lender of last resort. What is more, Hayek sees it as an undesirable, contingent but pervasive fact that the size of the state sector effectively precludes the bourgeois ideal of a separation between the framework and active policy (S4) aspects of the state's monetary activities: 'an effective monetary policy can be conducted only in co-ordination with the financial policy of the government' (Hayek 1960: 327). He also argues that the central bank, as the monetary framework authority, will end up under state control. Even for systematic liberalism, the total 'depoliticisation' of the monetary framework would appear to be an unrealisable ideal.

---

§11. Conflicts of the infrastructure

The state's intervention in the allocation of resources to the production of what it itself determines to be infrastructural goods and services has a contradictory impact on civil society. It involves the first interpellation by the state of use-value criteria into the decision making of the competition subjects whose necessary logic is that of value criteria. Such intervention could thereby make space for the extension of use-value criteria over and above those conducive to the value-form determined processes of valorisation and accumulation.

The value-form basis of the bourgeois state determines that its activities be pursued in accordance with value rather than use-value criteria. This determination is concretely reproduced either by subjecting them directly to market forces or by the administrative imposition of value criteria. However, the state qua universal social subject necessarily must have the discretion to dilute these value-form imperatives. What is more, the existence of the state itself requires that it act in accordance with the general interest as it conceives it, to which the value-form dominated economy has been shown in the very derivation of the state to be inadequate.

In the production of that category of infrastructural use-values which it sells as commodities (typical examples being various forms of energy and communications – §5) the state appears in the guise of capital. However, in pursuit of revenues, or of some other policy objective (such as counter-inflation, or the provision of cheap energy for its domestic industry) the state will be tempted to use its relative size in the markets in which it operates to charge other than market prices for its outputs, and to pay other than market prices for its inputs. This may lead to disruption of the efficient reproduction of valorisation and accumulation by market forces. It is thus internally contradictory for the universal *social* subject to take on the guise of a number of *particular* capitals, since it is then confronted internally with contradictory imperatives: value criteria and use-value criteria. As the employer of (potentially) productive labour the state will appear to everyday consciousness as just another capital attempting to maximise its appropriation of surplus value to the detriment of the existence based rights of its workers and the property rights of its customers. This will tend to undermine the state's legitimation.

Addendum: a. Value and use-value criteria

a. The terms 'value criteria' and 'use-value criteria' were coined in an earlier work by one of the authors (Williams 1982) where, however, they lacked an adequate value-form theoretic basis. They are a concretisation of the contradiction of value and use-value at the level at which subjectivity, in particular the social subjectivity of the state, has been introduced.

SECTION 4   THE AGENT OF POLICY

§12. Antinomies of the social context

The law, money and infrastructure have been derived as elements of the social context within which market regulated resource allocation can proceed. This context is the grounding of the necessary form of separation-in-unity (6§12), which has its contradictory existence in the mixed economy (S3). If the state's interface with civil society could be confined to law and the actions of rigidly rulebound bureaucrats, lacking all discretion to discriminate except as a priori specified by law, this would adequately reproduce the abstract formal equality of the essential relationship between state and citizen. Such a situation would exactly reflect the state as the universal social subject, transcending the contradictions of competitive society by separating itself off as the guardian of those (universal) aspects of civil society not subsumed under the value-form processes. However, concrete separation cannot be maintained: the putative 'framework' itself has been shown to bridge the separation, manifesting contradictions within civil society and within the state (S3). The contextual activities of the state thus reproduce more concretely the contradictions which gave rise to them. By potentially putting use-value criteria on the social agenda, the power of the state could disrupt the value-form determination of civil society. To the extent that the state appears in the guise of capital as consumer, producer, borrower and lender it undermines separation-in-unity.

§13. The conscious social subject: the state as agent of economic policy

Because the state cannot in fact maintain its separation from civil society, the mere existence of the mixed economy is contradictory. This contradiction exists more concretely in *economic policy*. The state is then further determined as *the agent of economic policy*. Economic policy is constituted as active intervention by the state, from outside civil society, into the subjectless and unconscious regulation of the economy of property owning and labouring persons by market forces reproducing the value-form.

Economic policy, the presentation of the systematic socio-economic determinants of which was an objective of our work, has now been derived abstractly. Chapters 9 and 10 provide further particularisations of economic policy and indicate the further development to conjunctural accounts.

§14. The value/use-value contradiction and the state as the agent of policy

The state in principle assumes responsibility for maintaining the provision of those useful goods and services deemed necessary to the reproduction of the economy which are not adequately reproduced as use-values in the value-form (SS1–2; 6S3). The fundamental contradiction between use-value and value is not thereby overcome, but rather separated out (6§11): it reappears in other phenomenal forms within civil society and within the state, as well as between the state and civil society. The mere existence of the state as social context inevitably involves separation-in-unity existing as the mixed economy of use-value as well as value criteria (§8). Economic policy further involves actively altering, to a greater or lesser extent, the criteria for the allocation of resources to the production of goods and services within civil society (and, relatedly, the distribution of access to these goods and services – Chapter 9) away from the pure, subjectively reproduced value-criteria essential to competitive society.

The principle of competitive society is private property in whatever one can gain by exchange in accordance with rightfully struck contracts, including for the sale and purchase of labour power, regulated and reproduced by market mechanisms. The very existence of the state, and therefore of taxation, confronts this principle with some other universal principle, which legitimates the appropriation of part of private property in the form of money to be paid to the state (S2). Taxation and state expenditure with a redistributive intent in pursuit of actualisation of the right to existence introduces use-value criteria, confronting from outside the value criteria reproduced within competitive society. The breakdowns and discontinuities in the value-form processes which give rise to the necessity for macroeconomic management (9S2) and microeconomic intervention (9S3), entail that these activities be concerned with *particular* interventions. As well as conflicting with the general abstract value-form processes of civil society such activities generate tensions within the state, which should confront individuals as the *universal* instance before which each is formally equal.

In order to actualise the inherently particular right to existence and to modify the purely value-form criteria of civil society, the state thus inevitably not only bridges its separation from civil society in trying to provide the social context for the economy, it also exercises its subjectivity by intervening in civil society as the agent of policy. The universal social subject cannot remain in its Platonic heaven, but must descend to the profane level of the struggles and conflicts of civil society, which are then in part fought out *within* the state and with the state as a protagonist.

Just as the form of law arises because of the inadequacy of the abstract processes of the value-form to the intrinsic particularity of the actualisation of the right to existence, the abstract formal processes of law are themselves inadequate to that actualisation. The actualisation of the right to existence depends upon discretionary discrimination on the basis of a complex of specific and particular use-value criteria, many of which cannot be isolated let alone quantified along the monodimensional value-form axis and so cannot be specified a priori in formal law. Those economic policy objectives concerned with redistribution and the recognition of collective rights (see Chapter 9) are intrinsically complementary to the *equal* treatment of unequals inherent to both the value-form and the form of law, in that they are intrinsically concerned with the appropriately *unequal* treatment of unequals.

The contradiction between state and civil society (6S3) reappears more concretely as the conflict between discretionary, discriminatory economic policy on the one hand and the rule of law and the individual economic freedom of private property upheld by it on the other. The working out of these conflicts through the welfare state, macroeconomic management and microeconomic intervention is the object of the presentation in Chapter 9.

Addenda: a. Economics and the value–use-value conflict; b. Morals and microeconomics; c. Hayek and moral concepts; d. Hegelians and the integration of morality; e. Offe and morality; f. De Brunhoff on the mixed economy

a. The conflict of the value-form and use-value criteria is reflected in microeconomics. The discovery of market failures in the form of externalities and public goods by welfare economics (see, for example, Baumol 1952 and Levacic 1987: ch. 6) is countered by the discovery of 'state failures' by public choice theory (for a survey see Mueller 1976), and the economic theories of politics (see, for example, Breton 1974) and bureaucracy (for a recent overview, see Jackson 1982). The significance of imperfect competition for the optimality of value-criteria is rebutted by the discovery of potential competition and contestable markets (Baumol 1982). It is perhaps unsurprising that the appropriate mechanism for the provision of 'public' goods is a matter of enduring controversy (Offe and Ronge 1976: 127). The social efficiency, not to mention equity, of the market reproduced value-form system is maintained even in the face of a 'principal-agent' problem (Jackson 1982: ch. 8) in competitive society as well as in the state, the lack of robustness of the results of contestable markets theory, and the dependence of the relation between efficient allocation and market regulation on perfect competition.

b. The inability of microeconomics to come to grips with the problems of the mixed economy stems from its refusal to incorporate moral concepts systematically into its discourse. In reflection of the individualism of competitive society from which it springs, 'true' economic science tries to purge moral considerations from its discourse. Microeconomics, and its welfare and public sector applications, reflect the necessity for the purging of civil society of other than self-interested behaviour in the fact that its Pareto optimality conditions rest upon the assumption of such conduct. If economic agents, even in competitive markets, pursue other than self-interested objectives (i.e. do other than maximise their self-perceived satisfaction) in their economic decision making, then they will be drawing upon non-tradeable sources of information, so that the consequent trade-offs constituted by the aggregation of the interaction of preferences and technologies will no longer be reproduced by competitive market prices (Arrow 1975 is the key theoretical work). Of course, objective functions incorporating the externality 'altruism' as an argument can be modelled, but supply in accordance with the demands so generated cannot then be optimised by purely individualistic self-interested (say, profit maximising) behaviour. As has been clearly shown in the many 'alternative' theories of the firm, in which the firm's conduct initiated by managers diverges from profit maximisation, the outcome in terms of resource allocation will not reflect the satisfaction of consumer demand at minimum cost. (The seminal works are: Berle and Means 1932; Simon 1959; Cyert and March 1963; Marris 1964 and 1972; Williamson 1964; Leibenstein 1966; Machlup 1967; Naylor and Vernon 1969. Useful surveys/collections are: Marris and Wood (eds) 1971;

Wildsmith 1973.) That is to say, what we conceive of as the market reproduced value-form processes will diverge from an outcome satisfactory in use-value terms, even if this latter is restricted to the individualistic revealed preferences of consumers. These problems may be traced back to Adam Smith's famous dictum: 'It is not from the benevolence of the butcher, the brewer, or the baker that we expect our dinner, but from their regard to their own interest. We address ourselves, not to their humanity but to their self-love, and never talk to them of our own necessities but of their advantages' (Smith 1776: i, 13).

c. Hayek argues that the sterilisation of civil society from all norms is necessary precisely *because* such norms and use-value criteria, applied concretely to particular persons, can be only the subjective opinion of some other individual agent, and thus can be imposed only by illegitimate coercion. Morality is thus reintroduced into the analysis in the form of the *primacy of individual liberty* (§1a). But this, paradoxically, enables the justification of the purging of all moral concerns from civil society and their alienation to a state legitimated only to act in accordance with general rules, so that in fact morality in the Hegelian sense of disinterested conduct ('Sittlichkeit') still gets no look in. Rather we are left with self-interested conduct in civil society overseen by the state in accordance with general rules which do not discriminate between concrete particular individuals.

d. Philosophical writings in the Hegelian tradition best express the complexities of the state–civil society contradiction from which derive the tensions of the contemporary mixed economy (see, for example, Benhabib 1984: 168–9). The *separation* out of the complex multiple use-value criteria underlying political intervention from the formal abstraction of the value-form transactions between individual competition subjects cannot be maintained. It is one of the strengths of the Hegelian tradition that it attempts to grasp moral criteria as moments of the totality. The problem of political identity for Hegel concerns the question: 'is there a coherent set of values which can link the economic and the political and thus provide the basis for political identity and thus for a secure political community?' (Plant 1984: 228). Modern 'critical theory' (for example, Habermas 1973) has taken this up in the form of the crisis of legitimation, and radical political science and political economy (see, for example, Offe 1984 and O'Connor 1973 respectively) have developed more concrete analyses of the (so-called) 'contradictions of the welfare state' and the 'fiscal crisis of the state' (Chapter 10). The conflicts of the mixed economy are thus another facet of the tension between the principle (moral imperatives) of civil society and those of communality (6§1) manifested only abstractly in the state (Plant 1984: 243). The basic conflict is that of the necessary attempt by the state as social subject to introduce conscious particular differentiation between persons that the universal value-form confronts as undifferentiated competition subjects (cf. Eldred 1984a: §§282, 313, 341–2).

e. Offe (1973: 50) describes the essential *amorality* of the value-form processes in civil society, and the legitimation problems this generates for a state intervening therein on the basis of non-value, moral or use-value criteria (Offe 1979: 82). The theoretical problem of the integration of morality into the totality reappears as a practical-political problem of managing consent formation via the structures of the inner state (6§12). The dilemma of this process is that it involves organising consent to collective institutions and activities by bourgeois persons, in a way which keeps such concerns out of civil society and located only as politics at the level of the state (Offe 1973: 60). The immediate source of tension for the inner state is that state power does not derive fundamentally from the electorate but from the revenues appropriated from competitive society (Offe and Ronge 1976: 121; cf. also Offe 1973: 58; and 1979: 67). However, the structuralist, systems-theoretic approach generates problems once again (see §8b). Whilst the sterilisation of the market from norms and morals is well expressed, the *a priori* disjunction between structurally separate spheres means that Offe fails to integrate the grounding of the state's legitimacy in the will of bourgeois persons.

f. De Brunhoff (1976: 102–110) argues that much modern economic policy is problematical for the value-form because it is neither determined solely in accordance with value-criteria, nor concomitantly executed within the form of law. Whilst it is at some stage initiated by legislation, economic policy takes on powers and functions which are neither within the form of law nor subject to market enforced commercial criteria. Once again, our critique of De Brunhoff's work is that it relies rather indiscriminately on historical rather than logical argument to support its conclusions, thereby implicitly identifying what *is* with what is *necessary* to the bourgeois totality.

SUMMARY

Separation-in-unity, the necessary form of the state-civil society relation is characterised by the necessity to satisfy the aspirations of bourgeois persons to the extent that they continue to legitimate the state (as well as by the concrete existence of the universal social subject as but one of many sovereign states embedded in the world economy). The contradiction of the universal social subject which is both separated from that over which it is subject and restricted to particular sovereignty, is grounded in the state as provider of the social context of law, money and infrastructure for the economy (Section 1). Provision of such a context entails physical existence for which the state is dependent on the economy, ultimately through taxation (Section 2).

The putative context for the economy is thus in fact inextricably linked with it, so that separation-in-unity has its contradictory existence in the mixed economy – the necessary coexistence of value

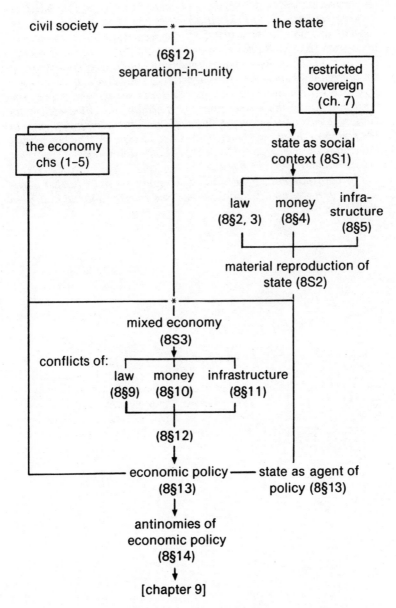

Figure 8.1 Concretisation and particularisation of separation-in-unity: the mixed economy.

and use-value criteria for resource allocation and subjective decision-making. *The state's contextual activities cannot be confined to the form of abstract, formal and non-discretionary law. Each moment of the social context is shown to generate conflicts with civil society (Section 3). Thus the very existence (and material reproduction) of the state makes space for the extension of use-value criteria beyond those directly conducive to valorisation and accumulation. The contradiction of the mixed economy is grounded in the state (social subject) as agent of active economic policy, intervening explicitly in the economy from outside civil society (Section 4). The conceptual development from separation-in-unity to the antinomies of economic policy is summarised in Figure 8.1.*

The contradictions of the mixed economy are to be further particularised in welfare, macroeconomic and microeconomic policy, in Part Five.

Part Five:

The Determination and Contingent Reproduction of Welfare and Economic Policy

Chapter nine

Welfare, Macroeconomic and Microeconomic Policy

PRELIMINARY REMARKS

The bourgeois state has been shown to constitute a contradictory unity with civil society, which separates out the basic contradiction between use-value and value in the bourgeois economy (Chapter 6). The state attempts to manage this relationship with welfare and economic policies. The first concretisations of the state as the social context for the market have addressed the inadequacy of the value-form to individual existence only indirectly, by providing the framework of law, money and infrastructure within which competitive society may more effectively reproduce the economy, and so the value-form as the specifically bourgeois mode of association of intrinsically non-self-reproducing individuals (8SS1–2). However, the economy remains dominated by value-form imperatives in contradiction with the use-value criteria implied by particular individual existence. As such, not all the conditions of existence of civil society have been grounded in particularisations of the state. The right to existence has only an alienated existence upheld by the state and separated from the value-form association of civil society (6§11). Even in a perfectly working market economy, along with its necessary frameworks of law, money and infrastructure, the ideal negative right of particular individual existence is under threat. The contradictions of the mixed economy as developed so far tend further to problematise the conditions of existence of particular individuals to the extent that they involve the undermining of the value-efficiency of competitive society. The state conceived only as the social context for the market cannot ensure – and indeed undermines – the reproduction of the ideal right to existence of bourgeois persons (8S3). This contradiction is expressed in the state as agent of economic policy (8S4), which is further particularised in this chapter.

231

The first particularisation of the state as agent of policy is the welfare state, characterised as the social subject intervening in civil society in pursuit of the realisation of the right to existence and, relatedly, the reproduction of competition subjects, in particular the labourer (Section 1). Welfare policy further grounds the legitimation of the state in the consent of citizens. The state as the agent of welfare policy reaches back across separation-in-unity, in pursuit of the realisation of the right to existence and the reproduction of an adequate supply of labour power.

Both the state (as social context and as welfare state) and its citizens depend materially on the success of the economic processes of valorisation and accumulation in civil society. This leads to the particularisation of the state as the agent of macroeconomic management (Section 2). The reappearance of the contradictions of separation-in-unity as the conflicts of macroeconomic management leads to the further particularisation of the state as the agent of microeconomic policy (Section 3). The success of valorisation and accumulation themselves depend upon the success of individual entrepreneurs regulated by market forces, which the activities of the state tend to undermine. Microeconomic intervention aims to facilitate this success, and to ensure the allocation of resources to infrastructural use-values.

However, the activities of the state as the agent of economic policy cannot overcome the contradictions of separation-in-unity, which reappear in the conflicts of different policies (Section 4). The welfare state undermines separation, generating legitimation crises and contributing to economic stagnation. In trying to enhance the conditions for valorisation and accumulation of national capitals as well as their welfare implications, macroeconomic management further confronts the value-logic of civil society with use-value criteria. Microeconomic intervention constitutes the most highly developed manifestation of the value/use-value contradiction characterising the bourgeois totality. Even in its most interventionist form, state policy cannot overcome but only abstractly ground the fundamental contradictions of the epoch in the form of policy. The contingent content of policy is then constituted by the states' attempts to manage the shifting manifestations of these contradictions.

Chapter 9 presents the policy targets of the state by identifying the contingent expressions of the contradictions which have, in the presentation of the economy and competitive society, been transcended in the existence of separation-in-unity. It also develops an account of the dilemmas, conflicts and antinomies of economic policy itself for civil society and for the state, as manifestations of the *state's attempts to manage the effects of the contradictions of the economy and of bourgeois society. The overarching problem for the state's activities is that they tend to undermine the separation-in-unity which transcends the contradictory existence of competitive society. In order to exist, provide a framework for the market, actualise existence right, manage the macroeconomy and intervene in the microeconomy, the state confronts the value-form processes of civil society with a variety of alternative use-value criteria for the allocation of resources. State intervention cannot resolve the contradictory tendencies of valorisation and accumulation. Indeed it may even exacerbate their manifestations. Moreover, it may tend to undermine its own legitimation by bourgeois persons, to the extent that it overrides property right, pursues its own self-interest and raises aspirations it is unable to meet. The state as the agent of policy can then be conceived as driven by the necessity to manage the conditions of existence of the reappearance of such contradictions (Chapter 10).*

SECTION 1   THE CONTINGENCY OF INDIVIDUAL EXISTENCE AND THE WELFARE STATE

§1. From ideal negative right to existence to actual positive right to welfare benefits

Because of the contingency of particular individual existence in competitive society, and the systematic threat to that existence from the crisis-ridden nature of the value-form determined reproduction of the economy, the negative right to existence in its inherent concrete particularity cannot be reproduced at the level of competitive society. This contradiction is transcended in the doubling of competitive society into civil society and the state (6§7). The contingent and systematic threats to individual existence appear in the shape of the inability of bourgeois persons as competition subjects to earn an adequate income from the deployment of their income source within competitive society (civil society conceived in abstraction from the state). The income source of last resort for those who do not own (sufficient) property is labour power (6§4), so that the ultimate threat to existence is the inability to sell labour power, or to be able to sell it only for an inadequate price.

The necessity that the state attempt to actualise the right to existence determines it as the welfare state. Welfare policies are concerned to improve the saleability of labour power, to regulate the conditions of its exchange and employment, and to provide income support or even income replacement (in cash or in kind) for the unsuccessful labourer. The qualitative and quantitative extent to

233

which particular existence is actualised in politically, legally and administratively determined welfare policies is not determined. The right to welfare benefit overcomes the purely economic determinations of competitive society – as, indeed, does the mere existence of the state itself. But it does so only as an abstract political, not as a substantive social, right (6§11). Consequently the mode and size of welfare benefits is contingently subject to the ebb and flow of the cyclical course of accumulation and crisis (Chapter 5), and the political, social and economic struggles as to what constitutes an entitlement to welfare assistance and what constitutes an adequate income.

In thus managing the manifestations of the contradictions of existence for the labourer, the state is also managing the supply of labour power available for integration into the expanding (and contracting) circuits of capital (2§5; 5S2), as well as the social consequences of the expulsion of labour from the circuits of capital (4S1). Given the existence of labour power as a unique element of production and income source that cannot be reproduced in the value-form, the state as the agent of policy (8S4) will be concerned with the reproduction of a consenting (§2), educated/skilled and healthy work force.

The particular instruments of welfare policy are contingent. They may include income support policies via transfers to the economically active as well as the inactive; compulsory and sometimes partially subsidised state or private insurance against loss or diminution of income from specific incapacities or from unemployment; and state interventions in the markets for labour power, involving such policies as regulation of health and safety at work, of employment contracts, of the conduct of industrial relations and collective bargaining, of the constitutions and activities of trades unions and of minimum wages payable. The provision of particular use-values relevant to the reproduction of existence in general, and of the consenting, educated/skilled and healthy labourer in particular, provide a welfare determination of infrastructural use-values (8§§5,11) which are not adequately reproduced in the value-form.

Addenda: a. Order of presentation and contingency of policy; b. Hegel on welfare; c. Economics and welfare

a. The particular policies by which the state actualises the imperatives of bourgeois right are not in themselves necessary. It is merely necessary that such an actualisation is maintained – that persistent contradictions have a form of existence, however contingent (0§§10–11). The increasingly concrete level of the presentation, together with the contingency of some grounding, also entails that ever more complex interconnections are being developed, calling for increasing numbers of cross-references cutting across the main line of the argument. For example: Keynesian macroeconomic management (S2) can be located as an attempt to deal with the welfare imperatives in a way which is less disruptive of the market regulation of value-form processes (Plant 1984: 241), though it nevertheless generates legitimation problems for the state (S4). The determinants of microeconomic policy (S3) could be supplemented by some of the determinants of welfare state policies presented here. State activities in the fields of health and education are determined as welfare state policies, and as aspects of macroeconomic management of the supply of labour power and of microeconomic intervention. The determination of welfare policies anticipates to some extent the determination of macro- and microeconomic policies, and successful macro- and micro-policies may reduce the demands for direct welfare support of incomes. Monetary policy may complement industrial policy (S3) by getting the banking system to favour the pre-validation of particular capitals, branches or sectors considered to be relevant to policy targets for infrastructure, growth, exports, import substitution and so on. This will also involve the state in other regulatory and persuasive interventions in the financial markets and in the banking system, which tend toward microeconomic intervention.

Some manifestations of the welfare state are indeed more fundamentally grounded in other areas of economic policy, being concerned to improve the opportunities for successful deployment of labour power by the labourer rather than to compensate for lack of such success. Nevertheless, economic policies which have a significant moment as aspects of the welfare state – that is, those which are involved directly with maintaining an adequate level of existence of individuals as persons or specifically as labourers – can be discursively separated from economic policies which are primarily determined as the social context within which the market can operate (8S1), and those which are concerned directly to manipulate competitive society to make it work more adequately (SS2–3). Clearly these latter policy packages will have existential implications for competition subjects by affecting their opportunities successfully to deploy their income sources.

The order of presentation from the mixed economy to the welfare state, macroeconomic management and microeconomic intervention has a subsidiary logic in addition to the main line of grounding transcendence: it expresses approximately a process of increasing degree of active intervention by the state in the reproduction of the value-form processes of civil society, as well as of the significance of such activities for the reproduction of the value-form determined totality. The contingency of particular policies means that a full grasp of why a particular policy is adopted at a particular time, in a particular state, would require – on the basis of value-form theory and the examination of the working out of contradictory moments of the value-form – the introduction of further (contingent historical and national) determinants.

b. For Hegel, welfare is the particular content which is to fill formal right, so that 'the Idea of the state is precisely the supersession of the clash between right (i.e., empty abstract freedom) and welfare (i.e., the particular content which fills that void)' (Hegel 1821: §336). And 'the right actually present in the particular requires ... that the securing of every single person's livelihood and welfare be treated and actualized as a right, i.e. that particular welfare as such be so treated' (Hegel 1821: §230; cf. Plant 1984: 232). Whilst the right of property secures the existence of the property owner, the actualisation of the universal right to particular existence requires an external separate instance, the state, and 'since I am inextricably involved in particularity, I have a right to claim that in this association with other particulars, my particular welfare too shall be promoted' (Hegel 1821: §229A). As expressed in terms reminiscent of Harold Macmillan's *Middle Way* (1938) by a modern commentator on Hegel: 'if poverty is the result of the operation of civil society and not a personal failing, and ... civil society on the whole works for everyone's advantage ... then a welfare system designed to compensate those who are made poor by the operation of the system could be seen as part of the necessary cost of maintaining the system' (Plant 1984: 242).

c. The analysis of the welfare state in orthodox economics focuses on the requirement for the production of certain kinds of goods and (more typically) services which cannot be adequately produced and distributed via market mechanisms, because of 'public goods' characteristics, 'externalities' (including altruism as an external benefit of consumption) and the general question of redistributive measures by the state. (For recent accounts see Barr 1987 and Levacic 1987: chs 12–13.) Microeconomics per se has in general a preference on efficiency grounds for redistribution in cash rather than kind: the former preserves the freedom of consumption choice, whilst the latter undermines it. In the light of Chapter 8, the preference for cash redistribution seems appropriate since it merely alters the framework within which markets work, except in the labour market where even cash transfers presumably alter the trade-offs between work and leisure. The preference does not, however (contrary to the beliefs of some economists) express any transcendental logic. Indeed, it has been argued that the attempted reduction of welfare policies to cash payments is internally contradictory:

> 'if the disadvantaged people had merely pointed out they had less money than the others, there would have been no suggestion that they should, therefore, be given more. It is only because they were asking for those things [specific welfare relevant goods and services such as 'education, health, safety'] that the discussion got going in the first place, and the idea came up that anyone should give them anything' (Williams, B. 1985: 145–6).

§2. Welfare, legitimation, labour and consent

The welfare state further grounds the legitimation of the state in the consent of citizens (6§§10, 12). Persons' consent is constituted by their acceptance of the mores, ethics, value-system and modes of calculation expressing the value-form and the rights-based state.

Given that acceptance, people will legitimate the state and concomitantly the value-form determined economic core of civil society, by demanding no more of it than that it uphold their (bourgeois) rights of property and existence and their formal equality as citizens and competition subjects. Given that labourers constitute the majority of the electorate in any state based on representative democracy an universal franchise (6§12), their consent is clearly a prerequisite of continued legitimation. Given that they constitute that unique element of valorisation, the direct producers, the potential industrial power of organised labour means that, even short of the development of bourgeois democracy, the state relies in principle on their de facto consent to its conception of what constitutes the general interest.

Addendum: a. Gramsci and consent

a. The concept of consent is adapted largely from the work of Gramsci, where it is closely related to that of hegemony. Gramsci uses the consent/hegemony couple in the analysis of the formation of effective class-consciousness and action, as well as in the discussion of the formation of popular fronts under the hegemony of the proletariat (thence with the consent of the other groups within the front). (See, for example, Gramsci 1971: 12, 80n, 170n, 181–2, 239, 242n, 258–9, 261–3 and 416–8.) For value-form theory, 'consent' is specifically that of persons to the dictates of the value-form determined economy, and to legitimate the form-determined state. It emerges only at that stage of the presentation when subjectivity is introduced.

SECTION 2 THE STATE AND MACROECONOMIC MANAGEMENT

§3. From fiscal state to fiscal policy

The state is necessarily separate from the value creating processes of the economic core of civil society (6§11). Its own existence as the social context for the economy (8S1), and its actualisation of the negative ideal right to existence in the face of the contingent and crisis-ridden opportunities for gaining incomes offered in civil society, therefore determines state intervention and the qualitative composition of expenditure and quantitative levels of state revenue (8§8). The existence of the state as social context of the mixed economy has been shown to be contradictory (8S3). The contradictions of separation-in-unity are further grounded in the state as the agent of macroeconomic management.

The state is intrinsically involved in expenditure and revenue-raising – it is the fiscal state. The revenue base of the state depends ultimately on the successful creation of value in civil society. Such economic success would also enhance the opportunities for adequate income earning by individual competition subjects, thus minimising the contingent and the systematic threats to particular, individual existence. It would further enable the welfare state better to maintain those who nevertheless do not succeed. Therefore, beyond the determination of expenditure and revenue raising by contextual and welfare activities, the state will adopt a fiscal policy stance.

The possibility of effective macroeconomic management arises from the non-necessity of the forms of appearance of the alternation of expansion and contraction (5§6). Crisis can in principle be avoided by management of the expressions of the contingent interaction of the tendency to over-accumulation of capital (TOC) and for the rate of profit to fall (TRPF) underlying cyclical development (5§4). Macroeconomic management is thus constituted by the attempt to stimulate the manifestations of those tendencies which reduce the amplitude of the cycle. It is concerned to prevent cyclical down-turns from degenerating into cumulative crises of accumulation and realisation (5§6). The basis of such management is the attempt to reproduce the conditions for the validation of extended accumulation in the light of the tendency of the rate of surplus value to rise (3§1), so as to manage the balance between the tendency to labour-shortage profit squeeze (3§3) and to under-consumption (3§4). Whilst welfare policy must manage the consequences of the expulsion of labour associated with the TRPF, macroeconomic policy tries to enhance the conditions for continued profitable accumulation. Maintaining growth in the context of the subjective reproduction of valorisation and accumulation entails maintaining an environment in which entrepreneurs and money-capitalists have optimistic profit expectations, and in which labourers consent to sell their labour power for a price relative to productivity which allows 'normal' profitability. The state's fiscal policy can contribute to this environment by maintaining economic growth, managing the level of aggregate demand and employment and controlling the rate of price change and rates of interest.

Addenda: a. Targets and instruments; b. Marxists on macroeconomic policy; c. De Brunhoff on macroeconomic policy; d. Macroeconomic theory and policy; e. Contingency of macroeconomic policy

a. A wide spectrum of actual and possible macroeconomic policies, targets and instruments has been exhaustively analysed in the economic literature. Value-form theory provides the basis for critical location of such policy by showing how it grounds the contradictions of the value-form, valorisation and accumulation, and the rights-based state which attempts to manage their economic, social and political conditions of existence. Chapter 10 will indicate the significance of such grounding for grasping the imperatives and constraints underlying the evolution and shifting phenomenal forms of economic policy within the bourgeois epoch. The choice of particular targets and instruments is contingent – it can be grasped only from a conjunctural and historical account of the conditions of existence of the value-form.

b. Marx could scarcely be expected to discuss macroeconomic policy per se, since the notion did not yet exist. However he appears to have anticipated Keynes's doctrine of effective demand, whereby money essentially mediates between individual needs and the expression of those needs on the market: '*Demand* also exists for those who have no money, but their demand is simply a figment of the imagination. For me or for any other third party it has no effect, no existence. For me it therefore remains *unreal* and *without an object*. The difference between effective demand based on money and ineffective demand based on my need, my passion, my desire, etc., is the difference between *being* and *thinking*, between a representation which merely *exists* within me and one which exists outside me as a *real object*' (Marx 1932: 378). For further discussion of Marx as a precursor of Keynes, see Robinson (1942).

Most (though not all, see Foley 1978 and 1986) recent Marxist accounts of macroeconomic policy have focused on a cyclical crisis-management role for the state. (See, for example, Gamble and Walton 1976: ch. 6; Fine and Harris 1979: part II; Campbell 1981: chs 5–7; Aaronovitch and Smith 1981: chs 8–9; Weeks 1981: chs V and VII; Burden and Campbell 1985; Thompson 1986). In general, these accounts make an ungrounded leap from the contradictions of the economy to the state, neglecting the conceptual development from competitive society to the state/civil society couple, and thereby the introduction of subjectivity (for example, Miliband 1969: 79). Relatedly they tend to utilise uncritically the classical Marxist conception of the state as the agent of the capitalist class, rather than as the rights-based upholder of private property mediated by the demands of existence right (Chapter 6), from which its support of capital accumulation takes the 'form of appearance of economic prosperity from which, hypothetically speaking, all could potentially benefit' (Eldred 1984a: §87). The point is not to deny the partial insights of such accounts, but to attempt to investigate their necessity or contingency with respect to the value-form determined totality.

c. De Brunhoff grounds macroeconomic policy in the *historical* development of the integration, in the 1920s and 1930s, of the bourgeois state's two necessary fields of action – the management of labour power and of money (De Brunhoff 1976: 64). Value-form theory disagrees with three aspects of De Brunhoff's account: the assumption of pre-existing structures implicit in the discussion of their articulation, the economistic reductionism of moving straight from the needs of capital accumulation to the state's functions, with no mediation by competitive society, and the explicitly historical nature of the argument. There is in her work a tendency to historicism, since it is undoubtedly also making conceptual points. The emphasis on money and labour as peculiar commodities, and so as objects of state policy, needs to be derived from the value-form and the rights-based state. The jump from economically determined classes to the state as an instrument of the capitalist class neglects the disappearance of classes from consciousness at the level of competitive society (6§4b), which enables the state to appear as the universal social subject. Value-form theory shows how the state can be the universal social subject for consciousness, without assuming its omniscience and omnipotence (De Brunhoff 1976: 83). It is the inner state apparatuses (6§12) which try, however imperfectly, to reproduce universal imperatives, grounding them in the shifting national interest.

The historical development of what active economic policy actually occurs (e.g. De Brunhoff 1976: 61ff), however illuminating, is contingent (0§§11–12). Any such history needs to be located in an account of the epochally necessary forms and functions of the state underlying shifting policy stances. This is a matter of conceptual, not historical, unfolding. Indeed the logic of De Brunhoff's presentation requires the conceptualisation of the epochally necessary moments of the state's economic policies. She implicitly assumes states to be a necessary universal moment of the bourgeois totality: 'even if they are entirely subordinated to private interest, managed in terms of criteria of profitability and deprived of stable frontiers, states cannot be "privatized" to such a degree that they become sub-businesses merely supplying more or less collective services' (De Brunhoff 1976: 96, 100). But whereas value-form theory can reconcile such assertions with the merely contingent historical shifts in the state/civil society relationship, it is not clear that De Brunhoff's theory can.

d. Most macroeconomic theory is, explicitly or implicitly, concerned to theorise the apparent inability of market forces to ensure an overall level of economic activity over time, compatible with full employment of labour, full utilisation of capacity, stable prices and a sustainable balance of trade. The microeconomic foundations of such analysis lie in the inadequacy of inter-temporal market resource allocation, based on the intrinsic imperfection of information about the future, and thus the existence of entrepreneurial myopia and uncertainty. There are few, and only highly specialised, microeconomic inter-temporal markets (insurance markets and various kinds of futures markets). Analysis of the breakdown at the aggregate level of the putative self-equilibrating characteristics of the market economy also addresses the determination of the demand and supply for labour and of the nominal wage in labour markets, which makes up the bulk of the most sophisticated and difficult part of the *General Theory* (Keynes 1936). The strategic objective of (Keynesian, if not Keynes's) macroeconomic policy then is to adjust aggregate expenditures in order to commensurate the division of income between consumption expenditure and savings, with the division of production between that for current consumption and that for investment for future consumption (cf. De Brunhoff 1976: 72). This theoretical analysis in fact also implicitly takes up many of Marx's remarks on the inadequacy of markets to the reproduction of valorisation and accumulation at the aggregate level. De Brunhoff takes up Keynes's concern with the uncertain future which subsequently gave rise to the more pro-market analyses of rational expectations (De Brunhoff 1976: 121). She points out that Keynes himself implicitly located the need for macro-economic stabilisation policy in the ubiquitous determination of the economy by the imperatives of the value-form, in the phenomenal guise of money: 'A monetary economy ... is essentially one in which changing views about the future are capable of influencing the quantity of employment and not merely its direction'(Keynes 1936: vii; cited in De Brunhoff 1976: 121). A similar point was made during the Keynesian/Monetarist controversy in the 1970s: 'The fundamental practical message of the General Theory [Keynes 1936] [is] that a private enterprise economy using an intangible money, needs to be stabilised, can be stabilised, and therefore should be stabilised by appropriate monetary and fiscal policies' (Modigliani 1977; cited in Schott 1983). Keynes conceived such stabilisation policy to be necessary for the reproduction of the capitalist system: 'Whilst, therefore the enlargement of the functions of government ... would seem ... to be a terrific encroachment on individualism, I defend it, on the contrary, both as the only practicable means of avoiding the destruction of existing economic forms in their entirety and as the condition of the successful functioning of individual initiative' (Keynes 1936: 380). Value-form theory, on the other hand, grasps it as a contingent transcendence of evolving contradictions, which reappear subsequently in a different phenomenal form. Such policies encouraged entrepreneurial 'flight from the present' in the boom sustained by pre-validation of value (via the credit system) and pseudo-validation (via the state expansionary policies) which eventually lead to stagflation (De Brunhoff 1976: 121-2; 28-9; and 5S3 above). Keynesian macroeconomic stabilisation is part of a package of policies orientated around the integration of financial into industrial capital (see S3) and the lifetime 'incorporation' of labour into the welfare state (cf. S1).

e. Conflicts over policy objectives may have their institutional expression in conflicts and rivalries between different institutions of the state, which may have privileged relations with different groups and corporations in civil society. For example, the Treasury and the Bank of England in the UK may be more closely linked with money capital than industrial capital, which in turn may have a privileged relationship with the Department of Trade and Industry. Different political parties may favour different groups. Whilst these linkages have to be empirically investigated, such relations are contingent and shifting. Certain broad imperatives can be derived from value-form theory in advance of conjunctural accounts. Macroeconomic management may be determined as a mode of state actualisation of the threatened right to existence which is in principle less subversive of the logic of competitive society than direct welfare expenditure. This insight goes right back to Hegel (1821) in his advocacy of public works rather than public charity, since the latter undermines the imperative to work.

§4. From monetary framework to monetary policy

As the framework for the market, the state must reproduce the currency as the general equivalent (8§4). The monetary framework is further determined by the state's management of the financing of its own existence (8S2) and activities. In order to reproduce money as a store of value the state must manage and stabilise the rate of inflation. Control of inflation is further necessitated by the need to reduce the diversion of capital into mere stores of value, which is concomitant to it (5§10). In order to stimulate investment and to provide orderly funding of its own expenditures, the state will be concerned to manage the levels and term structure of interest rates. A further determination of the form and quantitative levels of the state's expenditure and revenue raising will therefore be its monetary policy stance.

Monetary policy is a development of the monetary framework, and an important component of macroeconomic management. The state as the agent of macroeconomic policy must cope with the relationship between the value system expressed in monetary relations and its economic conditions of existence in terms of the allocation of resources – crucially labour power – to the production and distribution of use-values. Management of the system of credit (2§7) and banking (2§8), and interest rate policy (usually via a central bank) (2§11) are needed to ensure reproduction of the supply of money adequate for expanding circuits of capital (2§6). The state attempts to manage the acceleration of the cycle associated with the existence of credit (5§5) by reducing the interest rate burden in the downswing, and ensuring an adequate supply of credit in the upswing. More concretely, monetary policy may have to attempt to mediate the conflict between industrial and money capital to ensure that, especially in an inflationary environment, the former is offered credit on adequate terms (5§8). At the level of subjective reproduction, the state will be concerned to maintain a context conducive to entrepreneurial medium-term planning of investment programmes, by maintaining moderate (as perceived by investors) and stable rates of inflation (cf. 5§§7–8). It will in particular be concerned to prevent local ruptures in the circuits of capital multiplying into disruptions of the social circuit via the financial system (5§6), and to facilitate the restructuring of capital (4§6) by which the economy in itself adjusts to prevent, or recover from crises. During a wave of technological change the monetary system must be able to finance accelerated scrapping associated with the stratification that is the micro-condition of existence of the TRPF (4S2). The monetary authorities will be concerned to achieve a gradual and orderly decrease in the rate of pre-validation in the transition from inflation to deflation. This will involve the prevention or orderly management of threatened bank failure by easing liquidity and solvency problems

(5§§6, 10; 2§9) via regulation of money capital by the central bank and other financial sector regulatory agencies. This amounts to direct action by the social subject to socialise the individual losses arising from the cyclical course of accumulation (5S3).

Addenda: a. Monetary policy and value-form; b. Hayek and monetary policy

a. Monetary policy is more compatible with the universal value-form determined totality than fiscal policy. Its instruments are in principle universal and non-discriminatory, and thence in harmony both with abstract right and abstract value-form processes (cf. De Brunhoff 1976: 88–91). De Brunhoff expresses the relation between abstract right and the money-form thus: 'The extension of the commodity and money forms [into state activity] favours the redefinition of rights as a general expression of the public form of political power, rather than as a concrete privilege' (De Brunhoff 1976: 10). In order to be effective as the social subject of economic policy, the state must be integrated into value-form flows, so that monetary flows and calculation regulate the state's fiscal activities (De Brunhoff 1976: 103–4).

b. The congruence between the minimal rights-based state, monetary rather than fiscal or administrative regulation, and maximum autonomy for market regulation, is a central tenet of systematic liberalism (Hayek 1960: 334, 338–9). Hayek does, of course, have arguments against any interventionist discretionary monetary policy, on the grounds that monetary stability is necessary in order to provide a predictable environment for entrepreneurial decision-making. Ideally, therefore, monetary authorities should act in accordance with fixed, general (and preferably constitutionally sanctioned) rules. In practice, Hayek concedes that though 'the requirements for monetary stability are given first place and the rest of economic policy is adapted to them' (Hayek 1960: 337), the actions of the monetary authorities must remain at their discretion (Hayek 1960: 336–7).

SECTION 3   THE STATE AND MICROECONOMIC INTERVENTION

§5. From the state's activities to microeconomic policy

The state as social subject, having tendentially bridged the necessary separation of itself from civil society (6§11) through its contextual provision, welfare activities and macroeconomic management tends, in response to the antinomies of these activities, to be drawn into still more extensive and intensive *microeconomic* intervention in the economy.[1] The state's existence (8S2), and its ability to actualise the

1 For the *historical* argument that as the tensions of a mixed economy, with an overblown public sector, welfare state and macroeconomic policy are added to the inherent tendencies of capitalist accumulation, interventionist industrial policy comes into its own as one possible policy stance (see, for example, O'Connor 1973; Fine and Harris 1976; Williams 1982: 83–4).

243

right to existence and to support the market-regulated reproduction of valorisation and accumulation by means of contextual, welfare and macroeconomic policies, all depend on the success of the economy. The subjective reproduction of the economy depends on the success (on value criteria) of the activities of the capitalist entrepreneur in the shape of the company or firm (6§6).

At its least problematical, microeconomic policy is primarily a means of maintaining the conditions of existence of industrial capital so that it can successfully valorise and accumulate. Not only the state, but also the entrepreneur, the labourer, the landed-capitalist and the money capitalist depend for their revenue ultimately on the profitability of capital. Microeconomic policy is aimed at stimulating the successful company and supporting the temporarily unsuccessful. The entrepreneurial role is fundamentally to manage the relation between the production and realisation of value (the valorisation process – 1S5) and the production and distribution of use-values (the technical labour process – 1S5). In dynamic terms, it is clear that even to the extent that market regulation ensures that entrepreneurs act so as to reproduce valorisation, it may well not ensure the reproduction of the ever-changing composition of use-values demanded by changing technology and effective tastes. The infra-structural (8§5) or welfare significance of certain use-values, which cannot be or contingently are not adequately reproduced in the value-form, may motivate microeconomic measures to stimulate, support or take over their production.[2] Microeconomic intervention, focused on the money expression of labour (2§16), in order to manage the relation between the money and resource allocation aspects of the economy will also be concerned with regulation of financial institutions – and of the relation between money and industrial capital – to try to ensure that the former is responsive to the needs of (selected parts of) the latter. The state may then be constrained to deploy microeconomic policy to alleviate bottlenecks and scarcities in national and regional economies. The market reproduced value-form per se is also indifferent to the 'external' ecological and social costs of growth[3] which are therefore neglected by entrepreneurs, and so must be imposed by the state, in conflict with the imperatives of valorisation and accumulation. Since ecological concerns such as counter-pollution and management of non-renewable resources and land-use entail resource reallocation,

2 Marx mentions the possibility of nationalisation on the grounds of the inadequacies of functioning entrepreneurs to the production of infrastructural use-values (see, for example, Marx 1855: 288).
3 See, for example, Mishan 1967; Meadows *et al.* 1972; Hirsch 1977.

possibly into hitherto untapped areas of economic activity, they provide further pressure for, in general microeconomic, intervention.[4] At the level of many capitals (2S4), microeconomic policy will be concerned typically with balanced accumulation. It will attempt to rectify imbalances between different use-values, produced in different firms, industries, sectors, regions and national territories. Such policy will be directed at commercial, as well as industrial capital.

In trying to overcome the limits of accumulation, microeconomic intervention may attempt to facilitate the production of technology (2§4). In a dynamic context, the state may intervene to even out the waves of diffusion of technology by discouraging technology hoarding in the downswing (5§6), and by stimulating technical change and innovation, in the face of its tendential stagnation, arising from the decreasing range of stratification consequent on the tendencies of accumulation (5§7). Microeconomic instruments such as selective accelerated depreciation allowances may facilitate the devalorisation or restructuring of capital in the attempt to manage the manifestations of the TRPF (4§6). Microeconomic management of diffusion and innovation may be used to counter the inflationary pressures generated by rapid technological change, arising from the increased prices needed to meet rising amortisation demands, and the reduced possibilities of meeting over-capacity by price decrease, in the face of range decrease concomitant on rapid innovation (5§7).

Labour is the sole necessary factor of valorisation (1§9) and the income source of last resort (6§4). Microeconomic intervention in labour power markets may complement the macroeconomic attempt to manage the cycles of accumulation, by trying to ensure an adequate supply of labour and the successful redeployment of expelled labour, as well as (implicitly) to enhance capital's real subordination of labour (2§2). This may include policies to enhance the geographical and sectoral mobility of labour. Conversely it may involve regional policy designed to compensate for the immobility of labour, by altering the geographical location of accumulation. In attempting selectively to match wage to productivity increases, micro-intervention in labour markets can be seen as an extension of the macroeconomic concern to manage the dynamic balance between

---

4 Once they are so enforced, or if such issues are taken up by consumers with purchasing power, entrepreneurs will no doubt ensure that demands for reduction of the undesired side effects of growth, industrialisation, etc. are met as far as possible by valorising commodity production. However, it appears to be precisely the inadequacy of the value-form to the resolution of these kind of problems that it does not react until, very often, irreversible ecological and social damage has been done.

labour shortage profit squeeze (3§3) and under-consumption (3§4). It may thence also facilitate the macroeconomic management of the expressions of the interaction of the TRPF and the TOC (5§2). When unemployment is perceived to be a social problem, the aim may be an overall rate of accumulation high enough in relation to the rising value composition of capital (VCC) to increase the demand for labour. When over-accumulation and its consequences appear to threaten, the aim may be to enhance the tendency for the VCC to rise in order to offset the tendency to labour shortage profit squeeze (3§3).

Addenda: a. The circuit of capital and microeconomic intervention; b. Economics on micro-policy

a. The logic implicit in microeconomic assistance to valorisation may be indicated by reference to different transformations in the circuit of capital (2S1):

$$M - C\{MP;LP\} \ldots P \ldots C' - M'$$

Microeconomic interventions may thus facilitate the exchange $M - C\{MP;LP\}$ by improving the (spatial) availability of appropriate means of production and labour power. They may be targeted directly on improving the (potential) value productivity of the labour process, P, thus increasing quantitatively the ideal value produced, C'. They may attempt to improve the realised value of commodities C', by stimulating an increase in demand and so facilitating the exchange $C' - M'$. Micro-intervention aimed at enhanced accumulation will try to encourage the investment of the surplus-value $(M' - M)$ in a circuit of capital employing productive labour. More specifically, it may attempt to direct such investment to a particular firm, sector, branch or region characterised by some desirable use-value characteristic, by advanced technology, by specific local unemployment problems, or by balance of payments relevance. Or it may try to channel surplus value into research and development to stimulate innovation.

b. Microeconomics is concerned mainly theoretically to justify competition policy and the actual or surrogate influence of markets on resource allocation. Interventionist industrial and regional policies may be seen as a response to the insufficiency of instruments provided by welfare, fiscal and monetary policies for coping with the multiplicity and inter-dependencies of economic policy targets (see Tinbergen 1952). The ineffectiveness of market forces under the particular circumstances identified by the theory of externalities and public goods may provide a basis for state industrial intervention. In particular, the ubiquitous and crucially accumulation-relevant 'externality' quality of the production and application of knowledge appears to justify education and research expenditure, patent law, and micro-economic intervention aimed at supporting and complementing research and development expenditure by companies (see, for example, Carter (ed.) 1981; cf. Eldred 1984a: §88). (For a recent political economy of some aspects of microeconomic policy see Levacic 1987: chs 6, 11 and 14.)

§6. The execution of microeconomic policy and the inner state

Effective microeconomic intervention must discriminate between particular industries, sectors, companies and even individual entrepreneurs. Self-interested competition subjects may attempt to be classified as socially significant or welfare relevant, in order to be eligible for state subsidy or to avoid state regulation. The particular and contingent relations between different individual, or groups of, competition subjects, and different inner-state apparatuses and institutions, will affect the actual incidence of microeconomic policy activity. As an expression of the universal social subject, microeconomic intervention should be perceived as being implemented, in accordance with the universal criteria entailed by its objectives, by a professional, neutral, rule-bound bureaucracy with minimum discretionary powers. In bourgeois democracies the social subjectivity of the state is manifest in the political processes and institutions of representative democracy – such as parliament and its committees. These lay down in legislation objectives, instruments and rules for eligibility for state support, or liability for state regulation. On the other hand, specifically in the instance of microeconomic policy, the bureaucrats actually implementing policies may, to be effective, require considerable discretionary powers. The implementing institutions may then be given terms of reference within which to exercise such discretion which, in keeping with value-criteria, should mimic the commercial criteria enforced by market forces in civil society. To the extent that economic policy cannot present to everyday consciousness the formal equality of treatment characteristic of law, it must be seen to be regulated by surrogate market rationality.

SECTION 4   THE ANTINOMIES OF WELFARE AND ECONOMIC POLICY

§7. The welfare state and market reproduction of the economy

Welfare activity not only articulates with the expression of the tendencies of accumulation; more fundamentally, it conflicts with the value-form determined reproduction of the economy. State expenditure on transfers redistributes in favour of the (on value-criteria) unsuccessful, discouraging the deployment of income sources to the production of value. Welfare activity arising from some personal characteristic which is a bar to economic activity appears to be problematical only as a generator of state expenditure, which is in itself a drain on other incomes, in particular the value available for valorisation and accumulation. However, even welfare benefits for those declared unfit to work (because of age or health) reduce the ultimate reserve of labour available for work (and may even stimulate more people to become economically inactive), thus initially accelerating the cyclical course of economic development associated with the 'profit squeeze' expression of the tendency to over-accumulation of capital. Conversely, to the extent that welfare benefits are financed by taxation and other contributions out of surplus value, and that the institution of minimum wages puts a drain on surplus value, the cyclical course of development associated with the 'profit squeeze' expression of the tendency to over-accumulation initially slows down (3§3). The institution of welfare benefits ('unproductive consumption') also articulates with the expression of the tendency to over-accumulation in under-consumption. In the case of unemployment benefits in particular, welfare policy has the well known effect of automatic stabilisation in degree dependent on the way these benefits are financed (3§4). Finally, to the extent that welfare benefits put an upward pressure on wage costs, they may have the effect of reinforcing the speed of introduction of labour-expelling techniques of production (cf. 4S1; Reuten 1979b and Glombowski and Krüger 1984b).

More fundamentally, welfare activity directed at the intrinsically economically active contradicts the central principle of market regulated reproduction – that access to consumption should be dependent upon contribution made (in the last resort by labour – 6§4) to the production of value. The provision of some or all of a person's income irrespective of their contribution of labour distorts the trade-offs in, and so the operation of, labour markets. The more effective such a policy is in ensuring an adequate existence, the more disruptive of labour market resource allocation it will tend to be. Welfare policies generally involve redistribution from the successful (in terms of value) to the less successful. In a system based on material incentives this redistribution cannot but tend to generate a disincentive to deploy one's income source, be it capital or labour.

For civil society, income must be qualitatively dependent on contribution to the production, not of useful objects, and certainly not to the satisfaction of need, but of value. On the other hand, the logic of the state decrees that it must, in its actualisation of the right to existence and its support of an adequate supply of labour power, in fact take cognisance of consumption dictated by considerations of need. Welfare policy thus affects not only the size of the reserve of labour and the surplus value available for accumulation, but also the functioning of the labour market directly and indirectly through redistribution. Welfare policy thus threatens to undermine the reproduction of competitive society by the market. Conversely, it may also appear to assist reproduction by stabilising the cyclical course of accumulation (but cf. §9).

Addenda: a. Conflicting policy objectives; b. Welfare and social control; c. Microeconomics and welfare

a. Welfare goals may conflict with the other main targets of economic policy by increasing the costs of labour power and reducing the incentive to work and invest (Eldred 1984a: §84), and by undermining the real subordination of labour (Keane 1984: 17). The scope of redistribution may thus be limited by the deleterious effects of progressive taxation on 'Technical progress, the allocation of resources, incentives, social mobility, competition and investment' (Hayek 1960: 308). The mechanisms of entitlement to, and the quantitative levels of, welfare payments, etc. are 'designed to prevent the unemployed from losing everything and to permit them to continue to be consumers, but they are also intended to encourage the unemployed to stop being unemployed as quickly as possible' (De Brunhoff 1976: 73). Another inter-dependence then, is that between welfare expenditure and macro-economic management of aggregate demand.

b. The problem of attempting to substitute some administrative form of control for the market mechanisms tendentially undermined by welfare policy is embodied in the specific institutions which implement the policy. In the case of France, for example, the 'Agence nationale pour l'emploi' 'reproduced the usual capitalist norms regarding the waged labour force ... [and] the enormous gaps in the French public welfare ... are not the result of neglect or administrative insufficiency: they are instrinsic to the form of regulation itself. The unemployed have rights only in so far as they are potential wage earners ... and are thus subject to surveillance' (De Brunhoff 1976: 9). The welfare state must also have an, at least implicit, 'social control' aspect. A client must not only demonstrate need, 'but must also be a deserving client ... who complies with the dominant economic, political and cultural standards and norms of society ... [is] willing to keep themselves available for any alternative employment ... that eventually may be made available to them by employment agencies', so that 'the claim for welfare payments to the poor is everywhere made conditional upon their conformity to standards of behaviour which the better-to-do strata of the population are perfectly free to violate ... material benefits for the needy are traded for their submissive recognition of the "moral order" of the society which generates such need' (Offe 1981: 155–6). This also entails that systematic welfare provision be provided by the state, rather than by charity, 'to politically regulate who is and who is not a wage labourer' (Lenhardt and Offe 1977: 94–5).

For Hegel, too, state as opposed to charitable relief of poverty is to transcend the contradiction of the need to maintain the consent of the poor, and the principle of civil society that subsistence should be derived from income, from (in the last instance) labour (Hegel 1821: §245). To the extent that separation-in-unity is undermined, however, the contradiction reappears. The struggles over rights derivative from the right to existence – within the capital relation, in the economy, in competitive society, in civil society and within the state – can be conceived as strivings towards the transcendence of mere political emancipation towards social emancipation (on this distinction, see Marx 1844b; and 6§11). The point is that incipient moves towards the state imposing such social rights on civil society – for example, by minimum wage legislation – is an affront to the value-form determined processes of the competitive kernel of civil society. This is a rich source of the tensions manifesting the contradictions of the mixed economy, which provide the basis for an account of intra-epochal development of policy (initiated in Chapter 10). The conflicts between the defence of private property, and the demands of everyday consciousness for the implementation of policies consequent on the ideal right to existence, form an important organising principle for further concretisation of economic policy. It should be noted that these conflicts cannot be reduced to merely distributional problems between property owners and labourers, as some (mis)interpretations of Marxism would have it. Rather, they are to be grasped in their interconnectedness with the necessary processes of surplus-value appropriation at the level of valorisation and accumulation, which is then reflected more concretely in the real subordination of labour in the labour process, as well as in distributional struggle.

c. Political individualism and 'economic efficiency' considerations both predispose microeconomics to manage the antinomies of welfare demands via some kind of insurance principle, so that the level of benefit entitlement is related to the extent of contribution, thence reconstituting the link between effective participation in the value-form processes and material well-being. (For a well argued political economy on this viewpoint see Buchanan and Tullock 1965.) Many current welfare states incorporate such a principle, although it is noteworthy that the insurance fund is almost never adequate to the level and extent of benefits deemed appropriate, being almost everywhere topped-up by the general exchequer. The point is that if adequate existence could be supported by insurance markets, welfare could anyway be left to the value-form processes of civil society. Ultimately, those who cannot reproduce existence by contributing property or labour to valorisation are unlikely to be able to contribute to insurance funds sufficiently to generate actuarially sound levels of benefit entitlement, adequate to an acceptable level of existence.

§8. The welfare state and legitimation

The institutions of the inner state (6§12) must themselves generate actual welfare policies and the details of what constitutes an adequate existence. But it is upon the state's success in generating the implementing policies for the actualisation of the right to existence at some acceptable standard, without affronting property right, that continued reproduction of the state's legitimation by the will of its people depends (6§10).

The necessary form of the state/civil society relationship is that of separation, so that the state stands outside civil society confronting each citizen as equal. Legitimate state action in accordance with this form, is confined to the enactment, execution and adjudication of general, non-discriminatory law-like (8§2) rules which reproduce the abstract equality of citizens *vis-à-vis* the state. However, welfare policy is intrinsically concerned with differentiating individuals in accordance with some conception of the extent of their need. This differentiation involves treating unequals unequally – and, what is more, on the basis not of universal value-criteria but of particular-istic use-value criteria. The executive branches of the state become involved in discretionary adjudication as to individual eligibility, thus undermining the 'separation of powers' manifesting separation-in-unity in bourgeois democracy (6§12). Welfare policy then threatens the concrete separation of the state from civil society, as well as its universal form.

If the actualisation of existence right for the least well-off is to be adequate, any non-discriminatory system of general welfare benefits equally available to all is likely to generate quantitatively enormous appropriations of value by the state (and transformation of a huge proportion of labour into unproductive employment within the welfare state – see 10§4). The core process of welfare policy is redistribution, which must per se discriminate between persons on the basis of their concrete particular inequality, whilst the essence of the state's relationship to its citizens is their treatment abstractly as equals. Welfare policy must also discriminate against property owners (as well as better-off wage and salary earners) in favour of those who have only that income source of last resort, the ability to labour. It tends to discriminate even more specifically against capital accumulation in favour of consumption. On the other hand, to the extent that the state does not enact welfare policies, its legitimacy in terms of the consent of its citizens may be undermined since it fails to actualise the right to existence.

Addendum: a. Liberalism and the conflicts of welfare planning

a. Hayek is crucially concerned with the welfare state's threats to individual liberty, possessive individualism and economic efficiency. He acknowledges that 'There are common needs that can be satisfied only by collective action and which can be thus be provided for without restricting individual liberty' (Hayek 1960: 257), and that 'There is little reason why the government should not also play some role, or even take the initiative, in such areas as social insurance and education or temporarily subsidize certain experimental

251

developments' (Hayek 1960: 258). However, welfare 'measures which ...
could in aggregate destroy a free society ... really constitute an exercise of
the coercive powers of government and rest on its claiming exclusive rights in
certain fields' (Hayek 1960: 258), and as such are to be eschewed. He argues
that whilst the welfare state may 'facilitate the attainment of certain
standards of life by individuals', it may not 'make certain everybody attains
them' (Hayek 1960: 260), since then 'certain services become the exclusive
domain of the state' and 'nothing short of individualizing, paternalistic
treatment by discretionary authority with powers of discrimination between
persons will do' (Hayek 1960: 261; see also 257–60). What is outlawed is that
which involves the state in treating unequals unequally in pursuit of distributive justice, and thereby attempting to actualise as concrete social
particular rights, what should remain as abstract political rights, achieved
not by invidious comparisons of the socially determined differences between
individuals, but by some absolute, external, naturally determined minimum
subsistence level (Hayek 1960: 259). A 'free society ... is not compatible with
sharing out income according to some preconceived notion of justice' which
fails to preserve 'the impersonal method of adjustment under which people
can choose their occupation' (Hayek 1960: 303).

Hayek (1960: 203) perceives the free market on the one hand, and the rule
of law on the other, as the twin bastions of individual liberty. He then goes
on to posit the conflict between these principles and the welfare state, in the
face of what value-form theory has conceptualised as the essentially
universal state engaging in intrinsically *particularistic* interventions: 'A
government which cannot use coercion except in the enforcement of general
rules has no power to achieve particular aims ... and ... cannot determine
the material position of particular people or enforce distributive or "social
justice" without dirigism'. 'The restrictions which the rule of law imposes
upon government thus preclude all those measures which would be necessary
to ensure that individuals will be rewarded according to another's conception
of merit or desert rather than according to the value that their services have
for their fellows ... it precludes the pursuit of distributive, as opposed to
commutative justice' (Hayek 1960: 231). For value-form theory, the state – to
the extent that it successfully actualises the right to existence – comes into
conflict with its form as the universal social subject, and with its role as
defender of property right. The state cannot actualise the right to existence
without contradicting its form. Yet it cannot fail to actualise the right to
existence without undermining its legitimation. The conflicts of the involve-
ment of the state in welfare policy thus seem to mean that it is damned if it
doesn't and damned if it does (Offe 1973: 60; 1979: 68, 77). Offe also points
out that what he calls 'conservative' theories have identified the same tension
in the operation of the inner state which 'must necessarily frustrate the
expectations they generate' (Offe 1979: 68). Value-form theory bases these
conflicts in the contradictions of separation-in-unity.

§9. Macroeconomic management and the market reproduction of the economy

Macroeconomic management tends to dilute the coercive forces of the irregular cycle of boom and slump characteristic of capitalist accumulation (5S2), and thence to undermine the concomitant stimulation of restructuring of capital and disciplining of labour. The slump enables the devaluation of excess capital by its physical or institutional destruction, or by processes of merger and takeover (4§§4–6). Macroeconomic policy to reduce the unemployment consequences of cyclical down turns tends to dilute the disciplining of organised labour, and of over-enthusiastic extensions of the welfare state. Macroeconomic policy may thence exacerbate, prolong and change the phenomenal form of economic cyclical development.

The effects of macroeconomic management articulate in particular with the form of existence (4§4), and the expressions (4§§5–6) of the TRPF. Capital operating the most advanced technique of production, when added to an existing stratification, tends to generate either price decrease or over-capacity in the sector in which it operates. Macroeconomic management, to the extent that it successfully increases aggregate demand and thence capacity utilisation, counteracts concomitant falls in the rate of profit. However, to the extent that this occurs without inflation (thus increasing employment), it tends to produce a downward pressure on the rate of profit of the newly accumulated capital, and in the event may slow down the introduction of new techniques. All capitals benefit pro rata from aggregate demand increase, and if capitals at the bottom of the stratification are not scrapped then capacity utilisation is reduced for the top of the stratification, including the newly accumulated capital. This provides a disincentive for the introduction of new techniques, though it does not exclude it, even if the rate of profit falls, Further, during a wave of technological change (4§6) it will be difficult to maintain the bottom of a capital stratification in operation by stimulating aggregate demand increase without considerable inflationary pressures. Whilst inflationary macroeconomic management may generate an increase in the rate of profit for both the newly and the previously accumulated capital, it exacerbates the conflicts between industrial and non-banking money capital (5§8). Indeed money and industrial capital typically make conflicting demands on the state. In general, money capital wants low rates of inflation, high interest rates and a high and stable exchange rate, whilst industrial capital may want a moderate rate of inflation, low and stable interest rates and a lower exchange rate.

Industrial capital needs the framework expenditures of the state and the demand for its products generated thereby. Whether money capital profits from servicing a high level of public expenditure, or whether its source of profits in foreign investment makes it aware only of the tax burden of sustaining that expenditure, is a contingent matter.

Anti-inflationary policy may have a deflationary impact on incentives to accumulate (cf. 5§10), and indeed on the reproduction of existence. Macroeconomic management concerned with constraining money wages may ease the downward pressure on the rate of profit, concomitant on the articulation of the TRPF and the TOC (cf. 5S1). A downward pressure on wages may be facilitated by a (moderately) inflationary monetary policy. However, such a policy not only further exacerbates the conflicts between industrial and non-banking money capital, but it may also be deleterious to the competitiveness of national capitals in the world economy, if national exceed world inflation rates (see 10§2).

Intervention in money markets in pursuit of monetary policy disrupts their reproduction of money as the sole autonomous manifestation of value. Instruments such as interest rate policy have conflicting determinants (namely, lender of last resort versus control of monetary aggregates), tend to distort prices in money markets, and dilute the linkage with the profitability of industrial capital. Open-market operations beyond the mere funding of government debt also distort the operation of money markets. Monetary targeting invariably leads to the creation of new forms of money by money capital, which may divert resources from value-creating processes and make the quantity of different kinds of money responsive to state enforced use-value criteria rather than value-criteria. The ultimate dependence of the (national) monetary system on state power (7§§2–3) may enhance the ability of the state to borrow from the banking system, and thence facilitate an inflation financed expansion of the proportional size of the state. The combination of welfare state policies with fiscal stimulation of aggregate demand, in the face of tendencies undermining accumulation, may lead subsequently to the combination of stagnation and inflation. The point is that expansion of expenditure on welfare institutions and programmes, which seems sustainable in periods of buoyant economic activity, may be difficult to decrease sufficiently or rapidly enough to avoid inflationary pressures in the slump generated by that buoyant accumulation.

The state as the agent of macroeconomic policy contradicts the decentralised reproduction of the value-form by competition subjects regulated only by market mechanisms. Management of the level of capacity utilisation and of the funding of investment (and of state debt beyond a neutral framework) may disrupt capital market regulation of the processes of disinvestment and investment. Successful macroeconomic management undermines the micro-level allocative mechanisms of capital markets (and thus labour markets): companies sheltered from the full force of competition by state manipulation of macro-aggregates will have less incentive, and more diffuse signals, to disinvest from obsolescent, and invest in new industries. Labour with outdated skills, or located in declining regions, will then have less incentive to retrain or to be geographically mobile. The impact of this value-inefficiency will be enforced by world-economic competition. Active intervention in the processes of accumulation contradicts the world-wide logic of the value-form, which demands that capital flow freely throughout the world economy in pursuit of profits.

§10. Macroeconomic management and legitimation

The state, the upholder of the principal concretisation of the value-form in civil society – property right – necessarily infringes that right, in appropriating property without exchange and without contractual agreement, in the form of taxes (8S2). To the extent that this is merely a fiscal framework of appropriations in accordance with general interest criteria, within which competitive society continues to operate in accordance with value-criteria, it entails no additional conflict for the bourgeois state. However, given fiscality together with welfare state imperatives (S1), and the self-interest of the state, the latter will inevitably also engage in interventionist fiscal policy – macroeconomic management (S2).

By intervening in the processes of valorisation and accumulation in pursuit of macroeconomic policy, the state imports the contradictions of the tendencies of accumulation into itself. Macroeconomic management is faced with conflicting imperatives: maintaining an environment in which, on the one hand, capital is optimistic and, on the other, labour continues to consent to the sale of labour power as a commodity. In pursuing economic growth (determined as valorisation and accumulation) by policies financed by the appropriation of private property, the state is thus necessarily reproducing the contradictions of the value-form processes themselves. Their manifestations may then threaten its legitimation, and bridge the necessary separation of the state from civil society (6§11). To the extent that the competition subject perceives the state's activities (as opposed to merely the exigencies of civil society) as worsening the conditions for the successful deployment of its income source, the legitimation of the state by the will of the bourgeois person is potentially undermined. To the extent that the state's wages and taxation policy is perceived, more or less overtly in different conjunctures, to be partially benefiting capital or labour rather than to be guarding the universal general interest, its legitimation is potentially undermined.

To the extent that it systematically generates aspirations, to which it can in the outturn not live up – promises of macroeconomic stability which it cannot meet – macroeconomic management is also potentially threatened with the withdrawal of legitimation (see Chapter 10). The effects of declining legitimation are then played out in the mechanisms of the inner state (6§12; see Chapter 10). Overall it is not clear that macroeconomic policy can be contained within the bounds of a stable long-term context within which the value-form determined processes can operate. It is continually tempted to go beyond the provision of a soundly financed framework from the market, to intervene in its operation.

§11. Microeconomic intervention and the market reproduction of the economy

Microeconomic policy is the most direct manifestation of the conflict between the market-reproduced value-form logic of competitive society and the state imposition of use-values, attempting to rectify the inadequacies of the market reproduction of the value-form system for itself, and for the actualisation of the ideal right to existence. Even competition policy, intended to enhance the reproduction of the value-form by market forces, may prove a disincentive to accumulation by removing one of the fruits of its success – growth to a size enabling the wielding of economic, social and political power. Relative size and market power may be a prerequisite for technological innovation, upon which competitive accumulation may rest.[5] Industrial policy implemented by tax allowances and subsidies may also appear merely to alter the trade-offs in accordance with which competition subjects remain free to optimise their objective functions. However, it must distort the incentive and informational properties of market prices, and so may reduce the efficiency of the market reproduction of valorisation and accumulation. Exhaustive state expenditure for purchase of commodities is not directly regulated by capital market competition, and employs (mostly) unproductive labour (see 10§4). Administrative interventions usually involve a direct attempt to override value-criteria with use-value criteria, which may or may not be intended indirectly

5 See Schumpeter 1943, on 'creative destruction'.

to enhance valorisation. On the one hand, it might appear that distortion of the market could be minimised by universal monetary grants, subsidies and taxes, which are administered with little discretion, according to broadly defined eligibility/liability and narrow terms of reference, in accordance with criteria which override immediate commercial considerations only on clearly defined technical grounds. On the other hand, cost effectiveness is often better served by more specific measures, often 'in kind' rather than in cash, which are administered with highly discretionary discrimination, according to very narrowly defined eligibility/liability and wide terms of reference, and in accordance with criteria which frequently override commercial considerations on political and social grounds.[6]

Microeconomic policy brings into sharp focus the constraints on economic policy imposed by the value-form basis of the social totality. Microeconomic policy which is successful in increasing the rate of accumulation must exacerbate the manifestations of the contradictory tendencies of accumulation. Unsuccessful policy may contribute to the manifestation of the tendencies of accumulation in stagnation (§9) by, for example, diluting the incentives to restructuring. Microeconomic intervention, much more directly than macroeconomic management, interpellates use-value criteria into resource allocation decisions, determined primarily by the market-imposed needs of valorisation and accumulation. Attempts may be made to subordinate microeconomic policy to value-criteria, but the only ultimate value-criterion of the decisions of competition subjects (and of the state) is that they in fact lead to successful valorisation and accumulation. Chapters 8–9 have been concerned to argue that this itself may require the allocation of resources to the production and distribution of use-values which cannot be, or contingently are not, reproduced in the value-form. The proximate decisions to produce them are taken on use-value criteria, even if the ultimate criterion may be the successful reproduction of the value-form system. What is more, the state is also driven by political and social imperatives which go beyond the reproduction of valorisation and accumulation. Ecological concerns, for example, are inevitably imposed as costs on valorisation and accumulation, and frequently restrict the exercise of property rights.[7]

Management of technical change, innovation and research and development imposes social use-value criteria and may, by enforcing an inappropriately long time horizon, undermine the dynamism of

6 Cf. Williams 1982: 89.
7 Cf. for example, Beckerman 1974.

market forces. To the extent that research and development is stimulated by protection of intellectual property, diffusion may thereby be undermined. The tracing of these imperatives from contextual through welfare to macro- and microeconomic policy still leaves the state with the task of contingently managing the persistent conflicts grounding the fundamental contradictions of the epoch.

Addenda: a. Industrial policy and the contradictions of the mixed economy; b. Economics and the conflicts of microeconomic policy

a. The total or partial 'decommodification' implicit in microeconomic interventions raises for everyday consciousness the possibility of further modification of the value-form by use-value criteria, and thereby loosens the hold of bourgeois norms reproductive of the value-form and bourgeois right on that consciousness (Keane 1984: 21). Though radical political scientists like Offe share a number of the insights of value-form theoretic accounts of economic policy, they tend to lose any form determinations of the epoch in unwarranted assertions of secular irreversibility of, for example, subsidisation (for example, Offe 1973: 48). The rights-based state grounding the value-form can do whatever it can get legitimated by the will of competition subjects and citizens, including the reversal of any policy. What 'political power' cannot do is to evade the contradictions of 'organising material production according to its own "political" criteria' in a system in which 'property, whether in labour power or capital is private. Hence [where] ... private decisions ... determine the concrete use of the means of production' (Offe and Ronge 1976: 120).

b. The concern of microeconomics with administratively imposed surrogates for market resource allocation criteria (§5b) indicates the conflict of the state over-ruling market forces in the bourgeois epoch. For some macroeconomic, social or political reason the state has totally or partially taken over from the market in some domain of resource allocation. To the extent that this action is rationally based, it implies the (at least partial) imposition of some use-value criteria. Yet the recommendations of microeconomic welfare analysis are that devices such as long-run marginal cost based pricing, internal rate of return and net present value investment choice rules be used to mimic the value-form determined decision-making of the market.

---

§12. Microeconomic intervention and legitimation

In implementing any policy the social subject (6§8) threatens to come into conflict with the subjectless processes of the abstract universal value-form. Microeconomic policy is compatible with the rights-based state just so long as it is perceived as being based on the preservation and actualisation of the bourgeois rights of property and person. To the extent that the logic of the market is overridden, the more basic logic of the universal value-form may still be reproduced, in the universal forms of law and administration under which it is implemented. The effects of microeconomic policy on the reproduction of the legitimation of the state will depend on the success of the inner state in maintaining for everyday consciousness the identity between individual citizens' interests, the general interest espoused by the state and the self-interest of bureaucrats and politicians. At the same time, the apparent separation of political from economic processes has to be maintained. It has been argued that the state inevitably attempts to interpose use-value criteria in the value-form transactions of civil society. This constitutes contradictory activity for the state, bridging its concrete separation from civil society. Universality is transgressed by discretionary discrimination between particular citizens and between competition subjects other than by mutual agreement. Microeconomic policy may be perceived by no significant group in civil society (apart from the direct and obvious beneficiaries) as being in accordance either with the general, or with their own particular private, interest. If sufficiently large and powerful groups of such citizens are alienated, the legitimation of the state may come under pressure. For the same reasons that microeconomic intervention is potentially the most threatening to separation-in-unity, it is very often perceived by rival states and international organisations as crucially alien to the reproduction of the value-form through the free operation of international markets. It is thus peculiarly likely to be sanctioned by such organisations, and by those economically powerful states most likely to benefit from the free operation of such forces. This may generate further threats to legitimation (see 10§2).

The imperatives of microeconomic intervention may lead to the bypassing of the representative institutions of the inner state in favour of implementation by highly discretionary, technocratic and specialist bureaux, whose decisions over who is to benefit from, or bear the costs of, particular microeconomic interventions cannot be easily made accountable to the legitimate guardians of the general interest, in parliament and its committees. These tensions of microeconomic policy for the state manifest themselves in political struggles to re-establish parliamentary accountability, and to impose surrogates for commercial market criteria on the agents of that policy, so that they direct state assistance and regulation in accordance with expected profitability and value efficiency. Such moves merely pose the conflict again at the political level. If recipients are potentially commercially successful, then they are presumably illegitimate candidates for discriminatory state aid. If they are not, then such aid may be ineffective. What is more, the bureaucrats manifesting the universal social subject may be drawn into dangerously close relationships with the individual competition subjects with whom they deal, and so may face incentives and temptations to behave in accordance with their individual self-interest, rather than with the general interest. The social subject may appear to act as an individual competition subject, possibly in cahoots with one or more private competition subjects, to the disadvantage of others.

Whilst the state can do whatever it can get legitimated as being in the general interest, it cannot dissolve the fundamental contradictions of the value-form. In its microeconomic policies the state can be seen most clearly grappling with the manifestation of these contraditions. The value regulated economy cannot reproduce all its conditions of existence in terms of the adequate use-value composition of output for its expanded reproduction, whether in terms of the needs of continued technical production, or of the necessary reproduction of the unique factor of value production, labour power (1§6, 2S3). In order to reproduce the conditions of existence of civil society, and in particular the use-value based needs of persons and the economy, the state must reach back into civil society so that the contradictions reappear in the shape of the tensions of microeconomic policy, which tendentially undermine the legitimation of the state. These tensions become manifest in political struggles and the related policy stances of the state (Chapter 10).

Addenda: a. 'The road to serfdom'? b. Political economy of bureaucracy

a. It is a central tenet of systematic liberalism that any breach of the separation between state and economy leads to the inexorable trend to more and more intervention, which must ultimately threaten the democratic legitimation of the bourgeois state (see especially Hayek 1944). The conclusion that this process can and should be reversed depends on the neglect of (what value-theory argues to be) the necessary tendencies towards state intervention, based in the antinomies of the value-form economy, which may thus be expected to continually reappear as long as that economy persists.

b. The theory of public choice and the political economy of bureaucracy (see Jackson 1982, Mueller 1979 and Whynes and Bowles 1981 for surveys; the seminal works are Downs 1957 and Niskanen 1973) deals with the problems of aligning the behaviour of public servants with the imperatives of the general interest, by examining the objective functions of politicians and bureaucrats, and their consequent susceptibility to the blandishments of vested interests in civil society. (For a recent attempt to apply public choice theory to welfare and microeconomic policy see Levacic 1987: Part II.) The effectiveness of microeconomic intervention depends on the degree of discretion, monopoly of expertise and specialisation of the implementing bureaux. However, these same factors also provide the basis for the inter-pellation of the self-interests of particular groups of competition subjects into policy formulation and implementation. Once again, the basis of the behavioural conflicts that these theories assume to be aspects of human nature (or merely claim to observe empirically) is, for value-form theory, to be sought in the antinomies of the bourgeois totality. Bureaucrats and politicians are bourgeois persons, the first determination of whom is the self-interested competition subject, who may indeed be expected to seize opportunities for operating state bureaux in accordance with their personal objective function. Nevertheless, these same bureaucrats are also determined as citizens, specifically entrusted with implementing the general interest in accordance with universal criteria (cf. Van Winden 1981). Certain kinds of interventionist economic policy may enhance the opportunities for personal gain by exercise of discretion in favour of particular firms, as well as exacerbating the problems of administrative enforcement of general interest criteria. This problem may be expected to become worse as the size of the state bureaucracy, and the complexity of the tasks it is called upon to perform, are increased and made more remote from the parliamentary accountability. Nevertheless, policy recommendations focusing on reducing such intervention neglect its value-form determinants. The concrete power of capital to resist unwanted state intervention (identified by the parallel 'ungovernability' thesis of conservative political science) constitutes at least as great a threat to legitimation. The contradictions of the value-form, grounded in the separation out of the state from the economy are manifest in this conflict 'between the political reproduction demands of labour power and the private reproduction strategies of capital' (Offe 1979: 77).

SUMMARY

Within separation-in-unity, the state as social subject necessarily relates to civil society in four main ways: as provider of the social context for competitive – and, more broadly – civil society (8S1); as reproducer of its own material existence (8S2); as actualiser of the right to existence (Section 1); and as agent of macroeconomic management (Section 2) and microeconomic intervention (Section 3). The contradictions of the mixed economy (8S3) are grounded in the state as policy agent (8S4). In order to cope as it sees to be necessary with the contingency of, and systematic threats to, individual existence, active state policy is particularised first in welfare policies, concerned to enhance the conditions for the sale of labour power, and to provide income support or replacement for the unsuccessful labourer. The particular content of welfare policy is contingent, being reproduced by the effects of legitimation by citizens' consent (fundamentally that of the labourer), by the restricted sovereignty of the state, and by the national determination of civil society (see Chapter 10).

The welfare state is a contradictory form of existence of the mixed economy (itself the form of existence of separation-in-unity). Welfare policy generates conflicts since its actualisation of the right to existence tends to undermine the market regulation of labour markets, and is in general concerned with redistribution in accordance with other than value-criteria. It thus can affect the playing-out of the tendencies of accumulation. In its concern with differentiating between individuals in terms of particularities, and in raising aspirations which it cannot meet, welfare activity also conflicts with the state as universal social subject. The contradictions of the welfare state are the reappearance, with the emergence of the state as agent of economic policy, of the contradictions of separation-in-unity, themselves manifesting the fundamental contradiction of the value-form. The state's further attempt to manage the expression of these contradictions is particularised in macro-economic policy.

In maintaining its material existence as social context for the market and as welfare state, the state is necessarily the fiscal state. As part of the social context the state must provide a monetary framework. Active macroeconomic management provides further determinations of the state's fiscal and monetary activities. The restricted sovereignty of the macroeconomic agent further determines its policy towards its national economy, in the context of the world economy (7SS2–3). The attempt to manage the macroeconomy confronts its decentralised reproduction by competition subjects regulated by market forces. In addressing this reappearance of the contradictions of separation-in-unity, the state as the agent of policy is further particularised by its microeconomic intervention.

Microeconomic intervention attempts to enhance the market-regulated allocation of resources in pursuit of more efficient valorisation and accumulation, and of the use-value demands of contextual, welfare and macroeconomic policy. Once again its scope is restricted to its own national capitals throughout the world economy, plus all capitals operating within its domestic economy (7SS2–3). It manifests to the highest degree the expression of the contradictions of separation-in-unity, in the form of interventions by the state as social subject back into civil society. Microeconomic intervention conflicts with the value-form regulated economy in that it involves the direct interpolation of use-value criteria by the state. It engenders legitimation conflicts, since it involves discretionary discrimination between individual competition subjects and citizens, beyond that legitimated by law. Since it involves intervention aimed directly at overriding the outcome of market-reproduced value-form *processes, microeconomic policy poses the most persistent threats to separation-in-unity.*

The mixed economy (Chapter 8) has been grounded in welfare and economic policy. Market reproduction of the universal value-form, complemented by state activities under the rule of law, is found to be inadequate to macroeconomic management and microeconomic intervention. Such policies therefore tend continually to conflict with the imperatives of the value-form.

The presentation has had to integrate necessity with contingency (0§11). The forms of state and state–civil society relationship entailed by the right to property and existence, the derived need for the articulation of the general interest, for separation-in-unity and therefore for finance to perpetuate the existence of the state, and for macroeconomic management and microeconomic intervention, are all abstractly necessary. But whilst the form of policy is necessary, its content as revealed in the many different policies, institutions and apparatuses by which these abstract necessities are concretised, are contingent. It should be emphasised that there is no single point of the presentation at which necessity gives way to contingency. The content of rights-actualising laws will have contingent determin-ations. The reproduction of money and labour power are necessary, but the manipulation of this reproduction in pursuit of economic policies has contingent determinations. (cf. Hegel 1821: §299A: 'The proper object of universal legislation may be distinguished in a general way from the proper function of administrative officials or of some kind of state regulation, in that the content of the former is wholly universal, i.e. determinate laws, while it is what is particular in content which falls to the latter, together with ways and means of enforcing the law.')

Chapter ten

The Articulation of the Tendencies of Accumulation and Policy

PRELIMINARY REMARKS

In the course of the presentation, the contradiction between value and use-value has been grounded in valorisation and accumulation, and then separated out into the opposition between civil society and the state. But the contradiction is not resolved by this actual separation: it obtains forms of existence within the state, within the economy and in separation-in-unity. The state is both the facilitator of the value-form determined processes of valorisation and accumulation, and the reproducer of the right to levels and forms of use-value consumption adequate to realise the right to existence. This fundamental contradiction is endemic to the bourgeois epoch and cannot be resolved within it. It can only be transcended, to appear in other forms (cf. Williams 1982: 83). The changing manifestations of the fundamental contradiction provide the guiding thread for the account of the turns and twists of economic policy. The objective is not to hypostatise the bourgeois totality as some self-sufficient, harmoniously self-reproducing whole, but rather to lay bare the value-form determinants of the conflict-ridden course of development at the level of everyday consciousness (cf. Eldred 1984a: §74e). Whilst the form-determinations of the economy and the state are epochally necessary, they are grounded in a changing variety of particular state activity and policies which appear to be but contingent forms of existence of the contradictions manifested in the conflicts of the mixed economy (8§§8–12; 9S4). The most concrete necessary manifestation of the value/use-value contradiction is the intervention by the state as social subject in the value-form-regulated economy. As the agent of economic policy (8S4) the state is intrinsically involved in managing the form of existence of the persisting contradictions of the articulation of the tendencies of accumulation and separation-in-unity which have not been conceptually transcended.

264

The antinomies of the mixed economy for the economy and for the state are reinforced and reproduced by the existence of the state as but one of many, embedded in the world economy (7SS2–3). The value-form world order of the world economy and many states is per se indifferent to the spatial location of valorisation and accumulation, yet bourgeois persons exist as citizens of geographically specific states. The state is thus in principle only a restricted agent of macroeconomic management for its national segment of the world economy, and microeconomic intervention is concerned with the value-success of its capital wherever it is, and with domestically located capitals from wherever they come. Policy has contingent determinants derived from international economic competition and inter-state economic, political, diplomatic and military rivalry. Nevertheless, the concrete specification of what constitutes an adequate use-value determination of the realisation of existence right has national and regional components.

Whilst it is true that the fundamental value-form is indifferent to merely quantitative variations, which cannot then per se constitute a threat to its reproduction, it is nevertheless the case that value is purely quantitative form. The driving force of the economy is precisely that of valorisation. Whilst the state's quantitative encroachments on valorisation and accumulation are secondary to the form contradictions of separation-in-unity, they are thus nevertheless significant in grasping the evolution of the grounding of those contradictions in the articulation of the tendencies of accumulation, incipient stagnation, and fiscal and legitimation crisis.

The state's management of the manifestations of emerging contradictions appears in shifting conjunctural settlements, illustrated here by 'social-democratic corporatism' and 'conservative neo-liberalism'. Each settlement itself manifests the contradictions of the epoch in different ways, and it is these persisting conflicts which generate cycles of policy and political development. Likely proximate causes of cyclical turning points will be the cumulative failures of a policy stance resulting from the specific inadequacies of its reconciliation of the persistent contradictions of the epoch, leading typically to a policy shift, legitimation problems, and possibly a change of government. The contradictions of the mixed economy, articulated with the contradictory tendencies of valorisation and accumulation from which they derive, generate the cycles of economic activity and the fluctuations of economic policy which characterise the empirical development of bourgeois society. This indication of the form-constrained range of possible policy settlements brings to a close the systematic presentation of the moments and contradictions of the epoch, and at the same time initiates the move toward a conceptually adequate conjunctural account of the contingent historical development of economic policy.

SECTION 1   RESTRICTED SOVEREIGNTY AND POLICY

§1. Policy and the world economy

A major contingent determinant of the forms of the state's existence and policies is that it is grounded not in a single world state but in a multitude of states (7SS2–3). National civil societies and the bourgeois persons who inhabit them are determined by many particular national characteristics, so that the general interest exists only as particular national interests (7S2). And states have only geographically restricted sovereignty (7§5). The clash of sovereign social subjects, like the clash of right, can have no necessary grounding. Unlike the clash of right, in the case of the clash of sovereign states there is no universally recognised superior subject to whom recourse can be had. Any state's existence and activities are therefore proximately determined by its location within the world economy (7§6). The value-form processes of valorisation and accumulation are essentially indifferent to their geographical location and to the use-value needs of particular communities, economies, civil societies and states. Yet it is precisely these particularities which are the focus of any state's activities. States seek a self-defined adequate concretisation of the right to existence for their citizens, growth of domestic production and employment, a stable national currency, a balance or surplus on their own payments account, repatriation of the fruits of valorisation by their capitals abroad, the attraction of footloose multinational capital, and valorisation and accumulation of domestic capital.

The mere existence of the state as one of many generates additional contextual expenditure (8S1) on defence, diplomacy and international relations. The perception of what constitutes infrastructural use-values (8§5) to be produced within the national territory will often be affected by military – or, more broadly strategic – considerations. The extent to which the state can appropriate from civil society the resources it needs for its material reproduction (8S2) is constrained by the perceived and expected effects of this burden on the ability and incentives of its competition subjects to pursue the successful deployment of their income sources, and so reproduce the value success of the national segment of the world-economy (7§6). Conversely, the adequate performance of economic policies may help to isolate the national civil society from the constraints of the existence of other states and world-economy competition.

The concretisation of the right to existence as the adequate opportunity to deploy an income source, and the right to subsistence when that opportunity is denied, is predicated upon nationally specific conceptions of an adequate standard of life. The attempt to realise different standards of living by quantitatively and qualitatively differing welfare policies (9S1) may be constrained both by the effects on the value competitiveness of the national economy of increasing the cost of employing labour and the taxation burden (8§8), and by the response of rival states through international treaties.

The state as but one of many restricted sovereign macroeconomic managers (9S2) may expand its objectives to include the balance of payments, of trade and of international capital account, the enhancement of the international competitiveness of domestic capitals, and the attraction of economic activity to the national territory. Since the rate of profit demanded by money capitalists and entrepreneurs is determined only by pragmatically feasible alternative investments, it may be possible to maintain accumulation in a particular national economy in the face of the articulation of the TOC and the TRPF (Chapter 5) by imposing capital controls, in order to prevent the outflow of capital in pursuit of higher returns elsewhere. The significance of these international determinants of macroeconomic policy will depend on the extent and mode of integration of the national into the world economy, as well as diplomatic and strategic considerations affecting the viability of different policy instruments and the relative weight placed on different policy targets. National macroeconomic concerns for favourable international capital flows and balance on external accounts may conflict with welfare concerns, and themselves be in conflict with the fundamental indifference of value-form processes to spatial location.

Values constituted within national economies are articulated only externally one with another, through the contingencies of the world monetary system (7§7). Whilst the value-forms are world-wide in scope, the quantitative formation of values is interrupted by the transitions between national currencies at parities which are the result of the scrabble for an advantageous store of value, modified by intermittent contracts, agreements and treaties determined by the relative economic and other power of each state. States have to defend the external (as well as the internal – 8§4) value of their currencies, but there exists no world state to reproduce a world monetary framework. Since the prime mediation of the national into the international economy is via monetary processes, a state's pursuit of its own monetary objectives will have to take cognisance of the performance of its currency and monetary instruments in world markets and of monetary flows over its national borders. International relative rates of inflation, in relation to the production and realisation of national capital and the balance of payments, impose a limit on the national central bank's inflationary pseudo-social validation (2§10; 5S3). An imbalance of payments poses the problem of the international convertibility of currencies. The problem of inflation, which is raised from the level of private banks to the national level, is then reproduced at the international level where, just as at the national level, it undermines a currency as an adequate store of value. Currency reserves of central banks as a claim to the (future) social labour of other countries devalue along with the inflation. Such a devaluation of currency reserves is overcome to the extent that currencies are convertible at a fixed rate to commodities (as with a gold standard), or if at least one key currency is so convertible and may be used as currency reserve. But clearly this key currency fixed rate convertibility cannot be maintained if that currency devalues markedly because of its national inflation, and balance of payment deficits are built up. Convertibility cannot be maintained if the key currency is then in fact converted into commodities.[1]

An initial rupture in the circuit of capital (via a non-validated pre-validation by a private bank) may be closed at the national social level by way of the decrease in the purchasing power of a unit of money (via the central bank – 2§9). With a balance of payments deficit, and/or with other countries holding that currency as reserves, this circuit is not closed altogether at the national level, and part of the national social loss is shifted to the surplus country. The holding of gold as a reserve offsets this shift.[2] Exchange-rate policy may also be determined by the extent to which a state wishes to be able to try to pursue independent macroeconomic policy, or conversely to be constrained by the dictates of international value flows. The attenuation of international value processes at national boundaries implies that a different degree of discretionary activity is open to

1 Until the end of the 1960s the US dollar was not effectively converted because, on the one hand, a moderate inflation made it less urgent. But on the other hand the convertibility was merely fiducial, because the USA controlled the world stock of gold, and with it gold prices.

2 The abolition of the gold–dollar exchange standard in fact implies that since 1971 there has been no international general equivalent. There are only international means of circulation, which have no different status from any other instruments of exchange used by private capitals, because exchange rates in principle (that is, without central bank interventions) are fixed in terms relative to the balance of payments of each country only (cf. De Brunhoff 1976: 50).

states, contingent on their relative economic, political and military power on the world stage.

Microeconomic policy may be concerned to attract internationally mobile capital to invest in domestic industrial activity, to stimulate exports and import substitution, and to assist domestic capital in general by facilitating the provision of cheap inputs. The state may also have an interest in the value-success of its citizens wherever in the world-economy they be operating. Microeconomic policy may thus be aimed at enhancing the competitiveness of its capital wherever it is, as well as that of capital located in its territory, whatever its home state. To the extent that a basis of international political co-operation is the mutual recognition of the imperatives of the market-reproduced value-form, international treaties may, under the guise of outlawing unfair competitive practices, place constraints on the form and content of those microeconomic interventions which are seen as enhancing a particular nation's capitals' competitiveness. Those policies which undermine such competitiveness on world markets, on the other hand, will be constrained by the invisible hand of international competition. Competition policy (§7) may undermine the growth of domestic firms to a size adequate to international competition. Intervention in industry may undermine the dynamism of domestic firms by temporarily protecting them from such competition, as well as generating public expenditure aimed at attracting capital to specific locations. What is more, in the face of similar incentives to locate elsewhere, the spatial composition of capital may, in the event, be left unchanged.

The reproductive mechanisms of the value-form are powerfully reinforced by the imperatives of maintaining competitiveness in the world economy. But the specific effects of international competition on the formulation, implementation and outcomes of the policies of particular states are, in the absence of a world social subject, contingent.

§2. The world economy and legitimation

The world economy has no overarching universal social subject adequate to the value-form, only the complex of many individual states each determined by their specific formulations of the conditions of existence of their particular, geographically defined civil societies and concretisations of their citizens' rights to existence (7§5). Though the state must be a sovereign legitimated by the will of its citizens, its actualisation of policy in accordance with its conception of the national interest is restricted by its awareness of the existence of other states, and of the integration of its economy into the world economy. Whilst the value-form is in principle indifferent to national boundaries, states intrinsically cannot be. The state's policy is additionally determined by the interaction between de facto national political forms and the intrinsically world-wide value-form.

International competition (7§6) in the world capitalist economy and the constraints from rival states restrict the ability of an individual state to depart from the imperatives of the value-form in the formulation and implementation of its own concept of the national interest, as well as its ability to implement policies to realise it. Explicit restrictions may be imposed by international organisations, international treaties or pressure from rival states, and international competition may inhibit the extent of expenditure a state can undertake without destroying the international competitiveness of its capital. The forces of international competition reproduce the value-form imperatives upon a state's policy-making, which confront the use-value criteria derived from its contextual, welfare, macroeconomic and microeonomic objectives. It may be constrained to provide less by way of welfare than is appropriate to maintain its legitimation in the face of the demands of its citizens (§2; 9§2). Most actual states find that their monopoly of legitimate force is but a local one, which is deployed as much in defence against other states (with their own local monopolies of force) as in defence of its own citizens from each other internally. Significant groups of them may then disagree as to the identity of the foreign enemy and as to the appropriate extent of defence provision. The diversion of value flows, from both the circuits of capital and from expenditure on welfare services into defence and diplomatic expenditure, may further tax citizens' willingness to legitimate their state.

A state may attempt to overcome the antinomies of its existence as but one of many embedded in a world-wide value-form system by espousing free trade and free capital movement, and even free international mobility of labour. However, such a stance will tend to enforce the subordination of a state's policies to value-form imperatives imposed by international competition, at the expense of responsiveness to the demands of those of its citizens who do not see their interests as coincident with the needs of the world economy. To the extent that its economic policies favour domestic capital, its internationally orientated capital (commercial and money capital in particular) and the competition subjects dependent upon them may perceive such policies as failing to meet the general interest. The 'international community' may, by pressure through treaties and international organisations, impugn the legitimacy of its actions. To the extent that a state favours internationally orientated capital, domestic capital and the competition subjects dependent upon it may perceive that the general interest as they see it (i.e. the national interest) is being sacrificed to multinational capital. The citizens who legitimate the state may, as competition subjects, both be indifferent to any non-economic determinant of where they deploy their income sources, and yet demand the services of their state in their dealings with the citizens of alien states, wherever in the world they may operate. Which state has jurisdiction or the power to levy taxation, when territory and citizenship do not coincide, is a further basis of conflict between sovereign states.

The contradiction of restricted sovereignty can have no necessary grounding short of the evolution of a single world bourgeois state. This contradiction therefore exists in the form of various contingently conflicting determinations of specific economic activities and policies. A state may be unable to satisfy the legitimate demands of (enough of) its citizens adequately so that its legitimation in their eyes is maintained. The development of the multifaceted conflict between states (7SS2–3), its effects on the legitimation of states and on the development of policy is contingent – to be grasped by conjunctural examination of the articulation of the working out of the tendencies of accumulation and of the shifting policy settlements of the state, in the light of the multiple determinants which differentiate national civil societies.

SECTION 2   UNPRODUCTIVE LABOUR AND THE QUANTITATIVE MANIFESTATION OF THE CONFLICTS OF THE MIXED ECONOMY

§3. State activity and unproductive labour

The impact of the contradictions of the economy (Chapter 5) and of separation-in-unity (6§11) on the development of the mixed economy depends proximately on the quantitative extent of the trends[3] which ground them. Since the basic input into valorisation is labour (1§9), the effective size of the state and its activities is based on the extent to which it appropriates labour which would otherwise be available for integration into the circuits of capital (2S3). The material reproduction of the state requires that money be diverted from the circuits of capital (from the employment of productive labour) to state revenues (for the employment of at best, and however useful, labour unproductive of value).

The institutions of the state are by their nature removed from the

---

3 'Trend' here refers to any quantitative empirical regularity sustained over time (cf. 0§2).

direct imposition of value-criteria by market forces. Indeed the state's existence and reproduction is predicated upon the requirement for the imposition of use-value criteria in the general interest, as a condition of the continued reproduction of competitive society. Even the contextual apparatuses of the state (8S1) are concerned with the provision of useful services (and even goods) which cannot be (or contingently are not) adequately reproduced in the value-form. State sector workers are thus typically unproductive of value. They are employed for the use-value of the service they produce, either directly to the valorisation process, or on general interest criteria concerned with reproducing that process and actualising the ideal right to existence.

Thus, not only will state sector labour typically not be directly part of a valorising circuit of capital, it will also typically be difficult or impossible to regulate indirectly on value criteria via administrative management. In the first instance the output of such labour processes may not be measurable even in terms of immanent units, and secondly, even when such outputs can be quantified internally, they cannot be reduced to the single dimension of value. They cannot be evaluated simply in terms of money and so be immediately commensurated with other outputs and inputs. Consequently, there may be no way of explicitly (via management) or implicitly (via market forces) evaluating the productivity of state sector labour producing outputs which are not marketed. Such labour processes exist because of the non-self-sufficient nature of the value-form processes taken in isolation, so that the core activities and institutions of the state are intrinsically incommensurable through the value-form processes or their concrete reproduction via market forces. Of course, states undertake many activities which are not incommensurable in this way, and what concretely constitutes the irreducible core of state activities is the subject of dispute and struggle. Nevertheless that there is such a core is the very basis of the continued existence of the bourgeois state.

The state then constitutes a drain on value produced since it employs labour, the productivity of which cannot be regulated on mono-dimensional value criteria.

Addendum: a. Productive and unproductive labour

a. Baumol (1967, 1972) argues that since (much) state sector labour is not employed by capital and produces services the quality of which is closely related to the labour-intensity of their provision, it is not susceptible to productivity increases to match the social rise in wages. Consequently, because provision of these services cannot be (or is not) regulated by market mechanisms, so that rising costs are not reflected in rising prices, ever-increasing quantities of resources will have to be devoted to their production, from a decreasing economic base. This theory is also the basis of the so-called 'Relative Price Effect' whereby state-sector costs are expected to rise faster than those in the market sector. Value-form theory locates this persuasive account in a wider theory of the bourgeois totality, the contradictions of accumulation and the necessary yet contradictory relationships between the state and civil society.

Explicit use of the productive/unproductive labour distinction derived from Adam Smith is made by Bacon and Eltis (1978) in their argument that Britain increasingly suffers from 'too few producers'. On the basis of empirical trends they argue that an increasing proportion of the labour force is employed in producing un-marketed goods, and so does not produce a surplus over the total of resources used in maintaining and employing it. This generates economic stagnation and a 'fiscal crisis' of the state. The main weakness of this argument is that it is based on empirical trends, thus identifying what is to be theorised rather than providing an account of it. This is revealed very clearly in their search for an empirical index of 'unproductive' labour. A major strength is that they fix eventually on the notion of that labour which does not produce a marketed output (much of which is employed in the state sector). In doing so, they go beyond the materialism of Smith's distinction and, unknowingly, hit on something quite close to Marx's distinction – 'unproductive' labour as that which is not productive of surplus value, because its output does not take the form of value and thus does not enter the commensuration processes of the value-form system. This distinction is based on the social relations of production and exchange, rather than the use-value nature of output (cf. Marx 1904–10: ch. IV; Gough 1972, 1973; Fine 1973; Harrison 1973; Offe 1973: 44–5; Bullock 1974; Howell 1975). The value-form theoretic reconstruction of Marx synthesises the basis of the distinction in social relations and that in use-value. It is use-values necessary to the reproduction of the bourgeois totality but not adequately reproduced in the value-form which end up being produced by unproductive labour, typically within the state sector. Such labour processes are not only not regulated in accordance with value criteria by market forces, but cannot be managed even administratively in accordance with value criteria, and so cannot produce surplus value.

§4. The quantitative manifestation of the conflicts of the mixed economy — economic stagnation

The manifestations of the qualitative antinomies of the tendencies of accumulation and of separation-in-unity are contingently grounded in conflicts that have a quantitative dimension. Fundamental tendencies may impact upon conjunctural development only when they are grounded in trends of sufficient relative quantitative significance. If the state's activities are perceived to have grown too large, they threaten the subjective reproduction of the value-form processes of valorisation and accumulation regulated by the market. The state's appropriations and expenditures may be perceived as being of such a scale as to undermine the incentive to accumulate or innovate, or more generally for competition subjects to deploy their income sources as elements of production within the circuits of capital. The demands of restricted sovereignty and concomitant expenditures and taxation may exacerbate the drain on the value available for domestic and national valorisation and accumulation. Further, the state's relative size as an economic subject may make it both a suitable eventual home for 'hoarding' in the form of state bonds (2S2), and a very significant source of distortions of market signals, and of leakages of value which may motivate such withdrawals. Such distortions depend on the state's relative size as a competition subject in money-capital markets (8§7), and the relative size of its appropriations in the form of tax or inflationary finance.

Welfare activities specifically involve transfers to individuals independent of their contribution to the production of value (9§§7–8). The bourgeois state cannot offer substantial guarantees of the particular, integrated social existence (cf. 6§11), which would indeed entail specific quantitative, use-value determinants.[4] Again it is the relative size of this state-sponsored redeployment, determined by the conjuncturally specific standards of subsistence on the one hand, and the extent to which competitive society is able to provide this level on the other, which contingently determines the significance of its effects on the markets for labour power. Indeed the very concept of labour power as the income source of last resort may be partially undermined by the existence of quantitatively significant welfare benefits as a 'final last resort'. Whether welfare benefits increase the cost of labour power (by effectively providing a minimum wage floor or imposing supplementary costs of employing labour), or decrease it (by socialising some of the costs of subsistence in the 'social wage') is again quantitatively indeterminate short of detailed conjunctural investigation. Welfare expenditures appear to generate increasing demands for precisely those kinds of services which cannot be adequately produced in the value-form, and thus to generate upward pressures on the size of the welfare state. In a system in which the only accepted rationing system is the market, removal or easing of such constraints may be expected to generate excessive demand.

The state, in pursuit of its macroeconomic policy objectives (9S2), may well be led to deploy its relatively large size in money-capital

---

4 This distinction appears in everyday political discourse as the liberal commitment to equality of opportunity (that is, to enter the fray as an income source holding competition subject formally like all others), rather than equality (or even equity) of outcome.

markets, in factor markets (including labour) and in other markets in which there is a public sector presence. This may distort the trade-offs in those (and, indirectly, in related) markets from the market reproduced value-form ratios which would otherwise prevail. The appropriations and interventions of the state may exacerbate inflationary tendencies to the extent that the ex-nihilo creation of money involved in the financing of its expenditures is not subsequently socially validated by the performance of productive labour in a successful circuit of capital (2S2). Alternatively, depending on the economic conjuncture and the modes of state funding used, the state's appropriations and actions may contribute directly to stagnatory tendencies. These effects both depend on the size of the state's presence, and themselves may generate quantitative imbalances in these and adjacent markets.

Microeconomic policy entails further transfers without exchange of equivalents in the form of regional and industrial subsidies and enhanced tax allowances. Once again the scope of purely market-regulated commodity transactions is reduced, and the trade-offs facing competition subjects are distorted. The extent of such distortions is dependent on the size of the state's activities. What is more, whether attempts by rival regions to outbid each other in the incentives offered to footloose capital cancel each other out, leaving the spatial location of capital unaltered, is also a contingent question of relative magnitude.

Not only specific conjunctural settlements, but also the quantitative extent of the state and each of its activities is, within the overall form determination, contingent. What actually occurs is determined finally by aspects of the conjuncture manifested in economic, social and political struggles over the size of the state sector and what is to constitute the legitimate extent of policy activities.

§5. The quantitative conflicts of the mixed economy for the state — the threat of fiscal crisis

The state depends on civil society for the resources it needs (8S2). The contradictions of separation-in-unity are manifest as a series of quantitative legitimation problems, associated with the existence of the state and its different activities (8S2; 9S4). The quantitatively contingent expression of this undermining of legitimation is the shifting level at which resistance to the state's appropriations restricts the proportion of value created which is available to the state. At the same time the contradictions of the state's existence and activities for civil society may manifest themselves cyclically in economic stagnation, so that the base for state finance is also tendentially restricted. To the extent that the state must raise revenue from civil society by taxation, borrowing and inflationary finance, it comes into conflict with the right of property and the imperatives of valorisation and accumulation. This undermines both its legitimation (and thus the consent of citizens to finance it), and also the value-criteria success of competitive society (and so also the capability of the economy to generate the value from which state expenditures are to be financed). This undermining of consent and of the basis of state finance generates a threat of fiscal crisis.

Whilst some part of the cost of the welfare state may be imposed on the beneficiary by charges, welfare policy is concerned centrally with the provision of cash or services, if not 'free', then certainly at a price which does not cover costs. Such expenditure tends to generate increasing demands for its services precisely because they are not automatically regulated by the willingness to pay (§4). The demands for those welfare services – whose provision is typically mediated through the state – thus tend to grow continually, exerting an upward pressure on state welfare expenditure. The tendency to fiscal crisis of the state is thereby exacerbated. Consent to the welfare state may be reinforced by universally available benefits, but this is likely to prove extremely costly per unit of redistribution, especially in the light of the income elasticity of demand for such services as welfare, health and education. The fiscal crisis of the state itself tends to prevent the aspirations generated by the welfare state from being met adequately, so that the consent of the bourgeois person to taxation is further undermined: the self-reinforcing fiscal vicious circle is given another twist. In the slump, the demand determined components of welfare expenditure rise, whilst the state revenues required to finance them will tend to fall. This may generate pressure to reduce the scope and rate of welfare transfers (making them more discriminatory, less universal), and to make them more dependent on the demonstrated willingness on the part of the claimant to sell their labour power – to ever more scarce capitalist buyers.

The instruments of macroeconomic management are over-determined by the expenditure demands of the state itself and its framework and welfare activities. They are thus not susceptible to the kind of fine-tuning implicit in macroeconomic management. What is more, to the extent that it is successful in reducing the extent of slumps, macroeconomic management may undermine economic growth, generating a tendency to stagnation (9§9). Expenditure plans may then tend to outpace the ability of the economy to fund them. Macroeconomic policy may thus tend to exacerbate the tendency to fiscal crisis.

Microeconomic intervention also exacerbates the fiscal squeeze. It may involve transfers without exchange of equivalents, tending to increase the demand for more of these unproductive expenditures. At the same time it disrupts the subjective reproduction of the value-system, so reducing the revenue base of the state. Microeconomic policy also raises aspirations for regulation of the capitalist economy which cannot be met within the value-form determined bourgeois epoch. Once again legitimation is undermined because of the clash of politically manifested social aspiration and the inability of the economic base to finance it.

The settlement of the contradiction between the state enforced general interest and value-form regulated self-interest is influenced not only by the constellation of tendencies and contradictions in a qualitative sense, but also by the quantitative extent of the fiscal crisis of the state. The tendencies of valorisation and accumulation (Chapter 5), interwoven with the manifestations of the contradictions of separation-in-unity, appear in the phenomenal form of irregular cycles, one aspect of which is the threat of fiscal crisis of the state.

Addenda: a. O'Connor on fiscal crisis; b. Fiscal crisis and neo-liberalism; c. Empirical manifestations of fiscal crisis

a. The term 'fiscal crisis of the state' appears to have been first coined in O'Connor 1973 (but see, Schumpeter 1918 for a much earlier use of an apparently similar notion):

> We have termed this tendency for government expenditure to outrace revenues the 'fiscal crisis of the state'. There is no iron law that expenditures must always rise more rapidly than revenues, but it is a fact that growing needs which only the state can meet create ever greater claims on the state budget. (O'Connor 1973: 2)

From the point of view of value-form theory this influential work is often economistic and instrumentalist. The problems of the lack of systematicity are manifest even in this short early passage. What is the 'tendency' to fiscal crisis exactly, since it is not an 'iron law' yet it is based on a 'fact' (of ever-growing needs which only the state can meet) (cf. 0S3)? The rest of the book details many contributing empirical trends, but it does not conceptualise them in a systematic structure that would enable one to answer this crucial question.

b. Something like the fiscal crisis of the state is at least implicit in the conservative neo-liberal (§6) critique of the post Second World War mixed economy. (See, for example, Hayek 1975; Brittan 1977; Littlechild 1978; Burton 1979.) The argument re-emerges in the 'supply-side' economics concept of the 'Laffer curve'. In the face of increasing resistance to taxation and the increasingly stagnatory effect of such tax payments, it is concluded that it may be possible to raise total tax take by reducing tax rates (see, for example, Wanniski 1978; Canto, Jones and Laffer 1983; Bartlett and Roth 1984). The formal logic of the mechanism is far from impeccable, and it is a doubtful panacea for the problems of the bourgeois state. Value-form theory suggests that there are irreducible contradictions between state and civil society, which can be managed but not resolved by shifting the boundaries of the mixed economy in accordance with the conjunctural manifestations of these contradictions. Nevertheless, the Laffer curve illustrates the conflicts which constitute the fiscal crisis of the state.

c. Offe *describes* the working out of economic and political trends resulting in the quantitative fiscal crisis of the state, in which 'the borrowing and taxation powers of the state tend to impinge upon the profitability of the capitalist sector', and 'there is a contradiction between the ever-expanding costs associated with the welfare state's "socialization" of production and the continuing *private* control over investment and the appropriation of profits' (Keane 1984: 19). Consequently 'large and generally increasing portions of the gross national product [are converted] into "revenue" by withdrawing it from the process of surplus-value creation', and then 'Budgetary decisions concerning revenues and expenditures have the double function of creating the conditions for maintaining the accumulation process as well as partially hampering this accumulation process by diverting value from the sphere of production and utilizing it "unproductively" in the capitalist sense' (Offe 1973: 57). Offe also discusses the effects of the shortfall of economic and political performance from social aspiration (Offe and Ronge 1976: 124; Offe 1979: 67, 75).

SECTION 3   CONJUNCTURAL SETTLEMENTS

§6. Privatisation and deregulation

The maintenance of the social context for the market, actualisation of existence right, macroeconomic management and microeconomic intervention take contingently shifting institutional forms. Such shifts derive proximately from the working out of economic crisis, legitimation conflicts and fiscal crises, arising from the contra-dictions of separation-in-unity. This most concrete contingent grounding may be illustrated by two type of conjunctural settlement: 'conservative neo-liberalism' and 'social-democratic corporatism' (§8). Conservative neo-liberalism can be seen as the attempt to (re-) expose resource allocation within the state sector to market competition. It is an overt recognition of the conflicts of the mixed economy, leading to a decision to ameliorate them by increasing the domain of market regulated commercial criteria (manifesting value criteria). Those elements which cannot be left to the market are codified into the framework of law, based on the establishment and

278

clarification of property rights over such things as knowledge (for example, patent laws), and the right of individual or corporate competition subjects to litigate against anti-competitive practices.

Such a conjunctural settlement would be congruent with a minimal macroeconomic policy based on monetary targets, an attempt to minimise any state expenditure beyond the framework functions of defence and law and order, and the introduction of value-criteria for management and control throughout the state apparatuses. Elements of planning on use-value criteria give way as far as possible to management based on monetary flows. Microeconomic policy will tend to emphasise competition policy, attempting to increase the impact of market forces by control of monopolies and mergers, deregulation, privatisation, contracting-out of services, enterprise zones and the provision of a legal and administrative framework for litigation against anti-competitive practices.[5] Microeconomic industrial intervention, to the extent it is conceived as unavoidable, is subject to administrative regulation which mimics the commercial criteria of competitive market decision-making, and the direct relations of production in nationalised industries are made to mimic the capitalist wage relation.[6]

Addendum: a. The liberal case against state intervention

a. Hayek (1960: 486) presents the liberal case for minimal state discretion, deregulation and reliance on the rule of law. Given the postulated supremacy of the moral imperative of individual liberty, social regulation is to be confined as far as possible to free market forces, restricting state intervention to those measures which supplement rather than supplant market forces (Hayek 1960: 350-1). If actual or surrogate value-criteria (Hayek 1960: 224) cannot be brought to bear, then recourse must be made to the law (Hayek 1960: 351). Active intervention is not, per se, outlawed for liberalism, but it has to be justified in accordance with universal criteria – implicitly in terms of value or by reference to right (Hayek 1960: 264). Non-market regulation in the form of anything but the universal imperatives of law are necessarily arbitrary and thus open to abuse (Hayek 1960: 228). Value-form theory has suggested that this argument neglects the major threat to individuals' ability to fulfil their species being posed by the value-form determined market

---

5 Here the law takes a phenomenal form highly appropriate to the value-form, as a framework regulating the private market exchanges between competition subjects, which bourgeois persons can, if they chose, bring to bear on practices undermining the reproduction of the value-form by market mechanisms.
6 It should not be thought that neo-liberalism is confined to 'Thatcherism'. Offe describes what he calls '*re*-privatization' as a West German response to what so-called conservative theories characterize as 'ungovernability' (Offe 1979; 69–70; Lenhardt and Offe 1977: 112).

processes of valorisation and accumulation themselves (6§1b). It abstracts from the contradictory interconnectedness of the bourgeois epoch.

§7. Bureaucratisation and regulation

An alternative direction for policy attempting to grapple with the conflicts manifesting the contradictions of the mixed economy involves replacing the breached separation between civil society and the state by an administered separation between the executive bureaux implementing interventionist policy and the representative apparatuses. Policy implementation may thus become bureaucratised – subject apparently only to technical and economic rationale with the relation to the political institutions reduced to the letter of the law, and a rigid hierarchical system of administrative rules. Such technocratic bureaux may well become inter-linked with the corporations of civil society (trade unions, employers' federations, or even consumers' and environmental organisations). This further accentuates the shift of the political-economic divide from the state–civil society boundary to the division inside the state between representative apparatuses and implementing bureaux. Whilst the government may be represented on such corporatist bodies, their deliberations take the form of quasi-private negotiations of concessions to civil society interest groups, away from the publicly enforced need to reason in terms of the general interest. Indeed 'corporatism' plays a key role in reducing the scope of the general interest to the aggregation by negotiation of individual interests.

Microeconomic policy under this alternative will tend to take the form of industrial intervention via differential tax, allowance and subsidy regimes, preferential loans and purchasing policies, nationalisation, state holding companies and enterprise boards, indicative and town planning, and selective protection. Attempts are made to alter the allocation of resources from that thrown up by the market, in pursuit of economic or social objectives, by changing market trade-offs between the returns to specific branches, sectors, technologies, regions or even specific firms. The intrinsic conflicts of economic policy, most acute in such active microeconomic intervention, may facilitate the coming to power of a social-democratic type of government (6§12), and a concomitant corporatist form of relationship between the state and civil society. The inner state political structures of 'social-democratic corporatism' are typically influenced by a technocratic and managerial ethos. Corporatism allows the negotiation of minimum concessions required to maintain the consent of labourers, in a context in which value-criteria can be presented as the economic and technical imperatives of the economic system, upon which the material basis of such concessions and opportunities for deployment of income sources in general rests. Such a conjunctural settlement provides only a contingent form of existence of the contradictions of separation-in-unity.

Addenda: a. Corporatism; b. Corporatism and the economics of bureaucracy

a. Some contemporary forms of corporatism, sometimes seen as part of the problem of expanding intervention by the state, are also an institutional form which seeks to manage the concomitant breakdown of the state–civil society separation. They enable the incorporation of working class demands by negotiated settlement of concessions to them. Corporatism of this kind focuses on the partial truth that value-form imperatives are a technical economic constraint on what is possible, thus evading the tricky issue of the power of the state to support all its citizens' rights of property and person. The management of consent is isolated from parliamentary (or indeed any political) control, and confined to the borderline between state and civil society, as a second best to confining it to civil society (De Brunhoff 1976: 109; see also, Hegel 1821: §§270, 289, 295, 302, 303, 311 on the 'corporations' of civil society). Offe (1973: 50) explicitly relates the rise of corporatism to an expanding welfare state and 'excessive' intervention. The administrative apparatus is encouraged 'to become dependent upon powerful and organized social interests (for example, employers' associations, professional organizations, trade unions)'. The upshot is 'that the traditional liberal-democratic institutions of conflict articulation and resolution – elections, political parties, legislatures, judiciaries – are increasingly supplemented or replaced by informal "corporatist" schemes of functional representation and bargaining'; 'the effectiveness of welfare state policies [thus] comes to depend increasingly upon informal and publicly inaccessible negotiations between state planners and the elites of powerful social interest groups' (Keane 1984: 22). However, Offe sees privatisation and corporatism as complementary means of maintaining the separation between state and civil society, rather than as opposing strategies (Offe 1973: 50). Notwithstanding their incisive insights into the manifestations of the contradictions of the mixed economy, writers such as Offe tend to hypostatise different conjunctural settlements as necessary historical developments. Value-form theory identifies them as instances of the toing and froing of the bourgeois state (as agent of policy) in the face of the shifting manifestations of the contradiction between value and use-value. Offe *et al.* do provide evidence that indeed no strategy of 'reprivatization' succeeds in resolving the contradictions: the nature of state functions is such that the implementation of economic policy is bound to manifest, in new phenomenal forms, the contradictions from which they arise (Offe 1973: 59; 1979: 68, 73, 74, 76; 1981: 153). 'Corporatism' is also seen as problematical, and likely to succeed only under conditions of prosperity (Keane 1984: 28–9).

b. Corporatism's concern with the workings of the inner state place it in the domain of the theory of public choice, and in particular the economic theories of bureaucracy, which reflect the dominance of the economic in simply shifting the analysis appropriate to the economy into the very different sphere of state activity. However, state bureaucrats are faced with incentives, constraints and imperatives which cannot be reduced to self-interested pursuit of some mono-dimensional maximand, such as the size of budget under their control. Lenhardt and Offe (1977: 105–107) point out the need for empirical research to attempt to identify just what these incentives, etc. are in any particular conjuncture. But without some holistic conceptual framework, any such empirical research would have difficulty in separating the relatively trivial problems, which could be resolved by improved managerial structures or accounting practices, from the manifestations of the contradictions of the bourgeois epoch. The specific inadequacies of the economics of bureaucracy approach lie in its unmediated application of neoclassical microeconomic theory to the different imperatives (of reconciling value with use-value criteria) facing the state sector. The ideological weight of such theories lies in their provision of the basis for one particular putative resolution to the contradictions of the mixed economy – conservative neo-liberalism (§6). Value-form theory of the essential interconnection of the state's economic activities and the value-form determined economy, is able to grasp why the implementation of this programme in practice will be fraught with insurmountable problems (cf. Williams 1985b). The contradictions of the mixed economy are not overcome within the bourgeois epoch, rather their manifestations are managed.

§8. Intra-epochal development

Value-form theory suggests that there is no necessary transcendence of the contradictions of separation-in-unity in the mixed economy. Neither conservative neo-liberalism nor social-democratic corporatism (nor, apparently, any other conjunctural settlement) definitively resolves the conflicts of the mixed economy. Privatisation and deregulation, for example, neglect the use-value determinants of the interventions which they seek to undo. In general, increasing reliance on market reproduction of the capitalist economy must exacerbate the manifestations of the contradictions of the value-form. Conversely, corporatism may cope with the contradictions of separation-in-unity only by raising them to the political level within the state. What is more, such corporatisation dilutes parliamentary control, without increasing market disciplines, leaving ever more space in which the self-interest of the particular bourgeois persons staffing the bureaux and the corporatist bodies can triumph over general interest criteria. The increased hierarchical managerial control, and the construction of structures of effective incentives and sanctions needed to align the private interests of bureaucrats with the general interest, become ever more difficult and costly.

The state as social subject can adopt whatever form of economic policy it wishes, subject to its ability to maintain its legitimation. On the everyday surface of bourgeois reality, what appears to be at issue is the political feasibility of different state activities: from the framework of law and order, through the increasingly problematical macroeconomic (monetary) policy, macroeconomic (fiscal) policy and welfare state expenditures, to a spectrum of microeconomic competition and industrial policy, ranging from the most universal and non-discriminatory to the more particular and discriminating. However, it should be emphasised that, viewed solely at this level of appearance, this is nothing more than a descriptive taxonomy. The outcome of electoral struggle, social conflicts, the processes of the inner state and of the state's attempt to manage persistent contradictions are contingent, and may well contain contradictory elements.

The contradictions of the mixed economy do not normally manifest themselves in major constitutional crises, any more than the tendencies and the contradictions of accumulation (very often exacerbated by the state intervention meant to counteract them) generate continual economic crises. The normal expression of these contradictions will be no more dramatic than changing degrees of social disorder levelled at the state. More often they will consist merely of policy changes, accompanied or not by changes of the governing parties. The exact compositions of differing policy settlements is contingent, and no doubt they will sometimes be entirely novel combinations of policies. However, a range of the kinds of options which have prevailed in recent years is indicated by what has been characterised as the social-democratic corporatism of the post Second World War 'long boom', and the varieties of conservative neo-liberalism which followed it in many capitalist societies. The specific way in which the contradictions of the mixed economy manifest themselves in conjunctures in which social-democratic corporatism is dominant generate the forces for the subsequent swing to the 'right'. It is to be expected that the expression of the contradictions of the value-form under conservative neo-liberalism will eventually generate a swing to some new, transient conjunctural settlement. The value-form theoretic presentation has tried to indicate the bounds to the state's freedom of movement, imposed by its interconnections within the bourgeois totality (0§13).

Addenda: a. Marxist economics on persistent contradiction; b. The political transcendence of economic contradiction

a. Marxist economics poses the persisting contradictions of economic policy in terms of clash between the 'law of value' and conscious planning: 'in so far as the allocation of productive activity is brought under conscious control, the law of value loses its relevance and importance; its place is taken by the principle of planning ... Value and planning are as much opposed, and for the same reasons, as capitalism and socialism' (Sweezy 1942: 53–4). This formulation loses the sense of the bourgeois system itself as contradictory. The reproduction of competitive society, based on the 'law of value' both requires and is undermined by conscious 'planning' by the state.

b. Offe and Ronge (1976: 121), Lenhardt and Offe (for example, 1977: 111) and Offe (for example, 1979: 70, 83; 1981: 151–2, 158) discuss extensively the manifestation of the conflicts of the mixed economy in political/policy shifts. However, in concluding that the contradictions of the value-form can be definitively transcended at the political level, their argument relies on reducing the contradictions of the 'commodity form' to one of its poles – value with no use-value; the economy with no state. Such a reduction abolishes the contradiction, but ideally, by denying its existence! The state need not intervene because competitive society is self-sufficient; there is no problem of material resources for the state, because there is no need of the state (if there was, it would always be contradictory for it to appropriate value from civil society without exchange, however abundant such value may be); there are no problems of accumulation by definition; and there are no legitimation problems because there is no need for the state to exist, let alone breach its separation from civil society!

Offe (1973: especially 48, 50–5, 61; and 1979: 82–3) has also *described* many of the forms of appearance of the contradictions of separation-in-unity, such as 'the empirical side effect of depriving capital of either capital or labour power or the freedom to use both in profitable ways' (Offe and Ronge 1976: 126), 'organizations whose mode of operation is no longer subject to the commodity form' (Offe and Ronge 1976: 127), 'the subversion of the syndrome of possessive individualism' (Offe and Ronge 1976: 128–9), 'a burden of taxation and regulation upon capital which amounts to a *disincentive to investment*' and the granting of 'claims, entitlements and collective power positions to workers and unions which amount to a *disincentive to work*, or at least to work as hard and productively as they would be forced to under a reign of unfettered market forces' (Offe 1981: 149). These perceptive descriptions of the persistent conflicts and tendencies arising from the contradictions of bourgeois society are also related to conservative 'ungovernability' theories of crisis (Offe 1979: 75–8).

However, whilst he describes the *conflicts* of contemporary bourgeois society, Offe has no systematic way of developing them from persistent *contradictions*. Although he refers to 'underlying' contradictions, the analysis itself consists of the classification of the surface of bourgeois society into pre-existing systems and sub-systems on a structural-functionalist basis, and then of a description of the conflicts entailed precisely by his own postulated system of classification. The 'demonstration' of the 'oppositions' of capitalist society requires more than the empirical description of their manifestations. It requires a systematic account of how the reality of that society, as grasped by the everyday consciousness of bourgeois persons, reproduces the contradictory interconnections of the totality. Failing some such approach there can be only the postulated *external* oppositions between pre-existing systems or structures, manifesting not the specific contradictions of the bourgeois epoch, but the reproduction problems of any social system (for example, Offe 1973: 34). It is certainly the case that the manifestation of the contradictions of capitalist society as the tensions of the mixed economy involves the clash of different principles of organisation. But the more fundamental basis of these is the clash of value and use-value criteria. It is, for example, just inaccurate to characterise the economic system as the 'domain of the production and distribution of goods', as Offe does. Rather it is the domain in which the production and distribution of use-values is subordinated to the value-form and valorisation (and thus accumulation), as opposed to the state 'system' grounded in the interpellation of use-value criteria in pursuit of the reproduction of private property, the actualisation of the right to existence, and thus the reproduction of the bourgeois totality.

SUMMARY

There appears to be no necessary form and content of policy to resolve the contradictions of the epoch. Nevertheless contradiction cannot exist unreconciled; it must have a form and content in which opposites are reconciled, be it only contingently. These contradictions therefore reappear in the antinomies of the development of policy itself, leading to fluctuations between different conjunctural settlements. Thus over-determined, the actual outcome will be determined proximately by the contingent coming together of events which make up the history of a specific bourgeois society. The specific form, content and extent of the state's activities, and of its policy settlements, depend proximately on such events as the state of the world economy and the location of the national economy within it, the balance of class and other socioeconomic and political forces, the international balance of economic, diplomatic, political and military power, and the extant perception of ecological factors.

If a particular conjunctural settlement is perceived to fail to meet at least some of the legitimate aspirations of civil society, the state grounded in the government in power may lose the consent of citizens. The incipient economic problems and fiscal crisis, and consequent legitimation crisis may generate a more or less radical change of policy, which may eventually be confirmed by a change of govern-

ment to a party whose ideology is more in keeping with the new imperatives of policy. The grounding of the contradictions of separation-in-unity in intra-epochal development has been illustrated by reference to two conjunctural settlements, 'conservative neo-liberalism' and 'social-democratic corporatism'.

Part Six:

Summary and Conclusions: the Implications for Empirical Research

Summary and Conclusions

SECTION 1 THE CONTRADICTIONS OF THE BOURGEOIS EPOCH: SUMMARY

§1. The starting point

We have expressed our dissatisfaction with the method of mainstream economics (0S1), and constructed from within Hegelian-Marxist political economy the method of 'dialectical systematic theory' as a more adequate alternative (0SS2-3). Our presentation of the bourgeois epoch is itself developed from the fundamental logical categories of being and nothing (0§15). In this it differs from most Hegelian social theory, which tends to start with the social and economic categories in *The Philosophy of Right*. Sociation, necessary for the existence of individuals inherently incapable of self-production, is negated on the emergence of the bourgeois epoch by dissociation. The specifically bourgeois mode of association is postulated to be the value-form (0§16, 1SS1-3): the starting point (0§8) which the systematic presentation proper is to ground (0§9), and so to validate (0§12).

§2. The moments reproducing the economy

The value-form is the social universal form grounding the association of dissociated production and consumption in the capitalist economy. It is the necessary dimension of useful objects and of the activity of their creation, which thus each have a contradictory double reality – use-value and value (which constitutes the useful object as commodity), and concrete and abstract labour (which constitute the activity as labour), respectively (1SS1-3). Value is a purely quantitative form, whose sole autonomous social expression is in money as the general equivalent (1S4), and which is concerned only to valorise. Use-value, on the other hand, is multidimensional in terms of for what or for whom it is a use-value. It is the theorisation of the dialectical unity of value and use-value that marks our value-form reconstruction of the abstract labour theory of value. Its crucially dynamic nature is maintained in the introduction of ideal pre-commensuration anticipating exchange in production, which ensures that the form-determination imposed by ubiquitous exchange is internalised into the very organisation of production. The labour process itself thus has the contradictory double form of use-value production and valorisation. The production of use-values requires in general both labour and means of production. However, because only labour takes the value-form *and yet* is itself created outside the capitalist economy (in the private sphere – 7S1), it is the only element of valorisation. However, since capital is the necessary value-form of the elements of production as inputs, valorisation takes the contradictory form of valorisation of capital, which is thus contradictorily related to itself as self-valorising value, as expressed in the rate of profit (1S5).

The logic of the valorisation of capital is its futher expansion, which requires increasing control over the labour process by capital, and the investment of profits. The valorisation of capital thus entails its accumulation. The limits to accumulation are initially resolved in technical change (2S1). The accumulation of capital is grounded in the extended reproduction of labour power (2S3) and the credit system. Banks have been developed from the two forms of commercial credit – trade and production credit, doubling respectively into money of account and means of payment, and money capital and means of payment. The ex-nihilo creation of credit money by banks anticipates as a private pre-validation the successful production and social validation of commodities, and is thus a condition of existence of accumulation. Continuous pre-validation was itself grounded in inter-bank credit from which was derived the central bank and redeemability of credit money in legal tender. In this way (and contrary to most Marxist treatments) money (1S4) and the credit system have been developed without any recourse to commodity money (2S2).

The interaction of 'many capitals' – competition conceived abstractly – generates the tendencies to equalisation of rates of profit and to uniform wages and uniform prices. These tendencies, together with the compulsion to invest capital in cost-reducing and labour-productivity increasing techniques of production, establish that each branch of production tends to be composed of a stratification of capitals according to cost of production, and concomitant rate of profit differences (2S4). The concept 'money expression of labour' links the determinations of production, valorisation, accumulation and the interaction of many capitals, concretising the value-form of labour and useful objects. With it, all the moments of the economy have been presented in outline, and so also its (abstract) existence (2S5).

§3. The tendencies of economic development

In the process of accumulation the value–use-value contradiction is expressed in the tendencies of accumulation – that to over-accumulation (Chapter 3) and that for the rate of profit to fall (Chapter 4). With increase in the composition of capital blended out, the validation of extended accumulation requires an ever-increasing rate of accumulation, the condition of existence of which is an abundant labour force. However, an increasing rate of surplus value and its accumulation tend to deplete the reserve of labour, so that valorisation and accumulation tend to be extended up to the point where capital is abundant relative to labour (3S1). The tendency to over-accumulation of capital (TOC) is expressed either in labour scarcity profit squeeze or in underconsumption. The first is produced when labour scarcity gives rise to wage increase, squeezing profits and leading to a reduction in the rate of accumulation, until labour eventually becomes abundant again. Underconsumption is produced when labour scarcity does not generate *sufficient* wage increase to maintain effective demand, and so accumulation comes to stagnate. Underconsumption and labour shortage profit squeeze are usually put forward as mutually exclusive, but we have presented them as expressions of the same contradictory force whereby accumulation of capital is extended up to its negation in over-accumulation (3S2).

The tendency of the rate of profit to fall (TRPF) is predicated upon an increasing value composition of capital (VCC), concomitant on investment in labour-productivity increasing techniques of production. It contradicts the tendential increase in profit and the rate of profit generated by the accumulation of capital in new plants (4S1, cf. 2S1). This contradiction has been conceived by authors following Okishio (1961) as a theoretical inconsistency justifying the rejection of the TRPF. The dialectical systematic presentation reveals that the TRPF may be adequately grounded if it is conceived not as a comparative static, but as a dynamic process incorporating fixed capital. We have shown how this contradiction is transcended, and so can have existence, in the concretisation of capital stratification. When stratification is extended with composition of capital increasing techniques at one end, whilst sub-marginal plants are scrapped at the other, the new plant capital will tend to have a higher productivity and rate of profit than that of the capitals in the

291

previous stratification, whilst the capitals in the rest of the stratification experience devalorisation and declining rates of profit (4S2). One expression of the TRPF is in devaluation of capital. The price decrease typically concomitant on the TRPF counteracts the increasing VCC of newly accumulated capital, but at the same time falling means of production prices (and/or generalised over-capacity) devalue previously accumulated fixed capital, reducing the extension of accumulation. The TRPF is further expressed in restructuring and, contingently, in centralisation of capital. The more rapid and sustained the productivity increase, the more it generates scrapping of plants before the capital invested has had time to be fully amortised. As scrapping of the least efficient plants accelerates, the range of the stratification of capital is reduced, preventing the possibility of a smooth, gradual increase in the VCC. Instead, technical knowledge then tends to be implemented in waves, expressing the law of the TRPF in a tendential cyclical movement (4S3).

The tendencies of accumulation are articulated in the irregular cyclical course of *economic* development (Chapter 5). The increasing VCC concomitant on the TRPF counteracts the expression of the TOC in labour-shortage profit squeeze and underconsumptions. (5S1). The cycle of expansion and contraction of accumulation implied by each considered in isolation therefore tends to be extended. The character of the turning points is, however, indeterminate: alternation may occur either gradually or in the form of disruptive economic crises. Nevertheless the combination of the credit system (tending to increase the amplitude of the cycle), and the eventual cumulative expulsion of labour from the circuit of capital, tends to make the economy vulnerable to economic crisis, one important characteristic of which is the enforced manifestation of devalorisation and devaluation, and of restructuring and centralisation. The concomitant decrease in the range of stratification tends to generate 'hoarding' of technology, which may explain the wave-like implementation of new techniques (Schumpeter) (5S2).

The presentation of inflation (5S3) introduces (for the first time) a contingent moment, thus showing how the contingent may be linked with the systematic (0§11). Inflation is thus merely one *possible* process generated within the economy to overcome economic crisis (itself merely one possible manifestation of the contradictions of valorisation and accumulation). The inflationary reproduction of accumulation appears to overcome economic crisis, but it reinforces the tendency for the implementation of new techniques to come in waves. Whilst the revaluation of capital produced by inflation provides, in the form of windfall capital gains, compensation for devalorisation, it is offset by a loss in the purchasing power of the non-banking money capital lent to industrial capital. This causes the gradual withdrawal of such capital from industry, which has then to rely increasingly on short-term bank credit. This gives rise to an increasing share of interest in surplus value, reducing the inflationary compensation for devalorisation. Protracted inflation further enforces the cyclical manifestation of the TOC, imposed on an upward growth trend. The associated relative decrease in average rates of unemployment inhibits the regular disciplining of the labour force, affecting not only the level of the wage but also the intensity of labour, so that the rate of surplus value comes under pressure. The withdrawal of non-banking money capital from industry and the reinforcement of the TOC tend to put a further drain on profits, causing banks to slow down the increase in lending. This may be accomplished gradually, typically in the form of selective lending leading to a dual structure of a strong and a weak layer of capital. The resultant increase in the range of stratification puts a downward pressure on prices, which restores the tensions and conflicts that inflation was to overcome.

The contingent expression of the articulation of the TRPF and the TOC in protracted inflation undermines money as a store of value, so that not only is the position of banks within the circuit of capital undermined, but also the very associative function of money as general equivalent itself. Continuously increasing inflation therefore cannot persist, so that inflation cannot overcome but only modify the manifestations of the contradictions of the valorisation and devalorisation, and accumulation and devaluation of capital.

The presentation of the conditions of existence of the value-form as the bourgeois mode of association has thus been developed to the extent where necessity gives way to contingency. The value-form of association has been validated as the starting point of the presentation to the extent that it has been grounded in its abstractly economic conditions of existence. All the relations and forces conceptualised thus far are necessarily one-sidedly economic, and thus remain abstract, so the presentation must proceed to their further concretisation.

§4. Civil society and the state

In the presentation of the economy, subjects have had only an implicit and contradictory existence as the bearers of economic relations – subjects without subjectivity. This contradiction is transcended in competitive society, the unity of the abstract capitalist economy and the abstract social existence of free will (6S1–2). The bearers of economic relations and of abstract free will are concretised as competition subjects, with the abstract free will to deploy their income sources in pursuit of income within the constraints of the opportunities offered by the value-form determined economy. There are two categories of competition subject: subjects of property income sources and those of labour income sources. The particular subjective right to existence cannot be grounded within the capitalist economy as the value-form is immanently indifferent to it, and the tendencies of accumulation threaten it. Equally, the bourgeois right to property, derived from the free will of competition subjects to deploy income sources in pursuit of income, cannot be grounded within the capitalist economy. Therefore it is, as a system which is not self-reproducing, by itself contradictory (6S3). This contradiction is transcended in the doubling of competitive society into the state and civil society (6§7). Civil society is determined by the subject-less economic processes of valorisation and by the income-seeking activities of competition subjects, in the context of the separate existence of the state. The state is determined as the universal social subject which upholds the universal rights of property and existence (6§8). It is bourgeois in that the people it represents are essentially bourgeois subjects, in their two determinations as competition subject (with rights of property and, negatively, existence) and citizen.

The existence of the state is grounded first in its positing of right as law, and secondly in its legitimation by the will of bourgeois subjects whose consent depends upon their perception that the state is upholding their rights as constitutive of the general interest – that is, in universal forms. The legitimation of the state and the autonomy of the value-form require that the state be concretely separated from civil society, but also that its existence and activity be willed by bourgeois persons. This separation-in-unity (6§12) is the basis of the state's material existence (8S2), and of the contextual (8S1), welfare (9S1), macroeconomic (9S2) and microeconomic (9S3) activities in which the reproduction of the rights of property and person, and the market reproduction of the economy wherein lies their prime determination, require the state to engage.

§5. Economic policy

The contradiction of the universal social subject, which is both separated from that over which it is subject and restricted to particular sovereignty (7S3), is grounded in the state as provider of the social context of law, money and infrastructure for the economy (8S1). Provision of such a context entails physical existence, for which the state is dependent on the economy, ultimately through taxation (8S2). Separation-in-unity has its contradictory existence in the mixed economy – the necessary coexistence of value and use-value criteria for resource allocation and subjective decision-making. The contradiction of the mixed economy is grounded in the state (social subject) as agent of active economic policy, intervening explicitly in the economy from outside civil society (8S4). This intervention is further particularised in welfare, macroeconomic and microeconomic policy (Chapter 9). In order to cope as it sees to be necessary with the contingency of, and systematic threats to individual existence, active state policy is particularised first in welfare policies, concerned to enhance the conditions for the sale of labour power and to provide income support or replacement for the unsuccessful labourer (9S1). Active macroeconomic attempts to manage the cyclical manifestations of the tendencies of accumulation (Part Three) provide further determinations of the state's fiscal and monetary activities (9S2). The restricted sovereignty of the macroeconomic agent further determines its policy towards its national economy in the context of the world economy (7SS2–3). Microeconomic intervention attempts to enhance the market-regulated allocation of resources in pursuit of more efficient valorisation and accumulation, and of the use-value demands of contextual, welfare and macroeconomic policy (9S4). It manifests to the highest degree the expression of the contradictions of separation-in-unity, in the form of interventions by the state as social subject back into civil society.

As policy activities are predicated upon the reproduction of the value-form, they must inevitably reproduce the contradictions of that form (9S4). Welfare and economic policy involves the attempt to bring to bear a complex of use-value criteria on, in the first instance, necessarily value-criteria based commercial decision-making processes. Produced value is thereby diverted from the productive circuits of capital, and the pure logic of the value-form processes is distorted. Market prices become even less perfect bearers of information on the consumption, production and investment possibilities open to competition subjects, being contaminated by the effects of the activities of the state. The value-form is confronted in principle with the concrete particular social, rather than merely the abstract universal political, realisation of the right to existence. This, and the dilution of bourgeois property right, and of the connection between access to consumption and the effective contribution of labour power to the processes of valorisation and accumulation, appears to challenge the necessity of the unification of use-value with value in the commodity. It becomes possible for individual subjects

295

systematically to consume useful objects without the mediation of money, and to obtain money without contributing to their production.

§6. Legitimation

The citizen is a moment of the bourgeois person (6§10), itself determined by the contradictory existence of the competition subject characterised by pure *self*-interest. However, as citizen, the person must be persuaded to legitimate state activity grounded in the *general* interest. This creates a problem concerning the basis of legitimation in the will of the citizen, to the extent that the latter is to be confronted with state activity which actively discriminates against one in favour of another, albeit in the name of the general interest. In its necessary attempts to impose a system of morality ('Sittlichkeit') whose essential moment is disinterested conduct, upon a civil society grounded in the amorality of purely self-interested conduct, the universal social subject cannot help but threaten its own legitimation. More specifically, in trying to actualise the merely ideal right to existence the state is bound to fail, and thence to undermine its legitimation based upon the will of its citizens. To the extent that redistributive activities are successful, they undermine the value-form processes of the economy; to the extent that they are not, they undermine legitimation.

In order to carry out laws which enact economic policy the executive (6§12) invariably requires some discretionary powers in assessing which economic agents (competition subjects) fall under the provisions of a particular policy or regulation, and to what extent they are liable to bear its costs or are entitled to receive its benefits. It is a practical impossibility that such discretionary discrimination could be obviated by drafting laws so tightly that they could be implemented in an entirely automatic way by a rule-bound executive bureaucracy, with disputed liability or eligibility being decided by an independent judiciary. Indeed, cost-efficient implementation of economic policy in order to reduce the quantitative strain on accumulation (10S2), and the dilution of market reproduction of the value-form, demands that economic agents be subject to specialist scrutiny by bureaucrats to ensure the exact extent of their liability of entitlement. The state's role in supporting the value-form and the form of right both requires and abhors discretionary discrimination as between persons and groups of persons: it is contradictory. To have discretion, the *executive* must de facto *legislate* and *adjudicate*, and thus break down the separation of executive bureaux from the legislative and the judicial (8§§2–3). To the extent that the executive bureaux of the state are seen to act in the interests of one person or group of persons and against others, the state's legitimation grounded in the will of bourgeois persons is undermined.

By bridging the necessary separation between state and civil society (6§11), economic policy places on the social agenda intimations of principles for the allocation of resources and the regulation of the economic aspects of social life other than (and in conflict with) market reproduced value criteria. If this agenda were to be taken up consciously by large numbers of economically, socially and politically effective people, the dominance of the value-form, and of the power structure of vested interests which grounds it, might be threatened. The state's activities in the form of economic policies become the object of political, administrative and legal struggles in and around the state, which may not be confined to the legitimate form of parliamentary debate and legislation, but may reappear within the execution and adjudication of economic policy, as well as within civil society. It is these struggles, in the context of the constraints of international competition (10S1), and articulated with the working out of the tendencies of accumulation, which proximately determine the course of development of the mixed economy (10SS2–3).

SECTION 2 THE EMPIRICAL AS THE CONCRETE

§7. Actually existent contradiction

Modern mainstream social science finds it difficult to come to terms with the notion of an actually existing social system which is perceived as contradictory. For us, contradiction refers to the unity of opposites, and the point is to explain how they can coexist within a unity. Those contradictions that are not transcended necessarily, must have a contingent form of existence (0§§10–11). Both the contradictions of the capitalist economy taken in isolation and the contradictions of separation-in-unity developed from them work themselves out in the form of the irregularly cyclical course of development of the capitalist economy (Chapter 5), and of the developing and fluctuating forms of welfare and economic policy in which both economic and legitimation crises continually threaten (Chapter 9). The concrete *content* of these transcendent *forms* of existence of contradiction is, however, indeterminate (for example, 5S3; 10S3). The activities of the state more concretely grasped are constituted by its attempts to manage the conflicting manifestations of the working out of the contradictions of the mixed economy. Economic activity rises and falls, and policy targets and instruments

– and perhaps the governments espousing them – come and go.

Concrete accounts should thus be concerned to grasp how the contradictions of the crucial moments and tendencies of the epoch are momentarily resolved in the cyclically changing empirical phenomena of the conjuncture. It is in the actuality of everyday life, with its many contingent determinations, that contradictions are ultimately grounded. However, such contingent resolution cannot dissolve the contradictions of the bourgeois totality, which will persist until the latter is itself transcended. Our systematic presentation is concerned to trace out the relationship of the contingently actual to the necessary moments and tendencies, which is what is required for a theory of crises which could identify those processes which challenge the dominance of the value-form (Offe 1973: 38), as they manifest themselves in a cyclical course of development, rather than in an inevitable secular increase (cf. Offe 1973: 41; 1979: 80).

§8. Form and content

Because the content of the more concrete necessary moments is proximately determined only contingently, it would appear that the systematic presentation of the development of the bourgeois epoch cannot be extended beyond them. However, the immediate objects of conjunctural accounts of the mixed economy would consist of the form and content of the controversy, and economic, social and political struggle over such things as the appropriate scope and nature of state activity; the legitimate constituents of the social context for the market; the proper level and eligibility conditions for welfare benefits; the extent to which the state can and should attempt to manage the macroeconomy; the degree and substance of possible and desirable microeconomic intervention; the perceived trade-off between redistribution and efficiency; and the changing institutional forms of the inner state (6§12).

The restricted sovereignty of the agent of policy in the context of the world economy further contingently determines the outcome (10S1). The state provides the necessary conditions of existence of valorisation and accumulation in the shape of a social context and welfare, macroeconomic and microeconomic policy (Chapters 8ff). *Given* the existence of many states, in the light of the geographically indifferent value-form processes reproduced by world market mechanisms, how a concrete particular state manifests these policies will be modified by the external threats from other states. That is the object of the presentation in 7S3, which enables the subsequent further particularisation of the state–society relationship in the different categories of state policy in 10S1. We have argued that the existence of the state as many states is at a more concrete level than the determination of the state itself on the basis of the value-form. Further, we have postulated that this form of existence is contingent with respect to the reproduction of the bourgeois totality. The introduction of 'many states' is, however, only provisional.

§9. Systematicity and conjunctural accounts

The examination of any conjuncture can be effective only to the extent that it grasps the empirical detail concretely — that is, as interconnected within the totality – so grounding the abstract determinants. It is a condition of the possibility of a systematic conceptualisation of it that the object-totality (bourgeois society – 0§14) is a structured, coherent whole. Observed changes in the processes by which that system seems to reproduce itself are to be theorised in terms of their likely effects on the reproduction of its derived conditions of existence. To the extent that it is shown to be impossible to grasp significant aspects of any conjuncture on the basis of the contingent transcendence of the persisting contradictions of valorisation and accumulation, and of the rights-based state grounding the value-form, the presentation must be modified (0§12).

The presentation constitutes our argument for the correctness of our starting-point in the value-form as the specifically bourgeois mode of association, by grounding it. The authors would not be so immodest as to claim that further *intensive* development of the value-form presentation of the bourgeois epoch is not required. Particularly underdeveloped topics are the private sphere, the existence of the state as many states and the presentation of the world economy and (the lack of) world money (all provisionally presented in Chapter 7), but there are no doubt many other interconnections which have been neglected. Nor can there be any absolute certainty about the correctness of the order of presentation in all its details (0§12). The major next step in *extending* the presentation, however, must surely involve still further concretisation, to the investigation of everyday life. This, on the basis of adequate concepts, has proved troublesome for Marxist and Hegelian social science, as well as specifically for mainstream economics (0S1), so it is worth spelling out briefly the mode of investigation of policy at the level of the empirical concrete implicit in the method. The development of policy is, for value-form theory, to be theorised as an element of the state's attempts to manage the manifestations of the playing out over historical time of the contradiction between the ahistorically necessary satisfaction of particular human needs, and the socially necessary universal form in which that content appears in the bourgeois epoch: value. Such a development is the history of any particular state's attempts to manage, suppress, mediate and compensate for the phenomenal manifestations of these fundamental contradictions. The kinds of research questions suggested by value-form theory for interrogation of the empirical description of events and trends are: Does the observed removal or modification of some policy target or instrument mean that some derived necessary condition of existence is not being reproduced, or is being undermined? Is the system then degenerating (in terms of its own logic)? If so how? Or are alternative mechanisms (policies, or autonomous economic or social processes) emerging which will serve to reproduce that condition of existence? Or has the system developed in such a way that the threatened condition of existence is no longer necessary to its reproduction? Or was it perhaps wrongly identified as a necessary condition in the first place?

As with any theory of cyclical development, the most interesting questions concern the turning points: what kinds of manifestations of the persistent tensions of the mixed economy are likely to stimulate a reversal of policy strategy? In general, such turning points may be expected to result from the decreasing success of a strategy as the manifestations of persisting contradictions build up, faced with the rising expectations of the electorate generated by the promises of change and by its early successes. Whilst a sovereign state may do whatever it can get legitimated – and it is therefore *a state's* understanding of the tasks and problems facing it which proximately determine the intended objects and instruments of policy – the task of theory is to grasp those understandings in the light of a conceptualisation of the systematic whole that is bourgeois society.

Conjunctural accounts are not some optional extra, but are demanded by the methodological imperatives of value-form theory itself: contradiction must have a form of existence, however contingent its content. The procedure of systematic conceptual development and the programmatic interrogation of empirical information not only generate new insights as to contingent developments, but also provide a more adequate foundation for existing assertions about the basis of policy. Policy and political options can then be discussed on the firm basis of their interconnectedness within bourgeois society. One issue evolving from our presentation may clarify this. Value-form theory would argue that the diremption of society, and concomitantly of the individual (7S1), is manifest in the antinomy of pro-working class politics in the bourgeois epoch. It is clearly in the interests of labourers that civil society be economically successful, since economic growth enhances their possibilities of successfully deploying their capacity to labour, as well as of winning an increased 'social wage'. But such growth must of necessity be the successful reproduction of the value-form determined processes which inhibit people's potential for self-determination. 'Subjective individuals acquire objective recognition by means of these two factors (exchange and contract), and this recognition transforms their fortuitous possessions into property, and themselves into persons' (Kortian 1984: 201). For Hegel, as for Marx: 'human capacities and the potentialities contained in economic activity, can only be fully actualised in the context of a properly ordered social context' (Walton 1984: 250). According to value-form theory, in the bourgeois epoch that context's 'proper order' is fatally flawed by the diremption into economic, political and private spheres. The economic rationality which dominates bourgeois society is, in reality, but one, separated, moment of a conception of rationality adequate to humankind's species being – and, we have shown, can be comprehended as such. Nevertheless, whilst truth is in-itself political, it may only become for-itself political – thus freedom in-itself – if it is *comprehended* as in-itself political (0§13).

Bibliography

Note: The first date in parenthesis normally refers to the first edition in any language; subsequent dates in parenthesis indicate subsequent editions, marked with a superscript. We have normally also shown the date of first and subsequent translation of a work into English. All this is intended to facilitate the relative dating of different works when comparing the development of authors and their reception in the literature. Unless otherwise indicated in the text, the edition and print to which page numbers refer is the one next to the publisher's name.

Aaronovitch, S. and R. Smith (1981)
    The Political Economy of British Capitalism, McGraw-Hill, London 1981
Adarkar, B. P. (1934)
    Fisher's Real Rate Doctrine, *Economic Journal*, 1934, pp. 337–42
Aglietta, M. (1976)
    Régulation et Crises du Capitalisme, Calmann-Lévi 1976, Engl. transl. D. Fernbach, *A Theory of Capitalist Regulation; The US Experience*, NLB, London 1979
Altvater, E. (1972)
    Zu Einigen Problemen des Staatsinterventionismus, *Prokla* no. 3, 1972 pp. 1–53; Engl. transl., Notes on some Problems of State Inverventionism, *Kapitalistate* no. 1, 1973, pp. 96–116; no. 2, 1973, pp. 76–83
Armstrong, P., A. Glyn and J. Harrison (1984)
    Capitalism Since World War II; the making and break up of the great boom, Fontana, London 1984
Arrow, K. J. (1975)
    Vertical Integration and Communication, *Bell Journal of Economics* 6, 1975, pp. 173–83.
Arthur, C. J. (1970)
    Editor's Introduction, to K. Marx and F. Engels, *The German Ideology*, Lawrence & Wishart, London 1974, pp. 4–34
Arthur, C. J. (1976)
    The Concept of Abstract Labour, *Bulletin of the Conference of Socialist Economists* Vol. V (2), pp. 1–16

Arthur, C. J. (1988)
Hegel's theory of value, in M. Williams (ed.) *Value, social form and the state*, Macmillan, London 1988, pp. 21–41

Backhaus, H-G. (1969)
Zur Dialektik der Wertform, in, A. Schmidt (hsg.) *Beiträge zur Marxistischen Erkenntnistheorie*, Frankfurt a. M. 1969; Engl. transl. M. Eldred and M. Roth, On the Dialectics of the Value-form, *Thesis Eleven* I, 1980, pp. 99–120

Bacon, R. and W. Eltis (1977[1], 1978[2])
Britain's Economic Problem: too few producers, Macmillan, London 1978

Bader, V.-M., J. Berger, H. Ganssmann, T. Hagelstange, B. Hoffmann, M. Krätke, B. Krais, L. Kürschner and R. Strehl (1975)
Krise und Kapitalismus bei Marx, Band 1, Europäische Verlagsanstalt, Frankfurt/a.M./Köln 1975

Balibar, E. (1965[1], 1968[2])
The Basic Concepts of Historical Materialism, in, Louis Althusser and Etienne Balibar, *Lire le Capital*, Maspero, Paris 1965; Engl. transl. (1970) Ben Brewster, *Reading Capital*, NLB, London 1975

Bannock, G., R. E. Baxter and R. Rees (1978[2])
The Penguin Dictionary of Economics, Penguin Books, Harmondsworth 1979

Baran, P. A. and P. M. Sweezy (1966)
Monopoly Capital; An Essay on the American Economic and Social Order, Penguin Books, Harmondsworth 1970

Barr, N. (1987)
The Economics of the Welfare State, Weidenfeld & Nicolson, London 1987

Bartlett, B. and T. R. Roth (1984)
The Supply-Side Solution, Macmillan, London 1984

Baumol, W. J. (1952[1], 1965[2])
Welfare Economics and the Theory of the State, Bell and Sons, London 1965

Baumol, W. J. (1967)
Macro-economics of Unbalanced Growth, *American Economic Review* Vol. 57, 1967

Baumol, W. J. (1982)
Contestable Markets: an Uprising in the Theory of Industrial Structures, *American Economic Review* Vol. 72, 1982, pp. 1–5

Beckerman, W. (1974)
In Defence of Economic Growth, Cape, London 1974

Bell, P. F. (1977)
Marxist Theory, Class Struggle, and the Crisis of Capitalism, in J. Schwartz (ed.), *The Subtle Anatomy of Capitalism*, Goodyear Publishing Co., Santa Monica (Cal.) 1977, pp. 170–94

Benhabib, S. (1984)
Obligation, Contract and Exchange: on the Significance of Hegel's Abstract Right, in Z. A. Pelczynski (ed.) 1984, pp. 159–77

Berg, M. (1979)

(ed.) *Technology and Toil in Nineteenth Century Britain*, CSE Books/Humanities Press, London/New Jersey 1979

Berle, A. A. and G. C. Means (1932)
The Modern Corporation and Private Property, Macmillan, London 1932

Berlin, I. (1958)
Two Concepts of Liberty, in A. Quinton, (ed.), *Political Philosophy*, Oxford University Press, Oxford 1967

Berlin, I. (1972)
Nationalism: past neglect and present power, in Berlin, *Against the Current: Essays in the History of Ideas*, London 1979

Bhaskar, R. (1975[1], 1978[2])
A Realist Theory of Science, Harvester/Humanities, Sussex/New Jersey 1978

Bhaskar, R. (1979)
The Possibility of Naturalism; A Philosophical Critique of the Contemporary Human Sciences, Harvester, Sussex 1979

Bischoff, J., H. Ganzmann, G. Kümmel and G. Löhleen (1970)
Produktive und unproduktive Arbeit als Kategorien der Klassenanalyse, *Sozialistische Politik* 6-7, 1970

Blanke, B., U. Jürgens and H. Kastendiek, (1974)
Zur neueren marxistischen Diskussion über die Analyse von Form und Funktion des bürgerlichen Staates, *Prokla* 14-15, pp. 51-102; Engl. transl. M. Sohn-Rethel, On the Current Marxist Discussion on the Analysis of Form and Function of the Bourgeois State, in J. Holloway and S. Picciotto, (eds) *State and Capital, A Marxist Debate*, Edward Arnold, London 1978, pp. 108-47

Blaug, M. (1962[1], 1968)
Economic Theory in Restrospect, Irwin, Homewood, Illinois 1968

Blaug, M. (1980)
The Methodology of economics, or how economists explain, Cambridge University Press, Cambridge 1980

Bleaney, M. (1976)
Underconsumption Theories; A history and critical analysis, Lawrence and Wishart, London 1976

Bleaney, M. (1980)
Maurice Dobb's theory of crisis: a comment, *Cambridge Journal of Economics* Vol. 4, 1980, pp. 71-3

Boddy, R. and J. Crotty (1975)
Class Conflict and Macro-Policy: The Political Business Cycle, *Review of Radical Political Economics*, Vol. 7, 1975

Braverman, H. (1974)
Labour and Monopoly Capital, The Degradation of Work in the Twentieth Century, Monthly Review Press, New York/London 1974

Breton, A. (1974)
The Economic Theory of Representative Government, Aldine, Chicago 1974

Brighton Labour Process Group (1977)
The Capitalist Labour Process, *Capital & Class* no. 1, 1977, pp. 3-26

Brittan, S. (1977)
The Economic Consequences of Democracy, Temple Smith, London 1977
Brown, C. V. and P. M. Jackson (1978)
Public Sector Economics, Martin Robertson, Oxford 1978
Buchanan, J. M. and G. Tullock (1965²)
The Calculus of Consent, Ann Arbor, Michigan 1965
Bullock, P. (1974)
Defining productive labour for Capital, *Bulletin of the Conference of Socialist Economists* Vol. III (9), 1974
Burden, T. and M. Campbell (1985)
Capitalism and Public Policy in the U.K., Croom Helm, London 1985
Burton, J. (1979)
The Job Support Machine: a critique of the subsidy morass, Centre for Policy Studies, London 1979
Caldwell, B. (1982)
Beyond Positivism: Economic Methodology in the Twentieth Century, Allen & Unwin, London 1982
Callinicos, A. (1985)
Marxism and Philosophy, Oxford University Press, Oxford 1985
Campbell, M. (1981)
Capitalism in the U.K.: A perspective from Marxist political economy, Croom Helm, London 1981
Camus, A. (1942)
Le mythe de Sisyphe, Gallimard, Paris 1942; Dutch transl. Anton van der Niet, *De myte van Sisyfus*, De Bezige Bij, Amsterdam 1975
Cannan, E. (1893¹, 1917³)
A history of the theories of Production and Distribution in English political economy from 1776-1848, third edition, King & Son, London 1920
Canterbery, E. R. and R. J. Burkhardt (1983)
What do we mean by asking whether economics is a science?, in A. E. Eichner (ed.), *Why is economics not yet a science*, Macmillan, London 1983, pp. 15-40
Canto, A., D. H. Jones and A. B. Laffer (1983)
Foundations of Supply-Side Economics: theory and evidence, Academic Press, New York 1983
Carter, C. (ed.) (1981)
Industrial Policy and Innovation, (NIESR, PSI and RIIA, Joint Studies in Public Policy, 3), Heinemann, London 1981
Cass, D. and J. Stiglitz (1969)
The Implications of Alternative Savings and Expectations Hypothesis for Choices of Technique and Patterns of Growth, *Journal of Political Economy* July/August 1969
Clark, J. B. (1907)
Essentials of economic theory, as applied to modern problems of industry and public policy, Kelley, New York 1968
Coakley, J. and L. Harris (1983)
City of Capital, Basil Blackwell, Oxford 1983

Cohen, G. A. (1978)
Karl Marx's Theory of History: a Defence, Princeton University Press 1978; Chapter reprinted in Roemer (ed.) 1986
Colletti, L. (1974)
Marxismo e dialettica, *Intervista politico-filosofica*, Laterza 1974; Engl. transl. J. Matthews, Marxism and the Dialectic, *New Left Review* no. 93, 1975, pp. 3–29
Colletti, L. (1975)
Introduction to K. Marx, *Early Writings* (Engl. transl. G. Benton), Penguin/New Left Books, London 1975, pp. 7–56
Cutler, A., B. Hindess, P. Hirst and A. Hussain (1977)
Marx's Capital and Capitalism Today, Vol. 1, Routledge and Kegan Paul, London 1977
Cyert, R. and J. March (1963)
A Behavioural Theory of the Firm, Prentice-Hall, New Jersey, 1963
De Brunhoff, S. (1973)
La Monnaie chez Marx, Editions sociales, Paris 1973; Engl. transl. M. J. Goldbloom, *Marx on Money*, Urizen Books, New York 1976
De Brunhoff, S. (1976)
État et Capital, Presses Universitaires de Grenoble & Maspero 1976; Engl. transl. M. Sonenscher, *The State, Capital and Economic Policy*, Pluto Press, London, 1978
De Brunhoff, S. and J. Cartlier (1974)
Une Analyse Marxiste de l'Inflation, *Chronique Sociale de France*, no. 4, 1974, pp. 47–60
Desai, M. (1974)
Marxian Economic Theory, Gray-Mills, London 1974
Desai, M. (1979)
Marxian Economics, Basil Blackwell, Oxford 1979
De Vroey, M. (1981)
Value, Production, and Exchange in, I. Steedman, P. Sweezy *et al.*, *The Value Controversy*, Verso/NLB, London 1981, pp. 173–201
De Vroey, M. (1982)
On the Obsolescence of the Marxian Theory of Value: A Critical review, *Capital and Class* no. 17, 1982, pp. 34–59
De Vroey, M. (1984)
Inflation: a non-monetarist monetary interpretation, *Cambridge Journal of Economics* Vol. 8, 1984, pp. 381–99
Dobb, M. (1937[1], 1940[2])
Political Economy and Capitalism; some essays in economic tradition, Routledge & Kegan Paul, London 1968
Dobb, M. (1973)
Theories of value and distribution since Adam Smith: Ideology and economic theory, Cambridge University Press, Cambridge 1973
Domar, E. D. (1946)
Capital expansion, rate of growth and employment, *Econometrica* Vol. 14, 1946, pp. 137–47, reprinted in A. Sen (ed.), *Growth Economics*, Penguin Books, Harmondsworth 1970, pp. 65–77

Domar, E. D. (1947)
Expansion and Employment, *The American Economic Review* Vol. 37, 1947, pp. 34–55, reprinted in M. G. Mueller (ed.), *Readings in Macroeconomics*, 2nd edn, Holt, Rinehart and Winston, London 1971, pp. 227–93

Dow, S. C. (1985)
Macroeconomic Thought, A Methodological Approach, Basil Blackwell, Oxford 1985

Downs, A. (1957)
An economic theory of democracy, Harper, New York 1957

Driehuis, W. (1978)
Labour market imbalances and structural unemployment, *Kyklos* Vol. 31, 1978, pp. 638–61

Easton, L. D. and K. H. Guddat, (eds and transl.) (1967)
Writing of the young Marx on Philosophy and Society, Anchor, New York 1967

Edwards, C. (1985)
The fragmented world: competing perspectives on trade, money and crisis, Methuen, London 1985

Eldred, M. (1984a)
Critique of Competitive Freedom and the Bourgeois-democratic state; outline of a form-analytic extension of Marx's uncompleted system, Kurasje, København 1984

Eldred, M. (1984b)
A reply to Gleicher; history: universal concept dissolves any concept!, *Capital & Class* no. 23, 1984, pp. 135–40

Eldred, M. and M. Hanlon (1981)
Reconstructing Value-Form Analysis, *Capital & Class* no. 13, Spring 1981, pp. 24–60

Eldred, M., M. Hanlon, L. Kleiber and M. Roth (1982/85[1], 1984[2])
Reconstructing Value-Form Analysis 1, 2, 3, 4, *Thesis Eleven* no. 4, 1982; no. 7, 1983; no. 9, 1984; no. 11, 1985; modified as, A Value-form analytic reconstruction of 'Capital', Appendix to M. Eldred, 1984a, pp. 350–487

Eldred, M. and M. Roth (1978)
A Guide to Marx's 'Capital', CSE Books, London 1978

Elson, D. (1979)
The Value Theory of Labour, in, D. Elson (ed.) *Value; The Representation of Labour in Capitalism*, CSE Books, London 1979

Engels, F. (1880)
Socialism: Utopian and Scientific, English transl. by Averling, 1892; reprinted in Lewis S. Feuer (ed.) *Marx and Engels: Basic Writings on Politics and Philosophy*, Fontana, London 1969

Engels, F. (1884[1], 1891[4])
Der Ursprung der Familie, des Privateigentums und des Staates; Engl. transl., *The Origin of the Family, Private Property and the State*, in Marx and Engels, *Selected Works* in One Volume, Lawrence & Wishart, London 1973, pp. 449–583

Ergas, M. and D. Fishman (1975)

The marxian theory of money and the crisis of capital, *Bulletin of the Conference of Socialist Economists*, Vol. IV (2) 1975, pp. 1–15
Evans, T. (1985)
Money makes the world go round, *Capital & Class* no. 24, 1985, pp. 99–123
Fennema, M. (1982)
International Networks of Banks and Industry, Martinus Nijhoff, The Hague 1982
Feyerabend, P. (1975)
Against method, NLB, London 1975
Findlay, J. N. (1973)
Comment on Weil's 'The Hegelian Dialectic', in, J. J. O'Malley, K. W. Algozin, H. P. Kainz and L. C. Rice (eds), *The Legacy of Hegel, Proceedings of the Marquette Hegel Symposium 1970*, Martinus Nijhoff, The Hague 1973, pp. 65–71
Findlay, J. N. (1974)
Reflexive Asymmetry: Hegel's Most Fundamental Methodological Ruse, in F. G. Weiss (ed.) *Beyond Epistemology; New Studies in the Philosophy of Hegel*, Martinus Nijhoff, The Hague 1974, pp. 154–173
Findlay, J. N. (1975)
Foreword to Oxford edition of Hegel (1817), *Hegel's Logic*, Oxford University Press, Oxford 1975, pp. v–xxvii
Fine, B. (1973)
A note on productive and unproductive labour, *Bulletin of the Conference of Socialist Economists* Vol. II (6), 1973
Fine, B. (1975)
The Circulation of Capital, Ideology and Crisis, *Bulletin of the Conference of Socialist Economists* Vol. IV (12), 1975
Fine, B. (1982)
Theories of the Capitalist Economy, Edward Arnold, London 1982
Fine, B. and L. Harris (1976)
Controversial Issues in Marxist Economic Theory, in, R. Miliband and J. Saville (eds), *Socialist Register 1976*, Merlin Press, London 1976
Fine, B. and L. Harris (1979)
Rereading Capital, Macmillan, London 1979
von Flatow, S. and F. Huisken (1973)
Zum Problem der Ableitung des bürgerlichen Staates: die Oberfläche der bürgerlichen Gesellschaft, der Staat, und die allgemeinen Rahmenbedingungen der Produktion, *Prokla* no. 7, 1973
Foley, D. K. (1978)
State expenditure from a Marxist perspective, *Journal of Public Economics* no. 9, 1978, pp. 221–38
Foley, D. K. (1986)
Money, Accumulation and Crisis, New York, Monthly Review Press, 1986
Freedman, R. (ed.) (1961)
Marx on Economics, Penguin, Harmondsworth 1982
Freeman, C. (1974[1], 1982[2])
The Economics of Industrial Innovation, Frances Pinter, London 1982

Friedman, M. (1953)
The Methodology of Positive Economics, in Friedman, *Essays in Positive Economics*, University of Chicago Press, Chicago/London 1953, pp. 3–43; reprinted in D. M. Hausman (ed.), *The Philosophy of Economics, an Anthology*, Cambridge University Press, Cambridge 1984, pp. 210–44

Friedman, M. (1962)
Capitalism and Freedom, Chicago University Press, Chicago 1962

Friedman, M. (1976)
The Line we dare not cross: the fragility of freedom at 60%, *Encounter*, November 1976

Gamble, A. and P. Walton (1976)
Capitalism in Crisis; Inflation and the State, Macmillan, London 1976

Gerstein, I. (1976)
Production, Circulation and Value, *Economy and Society* Vol. 5, 1976, pp. 243–91

Geurts, J. P. M. (1971)
Het ervaringsgegeven in de natuurwetenschappen, kennistheoretische aantekeningen, unpubl. Ph. D., Utrecht 1971

Geurts, J. P. M. (1974)
Feit en theorie, inleiding tot de wetenschapsleer, Van Gorkum, Assen/Amsterdam 1974

Gleicher, D. (1983)
A historical approach to the question of abstract labour, *Capital & Class* no. 21, 1983, pp. 97–122

Gleicher, D. (1985)
A rejoinder to Eldred: Abstract Labour, the Rubin School and the Marxist Theory of Value, *Capital & Class* no. 24, 1985, pp. 147–55

Glombowski, J. (1982)
Marx en Keynes: Krisistheorie en 'alternatieve ekonomische politiek', *Tijdschrift voor Politieke Ekonomie* Vol. 5 (4), 1982, pp. 9–32

Glombowski, J. (1983)
A Marxian Model of Long Run Capitalist Development, *Zeitschrift für Nationalökonomie/Journal of Economics* Vol. 43, 1983, pp. 363–82

Glombowski, J. (1984)
Kritische Kommentare zur Akkumulationstheorie, *Mehrwert* no. 25, 1984, pp. 67–80

Glombowski, J. and M. Krüger (1984a)
Profit-Squeeze und Fall der Profitrate als Elemente eines integrierten Überakkumulationsansatzes, *Prokla* no. 14, 1984, pp. 40—54

Glombowski, J. and M. Krüger (1984b)
Unemployment insurance and cyclical growth, in R. M. Goodwin, M. Krüger and A. Vercelli (eds), *Nonlinear Models of Fluctuating Growth*, Springer-Verlag, Berlin etc. 1984, pp. 25–46

Glombowski, J. and M. Krüger (1986)
Generalizations of Goodwin's Growth Cycle Model, *Osnabrücker Sozialwissenschaftliche Manuskripte* no. 3/86, Universität Osnabrück, 1986

Glyn, A. and J. Harrison (1980)

The British Economic Disaster, Pluto Press, London 1980
Glyn, A. and B. Sutcliffe (1971)
The Critical Condition of British Capital, *New Left Review* no. 66, 1971
Glyn, A. and B. Sutcliffe (1972)
British Capitalism, Workers and the Profit Squeeze, Penguin Books, Harmondsworth 1972
Goodwin, R. M. (1967[1], 1972[2])
A growth cycle, in C. H. Feinstein (ed.), *Capitalism and Economic Growth*, Cambridge University Press, Cambridge 1967, pp. 54–8; revised and enlarged in E. K. Hunt and J. G. Schwartz (eds), *A Critique of Economic Theory*, Penguin Books, Harmondsworth 1972, pp. 442–9
Gorz, A. (1971)
Technology, Technicians and Class Struggle, (original publication in *Les Temps Modernes*, 1971, Engl. transl. J. Mepham) in Gorz (ed.), *The division of Labour: the Labour Process and Class Struggle in Modern Capitalism*, The Harvester Press, Hassocks 1976, pp. 159–89
Gough, I. (1972)
Marx's Theory of Productive and Unproductive Labour, *New Left Review* no. 76, 1972
Gough, I. (1973)
On Productive and Unproductive Labour – a reply, *Bulletin of the Conference of Socialist Economists* Vol. II (7) 1973
Gough, I. (1979)
The political economy of the welfare state, Macmillan, London 1981
Gramsci, A. (1971) (written 1929–1935)
Selections from the Prison Notebooks, eds Q. Hoare and G. Nowell Smith, Lawrence and Wishart, London 1976
Gransow, V. and C. Offe (1981)
Political culture and social democratic administration, translated and shortened from *Das Argument* no. 128, 1981, pp. 551–64, in Offe 1984, pp. 207–19
Haberler, G. (1937[1], 1958[4])
Prosperity and Depression, A Theoretical Analysis of Cyclical Movements, Atheneum, New York 1963
Habermas, J. (1973)
Legitimationsprobleme im Spätkapitalismus, Suhrkamp, Frankfurt a. M. 1973; Engl. transl., T. McCarthy, *Legitimation Crisis*, Heinemann, London 1976
Hahn, F. (1982)
Reflections on the Invisible Hand, The Fred Hirsch Memorial Lecture, Warwick University, 5.11.81, *Lloyd's Bank Review* no. 144, April 1982
Hanlon, M. (1983)
The Crisis in Marxis(t-Feminis)m, Marx Conference of Democrazia-Proletaria, Milan, December 1983
Hansen, L., K. Pedersen and T. Stenderup (1984)
On methodological problems in economic theory; a critique of aprioristic value theory, *Institut for Socialvidenskab Roskilde Universitetscenter, Instituttets skriftserie* no. 15, 1984

Harcourt, G. C. (1972)
Some Cambridge Controversies in the Theory of Capital, Cambridge
University Press, Cambridge 1972
Harris, D. J. (1983)
Accumulation of capital and the rate of profit in Marxian theory,
Cambridge Journal of Economics Vol. 7, 1983, pp. 311–30
Harris, L. (1976)
On interest, credit and capital, *Economy and Society* Vol. 5, 1976, pp.
145–77
Harrison, J. (1973)
Productive and Unproductive Labour in Marx's Political Economy,
Bulletin of the Conference of Socialist Economists Vol. II (6) 1973
Harrod, R. F. (1939)
An essay in dynamic theory, *Economic Journal* Vol. 49, 1939, pp. 14–23,
reprinted in A. Sen (ed.), *Growth Economics*, Penguin Books,
Harmondsworth 1970, pp. 43–64
Hay, D. A. and D. J. Morris (1979)
Industrial Economics, Theory and Evidence, Oxford University Press,
Oxford 1980
Hayek, F. A. (1944)
The Road to Serfdom, Routledge & Kegan Paul, London 1979
Hayek, F. A. (1960)
The Constitution of Liberty, Routledge & Kegan Paul, London 1960
Hayek, F. A. (1975)
Full Employment at any Price? Occasional Paper 45, Institute of
Economic Affairs, London 1975
Hegel, G. W. F. (1807[1], 1841[3])
Die Phänomenologie des Geistes (Einleitung: Vom wissenschaftlichen
Erkennen); (first Engl. transl. J. B. Baillie 1910), Dutch transl. P. Jonkers,
*Het wetenschappelijk kennen, voorwoord tot de fenomenologie van de
geest*, Boom, Meppel 1978
Hegel, G. W. F. (1817[1], 1830[3], 1970[4])
*Enzyklopädie der Philosophischen Wissenschaften im Grundrisse I, Die
Wissenschaft der Logik*, ed. E. Moldenhauer and K. M. Michel (1970),
Suhrkamp Verlag, Frankfurt a. M. 1986; Engl. transl. of the third edition
(1873[1]), W. Wallace, *Hegel's Logic*, Oxford University Press, Oxford 1985
Hegel, G. W. F. (1821[1], 1970[7])
Grundlinien der Philosophie des Rechts oder *Naturrecht und Staatswissen-
schaft im Grundrisse*, ed. E. Moldenhauer and K. M. Michel (1970),
Suhrkamp Verlag, Frankfurt a. M. 1975; Engl. transl. (first Engl. transl. S.
W. Dyde 1896), T. M. Knox (1942) from the 1821 Hegel edition, with
reference to the 1833 and 1854 Gans, the 1902 Bolland and the 1921
Lasson editions, *Hegel's Philosophy of Right*, Oxford University Press,
Oxford 1967
Hegel, G. W. F. (1833[1], 1840[2], 1940[3])
Einleitung in die Geschichte der Philosophie (of 1823, 1825, 1827) ed. J.
Hoffmeister 1940; Engl. transl. (first Engl. transl. of second edn E. S.
Haldane 1892) T. M. Knox and A. V. Miller (1985), *Introduction to the*

Lectures on the History of Philosophy, Clarendon Press, Oxford 1985
Hegel, G. W. F. (1837^1, 1840^2, 1955^4)
   Vorlesungen über die Philosophie der Geschichte, ed. J. Hoffmeister 1955;
   Engl. transl. selections (first Engl. transl. of second ed. J. Sibree 1875), H.
   B. Nisbet (1975), *Lectures on the Philosophy of World History,
   Introduction: Reason in History*, Cambridge University Press, Cam-
   bridge, 1984
Heinrich, M. (1986)
   Hegel, die 'Grundrisse' und das 'Kapital'; Ein Nachtrag zur Diskussion um
   das 'Kapital' in den 70er Jahren, *Prokla* Vol. 16, no. 4, 1986, pp. 4–33
Hicks, J. (1967)
   Critical Essays in Monetary Theory, Oxford University Press, Oxford
   1967
Himmelweit, S. (1977)
   The Individual as Basic Unit of Analysis, in F. Green and P. Nore (eds),
   Economics: An Anti-Text, Macmillan, London 1977, pp. 21–55
Himmelweit, S. (1974)
   The continuing saga of the falling rate of profit – a reply to Mario Cogoy,
   Bulletin of the Conference of Socialist Economists no. 9 1974, pp. 1–6
Himmelweit, S. (1984)
   The Real Dualism of Sex and Class, *Review of Radical Political
   Economics* Vol. 16 (1), pp. 167–83
Himmelweit, S. and S. Mohun (1978)
   The Anomalies of Capital, *Capital and Class* no. 6, 1978, pp. 67–105
Himmelweit, S. and S. Mohun (1981)
   Real Abstractions and Anomalous Assumptions, in, I. Steedman and P.
   Sweezy *et al.*, *The Value Controversy*, Verso/NLB, London 1981, pp.
   224–265
Hirsch, J. (1974)
   Staatsapparat und Reproduktion des Kapitals, Suhrkamp, Frankfurt
   1974; Engl. transl. of Parts 1 and 5, J. Holloway and S. Picciotto, The
   State Apparatus and Social Reproduction: Elements of a Theory of the
   Bourgeois State, in J. Holloway and S. Picciotto (eds), 1978, pp. 57–107
Hirsch, F. (1977)
   Social Limits to Growth, Routledge & Kegan Paul, London 1977
Hobbes, T. (1651)
   Leviathan, ed. C. B. Macpherson, Penguin Books, Harmondsworth 1968
Holloway, J. and S. Picciotto (1977)
   Crisis and the state, *Capital and Class* no. 2, 1977, pp. 76–101
Holloway, J. and S. Picciotto (eds) (1978)
   The State and Capital: A Marxist Debate, Edward Arnold, London 1978
Howell, P. (1975)
   Once Again on Productive and Unproductive Labour, *Revolutionary
   Communist* no. 3/4, 1975, pp. 46–68
Hume, D. (1739/40)
   An Abstract of a Treatise of Human Nature (eds J. M. Keynes and P.
   Sraffa) Cambridge 1938, reprinted in Hume (1748), ed. C. W. Hendel
   1955, pp. 181–98

Hume, D. (1748[1], 1777)
   An Inquiry Concerning Human Understanding (ed. C. W. Hendel), The
   Liberal Arts Press, New York 1955
Hunt, E. K. (1979)
   History of Economic Thought, a critical perspective, Wadsworth,
   Belmont Cal. 1979
Huxley, A. (1932)
   Brave New World
Huxley, A. (1936)
   Eyeless in Gaza, Bantam, London 1961
Ilting, K.-H. (1977a)
   Hegel's Begriff des Staats und die Kritik des jungen Marx, *Rivista di
   filosofia* no. 7–9, October 1977; Engl. transl., Hegel's concept of the state
   and Marx's early critique, in Z. A. Pelczynski (ed.) 1984, pp. 93–113
Ilting, K.-H. (1977b)
   The Dialectic of Civil Society, in Z. A. Pelczynski (ed.), 1984, pp. 211–66
Innes, D. (1981)
   Capitalism and Gold, *Capital and Class* no. 14, 1981, pp. 5–35
IJsseling, S. (1978)
   Filosofie als wetenschappelijk systeem, introduction in G. W. F. Hegel,
   Het wetenschappelijk kennen, Boom, Meppel 1978, pp. 7–35
Jackson, P. M. (1982)
   The Political Economy of Bureaucracy, Philip Allan, Oxford 1982
Jessop, B. (1977)
   Recent Theories of the Capitalist State, *Cambridge Journal of Economics*
   Vol. 1, 1977, pp. 353–73
Jessop, B. (1978)
   Democracy: the Best Possible Political Shell?, in Littlejohn *et al.* (eds),
   Power and the State, Croom Helm, London 1978
Jessop, B. (1982)
   The Capitalist State; Marxist Theories and Methods, Martin Robertson
   1982/Basil Blackwell, Oxford 1984
Jevons, W. S. (1871[1], 1879[2])
   The Theory of Political Economy, Penguin Books, Harmondsworth 1970
Johansen, L. (1959)
   Substitution versus fixed production coefficients in the theory of
   economic growth: a synthesis, *Econometrica* Vol. 27, 1959
Kahn-Freund, Sir O. (1968)
   Labour Law: Old traditions and new developments, Stevens, London
   1968
Kahn-Freund, Sir O. (1972)
   Labour and the Law, Stevens, London 1972
Kainz, K. P. (ed.) (1973)
   Round-Table Discussion on Problems of Translating Hegel, in, J. J.
   O'Malley, K. W. Algozin, H. P. Kainz and L. C. Rice (eds.), *The Legacy
   of Hegel, Proceedings of the Marquette Hegel Symposium 1970*, Martinus
   Nijhoff, The Hague 1973, pp. 253–67
Kaldor, N. (1957)

A model of economic growth, *Economic Journal* Vol. lxviii, 1957, pp. 591–624

Kaldor, N. (1971)
Conflicts in national economic objectives, *Economic Journal*, Vol. lxxxi, 1971, pp. 1–16

Kaldor, N. and J. A. Mirrlees (1961/62)
A new model of economic growth, *Review of Economic Studies* Vol. 29, 1961–2, pp. 174–90, reprinted under the title 'Growth Model with Induced Technical Progress' in A. Sen (ed.) *Growth Economics*, Penguin Books, Harmondsworth 1970, pp. 343–66

Katouzian, H. (1980)
Ideology and Method in Economics, Macmillan, London 1980

Kay, G. (1976)
A Note on Abstract Labour, *Bulletin of the Conference of Socialist Economists* Vol. 5 (13), 1976

Kay, G. (1988)
Economic Forms and the Possibility of Crisis, in M. Williams (ed.) *Value, Social Form and the State*, Macmillan, London 1988, pp. 80–95

Keane, J. (1984)
Introduction to C. Offe, *Contradictions of the Welfare State*, Hutchinson, London 1984, pp. 11–34

Keynes, J. M. (1936)
The General Theory of Employment, Interest and Money, Macmillan, London 1936

Keynes, J. N. (1891[1], 1917[4])
The Scope and Method of Political Economy, Macmillan, London, excerpts reprinted in D. M. Hausman (ed.), *The Philosophy of Economics*, Cambridge University Press, Cambridge 1984, pp. 70–98

Kirzner, I. M. (1973)
Competition and Entrepreneurship, University of Chicago Press, London 1978

Klant, J. J. (1972)
Spelregels voor Economen, Stenfert Kroese, Leiden 1972

Kleiber, L. (1981)
Zur Theorie des Privaten in der bürgerlichen Gessellschaft, *mimeo*, Sydney 1981

Knox, T. M. (1942)
Foreword (v–xii) and Notes (298–376) to Hegel's *Philosophy of Right*, Oxford University Press, London 1967

Kortian, G. (1970[1], 1984[2])
Remarques sur le rapport entre subjectivité et société civil, *Dialogue* IX, 2, 1970; revised and translated as, Subjectivity and civil society, in Z. A. Pelczynski (ed.) 1984, pp. 197–210

Kuhn, T. S. (1962[1], 1970[2])
The Structure of Scientific Revolutions, Chicago University Press, Chicago/London 1970

Leibenstein, H. (1966)
Allocative Efficiency versus X-efficiency, *American Economic Review* 56,

1966, pp. 392–415
Lenhardt, G. and C. Offe (1977)
Staatstheorie und Sozialpolitik – politische-soziologische Erklärungs-
ansätze für Funktionen und Innovationsprozesse der Sozialpolitik, in, C.
V. Ferber and F. X. Kaufman (hrsg.) *Kölner Zeitschrift für Soziologie
und Sozialpsychologie* no. 19, 1977, pp. 98–127; Engl. transl., Social
policy and the theory of the state, in Offe (1984) pp. 88–118
Lenin, V. I. (1917)
Imperialism, the Highest Stage of Capitalism (A Popular Outline), Zhizn i
Znaniye, Petrograd 1917, reprinted in Lenin, *Selected Works*, Progress
Publishers, Moscow 1975, pp. 169–262
Leontief, W. (1982)
Letter to the Editor, *Science* no. 217, July 9, 1982, pp. 104–105, reprinted
as Foreword, in A. S. Eichner (ed.), *Why Economics is not yet a Science*,
Macmillan, London 1983, pp. vii–xi
Levacic, R. (1987)
Economic Policy-making: its theory and practice, Wheatsheaf, Sussex
1987
Lipietz, A. (1983)
Le monde enchanté, Editions La Découverte, Paris 1983; Engl. transl. I.
Patterson, *The Enchanted World; Inflation, Credit and the World Crisis*,
Verso, London 1985
Littlechild, S. C. (1978)
The Fallacy of the Mixed Economy, Institute of Economic Affairs,
London 1978
Locke, J. (1690)
Second Treatise of Civil Government, in P. Laslett (ed.), *Locke's Two
Treatises of Government*: a Critical Edition with an Introduction and
apparatus criticus, Cambridge University Press, Cambridge 1960
Luxemburg, R. (1913)
*Die Akkumulation des Kapitals, Ein Beitrag zur ökonomischen Erklärung
der Imperialismus*; Engl. transl. A. Schwarzchild (1951), introd. J.
Robinson, *The Accumulation of Capital*, Routledge and Kegan Paul,
London 1971
Machlup, F. (1967)
Theories of the Firm: Marginalist, Behavioural and Managerial,
American Economic Review 57, March 1967
Macmillan, H. (1938)
The Middle Way, Macmillan, London 1938
Macpherson, C. B. (1962)
The Political Theory of Possessive Individualism; Hobbes to Locke
Oxford University Press, Oxford 1972
Macpherson, C. B. (1973)
Democratic Theory: Essays in Retrieval, Oxford University Press, Oxford
1977
Mandel, E. (1962)
Marxist Economic Theory, (Engl. transl. B. Pearce), Merlin Press,
London 1971

Mandel, E. (1970)
De geschiedenis en de bewegingswetten van het kapitalisme, in, Altvater *et al.*, *Het kapitalisme in de jaren '70*, Van Gennep, Amsterdam 1970, pp. 10–37

Mandel, E. (1983)
Competition, in, T. Bottomore (ed.) (1983), *A Dictionary of Marxist Thought*, Basil Blackwell, Oxford 1985, pp. 90–92

de Marchi, N. B. (1986)
Mill's Unrevised Philosophy of Economics; A Comment on Hausman, *Philosophy of Science* no. 53, 1986, pp. 89–100

Marglin, S. A. (1974)
What do bosses do? The origins and functions of Hierarchy in Capitalist Production, in, A. Gorz (ed.), *The division of labour: The Labour Process and Class-Struggle in Modern Capitalism*, The Harvester Press, Hassocks 1976, pp. 13–54

Marris, R. A. (1964)
The Economic Theory of 'Managerial' Capitalism, Macmillan, London 1964

Marris, R. A. (1972)
Why Economics needs a Theory of the Firm, *Economic Journal*, March 1972

Marris, R. A. and Wood (eds) (1971)
The Corporate Economy, Macmillan, London 1971

Marshall, A. (1890[1], 1920[8])
Principles of Economics, An introductory volume, Macmillan and Co., London 1930

Marx, K. (1844a)
Zur Kritik der Hegelschen Rechtsphilosophie, in A. Ruge and K. Marx (eds) *Deutsch-Französische Jahrbücher*, 1844, reprinted in *MEW 1*; Engl. transl. R. Livingstone (1975), A Contribution to the Critique of Hegel's Philosophy of Right; Introduction, in, K. Marx, *Early Writings*, Penguin/NLR, Harmondsworth 1975, pp. 243–57

Marx, K. (1844b)
Zur Judenfrage, in A. Ruge and K. Marx (eds), *Deutsch-Französische Jahrbücher*, Paris 1844, reprinted in *MEW 1*; Engl. transl. G. Benton, On the Jewish Question, in K. Marx, *Early Writings*, Penguin/NLR, Harmondsworth 1975, pp. 211–241

Marx, K. (1852[1], 1869[2], 1885[3])
Der Achtzehnte Brumaire des Louis Bonaparte, in *Die Revolution* (ed. J. Weydemeyer) 1852; 1869 and 1885 edn as book, reprinted in *MEW 1*; Engl. transl. D. Fernbach (1973), The Eighteenth Brumaire of Louis Bonaparte, in D. Fernbach (ed.), K. Marx, *Surveys from Exile*, Political Writings Vol. 2, Penguin/NLR, Harmondsworth 1977, pp. 143–249

Marx, K. (1855)
On the reform movement, in *Neue Oder-Zeitung*, 24 May 1955; Engl. transl. P. Jackson, in D. Fernbach (ed.), K. Marx, *Surveys from Exile*, Political Writings, Vol. 2, Penguin/NLR, Harmondsworth 1973, pp. 286–8

Marx, K. (1859[1], 1897[2]) (1859G = German edn)
Zur Kritik der Politischen Okonomie, MEW 13, Dietz Verlag, Berlin 1974; English edn (first Engl. transl. N. I. Stone (1904)) by Maurice Dobb, transl. S. W. Ryazanskaya, *A Contribution to the Critique of Political Economy*, Lawrence & Wishart, London 1971
Marx, K. (1867[1], 1887[3])
Das Kapital, Kritik der politischen Okonomie, Band I, Der Produktionsprozess des Kapitals; Engl. transl. from the 3rd German edn (1886[1]) by S. Moore and E. Aveling, *Capital, A Critical Analysis of Capitalist Production, Volume One*, Lawrence & Wishart, London 1974
Marx, K. (1867[1] first edn)
Das Kapital etc., Anhang, Die Wertform (pp. 764–84; dropped in subsequent editions); Engl. transl. (A. Dragstedt 1976[1]) M. Roth and W. Suchting (1978), The Value-form, *Capital & Class* no. 4, 1978, pp. 134–50
Marx, K. (1867[1]P, 1890[4]) (1867G = German edn)
Das Kapital, Kritik der politischen Okonomie, Band I, Der Produktionsprozess des Kapitals, MEW 23, Dietz Verlag, Berlin 1973; Engl. transl. (1886[1]) B. Fowkes (1976), *Capital, A Critique of Political Economy, Volume 1*, Penguin Books, Harmondsworth 1976
Marx, K. (1868)
Marx an Kugelmann, 11. Juli 1868, *MEW 32*, Dietz Verlag, Berlin 1965
Marx, K. (1885[1], 1893[2])
ed. F. Engels, *Das Kapital, Kritik der politischen Okonomie, Band II, Der Zirkulationsprozess des Kapitals, MEW 24*, Dietz Verlag, Berlin 1972; Engl. transl. (E. Untermann 1907[1]) I. Lasker, *Capital, A Critique of Political Economy, Volume II, The Process of Circulation of Capital*, Lawrence & Wishart, London 1974
Marx, K. (1888) (written 1845)
Thesen über Feuerbach, *MEW 3*, amended as 'Marx über Feuerbach', in F. Engels, *Ludwig Feuerbach und der Ausgang der klassischen deutschen Philosophie*, 1888; Engl. transl. of the original text, Theses on Feuerbach, in C. J. Arthur (ed.) K. Marx and F. Engels, *The German Ideology, Part One*, Lawrence & Wishart, London 1974, pp. 121–123
Marx, K. (1894) (1894G = German edn)
ed. F. Engels, *Das Kapital, Kritik der politischen Okonomie, Band III, Der Gesamtprozess der kapitalistischen Produktion, MEW 25*, Dietz Verlag, Berlin 1972; Engl. transl. (E. Untermann 1909[1]) *Capital, A Critique of Political Economy, Volume III, The Process of Capitalist Production as a Whole*, Lawrence & Wishart, London 1974
Marx, K. (1894P)
idem (1894); Engl. transl., D. Fernbach (1981), *Capital, A Critique of Political Economy Volume III*, Penguin Books, Harmondsworth 1981
Marx, K. (1903) (written 1857)
Einleitung (zu Grundrisse der Kritik der Politischen Okonomie), ed. K. Kautsky, *Die Neue Zeit* 1903, Engl. transl. (1904[1]) B. Fowkes 1973, see Marx 1939/53, pp. 83–111
Marx, K. (1904/10[1], 1956/66[2]) (written 1861–1863)
Theorien über den Mehrwert, 1st edn (1904/10) by K. Kautsky; selections

first translated 1951 by G. A. Bonner and E. Burns; 2nd edn (1956/66) by Institut für Marxismus-Leninismus, *Theorien über den Mehrwert, Teile I, II, III, MEW 26.1, 26.2, 26.3,* Dietz Verlag, Berlin 1973, 1972, 1972; Engl. edn, *Theories of Surplus Value, Part 1,* ed. S. Ryazanskaya and transl. E. Burns (1963), *Part II,* ed. and transl. S. Ryazanskaya (1968), *Part III,* eds S. Ryazanskaya and R. Dixon and transl. J. Cohen and S. Ryazanskaya (1971), Lawrence & Wishart, London 1969, 1969 and 1972

Marx, K. (1927) (written 1843)
Kritik des Hegelschen Staatsrechts, *MEGA I,* 1/1 1927 (*MEW I*); Engl. transl. R. Livingstone, Critique of Hegel's Doctrine of the State, in K. Marx, *Early Writings,* Penguin/NLR, Harmondsworth 1975, pp. 57–198

Marx, K. (1932) (written 1844)
Oekonomisch-philosophische Manuskripte, *MEGA I,* 3, 1932 (*MEW Ergänzungsband I*); Engl. transl. G. Benton, Economic and Philosophical Manuscripts, in K. Marx, *Early Writings,* Penguin/NLR, Harmondsworth 1975, pp. 279–420

Marx, K. (1939/41[1], 1953[2]) (written 1857–58)
Grundrisse der Kritik der Politischen Okonomie (Rohentwurf); Engl. transl. (1973[1]) M. Nicolaus, *Grundrisse,* Penguin/NLB, Harmondsworth 1973

Marx, K. and F. Engels (1848, 1872)
Manifest der Kommunistischen Partei, anonymous, London 1848, *MEW 4*; Engl. transl. H. MacFarlane, Manifesto of the German Communist Party, in *The Red Republican* 1850; *Das Kommunistische Manifest,* authorised, Leipzig 1872; Engl. transl., *Communist Manifesto*; cited as in Marx and Engels, *Selected works in One Volume,* Lawrence & Wishart, London 1968, pp. 31–63

Marx, K. and F. Engels (1902/3[1], 1965/66[2]) (written 1845/46)
Die deutsche Ideologie: Kritik der neuesten deutschen Philosophie in ihren Repräsentanten Feuerbach, B. Bauer und Steiner, und des deutschen Sozialismus in seinen verschiedenen Propheten; Excerpts first publ. by E. Bernstein, in *Dokumente des Sozialismus* 1902/03 and by G. Mayer in *Archiv für Sozial Wissenschaft und Sozialpolitik* 1921; First edn of ch. 1 of Part 1, 1924 (Russian) and 1926 (German); First complete edn 1932 *MEGA I,* 5 (*MEW 3*); Engl. transl. (excerpts 1938) W. Lough, C. Dutt and C. P. Magill, edited by C. J. Arthur (1970), *The German Ideology, Part One,* Lawrence & Wishart, London 1974

McCloskey, D. N. (1983)
The Rhetoric of Economics, *Journal of Economic Literature* Vol. XXI, 1983, pp. 481–517, reprinted in, B. Caldwell (ed.), *Appraisal and Criticism in Economics,* Allen & Unwin, Boston/London 1984, pp. 320–56

Meadows, D. H., L. Dennis, J. Randers, III Behmens and M. Williams (1972)
The Limits to Growth: a report for the Club of Rome's project on the predicament of mankind, Earth Island Ltd., London 1972

Meek, R. L. (1956[1], 1973[2])
Studies in the Labour Theory of Value, Lawrence & Wishart, London 1973

Miliband, R. (1969)
The State in Capitalist Society, Weidenfeld & Nicolson, London 1972

Mill, J. S. (1836[1], 1877[3])
On the Definition of Political Economy; and on the Method of Investigation Proper to It, *London and Westminster Review*, October 1836, repr. in J. S. Mill, *Essays on some unsettled Questions of Political Economy* (1844[1], 1877[3]) Longmans Green & Co., London 1948, pp 120–64

Mill, J. S. (1848[1], 1871[7])
Principles of Political Economy, with Some of Their Applications to Social Philosophy, Collected Works, Vol. II–III, ed. J. M. Robson, University of Toronto Press/Routledge & Kegan Paul, London 1965

von Mises, L. (1949)
Human Action, Yale University Press, New Haven 1949

Mishan, E. J. (1967)
The Cost of Economic Growth, Staples Press, London 1967

Modigliani, F. (1977)
The Monetarist Controversy or Should we Forsake Stabilization Policies? *American Economic Review* Vol. 67, no. 2, 1977, pp. 1–19

Moggeridge, D. E. (1976)
Keynes, Fontana/Collins, Glasgow 1976

Mueller, D. C. (1976)
Public choice: a Survey, *Journal of Economic Literature* 14, 1976, pp 395–433

Mueller, D. C. (1979)
Public Choice, Cambridge University Press, Cambridge, 1979

Müller, W. and C. Neusüss (1970)
Die Sozialstaatsillusion und der Widerspruch von Lohnarbeit und Kapital, *Sozialistische Politik* 6–7: 4–67; Engl. transl., The illusions of state socialism and the contradiction between wage-labour and capital, *Telos* 25, 1975, Extract: The 'Welfare-State illusion' and the Contradiction between Wage-Labour and Capital, in Holloway and Picciotto (eds), 1978, pp. 32–9

Nakatani, T. (1980)
The law of falling rate of profit and the competitive battle: comment on Shaikh, *Cambridge Journal of Economics* Vol. 4, 1980, pp. 65–8

Napoleoni, C. (1973[2])
Engl. transl. J. M. A. Gee, *Smith Ricardo Marx, observations on the history of economic thought*, Basil Blackwell, Oxford 1975

Nauta, L. W. (1971[1], 1980[4])
Wetenschap en waardevrijheid, in L. W. Nauta, *Argumenten voor een kritische ethiek*, Van Gennep, Amsterdam 1980, pp. 101–21.

Naylor, T. and J. Vernon (1969)
Micro-economics and Decision Models of the Firm, Harcourt, Brace & World, New York 1969

Niskanen, W. A. (1973)
Bureaucracy: servant or master?, Hobart Paperback No. 5, Institute of Economic Affairs, London 1973

Norman, R. (1976a)

Hegel's Phenomenology, A Philosophical Introduction, Harvester/ Humanities, Sussex/New Jersey 1981

Norman, R. (1976b)
On the Hegelian Origins, *Radical Philosophy* 14, 1976, reprinted in R. Norman and S. Sayers, *Hegel, Marx and Dialectic, A Debate*, Harvester, Brighton 1980, pp. 25-46

Norman, R. (1980)
The Problem of Contradiction, in R. Norman and S. Sayers, *Hegel, Marx and Dialectic: A Debate*, Harvester, Brighton 1980, pp. 47-66

Nozick, R. (1974)
Anarchy, State and Utopia, Basil Blackwell, Oxford 1974

O'Connor, J. (1973)
The Fiscal Crisis of the State, St. Martin's Press/St. James Press, New York/London 1973

Offe, C. (1973)
'Krisen des Krisenmanagement': Elemente einer politischen Krisentheorie, in M. Jänicke (ed.) *Herrschaft und Krise*, Westdeutscher Verlag, Opladen 1973, pp. 197-223; Engl. transl. 'Crises of crisis management': elements of a political crisis theory, *International Journal of Politics* Vol. 6, no. 3, 1976, pp. 29-67, reprinted in Offe (1984), pp. 35-64

Offe, C. (1975[1], 1984[2])
The Theory of the Capitalist State and the Problem of Policy Formation, in Lindberg *et al.* (eds), *Stress and Contradiction in Modern Capitalism*, D. H. Heath, Lexington Mass. 1975, pp. 245-59; revised as, Legitimacy versus efficiency, in Offe (1984) pp. 130-46

Offe, C. (1979)
'Ungovernability': the renaissance of conservative theories of crisis, German original in J. Habermas (ed.), *Stichworte zur Geistigen Situation der Zeit*, Frankfurt 1979, pp. 294-318; Engl. transl. in, Offe (1984) pp. 65-87

Offe, C. (1981[1], 1984[2])
Some Contradictions of the Modern Welfare State, *International Praxis*, Vol 1, no. 3, pp. 219-29, revised as in Offe (1984) pp. 147-61

Offe, C. (1984)
Contradictions of the Welfare State, (ed. J. Keane), Hutchinson, London 1984

Offe, C. and V. Ronge (1976)
Thesen zur Begründigung des Konzepts des 'kapitalistischen Staates' und zur materialistischen Politikforschung, in C. Pozzoli (ed.) *Rahmenbedingungen und Schranken Staatlichen Handelns*, Suhrkamp, Frankfurt 1976, pp. 54-70; Engl. transl. Theses on the Theory of the State, *New German Critique* 6, 1975, pp. 139-47, reprinted in Offe 1984, pp. 119-29

Okishio, N. (1961)
Technical changes and the rate of profit, *Kobe University Economic Review* Vol. 7, 1961, pp. 85-99

Okun, Arthur M. (1962)
Potential GNP: Its Measurement and Significance, *Proceedings of the Business and Economic Statistics Section of the American Statistical*

Association, 1962, pp. 98–104, reprinted in M. G. Mueller (ed.) *Readings in Macroeconomics*, 2nd edn, Holt Rinehart and Winston, London etc. 1971, pp. 401–10

Olin Wright, E. (1977)
Alternative Perspectives in Marxist Theory of Accumulation and Crisis, in J. Schwartz (ed.), *The Subtle Anatomy of Capitalism*, Goodyear Publishing Co., Santa Monica (Cal.) 1977

Palloix, C. (1976)
The labour process: from Fordism to neo-Fordism (Engl. transl. J. Mepham and M. Soneusher) in R. Guttmann and T. Putnam (eds), *The Labour Process and Class Strategies*, Stage 1, London 1976, pp. 44–67

Pasinetti, L. (1961/62)
Rate of profit and income distribution in relation to the rate of economic growth, *Review of Economic Studies* Vol. 29, 1961–2, pp. 267–79, reprinted in A. Sen (ed.), *Growth Economics*, Penguin Books, Harmondsworth 1970, pp. 92–111

Pelczynski, Z. A. (ed.) (1971)
Hegel's Political Philosophy: Problems and Perspectives, Cambridge University Press, Cambridge 1971

Pelczynski, Z. A. (ed.) (1984)
The State & Civil Society: Studies in Hegel's Political Philosophy, Cambridge University Press, Cambridge 1984

Pelczynski, Z. A. (1984a)
Introduction: The significance of Hegel's separation of the state and civil society, in Z. A. Pelczynski (ed.) 1984, pp. 1–13

Pelczynski, Z. A. (1984b)
Nation, civil society, state: Hegelian sources of the Marxian non-theory of rationality, in Pelczynski (ed.) (1984) pp. 262–78

Phillips, A. W. (1958)
The Relation between Unemployment and the Rate of Change of Money Wage Rates in the United Kingdom 1861–1957, *Economica*, Vol. 25, 1958, pp. 283–99, reprinted in M. G. Mueller (ed.) *Readings in Macroeconomics*, 2nd edn, Holt, Rinehart and Winston, London etc. 1971, pp. 245–64

Pilling, G. (1972)
The law of value in Ricardo and Marx, *Economy and Society* Vol. 1 August 1972

Plant, R. (1977)
Hegel and Political Economy, *New Left Review* no. 103–4, 1977

Plant, R. (1984)
Hegel on identity and legitimation, in Z. A. Pelczynski (ed.) (1984) pp. 227–43

Polak, N. J. (1940)
Goed koopmansgebruik in verband met de winstbepaling, *De Naamloze Vennootschap* 19, 1940/41, reprinted under the same title, Van der Marck, Roermond 1965

Quine, W. V. O. (1951[1], 1953[2])
Two Dogmas of Empiricism, *Philosophical Review*, January 1951, revised

in Quine, *From a Logical point of View: Logico-Philosophical Essays*, Harper & Row, New York 1963, pp. 20–46

Reichelt, H. (1974)

Einige Anmerkungen zu Sybille von Flatows und Freerk Huiskens Aufsatz 'Zum Problem der Ableitung des bürgerlichen Staates', *Gesellschaft, Beitrage zur marxistischen Theorie 1*, Suhrkamp, Frankfurt 1974, pp. 12–29; Engl. transl., On the Problem of the Derivation of the Bourgeois State, in J. Holloway and S. Picciotto, (eds) (1978) pp. 43–56

Reuten, G. A. (1978)

A concretization of the operation of the general rate of profit (:on the problem of the alleged transformation of values into prices of production), *Research Memorandum* no. 7801, Faculty of Economics, University of Amsterdam, 1978

Reuten, G. A. (1979a)

Meerwaarde en winst; over 'gedachtenkonstrukties' en 'theorie', *Tijdschrift voor Politieke Ekonomie* Vol. 2, no. 4, 1979, pp. 108–15

Reuten, G. A. (1979b)

Unemployment payments and the course of the depression, *Research Memorandum* no. 7913, Faculty of Economics, University of Amsterdam, 1979

Reuten, G. A. (1981a)

Reproduction scheme aggregates for the Dutch economy 1961–1977, Onderzoeknotitie no. 40 van de Vakgroep Macro-economie, Universiteit van Amsterdam, *mimeo* 1981

Reuten, G. A. (1981b)

On production distinctives of aggregate demand categories; method of analysis and results for the Dutch economy 1976, *Research Memorandum* no. 8104, Faculty of Economics, University of Amsterdam 1981

Reuten, G. A. (1986)

De neoklassieke theorie; consistentie en falsifieerbaarheid, in W. Driehuis and R. A. de Klerk (eds), *Economie als spel; Opstellen over economische methodologie*, Stenfert Kroese, Leiden/Antwerpen 1986, pp. 55–69

Ricardo, D. (1817[1], 1821[3])

On the principles of political economy and taxation, Dent & Sons, London 1933

Rima, I. H. (1978[3])

Development of Economic Analysis, Irwin, Homewood 1978

Robertson, D. (1933)

Saving and Hoarding, *Economic Journal*, September 1933, reprinted in D. Robertson, *Essays in Money and Interest* selected by J. Hicks, Collins Fontana, 1966, pp. 46–63

Robertson, D. (1934)

Industrial fluctuation and the natural rate of interest, *Economic Journal*, December 1934, reprinted in D. Robertson, *Essays in Money and Interest* selected by J. Hicks, Collins Fontana, 1966, pp. 64–74

Robinson, J. (1942[1], 1966[2])

An Essay on Marxian Economics, Macmillan, London 1969

Robinson, J. (1962)

A model of accumulation, in Robinson, *Essays in the Theory of Economic Growth*, Macmillan, London 1962; excerpt reprinted in A. Sen (ed.), *Growth Economics*, Penguin Books, Harmondsworth 1970, pp. 115–40

Roemer, J. E. (1979)
Continuing controversy on the falling rate of profit: fixed capital and other issues, *Cambridge Journal of Economics* Vol. 3, 1979, p. 379–98

Roemer, J. (1982)
New directions in the Marxian theory of exploitation and class, *Politics and Society* Vol. 11, nr. 3, reprinted in J. Roemer (ed.) 1986, pp. 81–113

Roemer, J. (ed.) (1986)
Analytical Marxism, Cambridge University Press, Cambridge 1986

Roll, E. (1938[1], 1973[4])
A history of economic thought, Faber & Faber, London 1973

Roll, Lord (ed.) (1982)
The Mixed Economy, Macmillan, London 1982

Roobeek, A. J. M. (1987)
De rol van de technologie in de ekonomische theorievorming, Economische Monografieën/Universiteit van Amsterdam no. 4, Scheltema Holkema Vermeulen, Amsterdam 1987

Rosdolsky, R. (1968)
Entstehungsgeschichte des Marxschen 'Kapital', Europäische Verlagsanstalt, Frankfurt a. M. 1968; Engl. transl. P. Burgess, *The Making of Marx' 'Capital'*, Pluto Press, London 1977

Rousseau, J.-J. (1762)
Du Contrat Social; Engl. transl. G. D. H. Cole (1913), in J. H. Brumfitt and J. C. Hall (eds), *The Social Contract, or Principles of Political Right*, in J.-J. Rousseau, *The Social Contract and Discourses*, Dent & Sons, London 1973

Rowthorn, B. (1980)
Capitalism, Conflict and Inflation: Essays in Political Economy, Lawrence and Wishart, London 1980

Rubin, I. I. (1928[3])
Ocherki po teorii stoimosti Marksa, Gosudarstvennoe Izdatel'stvo, Moscow 1928; Engl. transl. M. Samardźija and F. Perlman, *Essays on Marx's theory of value*, Black & Red, Detroit 1972

Ryan, A. (1984)
Hegel on work, ownership and citizenship, in Z. A. Pelczynski (ed.) 1984, pp. 178–96

Salter, W. E. G. (1960)
Productivity and Technical Change, Cambridge University Press, Cambridge 1960

Samuelson, P. A. (1948[1], 1970[8])
Economics, 8th edn, McGraw-Hill, New York etc. 1970

Samuelson, P. A. (1962)
Parable and realism in capital theory: the surrogate production function, *Review of Economic Studies* Vol. 39, 1962, pp. 193–206; reprinted in G. C. Harcourt and N. F. Laing (eds) *Capital and Growth*, Penguin Books, Harmondsworth 1971, pp. 213–32

Samuelson, P. A. (1966)
  A Summing Up, *Quarterly Journal of Economics* Vol. 80, 1966, pp. 568–83, reprinted in G. C. Harcourt and N. F. Laing (eds) *Capital and Growth*, Penguin Books, Harmondsworth 1971, pp. 213–32
Samuelson, P. A. (1974)
  Insight and Detour in the Theory of Exploitation: A Reply to Baumol, *Journal of Economic Literature* 1974, pp. 399–431
van Santen, J. (1968)
  De Marxistische Accumulatietheorie, Stenfert Kroese, Leiden 1968
van Santen, J. (1970)
  Economische kritiek en dialektiek, in L. Goldman *et al.*, *Dialektiek en maatschappijkritiek*, Boom, Meppel 1970, pp. 48–69
Schott, K. (1983)
  The Rise of Keynesian Economics, in D. Held (*et al.* eds) *States & Societies*, Martin Robertson/OU, Oxford 1983
Schumpeter, J. A. (1918)
  Die Krise des Steuerstaats, Zeitfragen aus dem Gebiete der Soziologie, Graz and Leipzig 1918, Engl. transl. W. F. Stolper and R. A. Musgrave, The Crisis of the Tax State, in A. T. Peacock *et al.* (eds), *International Economic Papers* no. 4 (Translation Prepared for the International Economic Association), Macmillan, London 1954, pp. 5–38
Schumpeter, J. A. (1934)
  The Theory of Economic Development, Harvard University Press, Cambridge 1934
Schumpeter, J. A. (1943[1], 1954[4])
  Capitalism, Socialism and Democracy, Unwin University Books, London 1966
Schumpeter, J. A. (1954)
  History of Economic Analysis, (ed. E. B. Shumpeter) Allen & Unwin, London 1972
Sen, A. (1983)
  The Profit Motive, *Lloyds Bank Review* no. 147, January 1983
Shaikh, A. (1978)
  Political Economy and Capitalism: notes on Dobb's theory of crisis, *Cambridge Journal of Economics* Vol. 2, 1978, pp. 233–251
Shaikh, A. (1980)
  Marxian competition versus perfect competition: further comments on the so-called choice of technique, *Cambridge Journal of Economics* Vol. 4, pp. 75–83
Simon, H. (1959)
  Theories of Decision Making in Economics and Behavioural Science, *American Economic Review* 69, 1959, pp. 253–80
Smith, A. (1776[1], 1791[6])
  An Inquiry into the Nature of Causes of The Wealth of Nations, Volumes i and ii, Dent & Sons, London 1933
Solow, R. M. (1970)
  Growth Theory, an exposition, Clarendon Press, Oxford 1970
Solow, R., J. Tobin, C. C. von Weizsäcker and M. Yaari (1966)

Neoclassical Growth with Fixed Factor Proportions, *Review of Economic Studies*, April 1966
Sraffa, P. (1960)
Production of Commodities by Means of Commodities; Prelude to a Critique of Economic Theory, Cambridge University Press, Cambridge 1975
Steedman, I. (1977)
Marx after Sraffa, New Left Books, London 1977
Steedman, I. (1980)
A note on the 'choice of technique' under capitalism, *Cambridge Journal of Economics* Vol. 4, 1980, pp. 61–4
Steindl, J. (1952)
Maturity and stagnation in American Capitalism, Monthy Review Press, New York/London 1976
Sweezy, P. M. (1942)
The theory of capitalist development, Modern Reader Paperbacks, London 1968
Taussig, F. W. (1911^1, 1915^2)
Principles of Economics, 2nd edn. Vol. I and II, The Macmillan Company, New York 1917
Thio, K. B. T. (1987)
On simultaneous explanation of long periodic movements and medium term business cycles, *Research Memorandum* 8717, Faculty of Economics, University of Amsterdam 1987
Thompson, G. (1986)
Economic Calculation and Policy Formation, Routledge & Kegan Paul, London 1986
Tinbergen, J. (1952)
On the Theory of Economic Policy, North-Holland, Amsterdam 1970
Veblen, T. (1908)
Professor Clark's economics, *Quarterly Journal of Economics* Vol. 22, 1908, pp. 147–95; reprinted in Veblen, *The place of Science in Modern Civilization*, 1919; excerpts reprinted in E. K. Hunt and J. G. Schwarts (eds), *A Critique of Economic Theory*, Penguin Books, Harmondsworth 1972, pp. 172–85
Walton, A. S. (1984)
Economy, utility and community in Hegel's theory of civil society, in Z. A. Pelczynski (ed.), 1984, pp. 244–61
Wanniski, J. (1978)
The Way the World Works, Basic Books, New York 1978
Weber, M. (1920)
Introduction to 'Gesammelte Aufsätze zur Religionssoziologie', in M. Weber (1904^1), *The Protestant Ethic and the Spirit of Capitalism*, Allen & Unwin, London 1968
Weeks, J. (1981)
Capital and Exploitation, Edward Arnold, London 1981
Whynes, D. K. and R. A. Bowles (1981)
The Economic Theory of the State, Martin Robertson, Oxford 1981

Wildsmith, J. R. (1973)
Managerial Theories of the Firm, Martin Robertson, London 1973
Williams, B. (1985)
Review of T. C. Schelling (1984), Choice and Consequence, Harvard University Press, *Economics & Philosophy* Vol. 1, no. 1, 1985
Williams, K. (1975)
Facing reality – a critique of Karl Popper's empiricism, *Economy and Society* Vol. 4, 1975, pp. 309–58
Williams, M. J. (1979)
The Theory of (the) Capitalist State(s), *Capital and Class* no. 9, 1979, pp. 67–70
Williams, M. J. (1980)
B. Rowthorn, Capitalism, Conflict and Inflation: Essays in Political Economy, *Capital and Class*, no. 12, 1980
Williams, M. J. (1982)
Industrial Policy and the Neutrality of the State, *Journal of Public Economics* 19, 1982, pp. 73–96
Williams, M. J. (1984)
A new German idealism?: a critical appraisal of value-form analysis (*mimeo*)
Williams, M. J. (1985a)
Analisi Del Capitale e Politica Industriale, in *Marx Centouno: Revista Internazionale de Dibattio Teorico* no. 1/2, February 1985
Williams, M. J. (1985b)
Privatisation's Progress: What is the Government's Denationalisation Programme for?, *Brunel University Discussion Papers in Economics*, no. 8504, 1985
Williamson, O. E. (1964)
The Economics of Discretionary behaviour: Managerial Objectives in the Theory of the Firm, Kershaw, Chicago 1964
Williamson, E. (1975)
Markets and Hierachies: Analysis and Antitrust Implications, Free Press, New York 1975
van Winden, F. A. A. M. (1981)
On the interaction between state and private sector; a study in political economics, dissertation 1981, North-Holland, Amsterdam 1983
Wolff, E. N. (1979)
The Rate of Surplus Value, the Organic Composition, and the General Rate of Profit in the U.S. Economy 1947–67, *The American Economic Review*, Vol. 69, pp. 329–41
Zelený, J. (1968)
Die Wissenschaftslogik bei Marx und das Kapital, Akademie Verlag, Berlin 1968, Engl. transl. T. Carver, *The Logic of Marx*, Basil Blackwell, Oxford 1980

Author Index

Subject Index